Economics in Disarray

Economics in Disarray

Edited by

Peter Wiles and Guy Routh

Basil Blackwell

First published 1984

Basil Blackwell Publisher Ltd
108 Cowley Road, Oxford OX4 1JF, UK

Basil Blackwell Inc.
432 Park Avenue South, Suite 1505,
New York, NY 10016, USA

British Library Cataloguing in Publication Data

Economics in Disarray.
  1. Economics
  I. Wiles, Peter   II. Routh, Guy
  330.1   HB171

  ISBN 0-631-13436-0

Library of Congress Cataloging in Publication Data

Economics in disarray.
  Includes index.
  1. Economics—Addresses, essays, lectures.   2. Neo-classical school of economics—Addresses, essays, lectures.
  I. Wiles, Peter John de la Fosse.   II. Routh, Guy.
  HB71.E28 1984   330   84–14652   HB
                                              71
  ISBN 0-631-13436-0   E28
                                              1984

Typeset by Fourjay Typesetters Ltd, Oxford
Printed in Great Britain

Contents

Preface

The New College, Oxford, conference on Economic Methodology in December 1982 assembled a hard core of people extremely worried by the state of economics, especially of its academic, high-theory nucleus; and a number of other people much more content. The papers in this volume were all presented, or subsequently written, by 'worried' people, and all discussants were 'more content'. On both sides we have tried to be very specific, and to avoid general denunciation.

The phrase 'neo-classical methodology' is used a great deal in these pages. What most of us on all sides mean by it is perhaps best expressed by Dennis Mueller on pp. 159–61.

All the pieces have been revised. Of the contributors, Lee, Perlman and Robinson did not attend the conference.

We have acted in the belief that econometrics is a separate subject. We have tried not to pass over this wavy boundary, and to confine ourselves to 'economics', except in the Gorman–Cross exchange.

The conference was financed by a grant from the Royal Economic Society and an advance from the publishers: enlightened patronage, which the contributors hope to have merited *ex post*.

1

Our Methodological Crisis

TERENCE HUTCHISON

I

For over ten years, a 'crisis' in economics, or in economic policy, or economic theory, has been widely discussed. In 1972 the then Presidents of the Royal Economic Society and of Section F of the British Association both voiced a profound dissatisfaction with the state and methods of research and teaching in the subject. Since then there has been the persisting world-wide policy crisis, with more than usually fundamental conflict in views about how to meet it. Then again, in 1981, there appeared an interesting collection of essays, by mainly American *illuminati*, proclaiming 'the crisis in economic theory', and exhibiting a significant number of completely contradictory points of view as to how it should be overcome (see Phelps Brown, 1972, and Worswick, 1972; also Bell and Kristol, 1981).

This decade or more of crisis talk followed one of the most extraordinary intellectual booms in the history of the subject, which had lasted through much of the preceding quarter-century, a period of confident pretensions and prestige comparable only with that of the English classical boom of more than a century before. As with the fluctuations of the real economy, some connections may perhaps be traceable between the illusions, excesses and duration of the preceding boom, and the severity, despondency and persistence of the ensuing depression. In any case, it might well be maintained that, intellectually, much of this despondency has been quite inappropriate. 'Crises' in economic theory may mark a very real kind of progress – a progress of ignorance, or of the realization of the real state of knowledge. A 'crisis' may constitute a much healthier intellectual condition than the preceding 'boom', with its excessive pretensions and pretences, and even fantasies, of knowledge, and of the power to plan and regulate. Economics, or political economy, is perhaps a subject which is only in a healthy condition when it is in a pretty profound depression, that is, when the true extent of ignorance becomes more apparent.

However, among the various aspects of this crisis, something describable as a methodological crisis may be discerned which has a fundamental bearing on the other more widely debated facets. The main feature of this methodological crisis has been latent, though occasionally recognized, for a very long time, and may be traced back to Ricardo, the great pioneer of the method of abstract deduction and 'model'-building on the basis of extremely simplified assumptions. This kind of crisis was in fact identified, or its possibility raised, by critics of the Ricardian or 'classical' method, in the course of two previous upheavals in the subject. It was recognized in the 1870s by Cliffe Leslie and in the 1930s by Keynes and others.

This methodological crisis centres on the simplified assumption regarding knowledge, expectations and uncertainty – or certainty – first explicitly deployed by Ricardo. What Joan Robinson admired so enthusiastically as Ricardo's 'habit of thought' (1973, p.155) amounts to the deductive manipulation pre-eminently – but of course not only – of this postulate regarding knowledge, expectations and certainty. This assumption is easily the most ubiquitous, as well as the most richly consequential, of the various simplifying assumptions about human behaviour employed by theoretical or analytical economists. It is clearly implicated not only with such fundamental concepts as those of competition, equilibrium, maximization or optimization, but also with concepts like the rate of profit for an economy. It has had a central role in the use of the deductive method and abstract model-building in economics. It is relied on in much classical and neo-classical, as well as (paleo- and neo-) Ricardian and Marxian analysis. It pervades and infests most textbooks, large parts of which, including most of the geometrical exercises, could not be compiled without it. Even some quite recent fashionable developments, like much of the immense expansion of the analysis of political or social choice (which is discussed below) are fundamentally dependent on the same kind of vastly simplified assumption, and, of course, subject to the limitations such a simplification imposes.

The most criticizable and unrealistic feature of 'The Economic Man' is not his materialism, or selfishness, which can be corrected for. His most fatal limitation, from the point of view of real-world applicability, is his omniscience. Moreover, it is this assumption about knowledge which keeps the analysis rigidly static, and it has to be abandoned if there is to be any advance towards a truly dynamic theory. As F. H. Knight observed, the presence, or absence, of uncertainty is 'the most important underlying difference between the conditions which theory is compelled to assume and those which exist in fact' (1921, p.51). The methodological crisis, therefore, is not a crisis simply of one particular brand or school of economics, or of political economy of one or other political stripe. It is not a crisis simply of 'orthodox' economics, on the one hand, or of 'unorthodox' on the other, however these are defined. Perhaps the only kind of economics not today involved in this methodological crisis is historical or institutional economics, whose pioneer in this country, Cliffe Leslie, discerned just over a hundred years ago something of the underlying, or impending, problem in his remarkable paper 'The Known and the Unknown in the Economic World' (1879).

II

The abstract deductive method, as classically codified by Senior, and nowadays elaborated with vast displays of almost totally irrelevant mathematical rigour, was that of deducing conclusions, or predictions, from a small number of allegedly obvious, common-sense assumptions, of which overwhelmingly the most important regarding economic behaviour was, as Senior himself expressed it, that 'every man desires to obtain additional Wealth with as little sacrifice as possible' (1836, p.28)

But nothing can be deduced regarding people's actions or decisions simply and solely from a generalization about their desires or aims. A further fundamental postulate has to be included that people have the requisite *knowledge* to fulfil this aim, or that their expectations regarding relevant historical developments turn out to be correct. It is extraordinary how far, for decade after decade, the essential role of this extreme assumption regarding knowledge, expectations and certainty was successfully overlooked by the followers of the Ricardo–Senior method – classical, neo-classical and Marxian. The removal of this comprehensive simplification largely removed with it the possibility of deriving significant general conclusions or predictions about people's choices, decisions or behaviour by the method of abstract deduction from a small number of obvious, common-sense postulates. For as soon as one cannot, or does not, continue to assume that people make the single 'right' or maximizing decision, one has to discover and justify the particular decision which they will make of the virtually infinite number of 'wrong' ones.

Deductive analysis cannot significantly help in discovering which particular kind of ignorance, or erroneous expectations, may be operative. Either an assumption has to be introduced on the basis of 'hunch', or it has to be 'plucked from the air', to use Sir Henry Phelps Brown's expressive phrase (1972, p. 3); or it will have to be tentatively formulated as an empirical, historical or institutional proposition about patterns of behaviour, of much less generality than the traditional fundamental assumption. Inevitably, a considerable shift of method would be involved, for the significant kinds of uncertainty, the patterns of expectations and the kinds of ignorance and error are constantly shifting with historical and institutional change. As Herbert Simon has emphasized, research into conditions where uncertainty, ignorance and erroneous expectations prevail

> requires a basic shift in scientific style, from an emphasis on deductive reasoning within a tight system of axioms to an emphasis on detailed empirical exploration . . . Undoubtedly the uncongeniality of the latter style to economists has slowed the transition . . .
>
> As economics becomes more and more involved in the study of uncertainty, more and more concerned with the complex actuality of business decision-making, the shift in programme will become inevitable. Wider and wider areas of economics will replace the over-simplified assumptions of the situationally constrained omniscient decision-maker with a realistic (and psychological) characterization of the limits on Man's rationality, and the consequences of those limits for his economic behaviour. (1976, pp. 147–8)

However, the Ricardo–Senior abstract-deductive method is, in many ways, much less expensive than the institutional and historical alternatives, both in research and in teaching and examining. So persistent attempts are made to justify its importance and prestige as the programme to which quantitatively and qualitatively a major share of research and teaching should be directed.

One long-standing argument to this end invokes the 'optimistic' idea (the adjective is, or was, Joan Robinson's) of successive approximations or decreasing abstraction. The idea is, or was, that one should start from some deliberately oversimplified case, introduce successive complications step by step, and so approach or arrive at the real world, or something usefully approximating to it. Up to a point, this kind of procedure seems sometimes to have worked out. It was used, for what it was worth, in the opening chapter of Ricardo's *Principles*, with regard to the extreme abstractions of his labour-embodied theory of value. Ricardo started by mentioning Adam Smith's primitive example of the beaver-and-deer hunting economy, and then attempted, surely not very usefully or successfully, to approach the real world by introducing some of the complications involved in the use of capital. Also, in his *Elements*, Walras proceeded (less unsuccessfully) in a somewhat similar way, starting from the extreme simplification of two-party and two-commodity exchange, and introducing step by step the successive complications of production, capital and money.

But for the most part this 'optimistic' procedure just has not worked out at all fruitfully, and, as regards our fundamental assumption about knowledge, expectations and certainty, *it seems that it simply cannot work out*. No fruitful way has emerged of gradually relaxing the certainty assumption step by step, or of getting from the first approximation to a second approximation significantly less distant from the real world.

Perhaps the most far-fetched attempt to justify the continuing employment of extremely simplified assumptions is the confused and confusing doctrine that the unrealism of assumptions simply does not matter. With regard to our fundamental assumption about knowledge, expectations and certainty, the implication (not always recognized) of this extraordinary, but understandably long-fashionable, doctrine seems to be that the ignorance, erroneous expectations and uncertainty of the real world (as contrasted with the full knowledge, correct expectations and certainty assumed in the model) have negligible effects on real-world outcomes. There is even some obscurity as to how some of the most serious politico-economic problems of the real world, including aggregate fluctuations and unemployment, can arise if politico-economic decisions are generally governed by 'rational' expectations – a highly imprecise term, and one admitted by those who use it to be unrealistic.[1]

However, for decade after decade, exponents of the programme of starting from extreme abstractions, and either asserting that the utter unrealism of the assumptions simply does not matter or promising that, by successive approximations, gradually the significant complexities of the real world will be accounted for in the model, have attempted, or claimed, to overcome the obvious limitations imposed by the original simplification. Thirty or forty years ago, it was 'welfare' analysis, and before that imperfect competition, which, it was promised, would achieve a breakthrough. More recently some champions of general-equilibrium analysis have promised highly significant advances; to discuss them may require the highest expertise, but it takes little more than common sense and attention to past experience to see that they are hardly likely to be achieved.

It must, however, certainly be recognized that the kind of theory, or analysis, which has emerged from this fundamental simplification did yield some genuine and lasting advances in understanding, and in prediction or predictive potential, when applied loosely, discreetly and with restraint. If one does not take the view that over, say, the past two centuries economists, by the application of their theories and analyses, have almost completely failed to contribute to the task of less unsuccessful policy-making, then such contributions as have been delivered must surely, to a significant extent, have been derived from theories or models in some way dependent on this fundamental simplification.

But some four qualifications may be made. Firstly, the theories, analyses or models have often *not* been applied with discretion and restraint. The basic oversimplification involved has spawned other oversimplifications. For example, the concentration on optimization, or maximization, has led, on both sides of the political argument, to gross misconceptions as to the nature of real-world policy issues. It can hardly be denied that the idea originated by Smith and Turgot of general interdependence, and even of a kind of tendency towards equilibrium, has been profoundly illuminating, and even the elaborate development of general-equilibrium analysis by Léon Walras may have yielded valuable conclusions. But it now seems to be regarded as the outstanding contribution to the understanding of real-world policy issues, forthcoming from the 'considerable', or even 'major intellectual', achievement represented by contemporary hyper-rigorous and sophisticated GE analysis, that it has definitively demonstrated 'that leaving allocation to market forces will not guarantee an optimal solution'. Surely, however, no one except an extreme apriorist, or someone intoxicated by the exuberance of their own mathematical virtuosity, could ever have entertained such a misconception as to the nature of the real-world policy issue. Regarding claims that in the real world there is 'a beneficent role for the invisible hand' (Bell and Kristol, 1981, p. 185), the introduction of 'a guarantee of an optimal solution' is vastly irrelevant and misleading.[2] Though realizable in the fantasy world of omniscience and certainty, guaranteed optima and maxima will always be up in the mathematical–Utopian clouds, above a world in which ignorance, uncertainty and erroneous expectations are and will be, to put it mildly, of some importance. For anyone who happens to be interested in real-world problems, the immensely complex and largely empirical and institutional question is whether or not the invisible hand may, over large areas, perform somewhat less unsuccessfully, oppressively or even disastrously than the historically and politically available forms of government regulation. Plentiful recent evidence would appear to suggest that this is not too ambitious a target at which the invisible hand might frequently be allowed to direct itself.

Secondly, though a significant part of any contribution to more successful policy-making, which may have been forthcoming from formal economic theory or analysis, to some extent depended on one fundamental simplification regarding knowledge, expectations and certainty, this source of insight – such as it may have been – has surely long been exhausted. For perhaps something approaching a hundred years, this orange has been squeezed dry, and what has emerged since has been mainly the squeaking of mathematical pips. Of course, further insights of this broad elementary kind may continue to be forthcoming, and may even long continue to provide a major part of such policy guidance as may be based on formal economic theorizing or analysis. But it does not seem reasonable to expect or promise that any further new conclusions are likely to emerge from still more rigorous or refined analysis, mathematical or otherwise, which will be of relevance to real-world policy-making.

An interesting example of how the introduction of the perfect-knowledge assumption can rapidly produce an abundance of ir-relevant, vacuous 'rigour', with a minimum of real-world applica-bility, is offered by some of the developments of public-choice analysis over the last two decades. Bruno Frey has pointed out how Schumpeter, using a predominantly institutional method, had anticipated nearly all the important contributions of contem-porary public (or social) choice analysis (1981, pp. 126ff.). But Schumpeter included, and emphasized, the possibility of mistakes and fraudulence (i.e. that a significant number of people do get fooled a significant amount of the time). On the other hand, more recently the field has been taken over largely by 'rigorous' but ir-relevant analysis based on the assumption of correct expectations or full knowledge. As a result, Frey maintains:

> Scientific journals containing articles on political economy – in par-ticular *Public Choice* – have become less and less interesting to read for anybody who wants to know about the real world . . .
>
> Schumpeter argues that unfair and fraudulent competition be-tween parties and interest groups cannot be excluded if the analysis is not to end up as an unrealistic ideal . . . But this is exactly where the axiomatic public choice theory of party competi-tion has come to! . . . As a result, most governments which have ever existed anywhere in the world are excluded from application of the models. (1981, pp. 134 and 137)

Thirdly, the fundamental oversimplification, pushed precisely and rigorously to its logical conclusion, simply rules out many or most of the serious economic problems of the real world. Under these assumptions economic processes take place in a kind of his-torical and institutional vacuum. In particular, among the institu-tions excluded is that of money, or a money and banking framework, and even, perhaps, firms. So long as economic theory and analysis is kept bottled up, with mathematical rigour, in this vacuum, it can hardly be hoped that its contribution to the economic issues of the day will make progress.

Fourthly and finally, the simplified, or oversimplified, model, based on knowledge, certainty and correct expectations, may have been more of a justifiable simplification, or genuine first approximation, in the (in some ways) apparently less unstable world of a hundred years ago. Then, in this country, there was something approaching price stability, and something approaching that 'stable general culture' which Pigou assumed to be a presupposition of the economic theory and analysis of his younger days. A hundred to a hundred and fifty years ago, when according to T.H. Huxley political economy was 'a peculiarly Anglican subject', it may have been considerably less unjustifiable that the far-reaching assumption pervading so much of its theory and analysis was one which largely precluded instability. A comparatively stable price-level, and a comparatively stable 'general culture', may well have provided the climate in which knowledge and expectations, though far, indeed, from the requirements of the oversimplified assumption (with regard, for example, to the recurring crises of the business cycle) nevertheless diverged less completely and continuously from it, so that the assumption of perfect knowledge could more or less validly be regarded as a genuine 'first approximation'.

III

In the course of the crisis in economics which took place in the 1930s the fundamental postulate about knowledge, expectations and uncertainty came under serious scrutiny from a number of economists, including Keynes. Briefly in his *General Theory* (1936), and more forcefully in an article of 1937, Keynes emphasized how this fundamental oversimplification more or less assumed out of existence the very serious real-world problems which were supposed to be under examination. Denouncing the extreme unrealism of the fundamental assumption, Keynes described the edifice of theory based on it as 'a pretty polite technique' which 'tries to deal with the present by abstracting from the fact that we know very little about the future'; and further that 'the hypothesis of a calculable future leads to a wrong interpretation of the principles of behaviour' (1937, pp. 186 and 192).

But taking his writings as a whole Keynes did not place the main emphasis of his criticism of what he called 'classical theory' on this fundamental oversimplification. Nor, for over a quarter of a century after his death, did Keynesian writers focus significantly on the limitations of this basic postulate. This fundamental line of criticism continued to be comparatively neglected, in spite of the writings of George Shackle, when, after the post-war adjustment process, a remarkable period followed of what looked like something approaching aggregate equilibrium, with very low levels of unemployment and only comparatively mild inflation. Criticism of the fundamental assumption regarding knowledge, expectations and uncertainty only re-emerged, among most Keynesians, with the profound maladjustments of the 1970s, and when a crisis in the subject itself was widely recognized.

Keynes himself had met simply by 'hunch' and brilliant improvisation the fundamental methodological problem to which he had called attention. He proceeded to introduce, at the relevant points, crucial assumptions regarding knowledge, expectations, uncertainty and maximization, basing these on his own insights regarding the particular processes and institutions of the Britain of his day, rather than on any more systematic investigation. There was nothing else he could have done in order to get the results he wanted. In this way he reached his conclusions: (1) on the impossibility, by cutting money wages, of achieving the cut in real wages required for a reduction of unemployment; and (2) as to how this necessary cut in real wages *could* be brought about by an expansion of aggregate demand. In this way Keynes presumably provided a relevant and serviceable theory for the Britain of his day – especially at a time of catastrophically *falling* prices. But it was very far from being a 'General Theory', because the assumptions regarding knowledge and expectations on which it was based were not general. Methodologically, Keynes was replacing a fundamental postulate which, although it constituted such an extreme oversimplification, nevertheless possessed, for what it was worth, a kind of broad generality, with assumptions which were inevitably much less general, and much more historically and institutionally limited, or relative.

Since Keynes, various attempts have been made to replace the classical general oversimplification with some other oversimplification, such as adaptive or rational expectations, so as to provide a basis for further abstract model-building. But as has been observed:

It is one thing to reject the 'perfect knowledge' assumption, but it is another entirely different thing to make a case for any given alternative. (Meckling, 1978, p.103; see Hutchison, 1981, p. 247)

For while there is only one way of being perfectly right, there are countless different ways of being somewhat or entirely wrong. The rational-expectations assumption, in its various forms, attempts to reconstruct the classical abstract-deductive method and conclusions. At least it has the virtue of recognizing the possibility that people may learn, and may possess knowledge as accurate as, or less inaccurate than, that of the government. But, *in its more extreme form*, the rational-expectations postulate is simply another sweeping oversimplification on which abstract-deductive analysis can elaborate and proliferate. It seeks to cope with the serious real-world questions, which it is presumed to be answering, by assuming that, in the main, they do not, or cannot, arise. That was how classical orthodoxy, as represented by J.S. Mill, treated the business cycle, surely a serious recurring problem of instability which was hardly compatible with strictly 'rational' expectations.

Moreover, there seems to be something of a paradox involved in reintroducing such an assumption as that of rational expectations at a time when the classical assumption, or condition, of something approximating to peacetime price stability may have disappeared for a long time to come, with constantly and very sharply changing rates of inflation the more realistic prospect. Furthermore, much more frequent changes in monetary institutions and their management have replaced what, down to about a decade ago, were relatively much less unstable arrangements. Patterns of expectations, and of reactions to changes, are bound to be frequently shifting, so that the historical and institutional element in economic processes, and in their explanation, obviously becomes increasingly important.

What has also not been sufficiently recognized is the profound methodological contrast between the structure of elementary microeconomics and that of the macroeconomics built up in the last half-century originally round Keynes's *General Theory*. The abstract-deductive method based on the fundamental Ricardian assumption of perfect knowledge, correct expectations and maximization under certainty, and drawing also on such basic

generalizations as diminishing utility, and variable factor proportions, worked effectively in the construction of an elaborate
edifice of general theory and analysis broadly applicable at widely
differing times and places. It is based on a core of propositions of
the widest generality, which yields conclusions, or allocation formulae, certainly somewhat tenuous in content, and sometimes reduced to tautologies, but which, for what they are worth, have
some validity for Robinson Crusoe, a private firm or a socialist
planner. There simply has not been discovered, and very probably does not exist, any such core of general propositions on
which to build, or from which to deduce, a body of macroeconomic theory of comparable generality and significance.

It may be that this contrast between the structure and generality of microeconomics and of macroeconomics should not be
pressed in the most absolute black-and-white terms. But it is certainly one of widely different shades of grey. Keynes attempted to
fill the fundamental void in the foundations of his macroeconomics with what he called his 'Fundamental Psychological
Law' regarding income and consumption, 'upon which we are entitled to depend with great confidence both *a priori* from our
knowledge of human nature and from the detailed facts of experience' (1936, p.96). Subsequently there were the various forms of
'Phillips curves'. But such propositions, though not useless,
simply do not possess the generality and reliability, or alternatively the empirical content, to provide the basic postulates for a
significant body of theory.

Finally, Paul Davidson may, of course, validly claim that:

> For members of the Post Keynesian schools the notions discussed
> above – historical time, uncertainty, expectations, political and
> economic institutions (especially money and forward contracts) –
> represent fundamental characteristics of the world we inhabit – *the
> real world*. (Davidson, 1981, p.171)

But if the problems to which these vital features of 'the real
world' give rise are to be grappled with, then the change in
methodological style, emphasized by Simon, will have to be more
fundamental than it has been undertaken so far. What Joan
Robinson so ardently admired as the 'precious heritage –
Ricardo's habit of thought', which depended to a large extent on
his assumption of perfect knowledge and correct expectations – will

have to be jettisoned. The aim will also have to be abandoned of establishing or re-establishing a, or the, 'General Theory' of macroeconomics (which most Keynesians, post- or neo-, seem to suppose that Keynes originally discovered); that is, if it is genuinely intended to recognize 'historical time' as an essential part of the real economic world. It has recently been stated that 'Keynes insisted on treating every patient as a separate problem rather than as one of a series of standard cases.' The Keynes here under discussion was, of course, not Maynard, but his brother Geoffrey. Economists may not have to go as far as did the surgeon Geoffrey Keynes in treating every case, or economy, at each different time in its history, as a separate problem. But, to take account of the historical element and 'historical time', they will need, in macroeconomics, to go much further in Geoffrey's direction than did Maynard with his attempt at *The General Theory*.

IV

Our discussion up to now of the existence, nature and source of a 'methodological crisis' has proceeded on the basis of some implicit assumptions regarding the objectives of economics, or of what economists do. Such assumptions hardly ever come to the surface, and might be claimed to go without saying. But there can hardly be a crisis, methodological or otherwise, in a subject unless there are objectives which are not being adequately, and within the limits of the possible, attained. Certainly, no crisis, methodological or theoretical, needs to be held to exist *simply* because economists cannot provide more or less agreed solutions showing how the appetites and ambitions of politicians and public are reconcilable with existing, or acceptable, institutions.

But for most of the history of political economy and economics, from Adam Smith to Keynes (and especially *before* Smith in the period of those whom Schumpeter called the 'consultant administrators'), one would suppose that a, or the, overriding aim was to discover, or construct, theories which would contribute, directly or indirectly, to less unsuccessful policy-making. That has been the presupposition underlying this chapter. But although this traditional assumption dominated until recent decades, today there seems to be a good deal of vagueness, and even fundamental disagreement, about objectives (which confusion may be another facet of the methodological crisis). This intellectual situation seems to have been growing up gradually, but with a considerable acceleration in roughly the last quarter of a century, with the immense growth in the number of academic economists. Ten years ago Sir Henry Phelps Brown and G.D.N. Worswick were complaining powerfully that much of economic teaching and research, and much of that claiming and receiving the highest priority and prestige, was based on such extreme abstractions, so remote from reality, as to signify an abandonment of the traditional objective of economists to construct theories which could contribute to less unsuccessful real-world policy-making. More recently we have the authority of Sir John Hicks for the observation that 'there is much of economic theory which is pursued for no better reason than its intellectual attraction; it is a good game' (1979a, p. viii).

Now there is no reason at all for supposing that any crisis, methodological or otherwise, exists, or need arise, with regard to the pursuit of 'good games', or with regard to 'economics for pleasure' (the title of one of George Shackle's books). As regards 'much economic theory', there is no need to question the further serviceability of the fundamental Ricardian simplification about knowledge, expectations and certainty, insofar as 'a good game' is the object of the exercise (like the game described by Mark Blaug as 'playing tennis with the net down'). In fact, 'the Ricardian habit of thought' will doubtless continue to be of great service in promoting 'good games'. But a methodological crisis has, and can only have, arisen if economic theorizing is regarded as furthering other objectives than that of providing 'a good game', such as contributing, in one way or another, to more successful real-world policy-making.

Now though one may possess one's own quite strong views as to what the aims of economics and economic theorizing ought to be, one should be firmly opposed to any dogmatic or censorious conclusions as to what should be the aims of other serious academic people, even if these amount to games-playing, or 'economics for fun', *provided that such an objective is quite clearly and frankly avowed.* In the first place, there are strong grounds in academic freedom for protecting serious academic interests which may, like pure mathematics, have no apparent relevance or relation to any kind of real-world fruitfulness or policy-making. Furthermore, it may be that the turn towards games-playing in 'much' of economic theory stems to some extent from a not completely unjustifiable scepticism about the contribution of further economic theorizing to more successful real-world policy-making: either because such theoretical advances are more or less out of reach, or because, whatever advances in relevant economic theorizing *might* be achieved, these will inevitably come through – the present democratic policy-making process being what it is – in some crude, oversimplified form which might well bring more harm than good. Already, nearly 50 years ago, in his later, more sceptical years, the once highly optimistic Pigou was expressing profound pessimism about the market for economists' wares (1939, pp. 220–1).

Moreover, one should not be dogmatic as to what may or may not contain a contribution to more successful real-world policy-making. Eventually a model or theory, however abstract or simplified, *may* find a real-world applicability and policy relevance not discernible at the present time. There is a considerable grey area here in which it might be dangerous and damaging to eliminate over-censoriously new theoretical developments, even though they may appear extremely oversimplified and remote from the real world.

However, we cannot often establish this kind of case on behalf of Hicks's 'much' (and, it would seem, more and more) economic theorizing that is being pursued more or less as a good game. It *might* perhaps sometimes be got away with if there were sufficient explicit frankness as to how extreme and consequential were the degrees of abstraction and unrealism often being employed, and if the long record of unfulfilled promises of eventual, real-world fruitfulness was acknowledged, not only in respect of opposing or contrasting politico-economic theories but in respect of one's own. For whatever else it may, or may not, be able to achieve, or at least seek, academic economics should surely give the highest priority to maintaining standards of intellectual lucidity and frankness in research and teaching, in respect of the significance, and applicability to the real world, of its theories.

We have already mentioned the kind of intellectual fudging and mudging with regard to 'the very great practical importance' (or lack thereof) of recent refinements in general-equilibrium analysis. Similar questions may be asked about the extreme other-worldly abstractions of 'Neo-Ricardian' analysis, which shares to some extent with general-equilibrium analysis the same Ricardian oversimplification regarding knowledge and certainty. It can hardly be for any testable, empirical or predictive content which could contribute to policy-making in any kind of real-world economy that neo-Ricardian analysis has been so assiduously cultivated for two decades or more. Indeed its defenders can be found denouncing as 'instrumentalist' any appeal to such criteria – while also making use of the usual self-sealing protective ploy that critics cannot be understanding the ultra-refined intellectual *mystique* involved.

Unlike, however, general-equilibrium analysis, neo-Ricardian analysis possesses the distinctive and, to some, highly attractive feature of a highly charged ideological penumbra which diffuses a pungent aroma of politico-moralistic disapproval of the distribution of income in a market economy, as contrasted, apparently, with that in some kind of centrally regulated East-European economy. Certainly the intensity of the ideological input contrasts strikingly with the tenuousness of the testable empirical or predictive output. But this blend of refined and arcane academic preciosity, with its overtones of austere politico-moralistic disapproval, obviously possesses powerful attractions for those for whom mere empirical reality comes in a very poor third. Anyhow the 'neo-Ricardian' analysis certainly scores very highly if the suggestion of value-judgements, or the diffusion of an ideological aroma, of one particular flavour or another, by those who regard their own expertise as entitling them to act as 'critics and judges',[3] is the main object of the exercise. There certainly need be no question of any 'crisis' in this particular sector of the subject if this is the only kind of objective being pursued.

Moreover even some of those who seem clearly to hold to the traditional aim of contributing (somehow) to real-world policy-making may well consider no kind of theoretical or methodological crisis to exist, *if* they are sufficiently confident in their own particular brand of theory to be able totally to disregard the wide range of contrasting or contradictory doctrines. For such economists, any crisis that exists is not theoretical or methodological, but one of public relations or public influence: that is, some other brand of theory is influencing policy, which derives, not from serious economists, such as themselves, but from 'cranks', 'amateurs', unprofessional 'dilettanti', non-mathematicians, or political ideologues of the wrong colour. Many Marxians, or neo-Ricardians, *some* neo- or post-Keynesians (or Keynesians, *tout simple*), *some* rational-expectations theorists, or general-equilibrium theorists (affirming confidently 'the very great practical importance' of their ideas), *some* Austrians, too, seem to share, more or less, the traditional aim of contributing to real-world policy-making; but they certainly do not seem prepared to recognize the existence of any methodological or theoretical crisis.

For example, a few years ago Lord Kaldor announced as follows:

> We are on the verge of evolving an integrated theory of inflation which should be capable of forging the tools necessary for securing prosperity combined with price stability, partly through intervention in commodity markets and partly through incomes policies in the industrial countries. (1978, p. XXXVIII)

No reports seem to be to hand as to whether 'we' are now still 'on the verge', or have now crossed the verge. But there can surely be no theoretical or methodological crisis for Lord Kaldor, or for those who agree with him, while certainly he holds wholeheartedly to the view that economic theorizing should contribute to more successful real-world policy-making.

V

Not only are there the obvious strident disagreements about policies and the theories underlying them; not only is there a great deal of vagueness and latent disagreement regarding the objectives of economic theorizing; there is just as much, or more, vagueness or disagreement among economists who apparently hold to the traditional objective of contributing to real-world policy-making, as regards how, or by what precise steps or methods, this aim can validly be approached. In some cases there seems to be a readiness to proclaim the traditional objective, while trying, at the same time, to cling to a kind of intellectual purity which effectively precludes the most important means by which theory *can* contribute to policy: that is, by improved prediction. But if one really wills the end of contributing to policy-making, one must recognize the possibility of really effective means to promoting this end, or public confusion will be further heightened.

The epistemological links between theorizing and policy-making are a large and complex area which belongs, at least in part, to philosophers. But only in part, because the vital task remains with economists of defining and interpreting the theories, arguments and propositions which have to be epistemologically assessed, as well as the objectives which policies are claimed to promote. On the subject of this demarcation question, a rather brusque exchange took place in the columns of *The New York Times* (3 January 1982), in the course of a debate on 'The Meaning of Social Justice', between the Keynesian, Nobel Laureate, Yale economist, James Tobin, and the conservative, individualist, Harvard philosopher, Robert Nozick. At one point Tobin felt moved to exclaim 'There's nothing more dangerous than a philosopher who's learned a little bit of economics.' To which Nozick replied, 'Unless it's an economist who hasn't learned any philosophy.'

Certainly the dangers from both of these types are immense. On the one side, the history of political economy and economics is full of examples of economists taking up, or making up, bits of philosophy, epistemology or methodology to support their own particular brand of theorizing, or to boost their scientific prestige or professional status or influence. On the other side, that of non-economist philosophers, there may be failures in interpreting economic theories due to a lack of grasp of the full politico-economic context. Alternatively, philosophers may take too much at face value the first political economist they meet whose views seem politically sympathetic. Again, there are obvious dangers in applying some very general philosophical viewpoint without allowance for certain highly special characteristics of political economy and economics, notably its intense and continual involvement in political issues and even in party politics. In another direction, those philosophers of science who have constructed their methodological doctrines from the example of the natural sciences, especially physics, may put forward as positive analysis, or as methodological norms, ideas which are hardly applicable to economics, because – among other reasons – of its historical dimension. Alternatively, some philosophers seem to go over the top in the opposite direction, in denying *any* parallels between economics and the natural sciences as regards methods or criteria, which may be even more dangerous than exaggerating the parallels and similarities.

But someone or other has got to take the risks and face up to the dangers, if a whole complex of fundamental questions is not to be left obscure and unanswered, questions to which reasonably sound answers are essential for the accomplishment of the traditional aims of the subject. These questions relate to precisely how contributions to less unsuccessful economic policy-making should be, or can be, derived from economic theories. There appears to be a great deal of disagreement and fuzziness on this question, insofar as it is explicitly dealt with.

One of the subjects on which both fuzziness and outright contradictions are frequent is that of prediction: whether it should be an aim or claim of economists, and how far economists can claim to provide effective guidance for policy-makers if they entirely reject prediction (see Hutchison, 1977, chapter 2). Certainly the spectacle seems educationally dubious: distinguished professors of the subject proclaim the impossibility of effective prediction in economics, while some of their brightest pupils go straight off to posts as 'economists', in government or business, in which their prime task which they will be paid to perform will be to contribute vitally to the allegedly impossible.

But there is another question which is, perhaps, still more fundamental, which is concerned with the nature, or source, of the authority which a professional economist, or 'expert', can claim on the basis of his command of economic theory. At present there seems to be a growing rejection, as 'positivist', of the kind of discipline which consists in requiring the formulation of theories in a testable, refutable or falsifiable way, and in seeking, as strenuously as is feasible, to test, refute and falsify. It is observed, quite correctly, that this is often or usually extremely difficult, or sometimes, practically speaking, outright impossible. (However, there is always the further (positivist?) norm, in the case of inadequate testing, of *withholding judgement*, which is impossible for politicians, but perfectly feasible for academics.)

Yet, while this kind of discipline is being rejected, no other effective code of discipline, such as roughly obtains in the natural sciences, is being proposed in its place, nor any 'principle of demarcation' as Popper called it. But because of its intense and unrelenting involvement in highly political, or party-political, issues, there is probably *no* subject claiming academic status which requires more urgently some kind of demarcation principle or code of discipline.

Nevertheless, some recent writings on the methodology of economics display a marked and increasing support for methodological permissiveness, and a rejection of any discipline through testing, falsifiability and falsification, as well as the dismissal of prediction as an aim. A position is thus becoming established which amounts, virtually, to that of 'anything goes', or the methodological anarchism of Feyerabend, without his explicit, cheerfully irresponsible abandon. But it must be noted that Feyerabend, in proclaiming his message of 'anything goes', was quite explicitly concerned with undermining the public influence of natural scientists, who he thinks are too 'pushy', and whom he regarded as having grossly misused their influence and prestige. But if claims to scientific discipline, or the possibility thereof, are undermined, then simultaneously claims to influence based on some kind of scientific authority, and indeed science's *raison d'être*, are also undermined. Economists must face the dilemma that insofar as they reject such disciplines as are implied in the obligations of testing and testability, or falsifiability and attempting to falsify, with no other proposed disciplinary code existing, in a subject so intensely involved in party politics, they are undermining claims to influence or to some kind of 'authority'. Some, economists and non-economists, might heartily welcome such an abandonment, but hardly anyone would do so who holds that the main aim of economic theorizing is to promote more successful policy-making.

Past economists, from physiocrats and Ricardians onwards, have claimed, rightly or wrongly, but sincerely, that they were concerned with a 'scientific' *discipline* (even one producing 'laws') and have claimed public influence on that basis. If it now emerges that no attempts at discipline, or at demarcation of 'science' from 'non-science', can be valid, or worth attempting, then it hardly seems that any claims to influence or authority can be upheld.

However, we now conclude by putting forward another aim for economists, which might be regarded as especially appealing, or even obligatory, for academics: that is the maximum feasible frankness and clarity in stating the aims and objectives of their subject and their theorizing: and in stating how far these aims are being, or are likely to be, fulfilled, together with *the kind of discipline* on which their conclusions are based. This, in other words – to quote the concluding line of a recent study – is the aim of making economics 'a more honest science' (Caldwell, 1982, p. 252). This aim is perfectly complementary with the traditional aim of contributing to real-world policy-making, and seems even more essential for effective teaching. If it is to be advanced, much needs to be done.

Notes

[1] Patrick Minford defends an extreme form of 'rational' expectations on the basis of the methodological justifiability of unrealistic assumptions: 'The rational expectations view has been widely criticised as "unrealistic", "not how people behave" . . . The answer is clear: *of course* it is unrealistic, it is meant to be. It is a very powerful assumption for generating predictions. This one assumption is a rich source of restriction in economic models. The criticism is quite simply irrelevant' (Minford and Peel, 1981, p. 3). Minford then expressed the view that the predictions generated by RE models had been 'rather successful' – a view around which it could hardly have been said that a consensus has formed. Earlier Minford had claimed: 'Within five years the standard macroeconomic model will be an equilibrium model in which expectations are formed optimally and contract arrangements respond to economic forces especially inflation' (1980, p. 24). It is not quite clear whether the rational-expectations assumptions are intended as 'negligibility' assumptions, 'domain' assumptions, or simply as heuristic, simplifying assumptions (to use A. Musgrave's valuable distinctions). But they seem in Minford's writings to represent the strongest form of the three, i.e. negligibility assumptions (see Musgrave, 1981, and Hutchison, 1981, pp. 288–91).

[2] See Hahn (1981a) and Davidson (1981) contributions to Bell and Kristol, 1981, pp. 126, 137 and 157–8.

[3] In support of the economist acting 'as a critic and judge', rather than as 'the positivists' passive and neutral observer', see Hollis and Nell, 1975, p. 241. With regard to 'High Theory', which, of course, today means 'High Mathematical Theory', the very serious advice of Alan Prest in his recent 'Letter to a Young Economist' should be pondered by young and old concerned with the state of the subject: 'The suggested Ph.D. thesis title "n solutions to n-1 problems" is a very promising theme for an academic career devoted to High Theory. Nowadays this is the super-highway to eminence and professional acclaim. And you will very quickly discover that your standing and status will rise in geometrical proportion to the irrelevance and obscurity of what you say and write. Abraham Lincoln was wrong here: you can fool all the people all the time – without much effort either' (1983, p. 131).

Comment 1

MARTIN HOLLIS: IN DEFENCE OF TWO DEMONS

Terence Hutchison issues a call to arms against the demons of abstraction and ideology. He bids economists reaffirm the aim of 'improved prediction' in the service of 'less unsuccessful policy-making'. The methodological crisis is to be resolved by proper attention to historical and institutional matters. The message is delivered with lucidity and common sense and his own work is a model of what he recommends. Yet I am not persuaded that the crisis can be so readily diagnosed or settled. With the due nervousness of a philosopher in a den of economists,[1] I shall endorse his concern for historical and institutional matters but shall suggest that, consequently, the crisis must get worse before it gets better.

Underlying the call for improved prediction is a view of science with eminent friends. In bare outline it goes, I think, something like this. Science explores an ordered realm, whose workings are independent of us, of the concepts which we apply and of our conjectures about it. We capture its order in statements of laws, describing what happens in given initial conditions. Whether or not its workings are controlled by forces and mechanisms, our knowledge of them is empirical and our conjectures have only the empirical warrant of observation and experiment. The warrant is issued when prediction succeeds, provided that success was not guaranteed *a priori*. Hence theoretical abstraction is useful only if it is finally the servant of experience: and anything with an 'ideological penumbra' and 'pungent aroma of politico-moralistic disapproval' is to be shunned. Economic science must neither stray far from the real world nor forget the fact–value distinction.

This outline is too bare to discriminate between, for instance, positivists and Popperians. But it does catch the shared presumption, which underwrites the primacy of prediction. This is the neutrality of observation. Conjectures or hypotheses are refuted when they get their predicted facts wrong, rather as a map-maker fails if he writes in dragons where there turn out to be none. A major component of the methodological crisis, it seems to me, is the subverting of this moment of empirical truth by Quine, Kuhn, Feyerabend and others, who argue that observation always presupposes theory. For, if there is no 'unvarnished news' (Quine's phrase), refutations cease to be decisive and no longer point the finger anywhere in particular.[2]

'Percepts without concepts are blind,' Kant remarked. Perceiving involves judging and in judgement the mind is active. Veridical perception is not something thrust on us but something achieved after discarding the irrelevant or spurious. In classifying data we winnow what is given and also project it by bringing it under concepts. Whatever the final merits of this line of thought, it is almost irresistible for economic facts. For instance whether GNP has risen depends not solely on eyesight but on a complex abstraction from many events in many markets with the aid of theoretical concepts. In abstracting and in discarding the irrelevant and spurious, the economist also regulates what he finds. At the moment of empirical truth the success or failure of prediction is, so to speak, a majority verdict by theoretical jurors.

In that case a simple logic of falsification is doubly indeterminate. In place of the basic schema

$$H \to O$$
$$not\text{-}O$$
$$\therefore \; not\text{-}H$$

we have nothing more basic than

$$(H_1 \text{ and } H_2 \text{ and } H_3 \text{ and } \ldots) \to (O_1 \text{ and } O_2 \text{ and } O_3 \text{ and } \ldots)$$
$$not\text{-}(O_1 \text{ and } O_2 \text{ and } O_3 \text{ and } \ldots)$$
$$\therefore \; not\text{-}(H_1 \text{ and } H_2 \text{ and } H_3 \text{ and } \ldots)$$

The finger of refutation points only after we have judged what the facts are, and it points nowhere in particular, until we have reached our majority verdict. Taken to the limit, the thought leads to an intellectual anarchy and I do not have space to discuss the problem of where to halt. But I defy Terence Hutchison to resist the starting point. If he cannot, then the relation of theory to experience is not as implied in the bare outline, and the rubric of empirical knowledge needs rethinking. At any rate, there is no mistaking the recent upheaval in the philosophy of natural science and it means that economists can no longer count on a consensus about the proper conduct of science. The crisis is in part a healthy sign of a resulting open-mindedness.

One way to respond to Hutchison's strictures would thus be to invoke rival accounts of the role of theory in physics. I shall make a small gesture in this direction but mainly I shall take the riskier course of doubting whether economics should seek to ape physics in any case. As has often been noted, economics carries the flag of the social sciences; and even in economics the search for laws has not gone with *éclat*. No doubt social life is complex but, after two centuries, the plea that economics is a young science wears thin. This, let me say roundly, is not to cast economists as Old Mother Hubbard. The cupboard is full of achievements: the doubt is solely whether laws are the bones we seek. Hutchison traces the crisis to 'the extremely simplified assumption regarding knowledge, expectations and uncertainty' on which so much of microtheory relies. He urges its replacement with something more realistic and that will require (he says, quoting Simon) 'a basic shift in scientific style, from an emphasis on deductive reasoning within a tight system of axioms to emphasis on detailed empirical explanation'. I think it will require more than that and shall next say why.

The 'knowledge' assumption is a key member of the set of rationality assumptions distinctive of microeconomic theory. On these assumptions rests an ingenious edifice which might seem perversely remote from real life. The starting thought for the edifice is, very reasonably, that the only way to make the buzz and bustle of real life manageable is to abstract to 'ideal types', which are instanced often enough to be interesting. Micro-economics does so and the process is taken further in general-equilibrium theory and welfare economics. To a charge of playing foolish games, the obvious reply is that physicists do the same and to great final advantage. The critic retorts that theoretical physics can prove its point by blowing us up, whereas theoretical economics has little to show. The theorist then usually claims a useful approximation to reality or replies darkly, 'Wait and see!' If that does not carry conviction, is there a better line, as hinted, in the renewed importance attaching to theory, when recent philosophy of science is taken seriously? Ideal-type constructs in physics model what happens in the absence of interference and where well-defined variables take a limiting value of zero. Their dizzying complexity reminds us how instructive tautologies can be. They are finally useful, because, when interferences and real-life values are fed in, they yield predictions.

Hutchison grants this (although he would jib at an anti-empiricist reading of it) but denies parallel merit to treating the knowledge assumption as a 'first approximation' in economics. I agree. Philosophically, the difference arises, in my view, because the physicist does not care about the mental life of the atom. Atoms do not attach subjective meaning to their experience, do not communicate it to other atoms and are not guided in their actions by what they expect other atoms to do. Nor does the physicist advise his atoms what values it would be best for the variables in the model to take and how to achieve their purposes better. When prediction fails, it is never because the atoms have behaved foolishly or, alternatively, have learned to outwit him.

As a result the 'predictions' of microeconomic theory are protected in a way foreign to physics. Microtheory implies, for instance, that a firm in perfect competition, producing with marginal cost below marginal revenue, will increase output. This unpacks into a tautology about the logical consequences of perfect competition and a 'prediction' of what will happen, if all conditions are satisfied. Failure of prediction cannot upset the tautology and is therefore to be blamed on the conditions. These fall, at first sight, into objective ones about market situation and subjective ones, including the knowledge assumption, about what the economic agents want and believe. As in physics, where defective materials or apparatus do not refute hypotheses, the theory can be defended against some failures. Unlike in physics, however, the remaining slack can be taken up by blaming the agents for their subjective defects.

It might seem that this is a peculiarity of the theory of perfect competition, which makes agents mindless in the ideal case and leaves all action to the market mechanism. But the theory of imperfect competition in fact does the same, despite its mention of institutions. The oligopolist's control of price is an extra item in his stock of perfect information and hence an extra source of possible incompetence, when prediction fails. It does not, however, yield a 'second approximation' or way of letting the 'knowledge' variable take a real-world value. He has more to learn than the seller in perfect competition but, since it remains (paradoxically) true that rational economic man knows everything but learns nothing, this makes no difference to the status of 'predictions'. While the point of reference remains physics, the crux is still that atoms are neither foolish nor cunning.[3]

Sometimes, then, the economist makes a move, which the physicist never makes, by judging that the failure of prediction is to be blamed on the agents' ignorance (or cunning). The bare outline of the view of science sketched earlier has no place for this move. It involves the idea that economic action is a skill. The relation of prediction to policy-making is correspondingly more complicated. It becomes one question how economic agents will respond to a piece of legislation and another whether the legislation would produce the desired effect, if people responded rationally. The latter question invites an ideal-type answer, in the sort of sense in which a theory of 'best play' in chess is ideal-type. Policy is assessed for merit by judging whether its effects, if as intended, would satisfy a normative goal. Theory is involved both in identifying the effects and in breaking down a general goal, like prosperity or distributive justice, into warranted criteria for scoring the effects. It is not false to say that better theory here leads to improved prediction but, since it is likely to be a precondition that people accept the new theory, learn it and put it into practice, it is not very helpful. Meanwhile theoretical work of this kind must proceed without aid from Hutchison's paper, if it is to proceed at all.

Nor is the crux here the value-judgement attaching to the choice of goal. Economic action occurs in an historical setting and explaining it sets some of the problems of writing history. This fact will be awkward, unless historical actors, at least in their economic dealings, act rationally in a sense consonant with microeconomics. That makes it natural to look to Max Weber's economics-inspired account of historical method. Weber recommended the construction of ideal-types, which let the historian decide what it would have been rational for actors in their setting to do, as a necessary prelude to explaining their failure to do it. In other words the first step in explanation is to decide what needs explaining and it suits economists to agree that what needs explaining is departures from what economic theory would lead us to expect. But what this is depends (or ought to) on specifying the historical and institutional setting – hence the variety of Weber's ideal-types. There are theories of physics which tell us what atoms *will* do in particular settings but none which tell us what they *should* (rationally) do.

There is still the direct question of how people will in fact behave in their setting, granted that the knowledge assumption is often false. The problem is well set by pointing out that perfect knowledge does not function as a first approximation, knowledge not being a variable which can take a range of measurable values. I cannot think of anything brief to say about it, except that it is unavoidable. It is unavoidable because the working of institutions depends on what people know, believe and expect. Consequently the distinction which I drew earlier between market conditions and actors' characteristics holds only *prima facie*. Market conditions too can be specified only with the aid of some assumption about actors' knowledge. In that way they are unlike laboratory conditions, again in ways awkward for the opening picture of unified scientific method.

'The profound methodological contrast between the structure of elementary microeconomics and that of the macroeconomics built up in the last half-century' has, as Hutchison says, much to do with the treatment of institutions. But the relation of institutional to microeconomic ingredients is troublesome. It is not as if macroeconomics had no psychology. If institutions, such as trade unions and corporations, are treated as if they were atomic units, then it is as if they had all and only the rational and maximizing properties of individual agents; and that seems an unpromising start on the task of allowing for differences of role and function both within and among institutions. But if differences of roles and functions are made central (for instance, those between production managers and sales directors or between unionized and un-unionized firms or between banks and factories) then a different psychology is needed. In that case macroeconomics is left struggling with two incompatible psychologies of human action, one abstracting to a pure individualism with famous difficulties and the other adding to it a conflicting account of socialized agency (I would be happy to argue that neither can microeconomics avoid this tension). Meanwhile macroeconomics is presumably not all psychology and, in urging microeconomists to take institutions seriously, Hutchison lands them with deep puzzles about the relation of social action, social system and social structure. The crisis deepens.

A sign of deep water here is the trouble caused for economic psychologies by institutional change. Such changes matter even for a microtheory which tries to treat them as exogenous. For if the search is for economic laws, projection from one place or time to another is reliable only if institutions remain constant in relevant respects. Without a dynamic model of changes (such as have occurred in the last half-century), we do not know which tautologies of microtheory to apply in understanding the states of an economy. Institutionalists tackle this matter; but it is one thing to allow for the impact of a given institutional practice and another to allow for likely institutional developments. As far as I know, we are without either a suitable institutional psychology or a detailed theory of underlying social forces which commands general assent. Hutchison has, in effect, urged orthodox economists to take to political economy and I have no quarrel with that. But it does deepen the crisis by requiring an improved psychology of social action with no analogue in physics.

Let me sum up with a word about the demons of abstraction and ideology. Hutchison is right, I think, to pick out the knowledge assumption but wrong to hope that, if it is simply made more realistic, economics can return to the straight and narrow of prediction. All sciences idealize experience by constructing theories which abstract from it and, if there is any merit in recent subversions in the philosophy of science, theory has an ineliminable role in the interpreting of observation and experiment. There is a long story to be told before prediction can resume its throne. Meanwhile the games which abstraction plays are continuous with attempts to understand actual economies. It is at present unclear, methodologically speaking, what is to be best assumed under the heading of 'knowledge'; and the need to assume something, where physics assumes nothing, should make us wonder whether a science of action is in the same line of work as a science of nature. Even without taking up so much of the floor, however, I am certain that theory in economics has more than the meagre place suggested by contrasting 'abstract' with 'realistic'. So let abstraction flourish!

Methodological puzzles about realism in science at large and in the social science of economics are not solved or by-passed by embracing the demon of ideology. But he, purged of the pungent aroma sprayed on by Terence Hutchison, is a reminder of the traditional concerns of political economy. These come into play as soon as institutions are admitted to be more than a frame or set of parameters within which transactions occur, but permeate the actions of the socially located actors. In that case the crisis goes very deep, since orthodox microtheory and political economy cannot merely be glued end to end; nor will a vague optimism about recent progress in macroeconomics serve as a connector. Political economy starts with other ideas of economic agency and these, on the evidence of Hutchison's paper, need exploring. Meanwhile I would not myself be inclined to lump together Marxians, neo-Ricardians, neo- or post-Keynesians, rational-expectations theorists, general-equilibrium theorists and Austrians for any purpose. Nor would I suppose that political economists were primarily ideologues. That is a rum way of ensuring that the devil has all the best tunes, while making it impossible to ask which of the devil's tunes are the best. The broadest methodological question here is how timeless theory shall engage with historical understanding and I welcome a crisis which makes it urgent. Let us hope that economics will emerge from the excitements as once again the moral science which it used proudly to be.

Notes

[1] Although still grateful for Peter Wiles's tutorial efforts 25 years ago, I lay no claim at all to proficiency in economics. But I have large debts to Edward J. Nell (fellow-author of Hollis and Nell, 1975) and Frank Hahn (fellow-editor of Hahn and Hollis, 1979). Since, it seems, one is in the grip of one demon and the other of the other, I take pleasure in the unlikely task of defending both at once. This has been made easier by Peter Wiles's helpful comments on my first draft.

[2] W. van O. Quine, 'Two Dogmas of Empiricism' in Quine, 1980. This article seems to me crucial for the debate about the realism of assumptions in economics.

[3] For a discussion of frictionless motion in physics, see Hollis and Nell, 1975, appendix to chapter 1, and, for a more general discussion of theory and prediction in economics, see chapters 1–5.

Comment 2

MARK BLAUG

In a letter to *Science* Wassily Leontief surveyed articles published in the *American Economic Review* in the last decade and found that over 50 per cent consisted of mathematical models without any empirical data, while some 15 per cent consisted of non-mathematical theoretical analyses, likewise without any empirical data, leaving 35 per cent of the articles using empirical analysis (see table 1).

TABLE 1   ARTICLES PUBLISHED IN THE *AER*

	1972–6 (%)	1977–81 (%)
1 Mathematical models without any data	50.1	54.0
2 Theoretical models without mathematical formulation and without data	21.2	11.6
3 Statistical methodology	0.6	0.5
4 Empirical analysis based on data developed by author	0.8	1.4
5 Empirical analysis using statistical inference on published data	21.4	22.7
6 Other types of empirical analysis	5.4	7.9
7 Empirical analysis based on artificial simulations and experiments	0.5	1.9

Source: Science, 217, 4555, 9 June 1982, p. 104.

This is one aspect of modern economics: to pursue economic theorizing like a game, making no pretence to refer to this or any other possible world on the slim chance that something might be learned which will one day throw light on an actual economy. There is another aspect however: to formulate theoretical hypotheses and to show that they are confirmed by empirical evidence, at the same time ignoring alternative hypotheses that might equally well have been confirmed by the same data. Putting these two tendencies together, we end up with a discipline that runs few risks of ever being shown wrong. In short, economists are very complacent about their subject. Of course, economists frequently disagree – witness the controversy between Keynesians and monetarists – but the participants in these furious debates spend more energy contrasting their respective ideological positions than formulating truly discriminating tests of their competing predictions. In consequence, such controversies persist for decades and even generations.

Specialists on economic methodology take two sharply opposing views of this state of affairs. Some argue that the business of the economic methodologist is to describe the actual practices of economists. Economists, they say, clearly place a high value on empirical research but only to confirm or disconfirm particular applications of economic theory; economists rarely abandon a theory because it has been repeatedly refuted and some economists even go so far as to argue that economic theory is true by the certainty of its fundamental postulates. In short, the methodology of modern economics is 'confirmationism' or 'verificationism' and there are still schools of thought in modern economics, like the modern Austrians, who remain 'radical apriorists'. In books like Ian M.T. Stewart's *Reasoning and Method in Economics* (1979), Fritz Machlup, *Methodology of Economics and Other Social Sciences* (1978), and Bruce Caldwell, *Beyond Positivism: Economic Methodology in the Twentieth Century* (1982), we get an exposition of economic methodology that is essentially defensive of modern economics, explaining that what economists do is to make the best of a bad job, which in the final analysis is not so different from what is done in the physical sciences.

In contrast to the descriptive role of economic methodology are books like those of Homa Katouzian, *Ideology and Method in Economics* (1980), Terence Hutchison, *On Revolutions and Progress in Economic Knowledge* (1978) and my own *Methodology of Economics* (1980), which argue that the role of the economic methodologist is to prescribe as well as to describe. Economists may well fall short of the best-practice methods they themselves preach and even the methods they advocate may be deficient. At any rate, these writers are frequently critical of what passes as modern economics, which is not to say that they agree precisely on where economics went wrong or how to put it right.

To illustrate this opposition between a 'defensive' and an 'aggressive' methodology, let me compare Bruce Caldwell's *Beyond Positivism* with my own account of *The Methodology of Economics*. Our two books are in striking agreement on most of the substantive issues in economic methodology: 'methodology' is not just a fancy name for 'methods of investigation' but a study of the relationship between theoretical concepts and asserted conclusions about the real world; in particular, methodology examines the procedures economists adopt for validating theories and the reasons they offer for preferring one theory over another; methodology is both a descriptive discipline ('this is what most economists do') and a prescriptive one ('this is what economists should do to advance economics'); finally, methodology does not provide a mechanical algorithm either for constructing or for evaluating theories and as such is more like an 'art' than a 'science'. We also agree that economic theories must sooner or later be confronted with empirical evidence as the final arbiter of truth, but that empirical testing is so difficult and ambiguous that one cannot hope to find many examples in economics of theories being decisively knocked down by one or two refutations. It is vain to seek an empirical counterpart for every theoretical concept employed, which is in any case an impossible objective, but we can achieve indirect testing by considering the network of fundamental concepts embedded in a particular theory and deducing their implications for some real-world phenomena. This is not to say, however, that predictions are everything and that it hardly matters whether assumptions are 'realistic' or not. Economic theories are not simply instruments for making accurate predictions about economic events but genuine attempts to uncover the causal forces at work in the economic system, that is, to depict things as they actually are.

Nevertheless, this is where the agreement between us stops. I argue more or less vehemently in favour of 'falsificationism', defined as 'a methodological standpoint that regards theories and hypotheses as scientific if and only if their predictions are, at least in principle, empirically falsifiable'. My reasons for holding this view are partly epistemological (the only way we can know that a theory is true is to commit ourselves to predictions about events and although a confirming instance does not prove truth, a disconfirming instance proves falsity) and partly historical (scientific knowledge has progressed by refutations of existing theories and by the construction of new theories that resist refutations). In addition, I claim that modern economists do in fact subscribe to the methodology of falsificationism: despite some differences of opinions, particularly about the direct testing of fundamental assumptions, mainstream economists refuse to take any economic theory seriously if it does not venture to make definite predictions about economic events, and they ultimately judge economic theories in terms of their success in making accurate predictions. I also allege, however, that economists fail consistently to practise what they preach: their working philosophy of science is accurately characterized as 'innocuous falsificationism'. In that sense, I am critical of what economists actually do as distinct from what they say they do.

Caldwell, on the other hand, doubts that falsificationism is a recommendable methodology: its strictures are so demanding that little of economics would survive if it were rigorously applied. In addition, he can see no evidence that economists practise falsificationism even innocuously. Instead, he advocates 'methodological pluralism', or 'let a hundred flowers bloom'. To me this seems to be tantamount to the abandonment of all standards, indeed the abandonment of methodology itself as a discipline of study. If all methodological views are equally legitimate, it is difficult to see what sort of theorizing is ever excluded. From the standpoint of 'methodological pluralism', it is not even obvious why we should require theories to be logically consistent, or to assert something definite about the real world, which after all carries the implication that they may be shown to be false. Caldwell is much too sophisticated not to recognize the dangers of ultra-permissiveness and the last few pages of his book are expressly devoted to answering possible objections to methodological pluralism. It is simply that I for one found his answers unconvincing.

Caldwell is clearly sympathetic to the methodology of falsificationism but he derives many of his dramatic conclusions – 'falsificationism has never been practised to any significant extent in economics'; 'there exist a number of specific and possibly irremovable obstacles to the practice of falsificationism in economics' (pp. 236, 237) – from the subtle distinction between the methodology of 'confirmationism' and that of 'falsificationism'. He notes that most modern economists believe 'that theories should be testable; that a useful means of testing is to compare the predictions of a theory with reality; that predictive adequacy is often the most important characteristic a theory can possess; and that the relative ordering of theories should be determined by the strength of confirmation, or corroboration, of those being compared' (p. 124). These four principles, he contends quite rightly, define the methodology of 'confirmationism' (or, as I would prefer to call it, 'verificationism') and not 'falsificationism'. Falsificationism is a tougher doctrine. In its simplest form, it can be stated in Caldwell's own words: 'Scientists should not only empirically test their hypothesis, they should construct hypotheses which make bold predictions, and they should try to refute those hypotheses in their tests. Equally important, scientists should tentatively accept only confirmed hypotheses, and reject those which have been disconfirmed. Testing, then, should make a difference' (p. 125).

Thus, the distinction between confirmationism and falsificationism rests partly on the degree to which theories are squeezed to yield risky implications, which are liable to refutation, and partly on whether refutations are taken seriously as possible reflections of fundamental error. Confirmationists make sure that their theories run few risks and, when faced with an empirical refutation, they set about repairing the theory or amending its scope; they never abandon it as false. Falsificationists, on the other hand, deliberately run risks and regard repeated failures to predict accurately as a sign that alternative theories must be considered. Obviously, these distinctions are differences of degree, not of kind, and two methodologists may honestly disagree as to whether modern economists are more appropriately characterized as 'confirmationists' or as 'falsificationists'.

Caldwell provides a valuable discussion of the factors that make falsificationism in economics so hard to practise (pp. 236–42) but he fails to point out that exactly the same factors operate in physics, chemistry and biology, albeit to a lesser degree. Indeed, the so-called Duhem–Quine thesis (see chapter 4) states that it is logically impossible decisively to refute any theory, since any test of a theory involves at least some auxiliary conditions besides the statements of the theory, so that a refutation can always be blamed on the auxiliary conditions. The way out of this dilemma is to lay down restrictions on what Popper calls 'immunizing stratagems' adopted solely to protect theories against empirical refutations. These restrictions are important features of the methodology of falsificationism, which Caldwell nowhere mentions or discusses.

Let us agree that there are no tests in economics, or for that matter in any other science, that are unambiguously interpretable. But is Caldwell asserting that disconfirming tests are always ignored in economics, or that they always lead to a repair-job designed to make sure that there will be no further disconfirmations? How then does he account for the wholesale abandonment of the Phillips curve in the 1970s, interpreted as a stable relationship between inflation and unemployment, such that one can be traded off against the other? Or how does he explain the repeated appeal to empirical evidence in the Keynesianism-versus-monetarism controversy? No doubt he would reply that the controversy has persisted for almost 20 years despite numerous refutations and counter-refutations. But, surely, what is remarkable is the insistence of all participants in these debates that they must be resolved by truly discriminating tests of the respective predictions of each school of thought, which so far have simply not been forthcoming. If this is not the methodology of falsificationism in action, what is it?

One difficulty is that Caldwell provides no case studies of economic disputes to illustrate his claim that economists typically adhere to confirmationism rather than falsificationism. His only report of empirical work deals with the attempt to construct a direct test of the fundamental rationality assumption of modern economics (pp. 150–62) and although this succeeds in demonstrating the inconclusiveness of such efforts, it has little bearing on the issue of confirmationism versus falsificationism. The book's central conclusion is stated in these words: 'The invocation to *try* to put falsificationism into practice in economics need not be dropped, although it seems there is little chance for its successful application. What must be avoided is the wholesale rejection of research programs that do not meet the falsificationist criteria of acceptability, for that would lead to an elimination, not only of alternative research programs like those proposed by Austrians and Institutionalists, but much of standard economic theory as well' (p. 242).

But the dreaded prospect of 'wholesale rejection of research programs that do not meet the falsificationist criteria of acceptability' is a red herring: there is no danger of wholesale rejection of anything in modern economics but rather the danger of never finding any common language of communication between an ever proliferating series of competing research programmes. It is not just Austrian and institutionalist economics versus mainstream economics but Marxism, radicalism, post-Keynesianism, behaviouralism, and so on, many of which purport to contain unique principles for validating their own findings and invalidating everyone else's. Can we really say nothing to appraise these competing research programmes except that 'anything goes' in methodology? Are there no minimum standards which we may demand of any species of economics claiming to be scientific?

'Methodological pluralism', I would contend, is a sham, an excuse for never making any final judgements about competing theories.

2

The Wider World and Economic Methodology

The Public Case for the Reconstruction of Economics

ROBERT NEILD

I want to address three questions. First, what is wrong with economic policy? Second, what, behind that, is wrong with economics? Third, how can we reconstruct economics?

Economic Policy

The economic policy of the present government is so amazingly naive that I find it hard to believe that I am not having a bad dream.

The policy rests on the fundamental belief that a market economy has automatic self-regulating properties of astonishing refinement – properties which if formally laid out make the performance of an automatic pilot in an aeroplane or the guidance mechanisms of an intercontinental missile look like child's play. There follows from this the belief that a policy of fiscal-cum-monetary restraint will reduce inflation without causing any involuntary unemployment. The market mechanism, so the story goes, will always ensure that there is a job available to anyone who will accept the right price.

The result of this policy is three million unemployed – obviously *not* all voluntarily unemployed – and a wastage and decay of human and physical capital that takes us back to the 1930s. In the south-east, in particular in a town like Cambridge where science-based industries are expanding, we do not see the wastage and decay. To see it you must travel north. I had occasion to drive through Sheffield while taking my daughter back to the University in Manchester. The sight of that town, with derelict steel plants, waste areas, run-down shops and a general air of bleakness, reminded me of being taken on holiday to Wales by my parents in the 1930s – though there was the difference that then you saw unemployed miners squatting on street corners gazing into space; nowadays the unemployed are indoors gazing at the television.

The government's reaction is to say that it cannot influence the real economy, except by improving competition and strengthening incentives. Secondly, they say that economic recovery will come, or is already upon us.

Yet the economic model of the economy operated by my colleagues in Cambridge, and every other economic model, except the Liverpudlian model, shows no hope of a significant recovery, unless there is a change in policy.

That this is plausible is confirmed by taking the simplest measure of domestic economic policy that all of us learnt as students. I refer to the Constant Employment Budget, otherwise called the Full Employment Budget. As you will remember, this measures what tax revenues at current tax rates and public expenditures with current expenditure programmes would be if employment were at a constant level, so that tax revenues were not depressed by the depression and unemployment benefits and other cyclical expenditures were not amplified by the depression. Since 1975, when Mr Healey turned to the IMF and monetarism, the Constant Employment Budget has been tightened by no less than about 10 per cent of GDP. That is much greater than the budgetary tightening undertaken in any other country in this depression. It is far greater than the budget tightening which occurred in the 1930s. Between 1929/30 and 1933/4 the Constant Employment Budget of central government was tightened by 4 per cent of GDP. By 1939–40 it had been relaxed again by no less than 16 per cent of GDP (Middleton, 1981, p. 280). I think there can be no gainsaying the proposition that there can be no marked recovery in economic activity until the budgetary policy as measured by the Constant Employment Budget is eased. I do not believe that one of you would dissent from that proposition.

Of course, it could be argued that the depression has been worth having. One such argument would be along the lines used by Schumpeter, to the effect that a periodic crisis in a capitalist system will squeeze out the inefficient like an ice age, and leave more vigorous animals to survive. It is a Darwinian argument. Another line of argument is that it has been necessary to spank the unions and workers in order to get them to be more moderate in their wage claims and more vigorous at work. That is the argument of the Victorian schoolmaster with the cane.

These arguments imply that the government is Machiavellian: that it knows that it is causing the depression, that its denial of the responsibility for unemployment is a calculated mistruth. But there is no evidence that the government is Machiavellian. Did anyone in the government calculate *in advance* that they would cause three million unemployed? The answer surely is no. And the reason for that is simple. Politicians come to believe their own propaganda, even if they have doubts about it to start with. And they select advisers who reinforce their beliefs.

I can testify to this from personal experience. I spent some years being economic adviser to Jim Callaghan. I was not a success. I tried to persuade him to devalue. But as time went by he made more speeches proclaiming that he would not devalue, and he shook more finance ministers by the hand and assured them that their sterling balances were safe. He became locked on the course he had chosen. If you told him that the policy would fail and that he must change it, the chances were that you would land in the doghouse for a stretch. He would listen to other advisers who did not express such discordant ideas.

If then Mrs Thatcher and her associates really believe in their policies, where did they get these extraordinary ideas? The answer is from economics. The ideas come from mainstream economic theory – to the embarrassment of some of the best theorists. If you ask how this has happened, the answer is that many of the cleverest men in the profession, who possess the greatest mathematical skill, have devoted their energies to building a model of a totally self-regulating economy. In doing this, they have followed in the footsteps of Walras, seeking to build a general-equilibrium model of the economy.

Their procedure is to start from the simple question, 'What conditions need to be fulfilled if an economy is to produce a Pareto optimum via the price mechanism only?' A Pareto optimum is, you will remember, a situation where no one can be made better off without someone else being made worse off. It implies that there is full employment. And it implies that there is an optimum allocation of resources.

The answer they produce is fantastical in an extraordinary degree.

They start from a world populated with atomistic individuals, whom they call 'agents', like detectives, who are assumed to be endowed with innate tastes, uninfluenced by those around them. They are assumed to possess a given 'factor endowment', meaning given human skills and capital. It is assumed that there are no economies of scale, an assumption which ensures that in every trade there is the multiplicity of firms required for perfect competition. It is assumed that there is no space – for if there is space every village shop and economic enterprise enjoys some degree of monopoly, caused by the cost of reaching another supplier. It is assumed there is no time, since if you admit time the machines you inherit from the past may not fit the demands of today. On the basis of these, and other fantastic assumptions, you then postulate a population so large that no one can influence any price and a society where people respond only to price signals in deciding what to buy and how much work to offer. There is then a massive series of auctions (taking no space) in which the 'agents' decide what to produce and what to buy, notionally scurrying timelessly from one market to another deciding how many shirts to buy once they have seen what price is emerging in the shirt auction, how many shoes to buy, once they have seen the price in that market, and how many hours of work to offer when they have seen what wage is being paid and how that compares with the prices of goods they propose to buy. To overcome the difficulty that all the markets interact and people might be rushing from one to another and endlessly revising what they did in one market in the light of what had just happened in another, it is necessary further to postulate a mighty super-auctioneer who arranges recontracting so that ultimately everyone is satisfied.

The explanations offered for undertaking this extraordinary exercise are of two kinds. There are those – though they seem to me to be a minority – who offer a negative explanation. Their purpose, they say, is to show how *unlikely* it is that a market economy will be self-regulating. The trouble with people who take this position is that they have no satisfactory answer when you ask them why on earth they go on with this kind of economics, since they must long ago have satisfied themselves, and everyone else, of this negative point. A reply they commonly offer is that their aim is progressively to relax the unrealistic assumptions until they return to a model sufficiently close to reality to permit policy conclusions to be derived. To which the objection, well made by Lord Kaldor, is that if you start dismantling the assumptions underlying a wildly fragile structure of this kind, the whole house of cards collapses.

The alternative, common in America, is to claim that the model is a good approximation to the real world. That, in my view, is a wholly irresponsible claim. But its validity is taken for granted in vulgar economics; and it has been taken for granted by the monetarists. Milton Friedman explicitly appealed to the Walrasian equations as the foundation for his assertion that monetary restriction would not cause any involuntary unemployment (Friedman, 1968). And others have followed in his footsteps. Here lies the source of our troubles.

Why do the economists behave like this? Why do they chase such a mad model of the economy? I think the best explanation is that they have been trying to be like physicists. They have been trying to be 'real scientists'. Listen to this description of physics. It was written by Bertrand Russell in 1927.

> Apart from pure mathematics, the most advanced of the sciences is physics. Certain parts of theoretical physics have reached the point which makes it possible to exhibit a logical chain from certain assumed premises to consequences apparently very remote, by means of purely mathematical deductions. This is true especially of everything that belongs to the general theory of relativity. It cannot be said that physics as a whole has yet reached this stage, since quantum phenomena, and the existence of electrons and protons, remain, for the moment, brute facts. But perhaps this state of affairs will not last long; it is not chimerical to hope that a unified treatment of the whole of physics may be possible before many years have passed. (Russell, 1927, p. 1)

Isn't that seductive! No wonder economists set about trying to 'exhibit a logical chain from certain assumed premises to consequences apparently very remote, by means of pure mathematical deductions'.

But in economics that approach has been hopelessly unscientific. In physics the assumed premises are realistic. If there is evidence that they are not realistic, or not close approximations to reality, they will be rejected; and at every step the propositions derived from theory will be tested by experiment and observation: all propositions made are subject to the test of falsification. In general-equilibrium economics, by contrast, the assumptions are the extreme opposite of realistic. They are mad. And as is unhappily the case with economics, the possibilities of subjecting propositions to the test of falsification are limited.

How to Reconstruct

The only way we can become more scientific, I suggest, is to start again, to demolish and reconstruct economics from scratch. Of course, there is a certain amount of knowledge of the world which we can redeploy, like old bricks from a demolished building. What is essential is that we should adopt a new and more scientific approach in the true sense of the word. Let me suggest some propositions by which we should be guided if we are to achieve that aim:

(1) We must recognize that economics is a 'soft science', not a 'hard science' like physics. We should regard it as an aspect of history in which an unusual amount of measurement is possible. We should regard it like demography, another area of history where a lot of measurement is possible but where our powers of prediction are limited. The reason in both cases is that we are dealing with social behaviour which is not repetitive in a simple manner.

(2) We must identify and acknowledge the frontiers of knowledge. The first step towards being a scientist is to discover what you do not know. Only then can you know what questions to ask and how to pursue research. In the hard sciences, the frontiers of knowledge are well defined and keep advancing. In one subject, regrettably, the tendency is to acknowledge no frontier to our knowledge. Instead, rival gangs of economists claim to know everything, like rival theologians.

(3) We must deal only with observable variables. To speculate about things you cannot observe is futile.

(4) We must develop a dynamic system, meaning a rigorous and coherent analysis of how successive periods grow out of each other.

(5) We must study behaviour. We must talk to firms, trade unions and other people engaged in economic activity, in order to develop hypotheses about behaviour. In this, we must follow the example set by Marshall, who set great store by talking to people engaged in all parts of the economy.

(6) In studying behaviour, we must start from social psychology. We must look at evidence about how people influence and manipulate one another and how group behaviour is formed; and we must look again at the work of Veblen and the institutionalists. We must stop accepting in every textbook and theoretical article the assumption that the world consists of atomistic individuals with 'rational behaviour', mean people who pursue a pleasure–pain calculus, simply regarding work as pain and consumption as pleasure. You need only look around you to see that many people work with an intensity that does not suggest pain – unless they are masochists. And the proposition that higher consumption always brings more happiness has been well demolished by Tibor Scitovsky in his review of the evidence on the psychology of satisfactions (Scitovsky, 1976).

(7) We must do what we can to test our hypotheses empirically, at whatever expense in clever people's time.

(8) We must face the dilemma that in building models of the economy the temptation to go for complex models must be tempered by the need to keep models so simple that you can exercise judgement. For we all know – indeed I am sure I need not remind you of this – any equation we produce to explain, say, some type of consumer spending, will be an extreme simplification of social behaviour in which we make spending depend on two or three variables and rely upon the association of those variables established over some past period. At any moment, that past behaviour may be changed by technological developments, by a change in inflation to a rate not recently observed, by an increase in unemployment to rates not recently observed, by a war scare, by a shock to relative prices, or other unexpected developments. At present, and for a very long time to come, there is only one

machine that can scan all those possibilities and suggest what their effects will be, and that is the human brain. All the time we need to keep examining any model we build in order to scan for the unexpected and exercise our judgement. If you make the model too big and too complex, that becomes impossible.

This programme offers immediate scope if you start with macroeconomics. Indeed the start has been made. My colleague Wynne Godley has in draft a book which makes an important beginning in this direction.

The theoretical heritage to start from lies in two elements in Keynes's '*General Theory*' which stand out today as having been of seminal importance. The first is the theory of effective demand, which tells us that supply does not create its own demand, it is the level of real demand which determines supply. Keynes's second enduring contribution, which seems almost to have been unconscious and is rarely recognized, is to have given us a theoretical system in terms of measurable variables such as investment and consumption, which fit a comprehensive system of national accounting. Most of the rest of the *General Theory* is in my view best discarded. The use of a static equilibrium framework, the notion that there are diminishing returns to capacity utilization in industry, the notion that the price/wage relationship is flexible in association with changes in demand – the notion that the money supply is exogenous – these and other points are part of the legacy of competitive equilibrium economics, in this case the Marshallian version, from which Keynes failed to escape. Indeed, the reconstruction of economics that I am suggesting can be seen as a response to the plea made by Keynes in the last paragraph of the Preface to the *General Theory* when he said:

> The composition of this book has been for the author a long struggle of escape, and so must the reading of it be for most readers if the author's assault upon them is to be successful – a struggle of escape from habitual modes of thought and expression. The ideas which are here expressed so laboriously are extremely simple and should be obvious. The difficulty lies, not in the new ideas, but in escaping from the old ones, which ramify, for those brought up as most of us have been, into every corner of our minds. (1936, p. viii)

The building blocks from which we must start are these:

(1) There is the accounting framework of both national and company accounts which has been tremendously developed in the post-war world. It has very rich and strong logical properties, which, as I think Wynne Godley will show successfully, have not been properly exploited. The flow relationships and stock-flow relationships of accounts have strong implications as to how one period is linked to another as well as strong implications as to how stocks, including the stock of money and financial assets, are related to flows.

(2) We know that in an economy like Britain's, the foreign-trade multiplier and the budget multiplier dominate the investment-savings multiplier. Or, in simpler terms, foreign-trade performance and budgetary policy are the main determinants of the level of employment.

(3) We know that manufacturing industry and services are worlds where oligopolistic competition rules; where there are increasing returns in the short and long run; where products are differentiated; where prices are administered – all points that Keynes got wrong and that must be embraced if macroeconomics is to be given a foundation in microeconomic behaviour and is not to be left floating in the air.

(4) We know that the primary sector, comprising agriculture and other extracting industries, has market-determined prices which are volatile – so volatile indeed that most market prices are now administered one way or another by government intervention.

(5) We know awfully little about the determination of the general level of wages.

(6) We know very little about the relationship between investment, productivity and growth, or about the determination of the distribution of income, although these have been subjects of intense theoretical research.

Starting from these foundations, you can derive some strong conclusions. And you can specify areas where research is needed.

Only if we strip down our subject to bare bones like this are we likely to advance. The proposal that we should do so is neutral politically. Those who believe in market economies do no service to the survival of market economies when they produce models of them so idealized and so unrealistic that the policies they advocate are destructive. Nor, on the other side, does the socialist improve the world or his reputation if he plugs on with a Marxist model which predicts that capitalism, like a ripe plum, must rot and fall into his hands. The only way to make up your mind about the merits of rival systems is to travel and look at them, to go to America, Russia, Eastern Europe and Western Europe and other parts of the world. I am sure you will then conclude that the middle way found in Western Europe is the best. But if we are to perpetuate that way, it is high time that we shed nonsensical economics and produced a more modest, pragmatic and firmly based body of economic theory, based on what we can observe.

To conclude, let me repeat my basic dictum. The first step to wisdom is to recognize how little you know and to proceed accordingly.

Note

Based on a speech made to the Society of Business Economists in Cambridge, 26 March 1982.

Comment

OLIVER HART

Robert Neild's paper contains three strands: criticisms of current economic theory; an attack on present government policy; and some proposals for reconstructing the subject of economics.

Let me begin with Neild's comments on economic theory. He is highly critical of mainstream economic theorists who, he argues, have been devoting their time to 'building models of a totally self-regulating economy' and to analysing 'what conditions need to be fulfilled if an economy is to produce a Pareto optimum via the price mechanism alone'. Neild argues that the assumptions theorists require in order to make progress on these questions, e.g. the existence of many small consumers and firms, the absence of space, time and economies of scale, are so unrealistic (he is less charitable and describes them as mad) as to render the whole exercise a waste of time. In fact he indirectly goes further since he claims that theoretical work of this sort provides intellectual support for the *laissez-faire* stance of the Thatcher government whose policies, Neild would argue, have caused much suffering.

Has theoretical work been at best useless and at worst positively damaging, as Neild suggests? I think not. First, the picture Neild paints of current theory is seriously inaccurate. In fact a great deal of work has been done relaxing the very assumptions he dislikes so much. Large parts of the recent literature are concerned, for example, with the consequences of imperfect competition (sometimes due precisely to the fact that firms are separated in space), economies of scale, and product differentiation. Much work has also been done on introducing uncertainty, imperfect information and more importantly asymmetric information into the picture (these are not areas Neild mentions). Finally, time plays an essential role in much modern theory (in fact, contrary to what Neild suggests, general-equilibrium models with time have existed since Walras).

This does not mean that theorists have a single general-equilibrium model of the economy which incorporates all these different features. Nor are they likely to in the near future. Rather they have a whole array of models (many of which are partial rather than general equilibrium in nature), each one focusing on a particular issue, e.g. imperfect competition or asymmetric information. These models are useful for understanding different aspects of the economy. One model, for example, might throw light on R and D activity in a concentrated industry, while another might be useful for understanding unemployment.

These models, since they concentrate on one issue, tend to make simplifying and hence often unrealistic assumptions about everything which is not the central focus. This is for reasons of analytical tractability. Neild would no doubt regard some of these assumptions as mad. This is, I suspect, because he does not understand what theories or models are all about. A theory or model is not a description of everything that exists in the world. It is a tool that helps us to sort out the wood from the trees. Any theory, if it is to get anywhere, must abstract from many (even most) aspects of reality. Otherwise it will simply be a complex and indigestible description of the economy. It is ironic that Neild criticizes theorists for building unrealistic models, and yet later argues for the need to keep models simple.

The current state of economic theory is very different then from what Neild seems to imagine. It is simply not the case that 'the cleverest men (or women for that matter) . . . have devoted their energies to building a model of a totally self-regulating economy.' Once, say, imperfect competition or asymmetric information is introduced, the economy will rarely be self-regulating in the sense of producing desirable outcomes.

What has this recent work taught us? First, it has increased our knowledge about various economic phenomena (this is the positive role of economics). For example, the research on asymmetric information has improved our understanding of the stock market, insurance markets and business cycles, among many other things; work on imperfect competition has improved our understanding of industrial organization. I also think that as a result of recent theoretical work on a number of the above topics, we understand unemployment better (although by no means well).

Secondly, it has allowed us to re-examine the question of whether market allocations are efficient. The answer here seems pretty unambiguous: they are rarely first-best efficient in the sense that a planner with complete information and total powers could not make everybody better off. Only if there is perfect competition, no externalities, symmetric information, complete markets, etc., is this the case. But what theorists have realized is that first-best efficiency is not really the issue. Is it reasonable, for example, to suppose that the central planner has perfect information when individual agents have imperfect information? Or (as Coase argued a long time ago) that agents face transaction costs in co-ordinating their actions to internalize an externality whereas the planner does not?

This leads to the concept of an allocation being constrained or second-best efficient, meaning that a planner *subject to the same constraints as the market* cannot make everybody better off. Are market allocations second-best efficient? The answer is again generally no. However, the way in which they are inefficient can be very complicated. In particular, it is clear that in order to improve on the market, the planner requires a great deal of information about the structure of the economy. To put it another way, it is not the case that for a large class of economies the market equilibrium is inefficient in a particular way and that the same intervention policy (e.g. tax or subsidy scheme) will correct things. Rather the type of inefficiency and intervention is very sensitive to the specification of the economy.

The conclusion then is not that the invisible hand always or even generally works (although Neild is right in suggesting that some economists who should know better take this extreme position). Rather it is that its failures are subtle, and that it may take a very sophisticated planner to do any better (or even half as well). Given the fallibility of planners in practice and the difficulty of controlling bureaucracies, it is not a big step from this to the conclusion that governments should be distinctly cautious about intervening.

Contrary to what Neild suggests, it is arguably this negative view of what planners or governments can achieve rather than a positive view of what the market can do that underlies the present government's popularity, if not their policies. Neild claims that the present government's economic policy is amazingly naive. It undoubtedly has some very naive features (for example, the obsession with getting inflation down when the theoretical and empirical case for the cost of inflation being large is slight). But what Neild does not acknowledge is that the policies of the opposition are also naive. The opposition believes that the current unemployment can and should be reduced by the application of old-fashioned Keynesian pump-priming policies. Is this not naive in view of the fact that neither they nor anybody else really has a satisfactory explanation for why this unemployment has occurred or for why pump-priming policies would work? Neild would no doubt argue that wages and prices are sticky. Yet over 40 years of theoretical work have failed to explain in a convincing way why this should be (some models of real wage rigidity have been produced recently but they are still very underdeveloped, while models of nominal wage and price rigidity are almost nonexistent). Furthermore, the empirical evidence on wage and price rigidity is, as in most cases in economics, ambiguous.

This would not matter if, whatever the causes of unemployment, there were a single appropriate intervention policy – Keynesian pump-priming say. As in the cases I considered earlier, however, this is unfortunately not so: the right intervention policy is crucially sensitive to the causes of the problem.

Let me turn finally and very briefly to Neild's proposals for restructuring economics. Perhaps not surprisingly in view of what I have said, I do not feel that the subject requires a radical restructuring. At the same time, improvements are no doubt possible. Some of the proposals Neild puts forward are worth considering (e.g. the study of group behaviour), while others are already being actively pursued (e.g. the development of dynamic systems, the empirical testing of hypotheses and the building of small models). As usual, it is one thing to make proposals and another thing to carry them out; the proof of the pudding is in the eating. Most importantly, however, I feel that Neild has dismissed too easily a large body of useful conventional economics.

3

The Good and Bad Uses of Mathematics

MICHIO MORISHIMA

> The empirical background of economic science is definitely inadequate. Our knowledge of the relevant facts of economics is incomparably smaller than that commanded in physics at the time when the mathematization of that subject was achieved . . . It would have been absurd in physics to expect Kepler and Newton without Tycho, – and there is no reason to hope for an easier development in economics. (von Neumann and Morgenstern, 1947, p. 4)

I

Economics – in particular that part of it known as mathematical economics in the sense of a discipline that uses a high degree of mathematical reasoning – has frequently been compared with physics.[1] If we measure the degree of scientific progress by the level of the mathematics utilized or the level at which systematic axiomatization is carried out, then the theoretical systems such as are being worked on by top mathematical economists in the 1980s bear favourable comparison with highly advanced theoretical physics, regarded as the queen of the natural sciences. Yet students who have read works on social choice or Arrow and Hahn's monumental book *General Competitive Analysis* (1971) are likely to be surprised at the remarkable resemblance between such works and Spinoza's *Ethica Ordine Geometrico Demonstrata*. The Arrow and Hahn work in particular is poor in terms of empirical content, despite its being a volume in the Mathematical Economics Text series, whose stated aim is expressed in the claim that 'students of mathematical economics and econometrics have . . . difficulties, [one of which] is that the theoretical and the empirical writings often make little reference to each other. The main object of this series is to overcome those difficulties. Most of the books are concerned with specific topics in economic theory, but *they relate the theory to relevant empirical work* [my italics].' Spinoza's work, which is at the same time metaphysics, epistemology, ethics and religious doctrine, persuasively demonstrates that axiomatization and scrupulous mathematical proof are by no means the monopoly of modern science, and that such techniques could also be used as weapons by the dogmatists, sophists and scholastics who were the enemies of modern scientists.

As Max Weber has said,

> the mathematically-based natural science of the West is a combination of two things: rational modes of thought developing out of the philosophy of ancient Greece; and technical 'experimentation', the specifically modern element in any naturalistic discipline, which originated during the Renaissance, and then not at first in the sphere of science but in the sphere of art. (1978, p. 439)

There is a qualitative difference between the ability to carry out observations and conduct experiments which will play an essential part in the progress of science on the one hand, and on the other the ability to construct a system of hypotheses which will provide a rational explanation of the results of such observations and experiments and the ability to clarify the logical implications of the system; so the two main pillars of science, fact-finding and theorizing, are usually strengthened and developed by people of two distinct groups with different talents.

Certainly it can hardly be expected that an individual who is ignorant of theory will conduct observations and experiments of major significance in the progress of science; likewise the consequences of an observation are likely to be different depending on what sort of theoretical light the facts are viewed in. It follows that observations can never stand in a perfectly neutral position, can never be isolated from theory. However, the history of science amply demonstrates that even those individuals who had been taught no more than existing theory could carry out important observations and experimentations which were yet sufficiently rebellious to encourage the modification of existing theories or to stimulate theoreticians to reject and relinquish them and create new ones. Theoreticians then went on to modify their hypotheses so as to explain in a thoroughly rational and systematic fashion the ever increasing wealth of objective observations and facts, and, where necessary, even to demolish utterly such extant hypotheses and replace them with completely new ones. Thus science differs from the non-scientific, metaphysical speculation which preceded it, in attempting to give a rational explanation of the natural world, which is firmly *supported by observed facts*. It is in this point that physics is distinguished from astrology, chemistry from alchemy.

Yet given that metaphysics is demonstrative in nature, science too is demonstrative. Here I mean by demonstrative the application of deductive logic to the system of hypotheses to predict phenomena which have hitherto never been observed; then at this point science gives foreknowledge likely to be far closer to fact than any foreknowledge based on metaphysics and dogmas; and this will be confirmed when observations are actually carried out. Science does not seek out a host of disparate laws governing various individual phenomena; it institutes as a basic principle several hypotheses which it takes as axioms, and then builds up a system of laws which are all derived from the axioms. Whether an axiom is or is not valid can be ascertained either through direct experimentation or by verification through the result of observations, or, if such a thing is impossible, the correctness of the axiom can be judged through the indirect method of verifying the laws which proceed from the axiom by observation or experimentation. (If the axiom is deemed to be incorrect it must be modified or instead a correct axiom must be found.) Such a correct axiom system will then guarantee the correctness of all the laws which logically proceed from it. It may be true that certain of these laws are only logically derived from the axioms and are not substantiated by experimentation or observation, but at some future time when demonstration of these laws through experimentation and observation has become possible, then as long as the axiom system is correct facts will be confirmed in accordance with the laws.

In this way modern science (in particular physics) is not only positive science but is at the same time characterized by being demonstrative science. For it to be demonstrative science, science must be constructed in an axiomatical format, and in order to ensure the positive correctness of the propositions (laws) which have been elicited demonstratively the hypotheses (axioms) must have been either directly or indirectly substantiated.

II

In view of this sort of development in mathematical natural science, the nineteenth-century economists conceived of the idea of 'mathematizing' economics, and the most advanced of them was Léon Walras.

William Jaffé's view, however, is that to regard Walras in this light is to distort the historical record (Jaffé, 1980). According to Jaffé, 'Walras' *elements*, instead of aiming to delineate a theory of any real capitalistic system, was designed to portray how an imaginary system *might* [Jaffé's italics] work in conformity with principles of "justice" rooted in traditional natural law philosophy, though the system remained subject to the same forces, the same "passions and interests", and the same material and technological constraints that govern the real world' (1980, p. 530). Jaffé states, 'in the *Elements* Walras was concerned with "a realistic utopia" . . . nowhere to be found in the actual world . . . ideally perfect in certain respects, and yet composed of realistic psychological and material ingredients' (1980, p. 530).[2] To make this sort of interpretation, according to Jaffé, is entirely consistent with the *Zeitgeist* of the time and he takes up my own proposition (Morishima, 1977, p.4) that the ultimate aim [of Walras's *Elements*] was to construct a model, by the use of which we can examine how the capitalist system works, delivering the following judgement on it:

> From the historical standpoint, it is within this setting of the intellectual life of nineteenth-century France that the *Elements* needs to be interpreted. To interpret it in a later setting (say, of a twentieth-century London School of Economics) is to commit a flagrant anachronism. (Jaffé, 1980, p. 533)

Such is the understanding of the translator, but the author of the *Elements* himself thought along the following lines: 'If necessary we shall divide political economy into a natural science, a moral science, and an art. To this end we shall first of all distinguish between science, art and ethics' (Walras, 1954, p. 57). Walras in fact divided economics into the three subsectors of pure economics, applied economics and social economics, in accordance with these three spheres, and attempted to advance in each one. He met with success only in the field of pure economics, and despite his tremendous interest in the other two, and despite his apparently having begun economic research because of what was an undoubted interest in moral problems, he was forced to content himself with a meagre yield for his efforts. The above quotation from Walras showed that he was attempting to establish economic theory, or what he termed pure economics, as a natural science – or, in other words, that he was trying to establish 'the study of facts' (1954, p. 13) concerning economic phenomena which 'observes, describes and explains' (1954, p. 13), so that it will bear comparison with natural science, in particular with Newtonian physics.

Walras's view of science very closely resembles that of Max Weber as mentioned above and that of H. Poincaré expressed in *La Science et l'hypothèse* (1902) and elsewhere. This is not something at which we should be surprised. Such writers were one generation younger than Walras, but they were active at more or less the same time.[3] The stipulation of science being a rational system of thought which is based on facts was one element of the *Zeitgeist* of the time, and Walras too possessed this way of thinking, as the following words of his show: 'No one can reproach our science with having taken an unduly long time in becoming rational as well as empirical' (1954, p. 47). In no sense whatever did Walras construct his general-equilibrium model in order to examine for its workability 'a realistic utopia' or 'an ideal fiction of "commutative justice"', as contended by Jaffé.

Jaffé states that Walras 'was faithfully following a tradition established by the "philosophes" of eighteenth-century France who were . . . believers in the sovereign efficacy of systematized reason in coping with social and political problems' (1980, p. 531), but rather than his having learnt such a method of thought from French philosophers, he must be seen as having acquired it from natural scientists such as Galileo, Newton, Laplace, d'Alembert and Lagrange; Walras adopted the method of 'systematized reasoning' in order to establish within economics a science which was 'rational as well as empirical'.

Whatever the case, the following passages do make it abundantly clear that Walras regarded pure economics as a discipline which through a reliance on empirical fact could elucidate the way in which the actual economy worked (cf. Morishima, 1980, p. 531).

Pure economics is, in essence, the theory of the determination of prices under a hypothetical regime of perfectly free competition. (Walras, 1954, p. 40)

We shall suppose the market is perfectly competitive, just as in pure mechanics we suppose . . . that machines are perfectly frictionless. (p. 84)

What physicist would deliberately pick cloudy weather for astronomical observations instead of taking advantage of a cloudless night? (p. 86)

It is perfectly clear that economics, like astronomy and mechanics, is both an empirical and a rational science. (p. 47)

The twentieth century . . . will feel the need . . . of entrusting the social sciences to men of general culture who are accustomed to think both inductively and deductively and who are familiar with reason as well as experience. The mathematical economics will rank with the mathematical sciences of astronomy and mechanics. (p. 48)

III

Walras's economic theory as indicated above is entirely sound and legitimate. It is entirely along the lines of the Report of the Evaluative Committee for *Econometrica* (1954), and given that this report was compiled by Samuelson, chairman, Koopmans and Stone, it could probably be said to represent the views of mainstream thinking among modern mathematical economists. This report states the following:

Without attempting here to define economics, we can say that it is concerned with the study of certain aspects of the actual world of our experience just as is physics or biology. Studies of this kind may be undertaken for their own sake, that is, to obtain a better understanding of the phenomena in question, or to assist in the evaluation, construction, or implementation of policy, in Pigou's phrase 'for light or for fruit.' However this may be, systematic investigation involves certain more or less distinct types of intellectual activity. One of these consists in the development of appropriate concepts and theories in terms of which observable phenomena can be described, classified, and related. This activity, mainly economic theory, results in statements about theoretical counterparts of actual phenomena, which statements may, in principle, be shown by experience to be false or to stand in need of modification. (p. 141)

We are convinced that the use of advanced or unfamiliar branches of mathematics should be no bar to the acceptance of an article provided that its economic relevance is clear and that it is of the requisite standard. (p. 142)

We do not believe that the mathematical character of an article is any reason for its rejection provided that the mathematics used form an appropriate language in which to discuss the subject matter of the article. (p. 144)

In discussing articles to be accepted for *Econometrica* the report went on to recommend an increase in 'the proportion of empirical studies of economic behaviour or technological structure' and 'the proportion of articles written in an expository style' (including the revival of the review articles surveying the existing state of knowledge in some particular area which appeared at more or less regular intervals in *Econometrica* before the war and including expository articles providing information about mathematical and statistical methods of relevance to economists).

Despite this, 27 years later Hahn was forced to recognize that 'theorists all over the world have become aware that anything based on this mock-up [i.e. competitive general-equilibrium analysis] is unlikely to fly, since it neglects some crucial aspects of the world, the recognition of which will force some drastic redesigning' (Hahn, 1981b). Walras's pure economics was the prototype of competitive general-equilibrium analysis, but even 70 years after his death it had failed to become a science which could 'rank with the mathematical science of astronomy and mechanics' (Walras, 1954, p. 48).

Of course, the redesigning of the Walrasian model has been attempted by a number of economic theorists. But the highly sophisticated mock-ups they have produced have not been objects which could fly either. If one calls those individuals working in the field of the microeconomic foundation of Keynesian economics Keynesian-economic theorists, then, as Hahn has said, these 'Keynesians were not much better'.

Despite the fact that many economic theorists have thus been aware of the deficiencies and defects of their own models and have made efforts to improve them, why is it, then, that no one has yet succeeded in producing a model which is at all 'airworthy'?

It is certainly true that there have, especially since 1960, been a great many attempts in this direction and variants of the competitive general-equilibrium model and alternatives to it have both been presented. Such things are in certain respects more appropriate than the original model, but as a whole they too have proved remarkably unsatisfactory. The most important reason for the continuing frustration which has beset the development of economic theory over the last 30 years or more is the failure of economic theorists to carry out sweeping, systematic research into the actual mechanisms of the economy and economic organizations, despite their being aware that their own models are inappropriate to analysis of the actual economy. Economic theorists randomly modify those parts of the original model which they themselves happen to consider inapplicable, each develops a model which emphasizes and exaggerates his own modifications with no sense of proportion, and they have ended up with a whole pile of models which are even more difficult to deal with than the original.

The original model presupposed a system where all prices were decided by *tâtonnement* with or without an auctioneer. In the real economy, however, the goods where such methods of deciding prices can be regarded as predominant are at most only the products of agriculture, forestry, fishing and mining. No auction market exists for the products of manufacturing industry. The production prices of such products are decided at each individual factory according to the full-cost principle, and each has its own channels of circulation through which it reaches its final customer. Under the classical models – and this is not merely true of that of Marx, of course, but even, contrary to what is generally assumed, true of Walras's general-equilibrium model of production – there existed, for each individual good (including agricultural, factory, marine and mining products), a cost–price equation according to which it decided its own price. But under the neo-classical, competitive general-equilibrium model the situation was quite the opposite, with the prices not only of agricultural, forestry, fishing and mining products but also those of the products of manufacturing industry being regarded as decided by auction with no cost–price equation. Furthermore, the price of labour (i.e. wages) was assumed to be decided in exactly the same way as was the price of fish. But is there any country in the world where the fish go on strike?

Moreover, in considering the method of fixing an exchange rate applicable for the conversion of the prices of imported goods into units of domestic currency, general-equilibrium analysis has had almost no useful observations to offer. The foreign exchange market is extremely competitive, and the inter-bank market, where the vast majority of exchange dealings are carried out, is not a *tâtonnement* market with an auctioneer. Economic theorists have very little idea of the precise rules according to which exchange rates are being decided. In order to decide the prices of products of the manufacturing industries which utilize as raw materials agricultural, forestry, marine and mining products imported from abroad, we must make clear how prices are decided in various different ways in different markets, such as commodity markets abroad (auction markets), exchange markets (competitive markets without auctioneers) and the domestic labour market (a kind of cross-trading market), and furthermore convert the prices which have been decided in these ways into the prices of products of manufacturing industry according to the full-cost principle adopted by manufacturing industry, but there has yet to be developed a multi-sectoral economic model which gives proper consideration to the structure of such price-fixing mechanisms.

Further problems are not only that competitive general-equilibrium analysis and its variations or alternatives do not give proper regard to the role of the labour unions and their limitations, but even banking activity is omitted from consideration. A general-equilibrium theory of money with no banks is running wild. In other words, the institutional foundation of these so-called highbrow economic theories is an extremely shaky one.

IV

Moreover, these models have neither 'nationality' nor historical character. It is well known that the farmers' co-ops of Poland and Yugoslavia and the kolkhoz of the Soviet Union differ from each other both institutionally and in their modes of operation. Furthermore, Soviet-type socialism, Hungarian market socialism and Yugoslav co-operationalism are all different. Economic theory for the countries of Eastern Europe must therefore take account of nationality, and even for the one country of Soviet Russia, in

economic theory we must distinguish between the period of the
NEP, the period of war communism, and theories for the period
since 1965 when important structural reforms were initiated.
Similarly, in the various countries of the so-called Western world
a single neo-classical theory cannot be regarded as equally applicable to the USA, the UK, West Germany, France and Japan. Not
only are the numerical values of the parameters of their demand
functions and production functions different, but they are also
qualitatively different in that they have economic structures
which are essentially quite different from each other, and for that
reason we must create for each of them models which are systematically distinct.

And this is not all. Economic theory must be developed in
terms of a logic appropriate to the economy with which it is concerned. Samuelson, for example, proved in the following manner
the proposition that Leontief's hypothesis of the fixed input
coefficients – which had been made by Leontief for the sake of
analytical simplicity – was compatible with the more general case
of production functions admitting of substitution, in the sense
that the actual input coefficients which were revealed after all the
necessary adjustments to market prices had been made were all
invariable with respect to changes in the composition of final demand and in the total quantity of labour (the so-called substitution theorem). Assuming that labour (regarded as homogeneous)
is the sole primary factor of production and providing that the
market for each product and the market for labour are competitive, Samuelson says that production will always be carried out on
the efficiency frontier. Considering as given the final outputs C_2,
$C_3 \ldots C_n$ of commodities $2, 3 \ldots n$ and the amount of labour used
x_{n+1}, he maximizes the final output of commodity 1, C_1: then the
$n \times n$ input coefficients a_{ji} and the n labour input coefficients $a_{n+1,i}$
will be decided by the first-order conditions for the maximum.
Since all production functions are assumed to be homogeneous of
degree one in all input variables, the a_{ji}'s and $a_{n+1,i}$'s as decided
above are independent of the assigned values of C_2, $C_3 \ldots C_n$,
x_{n+1}. (Providing these coefficients are kept constant then it is permissible to adjust the gross outputs $x_1, x_2 \ldots x_n$ such that:

$$x_j - \Sigma a_{ji} x_i = C_j, j = 2, 3 \ldots n,$$
$$\Sigma a_{n+1,i} x_i = x_{n+1}$$

Joint products, however, are assumed to be ruled out.)

These are the essentials of Samuelson's proof of the substitution theorem (Samuelson, 1951b)[5] from which it follows: The competitive prices in terms of labour which are determined under such conditions of efficiency are equal to Marx's labour values, and, therefore, the profit accruing to each capitalist under such conditions is zero.[6] Each capitalist combines labour with the means of production to produce his own particular product, but such activity on the part of capitalists must be undertaken by them without any remuneration!

Thus for production to be carried on in an efficient manner in the Samuelson world, capitalists must provide their services free of charge; but actually they are hardly likely to be philanthropists. Marx did not believe it to be the case that under a capitalist economy all prices would end up equal to their respective labour values, believing that such conditions would prevail only in simple commodity-production economies – petty producer societies preceding capitalism where the workers themselves owned their own means of production and exchanged their own commodities among one another. For that reason, even supposing the substitution theorem was valid under a capitalist economy, it must at the very least be said that Samuelson's demonstration is an inappropriate one.

My own opinion is that any static substitution theorem which disregards the existence of capital goods does not hold good for the real economy. However, given that this is not the point with which we are dealing at present, what means should we adopt for demonstrating that this theorem does have some validity for a capitalist economy? Evidently the logic we use must inhere in the economy.

Capitalists in each industry will fix their production coefficients so that the average cost of production of each product, $\Sigma\ p_j\ a_{ji} + p_{n+1}\ a_{n+1i}$, is at a minimum, subject to the production function $f_i(a_{1i}, a_{2i} \ldots a_{n+1i}) = 1$. The production coefficients are then given as functions of prices: $a_{ji} = a_{ji}(p, p_{n+1})$, $a_{n+1i} = a_{n+1i}(p, p_{n+1})$, where p is the n dimensional vector of prices excluding the wage rate p_{n+1}. Since capital migrates from one industry to another in search of the maximum rate of profit, profit rates will be equalized throughout n industries. Hence we will have

$$p = (1+\pi)[p\ A(p, p_{n+1}) + p_{n+1}\ a_{n+1}(p, p_{n+1})] \qquad (1)$$

where π is the uniform profit rate, $A\ (p, p_{n+1})$ the matrix whose elements are $a_{ji}(p, p_{n+1})$, and $a_{n+1}(p, p_{n+1})$ the vector with the components $a_{n+1i}(p, p_{n+1})$. The prices are normalized such that

$$p_1 + p_2 + \ldots + p_{n+1} \tag{2}$$

This can be demonstrated as follows. (a) If we assign to the wage rate a discretionary value such that $0 \leqq p_{n+1} < 1$, then any p, π which could produce (1) and (2) will be uniquely determined (see Morishima, 1964, Lemma 1, pp. 61–3). (b) When the wage rate p_{n+1} is set at 0 then π will be positive;[7] this value of π is denoted by π^*. (c) π is a continuous function of p_{n+1}; it takes on a negative value when p_{n+1} is set at a value which is very close to 1, and the limiting value of π where p_{n+1} approaches 1 is denoted by π_*. (d) A unique price set (p, p_{n+1}) associates with any assigned value of π between π^* and π_*. (e) It is then apparent from (a)–(d) above that π is a decreasing function of p_{n+1}.

Let us now assume the value of p_{n+1} which makes $\pi = 0$ to be p^*_{n+1}. If the wage rate is equal to or greater than p^*_{n+1} then the profit rate π will take on the value of 0 or minus; therefore capitalism cannot work.[8] Therefore the wage rate must be lower than p^*_{n+1}. If it is set at a p^0_{n+1} which fulfils this sort of condition, then π^0, p^0, p^0_{n+1} are accordingly fixed so as to satisfy (1). The establishment of such conditions as these under capitalism results from each enterprise selecting the technology that will minimize the cost per unit of output, capital migrating between industries in search of the greatest return, and as a result profits being equalized through industry as a whole.

With $A^0 = A(p^0, p^0_{n+1})$ and $a^0_{n+1} = a_{n+1}(p^0, p^0_{n+1})$ the output vector x and the volume of employment N are fixed by the equations

$$x = A^0 x + C$$
$$N = a^0_{n+1} x$$

C being the final demand vector. Consequently if final demand C_i is reduced the volume of employment N is also reduced. Should this create unemployment and the wage rate be pushed down, a new profit rate π^1 and prices p^1 are expected to prevail in accordance with the new wage rate p^1_{n+1}. The production coefficients become $A^1 = A(p^1, p^1_{n+1})$, $a^1_{n+1} = a_{n+1}(p^1, p^1_{n+1})$. Since it is not necessarily true that $A^1 = A^0$, $a^1_{n+1} = a^0_{n+1}$ the production coefficients in general change and the substitution theorem is violated.

For this reason, in order to effect the substitution theorem, apart from the conditions enumerated by Samuelson, it is necessary to have a situation where the wage rate remains unchanged even where there is an excess supply of (or demand for) labour. (And it is then found that such an assumption of rigid wages is necessary even in Samuelson's own theorem. As has been explained above, if his economy is a capitalist economy it can be regarded as a special case with $p_{n+1}^0 = p_{n+1}^*$ where π^* vanishes. However, it does not differ from the general case where any reduction in C produces unemployment, the appearance of unemployment pushes down the wage rate and the production coefficients are likely to change as a result.) Then if one recognizes the rigidity of the factor prices, the assumption of only one scarce primary factor (labour) which was maintained by Samuelson is no longer necessary for the theorem to be valid. Even should many factors of production exist this presents no problem providing all their prices are rigid.[9]

Whatever the case, the above argument illustrates the fact that when proving one of the theorems of mathematical economics verification must be in accordance with the economy presupposed by that theorem.[10] To substantiate the substitution theorem in relation not only to the input–output tables of the capitalist economy but also to the tables of the socialist economy, for the former the proof must be in accordance with the behaviour of enterprises under a capitalist economy, and for the latter the discussion must be based on the method of forming and carrying out economic plans in a socialist economy. But if the constancy of input–output coefficients is dependent on reasons which are entirely unrelated to the logic of the working of these systems (for example, technological reasons), then the proof of the theorem must lie in factors which transcend the system. Proof of a 'theorem' in economics is not like the same thing in mathematics, where a theorem is judged to have been proved providing there is no mistake in the formal argument. Samuelson's proof is also based on the characteristic of capitalism that production is carried out 'efficiently' in the economy. But is it really the case that capitalism is 'efficient' in the sense he maintains? In reality, in contrast with the implications of his substitution theorem, capitalists earn profits; labour values do not prevail as prices in the market.

V

So, despite the fact that the general-equilibrium analysis started by Walras has on the theoretical side developed into Hicks's sequential analysis of temporary equilibria, and as far as substantiation is concerned has led to the splendid empirical application of Leontief's input–output analysis (Hicks, 1939; Leontief, 1941); despite, moreover, the marked advance which has taken place in the mathematics used in economics since the last war, we have not yet, according to Hahn's judgement, reached a state of affairs where the thing will 'fly'.

What is the reason for this? The blame is often assigned to mathematics on the ground that people all too frequently make excessive use of over-advanced mathematics, but it is basically not with the mathematics that the fault lies. There is a 'kink' in people's demand for mathematics; they welcome enthusiastically the use of mathematics up to a certain level, but demonstrate a strongly hostile reaction to the use of mathematics over and above this point. At what level this 'kink' appears is decided by the mathematical capacity of each individual, and certainly is not something decided by the character of each individual sector of learning where attempts are being made to apply mathematics. Consequently introductory books should be written with their mathematics pitched at a lower level than that which lies within the mathematical ability of the average reader, while textbooks aimed at the more advanced university students should be written at a mathematical level slightly higher than the average student's ability. There should be no limit to the mathematics used in specialist writings.

However, as any economist knows, if any means whatsoever are used excessively their marginal productivity will decline. My own assessment is that in recent years mathematics has been over-used and its marginal productivity has decreased markedly, but the emergence of this phenomenon of a superfluity of mathematics stems not from the increase in the absolute quantity of mathematics at our disposal, but from the ever greater injection of mathematics into a fixed quantity of material. To the extent that there can be no comparison between the maximum principles from which each individual's and each firm's demand and supply functions are derived in the present era and those of Walras's period, these principles have been elaborated and refined with a self-satisfied air on the part of economic theorists, but any analysis of markets where these demands and supplies are matched is conspicuously backward. Needless to say, a market is a single institution, and all institutions have their own customs and rules which they must obey. General-equilibrium analysis is still remarkably backward in examining how a system works under a given institutional organization, since it is not seriously concerned with observing, formulating and analyzing these customs and rules. The antiquated theory that prices are fixed at the point where demand and supply coincide is still being used as hitherto, or else all we have is a plethora of new models and new theories based on ideas which assume crude institutional arrangements conceived from highly superficial observations. Since this is the state of affairs even with the market, other institutions are all disregarded in the mock-up created by the general-equilibrium theorists in spite of the fact that institutions such as banks, the central bank, labour unions, the government and capitalists' organizations play a highly significant role in the actual economy. My own belief is that the major factor due to which mathematical economics has been caught in its present remarkably 'anaemic' situation is that empirical institutional knowledge and mathematics have failed to sustain a good, co-operative relationship. In other words, institutional-analytical economics in the sense of abstracting from empirical information concerning actual institutions to conceive ideal-typical institutions and analyse their working in a rational, mathematical fashion, is either absent or else extremely underdeveloped.

In this respect the course of development followed earlier by 'Japanese mathematics' – known as *wasan* – offers a very salutary lesson.[11] In Western Europe mathematics developed in close conjunction with natural science, in particular with physics. Physicists observed the rationality within nature and mathematicians developed it in the form of mathematics. For the Japanese government, which imported Chinese mathematics (originally developed as arithmetic for administrative purposes), such an opportunity never existed. Chinese mathematics developed as a mathematics which used tools – in this sense Chinese mathematics can be regarded as the prototype of modern computer science –

tools perfected into the abacus. At the beginning of the seventeenth century, quite independently of the West, Japanese mathematicians succeeded in using symbols to express mathematical formulae. Algebra subsequently showed a remarkable degree of development in Japan. During the seventeenth century, again independently of the West, Japanese advances included the demonstration of Pythagoras's theorem, research on the ratio of the circumference of the circle to the diameter, and the discovery of various theorems concerning determinants. Seki Kōwa, a contemporary of Newton and Leibnitz, even initiated his own particular brand of differential and integral calculus.

Seki, however, achieved nothing in the way of mechanics and physics, and right up to the Meiji Revolution (1867–8) Japanese mathematics continued to pursue a development totally independent of natural science. It is true that during the last years of the Tokugawa period (1850s to 1860s) works on navigation, surveying and astronomy were imported into Japan, and the Japanese gained a limited acquaintance with Western mathematics, but Japanese mathematics in the sense of *wasan* remained virtually uninfluenced by Western mathematics and continued its own autonomous development. *Wasan* developed as an accomplishment or a pastime, for the sake of purely intellectual amusement, and mathematicians made their living by taking tuition fees from their pupils in just the same way as did masters of the tea ceremony, flower arrangement, *kendō*, *go* and *shōgi* (Japanese chess). The position in society occupied by mathematicians was a lowly one, and mathematics was no more than a piece of 'culture' liked as an intellectual amusement, mainly among townspeople rather than samurai. The Japanese merchant, unlike the Western bourgeois, was neither aggressive nor innovative in using modern technology. *Wasan*, therefore, had little bearing on production techniques or natural science, and its relationship with philosophy or any aspect of thought was also a tenuous one. It is not surprising that all it did was contract within its own world and end up by becoming a useless science. In 1872 the new Meiji government issued the Education Law, which ordered that '*Wasan* (Japanese Mathematics) shall be abolished and *yōsan* (Western mathematics) only shall be used'; as a result *wasan* died completely.

Similarly, if pure economics makes light of any application to the actual economy and neglects to base itself on abstractions from things of which we have actual experience, its future will be as wretched as the fate of *wasan*. However beautiful or however elegant the whole system may be, those who devote themselves to a learning which is useless are inevitably just playing at a pastime, and it is likely that before long its learning will come to a standstill. General-equilibrium analysis was started by Walras with a theory of the determination of prices under the hypothesis of perfectly free competition, as a first approximation to reality; pure economists must carry on in the same spirit by making abstractions from a large number of actual, non-competitive elements, and taking into account more relevant observations and experiences. They should come up with an airworthy theoretical system which will be of use in considering the actual economy and can be applied to it. Needless to say, economics is not something which exists to rationalize a specific ideal, be it *laissez-faire* or communism.[12]

Physicists have applied existing mathematics to elucidate physical phenomena; but they have in addition turned up hitherto undiscovered mathematics which has been concealed in physical phenomena, and with the devising of new mathematics (for example the theory of differential equations) both mathematics and physics have been advanced. If mathematical economists wish to make this sort of outstanding contribution, it is essential that they are prepared to make rather better observations of the actual economy and come to grips with reality. What is in any case necessary is an in-depth study of fact – and for that purpose we must know a great deal more about such things as history, sociology and institutions – and pursuit of mathematization in accordance with fact. Until such a thing is realized, mathematical economists must for the present not only be careful of using mathematics to over-engage in fancy speculation but must at the very least for a time retreat from the more dazzling varieties of mathematics. What we have to do most of all in this respect is not to build up highly sophisticated models, but to establish a reliable model whose foundations are firmly placed in the midst of reality, and which can serve a practical use, and so also serve as a base for the future development of defensible theory.

The mathematical economics of today is constructed on an axiomatic basis, and excessive stress is laid on its aspect as a deductive science. As Walras has said, it is certainly true that 'economics is a science in which the process of reasoning makes up for the ambiguities and the deficiencies in our experience' (1954, p. 367), but in saying so he was mistaken in giving people the impression that mathematical reasoning was the be-all and end-all. The conclusions arrived at by deductive reasoning can be held to be valid without turning to experience for confirmation only, as has been said above, where the axiom system which has been created is compatible with reality. A proposition which arises from an axiom system isolated from actual fact has no capacity for prediction. However magnificient theory may be, this sort of 'science' can never be anything more than a house built on sand.

In this chapter we have concentrated our attention in particular upon general-equilibrium analysis, discussing why it still remains in an incomplete, semi-scientific state, despite its being more than a hundred years since the idea was first conceived. There are possibly parts of the other branches of mathematical economics where the situation is not this bad, but there are fields which, for exactly the same reasons as apply to general-equilibrium analysis, are to the same degree unscientific and dogmatic, as well as fields in which mathematical economists devote themselves entirely to technical problems which in economic terms are not that important. These branches conduct a 'theoretical inquiry' which operates a plausible logic, but its positive basis of argument is weak and open to doubt. Furthermore, since general (dis)equilibrium analysis is a field which must occupy a focal position within economic analysis, for a field of such importance to be in such a state of affairs is a matter of grave significance.[13]

What I should perhaps put down here is my own evaluation of general-equilibrium theory. Despite the failings which I have mentioned I still believe general-equilibrium theory to be the theoretical kernel of economics. The traditional general-equilibrium theory makes clear such things as whether, after the various conditions for equilibrium are expressed in mathematical terms, such a mathematical system has an equilibrium solution, whether an equilibrium solution is stable, and whether an equilibrium solution is a point of Pareto-optimum. But it is probably evident from what I have said above that I do not set great store by this kind of stereotyped question. If economists successfully devise a correct general-equilibrium model, even if it can be proved to possess an equilibrium solution, should it lack the institutional backing to realize an equilibrium solution then that equilibrium solution will amount to no more than a utopian state of affairs which bears no relation whatsoever to the real economy. Disequilibrium is likely to persist in many parts of the actual economy, and at the very most only partial equilibria will be realized in several sectors. This being the case, the proposition that 'general equilibrium is Pareto-optimum' cannot be refuted in the light of the facts, so it can no longer even be called a scientific proposition.

Regarding this point it is significant that Walras, having elucidated the fact that his general-equilibrium model possessed a mathematical solution, then argued for 'solution in practice' attempting to show that 'the theoretical solution is identically the solution worked out by the market' (1954, pp. 170–2 – cf. note 1). Unfortunately Walras's solution in practice was a highly superficial one, and since it was not suitably based on the actual market mechanism Walras was satisfied with a verification which was mistaken as to the identity of the mathematical solution and the market solution. Had Walras, however, rendered his solution in practice less superficial and succeeded in bringing it rather closer to reality then the unreality of his general-equilibrium mathematical solution would probably have been more apparent.

But I regard general-equilibrium theory as being significant in a totally different sense. According to general-equilibrium theory the whole economy is conceived of as a system. Without this sort of framework it is impossible to elucidate in any systematic fashion what sort of repercussions on what part of the economy will result from a disturbance arising in one part of the economy. What I mean by general-equilibrium theory (and there will no doubt be some people who regard this designation as inappropriate) is this sort of theory concerning the framework of the economy. This framework is likely to be different for different countries, and apt to change when times change. In my 'general-equilibrium theory', therefore, mathematics too is, to a certain degree, important, but more important are such things as knowledge and observation of the economic system itself and a considerable interest in history and sociology.

In any case, the reason for present-day economics having lapsed into the wretched state of affairs we have noted above is the fact that so deep and extensive has been the mathematization of economics since 1940 that it has lost all sense of balance, becoming divorced from knowledge of economic systems and economic history. There is only one medicine which will cure this malaise, and that is for theorists to make a serious effort in the direction of the institutionalization of economics, in the sense of slowing the speed of all development towards mathematization and developing economic theory in accordance with knowledge of economic organizations, industrial structure and economic history.

However, I am not sufficiently optimistic to think that economists who have been successful in the field of mathematical economics will easily co-operate in pursuing this kind of methodological transformation. As Peter Wiles has said (1979–80), 'human capital is just as nonfungible (clay not putty) as physical capital', and to bring about any reduction in the role of mathematics in economics would serve to render obsolete the human capital which the mathematical economists themselves constitute. It is certainly the case that mathematics is no more than a language of science, and mathematical economics an extension of the verbal – logical Ricardian abstract economics, but because mathematics is powerful it will always become an object of fetishism, unlike abstract reasoning in words. Propositions congealed into the form of 'theorems' are not more than logical conclusions from assumed hypotheses, but create the illusion of being scientific discoveries. Mathematical economists construct a mountain as it were from these sorts of quasi-scientific (or pseudo-scientific) pieces, and worship as gods those who have contributed to making the mountain a high one.

What is also a bad thing is, again in the words of Peter Wiles, that 'theoretical, especially algebraical, articles take less time to write. Their correctness – though not, of course, their value – is more easily assessed' (1979–80). Therefore in order for mathematical economists to maximize the rate of return on their own human capital they have worked hard to produce quasi-scientific articles and succeeded in making the mountain higher and higher. We have in our discipline been led up the wrong path by the invisible hand of the demon, and because it takes both time and money to make an engine we are producing on a large scale 'aeroplanes' which have no engine.

The following words of Keynes, which I have quoted elsewhere, sum up admirably what sort of mix of ingredients the talents of an economic theorist must show, and consequently the fact that economics is an 'orchestral' field of study made up of a balance of various different methods of approach and disciplines.

> The master economist must possess a rare combination of gifts. He must reach a high standard in several different directions and must combine talent not often found together. He must be mathematician, historian, statesman, philosopher – to some degree. He must understand symbols and speak in terms of the general, and touch abstract and concrete in the same flight of thought. He must study the present in the light of the past for the purpose of the future. No part of man's nature or his institutions must lie entirely outside his regard.(Keynes, 1972, pp. 173–4)

Nor should mathematical economists such as ourselves forget Keynes's following warning:

> Unlike physics, for example, such parts of the bare bones of economic theory as are expressible in mathematical forms are extremely easy compared with the economic interpretation of the complex and incompletely known facts of experience, and lead one but a very little way towards establishing useful results. (ibid.)

Notes

Translated from the original Japanese text by Janet Hunter. The author is grateful to P.J.D. Wiles for helpful comments on an earlier version of this paper.

[1] This paper originally had the subtitle 'With Special Reference to General Equilibrium Analysis'. The reason for my selection of this field was the fact that, of all the various branches of mathematical economics, this was the one with which I am most conversant. It was also, however, because it is general equilibrium analysis which lies at the very heart of mathematical economics. What I have to say in this paper will, subject to the addition of appropriate modifications and changes in emphasis, more or less hold true for other branches as well.

[2] Jaffé calls attention to the fact that whereas Walras had written in the preface to the second edition of the *Elements* 'my theory . . . is indeed the faithful expression and exact explanation of facts of the real world', in the fourth edition this had been rewritten as 'the abstract expression and rational explanation of facts'. Jaffé's conclusion is that 'this only confirms Walras's constant preoccupation with creating a model of terrestrial utopia in contrast with the otherworldly utopias of the early French socialists' (1980, p. 531). This kind of interpretation, however, is devoid of any understanding of theory. For those who believe, like me, that Walras's theory had an eye to the actual world and not to a utopia of any kind, Walras's rewriting of the sentence is not merely extremely natural but also essential. The reason for this is that a theory geared to the actual world provides 'the abstract expression and rational explanation' of facts of the real world; it can

certainly not provide 'the faithful expression and exact explanation' of such facts. The passage was rewritten because it had to be.

[3] Max Weber (1864–1920), Henri Poincaré (1854–1912), Léon Walras (1834–1910).

[4] It is true that Walras designates pure economics as economic theory under the hypothesis of perfectly free competition, but the following passage makes it clear that he did not in fact apply such a narrow definition as this to pure economics: 'Varied as the topics are in this [non-competitive or imperfectly competitive] part of pure economics, they are at present completely ignored, but they will be developed little by little as a fuller knowledge of the general case makes possible a more detailed study of every kind of exception' (1954, p. 431). Moreover, in view of his statement that 'It is the part of applied economics to inquire whether free competition is always the best means' (p. 40n), even supposing he had been analysing Jaffé's so-called realistic utopia (this phrase does not appear in the *Elements* at all), it is unlikely that Walras regarded such a thing as a subject for pure economics.

[5] The volume containing Samuelson, 1951b, also contains alternative proofs by T.C. Koopmans, K.J. Arrow and N. Georgescu- Roegen, but the essence of these is not substantially different from Samuelson's proof.

[6] Let us denote the vector of the Samuelson prices in terms of labour by P, the Leontief input coefficient matrix and the labour-input coefficient vector by $A(P)$ and $a_{n+1}(P)$, respectively; then it can be proved that $P = P A(P) + a_{n+1}(P)$. Next let Λ be the labour value vector corresponding to the case where the technology $(A(P), a_{n+1}(P))$ prevails. We then have $\Lambda = \Lambda A(P) + a_{n+1}(P)$ by definition; hence it is immediately apparent that $P = \Lambda$. Thus the labour theory of value which Samuelson criticizes and rejects throughout his articles on Marx is valid where his substitution theorem holds true!

[7] But the assumption is that $A(p,0)$ is productive.

[8] Prices in accordance with p^*_{n+1}, are denoted by p^*. Since the profit rate is 0 the equation

$$p^* = p^* A (p^*, p^*_{n+1}) + p^*_{n+1} a_{n+1}(p^*, p^*_{n+1})$$

holds true. Since A and a_{n+1} are homogeneous of degree zero in p, p_{n+1} the above formula may be written

$$P^* = P^* A(P^*) + a_{n+1}(P^*).$$

Here $P^* = p^*/p^*_{n+1}$. P^* is therefore equivalent to Marx's labour value vector Λ, and as I have already explained this sort of situation is produced in a simple commodity production economy but does not appear in a capitalist economy.

[9] Concerning the above kind of interpretation of the substitution theorem see Morishima, 1956.

[10] In order to check how far this is so, mathematical economists must, as Tomonaga has said in relation to theoretical physics, 'at various stages of the mathematical process, return from the world of mathematical formulae to the world of the phenomena those mathematical formulae are attempting to represent, and remember the meaning of those formulae' Tomonaga, 1979.

[11] For information on what follows, see Ogura, 1940.

[12] If this should be the meaning of the following statement by Hicks I am in total agreement with him: 'I have felt little sympathy with the theory for theory's sake, which has been characteristic of one strand in American economics; nor with the idealization of the free market, which has been characteristic of another' (Hicks, 1979b). In the preface to *Value and Capital*, 1st edition (1939) Hicks had already stated: 'the place of economic theory is to be the servant of applied economics'; so this kind of spirit can be regarded as consistently running through all his theoretical research. It is this spirit, too, which separates him from the post-war (mainly American) mathematical economics. See also his *Classics and Moderns* (Oxford: Blackwell) 1983, pp. 355–64.

[13] With regard to disequilibrium analysis, see, for example, Barro and Grossman, 1976, and Malinvaud, 1977. The systemic background of their models, however, is sparse, and my own feeling is that Kornai, 1971, is a more useful key than are these two works to the development of disequilibrium analysis.

A Reply to Gorman (see chapter 11)

MICHIO MORISHIMA

Arrow-Hahn

Gorman feels that my making examples of Paul Samuelson's substitution theorem and Kenneth Arrow and Frank Hahn's *General
Competitive Analysis* leaves something to be desired, but there
was no ulterior motive in my selection of them as objects of criticism. If there had been it would have been because of their
wellfounded reputations, and also because while I may criticize
them I can at the same time express my own firm conviction of an
unchanging friendship and respect for them.

Gorman forgets that both Arrow and Hahn are the editors of
the mathematical economics series. The fact that they failed in
their own book to 'relate the theory to relevant empirical work'
may be the result of one of three things: either they were forgetful
of their own editorial manifesto; or this manifesto was no more
than publicity aimed at prospective readers; or the task of producing theories backed up by empirical work and real facts proved far
more difficult than simple mathematical work (however outstanding and rigorous this might be). My own belief is that it was
neither of the first two factors. But, supposing it was the last of
the three, and if, moreover, large numbers of theorists dodge this
difficult task, then high level mathematical economics will remain
for ever metaeconomics.

Samuelson

In the normal run of events there are several alternative proofs
for many theorems. In the case of mathematics, the merits or de-
merits of these proofs are judged from a mathematical–logical

standpoint. In the case of the theorems of mathematical economics, this does not have to be the case. Observations must be made concerning the way in which the actual economy works, and the theorem proved in line with these observations (or in line with the logic of the real economy). I chose Samuelson's substitution theorem as an example in developing this kind of view.

Walras

I am entirely in agreement with Gorman's view that 'Walras has been a Morishima–Walras at one time, and a Jaffé–Walras at another, or both at once'. It is not here, however, that our problem lies. As has already been stated, Walras subdivided political economy into 'a natural science, a moral science and an art', or into 'pure economics, social economics and applied economics', and he himself had planned to carry through his ideas in each of these three branches. The question is whether his pure economics was Jaffé–Walras or Morishima–Walras. There is no doubt that his *Elements* includes Jaffé–Walras elements, but that particular part (Lessons 26, 27 (pp. 296–306)) is not only lacking in mathematical lucidity, it is also no more than a very small part of the total text of the *Elements* (447 pages in all). Walras directed his *Elements* at the Morishima–Walras, and even supposing he had accomplished a considerable mount of work along Jaffé–Walras lines, he would have consigned it to the sphere of 'social economics'.

It is largely since 1950 that general equilibrium analysis has been developed along Jaffé–Walras lines. It was unfortunate that at a time when the Morishima–Walras type of model had yet to be perfected to a level where it could 'fly', economists' interests were switched in the direction of the 'realistic utopia'.

History

When Gorman recommends the combining of 'mathematics with history rather than science at school', he is not too far from the whole point of my argument. On the grounds that heaven does not bestow more than one gift and that those who like history tend to dislike mathematics (as I myself did) and vice versa, I myself have some doubts as to the popularity of a Gormanesque combined course at A level (or High School) student level, but not merely I myself, but many others as well, have no objection whatsoever to such a course, as a good combination preparatory to the study of economics. It seems, however, that Gorman believes that mathematical economics + history = good economic theory, whereas the ability to list persons and dates within the space of a few minutes (an ability acclaimed by Gorman in the original draft of chapter 11) does not prove one's ability as a historian at all. It merely proves either that one has a bad sense of what history is, or, at best, that he could become a candidate for 'Mastermind'. Even a large personal history library proves little. The question is whether a knowledge of history is reflected in economic theory. What I am emphasizing is the need to construct theories compatible with history, and to modify and improve theories in accordance with historical development. A mere knowledge of facts, while possibly worthy of admiration, is insufficient to secure an individual respect as a scholar. What I must reiterate is the need to build up economic theories based on a knowledge of history, institutions and society and compatible with them. For this we need not merely the division of labour stressed by Gorman, but also cooperation between various disciplines. To do this the economic theorist himself must be like the conductor of an orchestra, commanding a knowledge of many disciplines, and able to use the various tones to produce his own music – in this case his own theory. (This ability was possessed by the early economists, Adam Smith, for example.) To accomplish work in the field of economic theory which will be 'social study' in the true sense of the term requires 'imagination, fertility and open-mindedness' far in excess of that needed to prove new mathematical propositions.

More Mathematicians?

Finally, Gorman's conclusion appears to be that we need 'more mathematicians, not fewer', but I don't care much one way or the other about that sort of thing. At the LSE I work in the International Centre for Economics and Related Disciplines, as well as being in the Economics Department. I would not care in the least if this centre were 100 per cent occupied by mathematicians, as long as these mathematicians were capable of furthering the study of economics by using the achievements of related disciplines, and as long as this is what they actually did. Hitherto the development of economics has owed much to the Econometric Society's idea that there should be a trinity consisting of mathematics, statistics and economic theory. We have now reached a stage where the mathematization of economics is excessive, and it is the trinity of economic theory, statistics and related disciplines on which emphasis should be placed. Gorman himself is unlikely to be opposed to such a new trinity. He has already recognized the significance of history, and in the original draft of his comments wrote 'econometrics (my "statistics" – MM) is the methodology of economics in a much fuller sense than mathematics is.'

4

Monetarism and Duhem's Thesis

ROD CROSS

This paper is concerned with the problem of how to appraise theories in economics: are there 'rational' grounds for preferring one theory to another? Our starting point is Duhem's thesis which states that, because our theories are invariably conjunctions of hypotheses, evidence can only justifiably be used to falsify the claims made by conjunctions of hypotheses rather than the claims made by individual hypotheses. In response to the claims of a theory being found to be in conflict with the evidence, 'we learn that this theory should be modified but we are not told what must be changed . . . it may be good sense that permits us to decide . . . but these reasons of good sense do not impose themselves with . . . implacable rigour . . . there is something vague and uncertain about them . . . hence the possibility of lengthy quarrels' (Duhem, 1906, pp. 216–17). Here Duhem presents a challenge: are there 'rational' grounds – reasons of good sense – for preferring one theory to another which can be articulated and justified; or is theory-appraisal necessarily fraught with the vagueness and uncertainty surrounding Duhem's unarticulated good sense? Of the several attempts which have been made to articulate such 'rational' grounds for preferring one theory to another, this paper will argue the case for using the Lakatos criterion of corroborated content. In particular it will argue that this criterion is to be preferred to the other criteria for appraising theories in economics which have been articulated.

To paraphrase Kant, a discussion of theory-appraisal in economics without a discussion of the history of economic theories would be empty, and a discussion of the history of economic theories without a discussion of theory-appraisal would be blind. The theoretical controversy we shall discuss is that between 'monetarism' and other theories in macroeconomics. We will argue that the Lakatos appraisal criterion allows us to state 'rational' grounds for appraising the way 'monetarism' has developed since its resuscitation by Milton Friedman in the mid-1950s, relative to the way other macroeconomic theories have developed; and that this appraisal criterion is more illuminating than the criteria conventionally employed in macroeconomics. The term 'monetarism' means different things in different contexts, and different things to different people. Before proceeding further I will discuss what I mean by 'monetarism' in the context of this paper.

Monetarism

The term 'monetarism' was, as far as I know, coined by Karl Brunner to refer to the set of ideas which claims that variations in the money stock are the dominant source of variations in nominal income (Brunner, 1968). As in the case of messages passed down the line, however, the meaning of the word 'monetarism' has experienced considerable transmutation in its subsequent travels in academic and political arenas of discourse: 'like beauty "monetarism" tends to lie in the eye of the beholder' (Laidler, 1981, p. 1); 'the word "monetarism" [came to be used] . . . as a generalised term of abuse for the policies associated with Mrs Thatcher . . . many, in other ways educated, citizens believed the principal tenet of "monetarism" to be support for Latin American dictatorships employing torture . . . those of a more charitable disposition supposed it to be a label for hardships deliberately imposed on peoples by governments to punish them for laziness or poor productivity' (Brittan, 1982, pp. 16–17). In the eye of the present beholder 'monetarism' is taken to be a series of theories linked by the heuristic, or method of solving problems, 'Explain sustained variations in the rate of inflation by sustained prior variations in the rate of monetary expansion'. This series of theories was resuscitated in the post-1945 era by Milton Friedman's reformulation of the quantity theory of money (Friedman, 1956). Major subsequent developments have included the introduction of the 'natural' rate theory of what determines equilibrium output and employment (Friedman, 1968); and the extension of the theory to open economies by way of the monetary theory of the balance of payments or exchange rate (Johnson, 1973, for example).

The Competition to Monetarism

The competition to monetarism came, in the first instance, from the 'orthodox' or 'hydraulic' Keynesian (see Coddington, 1976) theory which monetarism sought to challenge. Orthodox or 'hydraulic' Keynesian theory is, or so I would argue, a series of theories linked by the heuristic 'Explain fluctuations in output and employment by reference to the factors which determine the aggregate demand for output'. A major development in this theory occurred in the late 1950s with the introduction of the Phillips curve, thus linking the output and employment levels determined within the theory to the rate of inflation (Phillips, 1958). Observations of the rate of inflation since the mid-1960s have been higher than is consistent with the Phillips curve, and the reaction has been to replace the Phillips curve with institutional theories of the determinants of the rate of inflation (see Hicks, 1974, for example). An influential UK offshoot from the hydraulic theory is the New Cambridge theory with its heuristic 'Amend the propositions of the "hydraulic" Keynesian theory to take account of the effects of financial assets on expenditure'.

A rival to the 'hydraulic' Keynesian theory emerged in the early 1960s, and was motivated by concern that the 'hydraulic' theory did not do justice to the revolutionary nature of Keynes's analytical system in rebutting the 'classical' Walrasian conception of economic systems as being sufficiently well co-ordinated to ensure that trade takes place at equilibrium prices. 'Keynes either had [disequilibrium trading] at the back of his mind, or most of the *General Theory* is theoretical nonsense' (Clower, 1965, p.290). This 'disequilibrium' Keynesian theory can be encapsulated in the heuristic 'Explain fluctuations in output and employment by analysing trading sequences taking place at disequilibrium prices'. Whilst considerable work has been done on the implications of disequilibrium trading for the functioning of macroeconomic systems (see Malinvaud, 1977, for example), less work has been done on outlining the relative price history of specific economies to give the theory content which could be challenged by evidence. A theory which makes more thoroughgoing claims for the revolutionary nature of Keynes's departure from 'classical economics' is the 'fundamental' Keynesian theory (see Coddington, 1976). The heuristic 'Explain economic fluctuations by reference to fluctuations in expectations formed in the face of untractable uncertainty regarding the future state of the economy' encapsulates the thrust of Keynes's own reply to reviewers of the *General Theory* (Keynes, 1937), and has been central to the criticism levelled at other theories by Joan Robinson, George Shackle and others. Taken literally, adherents to this theory 'guarantee and trivialise their scepticism by adopting unattainable standards for beliefs to qualify as knowledge . . . Keynes (himself) was not reduced to the state of puzzled indecision that a whole-hearted adoption of such standards would entail' (Coddington, 1982, p. 484). If the 'fundamental' Keynesian theory has content which can clearly be challenged by evidence, it is difficult to discern.

In monetarism the adjustment to a long-run or 'natural' rate equilibrium 'may well extend over decades' (Friedman, 1977, p. 465), with disequilibrium trading characterizing the period of adjustment. The new classical macroeconomics provides an alternative theory in which market-clearing equilibria are established in the short as well as long run. The foundations of this theory were laid by Robert Lucas in 1972 and can be summarized in the heuristic 'Analyse economies as being in a continuous state of market clearing equilibrium with output and employment fluctuations reflecting errors in rationally formed expectations regarding prices'. Heavy reliance is placed on the theory of rational expectations outlined by John Muth (Muth, 1961), errors in such expectations being used to explain observed cyclical fluctuations, though an *ad hoc* hypothesis of autocorrelation in output is introduced in order to explain the persistence of such fluctuations over time (see Gordon, 1981). This theory shares the monetary explanation of inflation involved in monetarism, but diverges in that it offers a supply-side explanation for short-run as well as long-run output and employment. The theory has novel content, for example in its prediction that only unanticipated policy measures and other shocks will affect output and employment. It remains to be seen whether the equilibrium explanation for prolonged depressions amounts to anything more than the invocation of *ad hoc* hypotheses – that is, hypotheses designed for the sole purpose of explaining adverse evidence and leading to no additional implications which can be tested.

An influential theory sometimes confused with monetarism is the neo-Austrian theory associated with F.A. Hayek. As far as I understand it, this theory can be summarized in the heuristic 'Analyse economies as inherently tending towards equilibrium, economic fluctuations reflecting disequilibrium processes of adjustment which can be hampered by barriers to the free play of market forces.' This Mt Pelerin view of the economic world (see Hayek, 1980, for example) is derived from such startling hypotheses as that human action is 'purposeful', and the theory is immunized from empirical criticism by the argument that its postulates are known to be true *a priori* (see von Mises, 1949, for example). All observations of the empirical world serve to confirm the truth of the theory, a result which no doubt is convenient for politicians who wish to defend a Mt Pelerin view of the world in the face of adverse evidence, but not so appealing to those who would have 'reasons of good sense' arbitrate in disputes between rival theories. For further discussions of rival theories in macroeconomics, see Cross (1982b).

Duhem's Thesis

Duhem pointed out that 'an experiment in physics can never condemn an isolated hypothesis but only a whole theoretical group' and that 'a "crucial experiment" is impossible in physics' (Duhem, 1906, pp. 183 and 188). An isolated hypothesis could only be held to be refuted by adverse evidence if we were justified in taking the auxiliary hypotheses with which it is conjoined to hold with certainty: we are clearly not justified in so doing. In principle any of the constituent hypotheses – or any conjunctions of such hypotheses – could be responsible for the adverse evidence, and there will not usually be any clear way of allocating the blame. This thesis is sometimes known as the Duhem–Quine thesis. Quine refers approvingly to Duhem when arguing that 'our statements about the external world face the tribunal of sense experience not individually but only as a corporate body' and expresses the thesis as follows:

> total science is like a field of force whose boundary conditions are experience. A conflict with experience at the periphery occasions readjustments in the interior of the field. Truth values have to be re-distributed over some of our statements. Re-evaluation of some statements entails re-evaluation of others, because of their logical interconnections . . . there is much latitude as to what statements

to re-evaluate in the light of any single contrary experience. No particular experiences are linked with any particular statements in the interior of the field, except indirectly through considerations of equilibrium affecting the field as a whole . . . (Quine, 1953, pp. 41 and 43)

This 'holistic' version of the Duhem thesis might be taken to mean that we face the empirical world with the whole of scientific knowledge, thus making it difficult if not impossible to bring the critical scrutiny of evidence to bear on particular theories. In a foreword to a recent edition of his 1953 book, Quine points out that this 'holism' 'has put many readers off . . . [but the] fault is one of emphasis. All we really need to say in the way of holism is that empirical content is shared by the statements of science in clusters and cannot for the most part be sorted among them. Practically the relevant cluster is indeed never the whole of science; there is a grading off' (Quine, 1980, p. viii). This 'grading off' would allow us, for example, to avoid testing theories of gravitational attraction and inertia along with our economic theories, even though such theories might be the way we explain why economic activities tend to stay located where they are.

All this means that arguments of the form $[H_o \rightarrow O . \sim O] \rightarrow \sim H_o$ are not justified, where H_o is a single hypothesis we are testing, O is the observed evidence, and the symbols $\rightarrow$, . and $\sim$ mean 'imply', 'conjoined with' and 'not'. Instead such arguments can only justifiably be phrased in the form $[T_o \rightarrow O . \sim O] \rightarrow \sim T_o$, where $T_o \equiv H_o . A_o$, where T_o is a particular theory and A_o is a set of auxiliary hypotheses which, when conjoined with H_o, produce the theory T_o. If H_o was a hypothesis that the rate of inflation is determined by the prior rate of monetary expansion, the auxiliary hypotheses would include: hypotheses serving to define a 'relevant' set of explanatory variables for the rate of inflation; hypotheses saying how variables codetermined with the rate of inflation are determined; hypotheses as to how to measure the variables contained in the theory; hypotheses as to how to identify the behavioural relationships from the data available; hypotheses as to how to draw inferences from the evidence; hypotheses regarding the time lags involved in the relationships; hypotheses as to the algebraic or geometric form of the relationships; hypotheses as to the stability of the economic system; and *ceteris paribus* or *mutatis mutandis* hypotheses. For a more detailed outline of the auxiliary hypotheses which are brought into play in order to test a particular hypothesis, see Cross (1982a). This means that if the H_o monetary explanation of inflation encounters adverse evidence it could well be any of the auxiliary hypotheses, or any conjunctions thereof, which are at fault, and not necessarily the H_o hypothesis itself. An alternative theory T_N containing H_o and some different A_N set might well be consistent with the evidence.

Given that a large set of auxiliary hypotheses A is being jointly appraised with H_o, there is much latitude for revising the A hypotheses should we wish to hold on to H_o. The question then is one of whether we can articulate 'reasons of good sense' critically to appraise the amendments made to theories in the face of adverse evidence. If we can apply such 'reasons of good sense' not only to the appraisal of a particular theory but also to the appraisal of competing theories we would have a means of appraising monetarism relative to competing theories which might be illuminating.

Appraisal Criteria

Duhem himself offered only 'reasons of good sense' which would be 'vague and uncertain' as criteria for appraising amendments to theories. The problem here is that vague and uncertain criteria for theory-appraisal are likely to produce vague and uncertain assessments of the merits of competing theories. In what follows we will argue that it is possible to justify appraisal criteria which are not as vague or uncertain as the 'reasons of good sense' outlined by Duhem. In particular we will argue that the Lakatos criterion of corroborated content 'has more teeth than Duhem's conventionalism: instead of leaving it to Duhem's inarticulated common sense to judge when a [theoretical] "framework" is to be abandoned [this approach injects] some hard Popperian standards into appraisal of whether a [theory] progresses or degenerates, or whether one is overtaking another' (Lakatos, 1978, I, p. 122). Before outlining this approach to theory-appraisal it is instructive to consider in general terms the considerations which might lead us to prefer one theory to another. To do this we need to ask what it is we require of our theories.

Arguably the most widely held theory of scientific method is the hypothetico-deductive approach to be found in such as Carl Hempel (1945). In this approach a problem is identified; a hypothesis is formulated to address the problem; the implications of the hypothesis are deduced; these implications are checked against observations; and the hypothesis is either found to be confirmed, in which case the hypothesis is accepted; or found to be disconfirmed, in which case the hypothesis is rejected. Thus science proceeds by challenging the implications of theories with evidence, and the preferred theory is that which offers the 'best' evidential account of itself. Phrased in this manner, the problem is to articulate what we mean by the 'best' evidential account. Other ways of posing the appraisal problem are, of course, possible – politically committed theorists may choose the theories whose implications accord most with their political view of the world, aesthetes may prefer the more elegant theories. In what follows we will confine our discussion to evidential 'reasons of good sense'.

Evidential Criteria

The following are some of the evidential criteria which could be used to state grounds for preferring one theory to another (see Horwich, 1982, for further discussion). First, we could prefer theories which have passed more severe tests: thus a theory which stated that the rate of inflation would rise by x per cent in response to an increase in the rate of monetary expansion of y per cent might be preferred to a theory which stated that the rate of inflation would merely rise. Second, we could prefer theories which imply novel facts which were not known when the theories were formulated: thus a theory which predicted something such as a convergence of inflation rates across countries might be preferred to theories which did not yield such a novel implication. Third, we could prefer theories which have the more surprising implications: thus a theory which implied that the rate of inflation would rise during periods of wage and price controls might be preferred to theories whose implications were not so surprising. Fourth, we could prefer simpler theories: thus the theory which accounts for the interaction between output, employment and prices with the lowest number of explanatory variables or parameters might be preferred. Fifth, we could prefer theories which are not *ad hoc*: thus we might prefer theories which are not designed simply to account for, say, the rise in unemployment during a particular epoch, but which instead yield implications which can be tested on other epochs. Sixth, we could prefer theories which account for diverse bodies of evidence: thus theories having implications for Soviet-type economies and Third World countries might be preferred to those having implications for Western industrial economies alone. Seventh, we could prefer theories which predict as well as explain: thus a theory which was able to predict a climacteric in the rate of economic growth in the future might be preferred to theories which merely explain past climacterics. Finally, but by no means exhaustively, we could have a preference for theories which yield empirical tests which can be easily replicated and checked by others working in the field.

The Lakatos Criterion

The argument here is that the Lakatos criterion of corroborated content provides a convenient and coherent method of summarizing the evidential *desiderata* we might demand of theories, as outlined above. Lakatos's appraisal criterion is part of his theory of the methodology of scientific research programmes. In an earlier paper we argued that it is possible to separate the Lakatos appraisal criterion from his theory of scientific methodology taken as a whole (see Cross, 1982a), and in what follows we will consider the appraisal criterion on its own.

Theories are seen as evolving over time in response to logical and empirical challenge, and appraisal of theories is based on observation of their paths of development. The evolution of a theory will generate:

a series of theories $T_1, T_2, T_3 \ldots$ where each subsequent theory results from adding auxiliary clauses to (or from semantical reinterpretations of) the previous theory in order to accommodate some anomaly, each theory having at least as much content as the unrefuted content of its predecessor. Let us say that a series of theories is *theoretically progressive* . . . if each new theory has some excess empirical content over its predecessor, that is, predicts some novel, hitherto unexpected fact. Let us say that a theoretically progressive series of theories is also *empirically progressive* . . . if some of this excess empirical content is also corroborated, that is, if each new theory leads us to the actual discovery of some *new fact*. Finally let us call a problem shift *progressive* if it is both theoretically and empirically progressive, and *degenerating* if it is not. We 'accept' problem shifts as 'scientific' only if they are at least theoretically progressive; if they are not, we 'reject' them as 'pseudoscientific'. Progress is measured by the degree to which a problem shift is progressive, by the degree to which the series of theories leads us to the discovery of novel facts. We regard a theory in the series as 'falsified' when it is superseded by a theory with a higher corroborated content – no experiment, experimental report, observation statement alone can lead to falsification. There is no falsification before the emergence of a better theory. (Lakatos, 1978, I, pp. 33–5)

Thus we are enjoined to prefer some theory T_1 to another theory T_2 if $C(T_1) > C(T_2)$, where $C(T)$ is corroborated empirical content, and if T_1 contains some novel implication not contained in T_2. The notion of a novel implication carries with it certain problems. Does novelty mean 'not used in the formulation of the theory', 'not known to the proponent of the theory', 'not directly relevant to the initial problem faced', or what? (See Gardner, 1982, for discussion.) Despite this I would argue that this notion encapsulates many of the evidential reasons one might have for preferring theories which are adventurous in the sense that they look forward and are able to predict phenomena, or relationships between phenomena, which have not yet been observed. *Ad hoc* theories do not have such a property, nor do theories which have unsurprising implications, theories which cannot account for diverse bodies of evidence, theories which cannot predict and theories which can merely pass the often unsevere test of explaining well-known observations. The Lakatos criterion does not account for why we might prefer simpler theories, but here there are severe dificulties in trying to articulate what we mean by a simpler theory (see Glymour, 1980, for example).

One aspect of theory-appraisal is the assessment of the series of groupings of hypotheses linked by a single heuristic which constitutes a particular theory. A second aspect is the assessment of the merits of different theories with their different heuristics. A major problem here is that of comparing like with like, for theories not only have implications which are 'true' or 'false' but also have no implications, or are 'silent', regarding certain phenomena (see Koertge, 1979). Given this, are we to prefer a theory which has 'false' implications regarding certain phenomena to a theory which is 'silent' regarding such phenomena? For example, it could be argued that 'false' implications are preferable because we can learn from our errors. This problem suggests that a weighted rating index of the content of theories might be required, such as $R = R[N_T, K_T, N_F, K_F, Q, S]$ where R is the rating index, N_T is novel implications which are 'true', N_F is novel implications which are 'false', K_T is known implications which are 'true', K_F is known implications which are 'false', Q is implications not yet checked and S is silence. Thus the way we appraise different theories depends on the weights we attach to the different types of empirical content contained in theories.

An objection which might be raised to the appraisal criterion of corroborated content (see Peter Wiles, pp. 304, 308 this volume) is that it is too lax: the criterion allows a theory to stand unrejected even if it offends against some known fact. The notion that theories should be consistent with the facts is an admirable one to which many would subscribe. The more specific injunction that theories should be rejected if they offend against even one known fact, however, would lead to the rejection of all theories of which I am aware. The injunction is misguided for several reasons.

First, most if not all theories are inconsistent with at least some known facts at birth. This was true of Newtonian theory and true of all the theories discussed in this paper. The interesting question here is one of how theories evolve in relation to the challenge of being inconsistent with at least some known facts. The criterion of corroborated content permits severe not lax criticism of the amendments which are made to theories in the light of anomalous evidence: *ad hoc* amendments, for example, are severely criticized. Secondly, the facts themselves are theory-laden, so the injunction would allow theory-laden observations to be used to reject theories. To take an example, there are several different theories which deal, *inter alia*, with unemployment, and several different theories as to how to measure unemployment. Would it make sense to reject a particular theory of unemployment on the basis of observation statements derived from surveys which appear to demonstrate that those not in jobs are not actively seeking work, even though there exists a substantial number of people registered as seeking work at employment exchanges? Thirdly, the injunction fails to take account of the fact that uncertainty surrounds our knowledge of facts as well as of theories. Is there really another planet in our universe; has the system of weights used not underestimated the growth in output over the last decade? Finally, but by no means exhaustively, the very tenacity which leads proponents of theories not to abandon their theories in the face of seemingly anomalous evidence can in itself be a source of creative energy in the formulation of amendments to theories which lead to new discoveries about the nature of the empirical world.

I would agree that economists do not pay careful enough attention to the measurement of the phenomena with which they deal. To suggest that they should abandon their theories at the first hint of a refutation is another matter.

Probability Criteria

A contrast exists between evidential appraisal criteria which are derived from an assessment of the content of a theory, and evidential criteria based on an assessment of the probability that a theory is true. A bold, ambitious theory will tend to have high content but low probability, a timid theory of limited ambition to have low content but high probability. To see this, consider the case of a theory T_1 which explains the rate of inflation in both fixed and flexible exchange rate economies, and a theory T_2 which has the same content as T_1 with regard to fixed exchange rate economies but which confines its attention to fixed exchange rate economies. Then over some set of empirical evidence e, we will have $C(T_1|e) > C(T_2|e)$ where C is corroborated content. In terms of probability, however, we have $p(T_1|e) \leqslant p(T_2|e)$ given that the total class of instances over which T_2 could be confiirmed is smaller than that for T_1. The tension between these two approaches to theory-appraisal (see Rosenkrantz, 1977, chapter 6, for example) arises in large part from the tendency of probability concepts to be backward-looking in the sense that they summarize how well a theory explains existing evidence, whereas content concepts are forward-looking in that they attempt also to summarize how much evidence could be used to appraise the theory in the future. In other words, content concepts tell us more about the *fecundity* of theories than do probability concepts.

Statistical Inference

Most attempts to appraise the evidential support for theories in economics have used probability concepts to yield appraisal criteria. Before considering the econometric methods usually employed it is useful to consider some of the main approaches to statistical inference which could be used in testing hypotheses in economics. Hypotheses is a key word here, because the methods of statistical inference available are largely concerned to appraise single hypotheses relative to other single hypotheses. Such methods do not capture the conjointness of hypothesis-testing other than by trivializing Duhem's thesis by assuming that auxiliary hypotheses hold with certainty. This means that such statistical methods of appraisal will not be able to deal with the linked series of groupings of hypotheses which constitute our theories. Nor will they be able to cope with the task of appraising the merits of competing theories and their heuristics. The appropriate role of methods of statistical inference in theory-appraisal is the limited one of assessing whether the specific implications of theories are consistent with specific sets of data.

The significance-test approach of R.A. Fisher is concerned with the evidential appraisal of a null hypothesis which does not represent any positive hypothesis as to a behavioural relationship, but rather represents some opposing hypothesis to the effect that there is no behavioural relationship, or that chance determines what happens – if 'determines' is the right word in this context. 'Every experiment may be said to exist only in order to give the facts a chance of disproving the null hypothesis' (Fisher, 1935, p. 19). The test procedure is usually to estimate a 'critical region' to either side of the outcome implied by the null hypothesis, and to see whether the observed outcome lies within this critical region – if not reject the null hypothesis. Fisher's account of significance tests leaves several important questions unanswered. 'First, in any experiment there may be several possible critical regions with the same significance level. How is one to choose? Second if the observed result does *not* fall in the critical region, what can one conclude? In particular, can one *accept* the (implicit positive counter to the null) hypothesis being tested? And if not, why not?' (Giere, 1979, p. 505). As I understand it, Fisherian significance tests are the orthodox means of testing for the significance of behavioural relationships in econometrics: regression planes attempt to establish, *inter alia*, whether the null hypothesis that a partial derivative is zero can be rejected on the basis of particular data sets. Elsewhere many have argued that Fisherian significance tests are more misleading than helpful – see Morrison and Henkel, 1970.

Jerzy Neyman and Egon Pearson (1967) dealt with the problems arising from the Fisherian tests by insisting that a positive set of hypotheses alternative to the null hypothesis, H_o, being tested be stated explicitly. The Fisherian significance level is then interpreted as the probability that H_o is mistakenly rejected if it is true – Type I error; and the explicit statement of the positive set of alternative hypotheses allows the definition of a second error probability, the probability that H_o fails to be rejected when some alternative H_N is true – Type II error. If the Neyman–Pearson approach is seen as yielding a decision rule regarding the rejection or acceptance of hypotheses, some criterion for weighting the disutilities attached to mistaken acceptance or rejection of hypotheses is required – see Wald, 1950. Expected utility theory can be used for this purpose, but raises the question of which of the possible expected utility functions should be used. The minimax rule adopted by Wald 'minimises the maximum possible disutility due to a mistaken choice . . . but while this rule makes some sense in game theory, where one assumes an opponent trying to "win", it seems unduly conservative when one seeks merely to learn the truth about an unconcerned universe' (Giere, 1979, p. 506). As far as I am aware, most econometric tests ignore Type II errors. This means that in the orthodox 'significantly different from zero' test no weight is attached to the probability that the 'zero' hypothesis fails to be rejected when some 'non-zero' hypothesis is true.

The other main approach to the evidential appraisal of hypotheses is that which employs Bayes's theorem. The argument here is that, although objective probabilities cannot justifiably be attached to the comparative likelihood of hypotheses, subjective probabilities can. Bayesian procedures have subjective probabilities revised in the light of the evidence, yielding *ex post* or *posterior* probabilities which reflect how subjective prior beliefs are affected by the weight of evidence. Bayes's theorem can be written as:

$$P(H|E) = \frac{P(H)\,P(E|H)}{P(E)}$$

Thus the posterior probability of a hypothesis given the evidence $P(H|E)$ is equal to the ratio of the prior probabilities of the hypothesis $P(H)$and the evidence $P(E)$ multiplied by the posterior probability of the evidence given the hypothesis $P(E|H)$. The major problem with this approach concerns the prior probabilities. Where do these probabilities come from, what do they mean and can evidence 'swamp' such prior probabilities? A non-monetarist, for example, could place a very low prior probability on a monetarist hypothesis and a very high prior probability on a competing non-monetarist hypothesis. Could a set of evidence which markedly favours the monetarist hypothesis have 'much effect' on such prior probabilities or beliefs? Consider a monetarist hypothesis: H_M – an increase in the rate of monetary expansion leads to an increase in the rate of inflation in 95 per cent of the possible cases, no change in the rate of inflation in the rest. And consider a non-monetarist hypothesis: H_K – an increase in the rate of monetary expansion leads to no change in the rate of inflation in 90 per cent of the possible cases, an increase in the rate of inflation in the rest. Suppose that observations taken in fifty different countries produce the evidence that an increase in the rate of inflation follows an increase in rate of monetary expansion in forty of the countries and no change in the rate of inflation in the other ten countries. Using Bayes's theorem

$$\frac{P(H_M|E)}{P(H_K|E)} = \frac{P(H_M)\;.\;P(E|H_M)}{P(H_K)\;.\;P(E|H_K)}$$

$$= \frac{P(H_M)}{P(H_K)}\;.\;\frac{\left(\frac{19}{20}\right)^{40}\left(\frac{1}{20}\right)^{10}}{\left(\frac{2}{20}\right)^{40}\left(\frac{18}{20}\right)^{10}}$$

Thus radical disagreement about the prior probabilities $P(H_M)$ and $P(H_K)$ will have to be accompanied by a very large amount of evidence favourable to one hypothesis and unfavourable to the other in order that the posterior probabilities $P(H_M|E)$ and $P(H_K|E)$ are 'swamped' by the weight of evidence, as in this example. In economics we perhaps do not have enough evidence regarding hypotheses to allow radical disagreements regarding hypotheses to be 'settled' by the evidence. Part of the problem is that the initial conditions outlining the circumstances under which hypotheses hold are likely to be violated once we lengthen the time series at which we look (see Hutchison, 1981). Another part of the problem is that some of the evidence we would require has simply not been thrown up in history. For interesting applications of Bayesian methods to theory appraisal, see Horwich (1982) and Jon Dorling (1979); for criticism, see Glymour (1980).

Econometrics

Theory-appraisal in economics is usually seen as being a job for econometrics. There are good reasons for arguing that econometric methods on their own do not, and could not, do the job adequately. First, the Fisherian significance tests often involved do not contain an account of the hypotheses being tested in competition with the null hypothesis, and reveal very little. Second, such tests do not capture the conjointness of hypothesis testing and so can throw very little light on the relative merits of theories considered as whole groupings of hypotheses linked by a heuristic. Third, econometric methods of testing hypotheses are too permissive in allowing specification searches for 'best-fitting' relationships about which very little of significance can be said (see Leamer, 1978). Fourth, econometric techniques employ probability concepts that do not allow for the preferences we might have for, for example, bold hypotheses which have high content but low probability. Fifth, most economic theories yield only sign restrictions on, rather than quantitative relationships between, the relationships between economic phenomena: it is not obvious that it is more productive to test quantitative versions of qualitative hypotheses rather than to test the qualitative hypotheses themselves.

It would be grossly misleading to suggest that all econometric appraisals of hypotheses are tarred by the same brush. Not all econometric studies amount to an inane application of Fisherian significance tests to pre-searched data. In Davidson and Hendry (1981), for example, the approach is to explain the successes of previous hypotheses as well as to advocate evidential reasons for preferring a particular behavioural relationship. The point remains, however, that econometric appraisals of hypotheses have not succeeded in providing clear means of arbitrating in such major disputes as that between monetarism and Keynesian theories. It could be that the nature of the appraisal problem in economics is such that no appraisal criteria can provide clear 'reasons of good sense' for preferring one theory to another. In what follows we will illustrate how the Lakatos criterion of corroborated content at least provides a framework which permits some of the 'reasons of good sense' we might employ in theory appraisal to be taken into account.

Appraisal of Monetarism

The first phase of monetarism, $M_{1956} \ldots M_{1967}$, involved a reformulation of the quantity theory of money, and the content created was largely corroborated in studies of the demand for money function and of the relationship between the money stock and nominal income. The second phase, $M_{1968} \ldots M_{1972}$, saw the incorporation of the 'natural' rate theory, and much of the new content was corroborated: error-learning hypotheses regarding the formation of inflation expectations could explain the upward shift of short-run Phillips curves, and the replacement ratio hypothesis regarding the 'natural' rate of unemployment could explain much of the upward shift in the rate of unemployment consistent with steady inflation. The 'natural' rate theory was formulated before the sharp rise in both unemployment and inflation in the late 1960s, and so anticipated the evidence rather than patched up the theory to explain the evidence after the event. The M_{1973} version of monetarism saw the incorporation of the monetary theory of the balance of payments or exchange rate, and the content added in this third phase was largely successful in explaining the simultaneous rise in inflation rates in the late 1960s as arising from the increase in the world money supply created in large part by the US financing of its escalating involvement in Vietnam.

Further, a largely novel fact, the tendency of inflation rates to converge in economies operating fixed exchange rates was predicted by M_{1973}, and this prediction was corroborated. Seen in this light the story of monetarism from M_{1956} to M_{1973} is one of increasing content, most of the new content being corroborated, 'novel' relationships between economic phenomena being predicted and all of this arising from a pre-stated heuristic – the story of a progressive theory, to use the Lakatos terminology.

Since around 1973, however, there have been virtually no developments in monetarism which have created new content, and the story has been largely one of the theory being patched up with *ad hoc* hypotheses to explain adverse evidence – the story of a degenerate theory. Adverse evidence has appeared in the form of holdings of money balances in such countries as the UK and US which are higher than stable demand for money functions would suggest; in the form of dramatic movements in exchange rates such as the depreciation of sterling in 1976 and the appreciation of 1979–81 which are not explained by the monetary theory of exchange rates; and most importantly, in the form of the massive increase in unemployment rates in the late 1970s and early 1980s which is not explained by the factors which were invoked to explain the natural rate of unemployment, replacement ratios, for example, tending to fall during this period. The reaction to such adverse evidence has been the invocation of *ad hoc* hypotheses which have not increased the content of monetarism, and which have little to do with its heuristic. Thus 'structural change in the monetary system', 'mismanagement of monetary policy' and 'increased uncertainty' have been invoked to explain the anomalously high holdings of money balances; 'confidence factors', 'mismanagement of foreign exchange market intervention' and 'overshooting' hypotheses have been invoked to explain the sharp movements in exchange rates; and 'the emergence of new industrial economies', 'real wages being too high', 'supply shocks' and 'the world recession' have been invoked to explain the massive increases in unemployment rates in individual countries. There is little or no attempt to explain why such hypotheses were not relevant to the determination of economic phenomena in earlier periods, the implication being that monetarism is being wise after the event and is not anticipating the evidence. Monetarism has retained its ability to explain the broad time path of the rate of inflation and we could not rule out the possibility that some future theoretical developments in the theory could explain the recent adverse evidence in a manner which would also add new empirical content to the theory. As things stand, however, monetarism has 'degenerated' during the last decade. What of the competition to monetarism?

Hydraulic Keynesian Theory

Orthodox or 'hydraulic' Keynesian economics 'went cantering briskly through the fifties and early sixties . . . faltered sometime in the middle sixties . . . stumbled into the seventies' (Coddington, 1976, p. 1264), and has not shown many signs of regaining its footing since then. The path of development HK_{1945} . . . HK_{1957} saw the refinement of Keynesian hypotheses regarding the individual components of aggregate demand, and the overall theory that government intervention could ensure the maintenance of a 'full employment' level of aggregate demand was not so much taken to be corroborated as taken to be not open to question in the light of the historically low unemployment rates and high growth rates experienced in most Western industrial countries. The articulation in this period of the Keynesian theory of the balance of payments allowed the theory to explain balance of payments 'crises' in such countries as the UK in terms of governments permitting aggregate demand to expand too rapidly. The idea that government fiscal deficits, rather than such factors as the growth in world trade, were responsible for 'full employment' was seen as being self-evident (see Matthews, 1968).

The introduction of the Phillips curve into the hydraulic Keynesian theory in 1958 produced a substantial increase in the content of the theory, the rate of inflation now also being determined inside the theory by way of the effect of aggregate demand on employment. The path of development HK_{1958} . . . H_{1967} was accompanied by largely successful attempts to identify Phillips curves in different countries, with HK reaching a peak of corroborated content somewhere in the mid-1960s. Observations of the rate of inflation since the mid-1960s, however, have been far in excess of what simple Phillips curves would suggest. The reaction to such adverse evidence has been mainly to postulate that factors of an institutional nature determine the rate of inflation. Most of the institutional theories postulated refer to factors which affect wage bargaining, such as 'workers target real wages' or 'union militancy'. The problem here is that we are not given a coherent explanation as to why such factors should have exerted upward pressure on the rate of inflation since the mid-1960s but not earlier, nor are we told why such factors should have come into play in different Western industrial countries more or less at the same time. Thus the replacement of the Phillips curve by institutional theories of inflation has reduced the corroborated content of HK. The theory has also encountered severe difficulties in explaining why expansionary aggregate demand policies have had smaller and less sustained effects on output and employment than the theory would predict in circumstances of less than 'full employment'. Such policies have been followed by increases in the rate of inflation and/or exchange rate depreciation – consequences not implied by the theory – which have usually led the policies to be reversed. The hypothesis that expansionary demand policies will achieve a sustained increase in output and employment only if there is a successful incomes policy is a tautology in that 'successful' is defined to ensure that the hypothesis will hold. Thus in this area there has also been a reduction in the corroborated content of hydraulic Keynesian theory, implying that HK_{1968} . . . has been a 'degenerate' theory.

Disequilibrium Keynesian Theory

The foundations of this theory were laid in the early 1960s, before the corroborated content of the HK theory began to decline (see Clower, 1965). Shortfalls of output and employment from full employment levels are traced back to economies not being sufficiently well co-ordinated to ensure that trade takes place at equilibrium prices. At any given 'wrong' price, the quantity traded is usually taken to be the minimum of that which can be effectively supplied or demanded at such a price. Much of the work on this DK theory to date has been concerned with unravelling the implications of the heuristic employed. Here the content of the theory is heavily dependent on the way in which relative prices are 'wrong'. In one taxonomy of such possibilities, for example, shortfalls from 'full employment can arise from real wages being 'too high' – 'classical' unemployment; from output prices being 'too high' – 'Keynesian' unemployment; and from output prices being 'too low' – repressed inflation (see Malinvaud, 1977). Such taxonomies have produced a DK theory whose content is heavily dependent on initial conditions describing in which way relative prices are out of line. This content is consistent with several known facts regarding Western industrial countries, such as the pro-cyclical relationship between employment and real wages, and in cases where it is clear in which direction relative prices are 'out of line', as in the case of UK output prices in 1920–5 and 1979–81, the content of the theory is unambiguous and can successfully explain the qualitative facts regarding output and employment. The detailed accounts of the relative price history of specific economies required to specify the initial conditions necessary for the DK theory to have refutable content are, however, still rather thin on the ground – the main exceptions being largely successful applications of the theory to Soviet-type economies. Thus the story of the theory DK_{1965} . . . has been largely one of a theoretically 'progressive' theory which has generated substantial content, some of which has been corroborated, but much of which has not been tested because of the lack of specification of initial conditions.

New Classical Macroeconomics

This theory also emerged from the critical examination of another theory, in this case monetarism, again at a time when the other theory was reaching a peak of corroborated content (see Lucas, 1972). During its path of development NCM_{1972} . . . the theory has predicted several novel features of economic systems, such as that only unanticipated changes in economic policy will affect output and employment and that changes in policy regimes will change the optimizing strategies adopted by 'economic agents'. Some of these novel facts have been corroborated, so in this respect we have a seemingly progressive theory to compare with the theoretically progressive DK and the degenerate M and HK theories. To state evidential grounds for preferring the NCM to other theories, however, we would have to show not only that

NCM had successfully predicted 'novel' facts but also that NCM had explained already known facts through its pre-stated heuristic. This heuristic of 'continuous market clearing equilibrium' encounters severe difficulties in explaining why certain markets are characterized by fixed rather than flexible prices, why certain markets do not exist, why the deviations of output from equilibrium associated with expectational errors persist over time and so on (see Gordon, 1981). The hypotheses so far advanced to explain such phenomena are largely *ad hoc* and bear no intrinsic relationship with the heuristic of NCM. Signs of degeneracy are also present in the way NCM theory has explained the massive increase in unemployment rates since the mid-1970s. The supply-side hypotheses advanced to explain the prolonged depression experienced in many countries either do not hold water or have merely patched up the NCM theory without creating additional content (see Cross, 1982b, for further discussion). Thus the NCM theory has successfully gained ground on monetarism through predicting novel facts, but shares much of the degeneracy associated with the response of the M theory to the adverse evidence which has emerged since the early 1970s.

Conclusion

Theory-appraisal is not an easy task, perhaps particularly so in economics where theories do not seem to experience increases in corroborated content for very long. In this paper we have asked how evidential criteria can justifiably be brought to bear on theory-appraisal in economics. We would argue that the Lakatos criterion of corroborated content permits severe evidential criticism of economic theories; that such criticism is illuminating in relation to the critical devices normally employed; and that such criticism is constructive in that it outlines how theories such as monetarism 'go wrong'.

Note

I am most grateful to several participants at the conference, and to members of the staff seminar at Edinburgh University, for comments on this paper.

Comment 1

BRIAN McCORMICK

In volume 13 of *The Collected Writings of John Maynard Keynes* is to be found a draft preface to *The General Theory* which appears to have much in common with the views of Duhem (Keynes, 1973, pp. 469–71). Keynes observes that economists have found it convenient to express their views in a quasi-formal style but that this mode of communication has disadvantages: there is a lack of precision, and analysis tends to be conducted at different levels of abstraction. 'It is, I think, of the essential nature of economic exposition that it gives not a complete statement, which even if it were possible, would be prolix and complicated to the point of obscurity, but a sample statement, so to speak, out of all the things which could be said, intended to suggest to the reader the whole bundle of associated ideas, so that if he catches the bundle, he will not in the least be confused or impeded by the technical completeness of the mere words which the author has written, taken by themselves.' And later he added that: 'In economics you cannot *convict* your opponent of error; you can only *convince* him of it.'

Rod Cross, following Duhem, believes that economists, especially monetarists, have not sought to test the 'bundle of associated ideas'. Elsewhere (Cross, 1982a) he has referred to the tendency to test single-target hypotheses, such as the stability of the money-demand function, and to infer from such tests the advantages of monetarism over Keynesianism. But it is not obvious that economists have been guilty of such methodological ineptitude. Thus Laidler (1978), surveying the empirical literature on the demand for money function, noted that any conclusions derived from empirical studies on the money-demand function were dependent upon the nature of the consumption and investment functions, and other theorists have taken a similar position on empirical work.

The attack on Keynesian economics was directed at the hypotheses concerning the stability of the consumption function, the investment demand function and the demand for money function. The initial testing examined the stability of the consumption function as compared to the demand for money function which suggests an awareness of the conjunction of hypotheses. It is of course true that the division of labour sometimes dictates the testing of particular hypotheses but those tests should not be confused with the tests of the major theories. Rejection of Keynesian economics arose because it was felt that the hypotheses regarding all of the functions specified no longer seemed plausible. Indeed, the general-equilibrium basis of macroeconomics directs attention to the auxiliary hypothesis, especially the horizontal hypothesis, concerning what is happening in other markets. In the absence of laboratory experiments we are forced to examine other markets for corroborative evidence. Hence I conclude that economists do not need to pay much attention to Duhem.

Duhem's proposal leads naturally on to Lakatos's methodology of scientific research programmes. In Cross's work we are asked to distinguish between the following programmes.

(1) Orthodox or hydraulic Keynesianism
(2) Disequilibrium Keynesianism
(3) Fundamental Keynesianism
(4) New Cambridge Keynesianism
(5) Orthodox monetarism
(6) New classical macroeconomics
(7) Neo-Austrian theory

Are these programmes distinct? Is the list complete in the sense that it faithfully portrays post-war developments? Can we accept Cross's evidence for progress and degeneracy in programmes? An initial difficulty is that rival research programmes frequently borrow from each other. Thus Friedman borrowed from Keynes in developing the arguments of his money-demand function. Meade (1978) lists no less than 30 hybrid versions of monetarism and Keynesianism and has produced a macroeconomic model which derives its supply side from Keynesianism and its demand side from monetarism (Meade, 1981b).

But leaving the problems of cross-fertilization aside, can we accept Cross's treatment of progress and degeneracy in the

Keynesian programme? Does, for example, disequilibrium Keynesianism represent an advance over hydraulic Keynesianism? The essence of hydraulic Keynesianism is its use of comparative statics and, in correspondence with Ohlin, Keynes defended comparative statics against the seemingly more realistic period analysis which can be regarded as a forerunner of disequilibrium analysis. Similarly, hydraulic Keynesianism accepts the existence of autonomous expenditure which is the essence of fundamental Keynesianism. There is, therefore, a problem of assessing the usefulness of the different strands of Keynesianism for tackling different issues. Thus disequilibrium Keynesianism with its emphasis upon the nature of contracts seems not only fundamental to an understanding of the path to equilibrium in Keynesian economics but also in monetarism and its offshoot, the rational-expectations hypothesis. Furthermore disequilibrium Keynesianism has developed a lively research agenda (Clower, Barro and Grossman, Malinvaud) which does seem to admit of empirical work on, for example, the extent to which labour markets are auction markets (Brown, 1982).

Cross's assertion of degeneracy in the Keynesian research programme also tests upon his assumption that his classification is complete. It is not. During the 1950s there developed supply-side Keynesianism (or what is sometimes referred to as post-Keynesian economics as distinct from new Keynesianism associated with Meade (1981) or new Cambridge Keynesianism as developed by Godley, Cripps and Tarling) associated with the work of Joan Robinson and Nicholas Kaldor and combining the ideas of Keynes and Kalecki. This theory was quite capable of explaining both slow growth and cost-push inflation, did distinguish between the determinants of raw material and manufacturing prices and in its recent versions (Tylecote, 1981) is capable of explaining the simultaneous existence of inflation in different countries and the reasons why inflation rates in different countries have varied. Of course, these theories may provide the wrong explanation but the point that I wish to establish is that Cross's list is incomplete and omits what many consider to be the agenda of progressive Keynesianism or even the mixture as before.

I turn now to monetarism. Cross states that the research programme has degenerated since 1973 because it has resorted to *ad hoc* explanations and because, as in the case of oil-price changes, those *ad hoc* explanations have not been applied to earlier price changes. Now the rational-expectations hypothesis, which may be regarded as an offshoot or extension of monetarism, was mainly developed through the 1970s and is still undergoing considerable development. Indeed, the RE hypotheses may be said to provide an explanation of why the causes of macroeconomic disturbances should be *ad hoc*. And in the 1970s both the British and American economies have been subject to severe shocks. Thus Britain experienced *Competition and Credit Control* and the American economy has undergone a revolution in its financial institutions. In drawing up the money-demand function it is customary to take the technology of exchange as given but the theory does take it for granted that if it does change then the money-demand function will shift. It is, therefore, not *ad hoc* to pinpoint the cause of instability as stemming from previously assumed parameters becoming variable. What might indicate degeneracy would be the use of arguments not previously encompassed by the demand function. And, as Laidler's recent work suggests, the monetarist programme is seeking to establish the theory underlying the short-run demand function; to that extent, therefore, it must be deemed progressive.

Should the monetarist programme have predicted the oil-price rises of the 1970s? Cross seems to think it is reasonable to invoke an *ad hoc* explanation but notes the absence of such explanations for earlier oil-price rises and falls. Now in some instances, those of the late 1940s and early 1950s, it seems plausible to assume that oil was relatively unimportant as compared with coal, and coal strikes were important in 1947 and 1956. And the fall in oil prices from 1957 onwards until the mid-1960s would surely be accepted by both monetarists and Keynesians as being a contributing factor to that decade's prosperity. However, research programmes do catch up on the questions and Hamilton's work on 'Oil and the Macroeconomy since World War II' finds that price changes did have a significant effect on the US economy and, being politically inspired, have to be considered as extraneous to economic analysis.

It is not easy to establish cases of progress or degeneracy and any evidence seems to be based upon the stance adopted. If you are a neo-classical economist then there are no revolutions in economic thought, merely a filling in of content. Perfect competition is, as Stigler once observed, a highly flexible paradigm. And, as Cross observes, perhaps we have had since *The Wealth of Nations* one research programme. I am not sure that economists have much to gain from studying Duhem on Lakatos and perhaps Sir Dennis Robertson's statement that he always associated methodology with Germans is something we should bear in mind and maintain. There are, of course, problems with the RE hypothesis. The bouts of unemployment or full employment seem more persistent and protracted than the thesis would seem to predict. Wage contracts do seem to be fixed more in terms of cost of living than the excess supply of labour might warrant. But both RE and disequilibrium Keynesianism have promoted the analysis of labour-market contracts and an examination of sources of error. Perhaps all one can ask of a research programme is that it contains the seeds not only of its own destruction but also of its replacement.

Comment 2

ANDREW HARTROPP and DAVID HEATHFIELD

Rod Cross's paper points out an obvious yet unaccepted truth: namely that macroeconomics abounds in controversy despite the extensive use of empirical work aimed at resolving issues. Cross claims that this inability of empirical work to resolve issues is due to the problem raised by Duhem. Having identified the problem, he suggests a solution similar to that of Lakatos.

Duhem said that it is never possible to test empirically a single hypothesis. Rather, it is always a grouping of conjoint hypotheses which is being tested. (Note that such a conjuntion of hypotheses is what Cross means by a 'theory'.) Hence one cannot use in science the logic of simple falsificationism: empirical evidence against a certain grouping of hypotheses does not compel any-body to reject any particular one of those hypotheses; rather, an adjustment to any of them could explain away the anomalous evidence.

The implication of this might seem to be that empirical testing is irrelevant to all disciplines, including economics. Cross does not want to accept this, however, and suggests instead that there are various criteria – rational criteria – for choosing between theories in economics. One such appraisal criterion is the elegance of the rival theories. Cross rejects this, however, and focuses on various evidential criteria. These include: the severity of the empirical tests passed by a theory; the number of novel facts it predicts; the extent to which its implications are surprising; the simplicity of a theory; whether a theory is not *ad hoc*; the diversity of the evidence it explains; and the ability of a theory to predict not just explain.

Cross then argues that the appraisal criterion proposed by Lakatos is useful because it embraces each of these seven evidential criteria except simplicity. The Lakatos criterion is that 'we are enjoined to prefer some theory T_1 to another theory T_2 if

$C(T_1) > C(T_2)$, where C is corroborated empirical content, and if $C(T_1)$ contains some novel implication not contained in $C(T_2)$'.

It must be noted, however, that Cross does *not* go on to propose, accordingly, that rival macroeconomic theories (i.e. research programmes, or conjunctions of hypotheses) should be compared *with each other* in terms of their corroborated empirical content. Rather, his procedure is to analyse rival theories separately, and to say that e.g. theory A did have corroborated empirical content in the years x through to y, but did not in the years y to z. In other words, Cross does not ask whether the content of theory A exceeds that of theory B. Instead, he asks whether A's own corroborated content increases through time. If it does, and if B's does not, then one has rational grounds for preferring A to B. He then goes on to apply this approach to monetarism and various alternative macroeconomic theories.

We begin our comments by noting Cross's decision to ignore the 'hard-core' aspect of Lakatos's work. Cross elsewhere justifies this decision (Cross, 1982a) by saying that to state the heuristic of a research programme (RP) is a sufficient condition for identifying that RP. It is not necessary for this task to define the RP's hard core: hence hard cores can be left out of this sort of analysis.

It seems to us, however, that hard-core statements are a crucial part of RPs, and in particular of macroeconomic theories: to ignore them is a step which may have serious consequences.

We would argue, for example, that monetarism's hard core may be stated as: (1) the economy always tends towards the natural-rate, market-clearing outcome, despite exogenous shocks; (2) monetary policy is incapable of altering real variables in the long run and must (eventually) affect only nominal variables; (3) economic agents are influenced by their perception of real rather than nominal variables.

Recognition of this hard core should lead to a better understanding of what monetarism is. It also hints at the importance in macroeconomics of value-judgements concerning the role of government in the economy.

Further support for this possibility comes from Cross's own reference to the relationship between the appraisal and the history of theories. We would suggest, in fact, that Cross has not taken his paraphrase of Kant to heart: 'a discussion of theory-appraisal in economics without a discussion of the history of economic theories would be empty, and a discussion of the history of economic theories without a discussion of theory-appraisal would be blind.' In particular, the history of economic theories shows that – whether we like it or not – economists sometimes choose between theories on normative/prescriptive grounds rather than positive/descriptive grounds. This does not mean that objective descriptions of an economy are impossible. It does mean that economists are interested in what *ought to be* – as well as what is. However, Cross says he is discussing only evidential criteria for theory-choice, and thereby rejects normative criteria.

It is interesting that Cross's problems in defining monetarism (pp. 94–6) actually make this point clearer. The debates amongst economists and politicians about monetarism have indeed been to do with prescriptions and political value-judgements. An analysis which pretends that monetarism is *only* a descriptive theory relating the money supply to inflation and money income is therefore likely to be somewhat empty.

Following on from this, the appraisal criterion which Cross proposes seems to us to be rather weak, and hence will probably be overridden by the much stronger pressures from prescriptive values. That corroborated content is a weak criterion can be seen in three ways. Firstly, there is no necessary link between *content* and *truth*. Content is a relative concept: it compares the scope or coverage of some theory T_1 with that of theory T_2. Truth, however, is to do with the objective relationship of a theory to the real world. It is fair to say that Cross's focus is on *corroborated* content, and this clearly is more to do with the objective rather than relative merit of a theory. Nevertheless, the danger is that one observes a theory T_1 with greater content than T_2, one also observes corroboration of *some* of the excess content of T_1, and one concludes that T_1 as a whole is better than T_2. The reason why this is dangerous is that the explanation given by T_2 of its (limited) area of inquiry may actually be true. T_2 should not therefore be rejected – and it should certainly not be rejected just because T_1 comes up with a new idea which explains T_2's evidence differently and has some excess corroborated content. The focus should be more on the truth of theories as they stand, rather than on the somewhat relativist notion of 'progress' through corroborated content.

A second, related weakness of the proposed criterion is to do with the merits of *ad hoc* hypotheses. What ought to matter to a politically neutral outsider's appraisal of alternative theories is the objective merits of the rival explanations. Just because a hypothesis is *ad hoc* – i.e. (on the Cross–Lakatos definition) comes after rather than precedes the evidence – does not necessarily say anything at all about the truth of that hypothesis. According to Cross's criterion, however, any *ad hoc* hypothesis is a symptom of a degenerate theory.

Corroborated content is weak, thirdly, in that the assessment of rival theories on this basis by no means leads to a clear-cut evaluation of their objective merits. Instead, the picture given by Cross's assessment is that each theory has good points and each has bad points (see pp. 86–8). This may of course be a correct assessment – but not a particularly novel or illuminating one.

Nor, more importantly, is it an assessment which is likely to dissuade someone who is concerned about normative/prescriptive factors from supporting a particular theory. Even a clear-cut evaluation of the descriptive merits of various macroeconomic views would fail to persuade some proponents. All the more so for a fuzzy evaluation. Similarly, the weakness of the criterion of corroborated content as regards its relationship to truth is (quite rightly) unlikely to cause people to give up their prescriptions.

A particular example of the power of normative value-judgements is seen in the popularity of the rational-expectations (RE) hypothesis and its role in the new classical macroeconomics (see Heathfield and Hartropp, 1982). We analyse there two types of argument which are thought to support RE. One is *a priori* reasoning – the view that RE is the most plausible theory of expectations-formation currently available. We argue, however, that RE makes highly *im*plausible assumptions, e.g. that economic agents generally agree that *a* particular model X is *the* relevant and correct model of the economy. This assumption is held despite the wide range of alternative macroeconomic models clearly in existence today.

A second (instrumentalist) justification for RE takes a different view and says that the realism of assumptions is of no importance: rather, what matters is the accuracy of a theory's predictions.

Again, however, this argument falls down when applied to RE: there is no such empirical support currently available.

We argue instead, therefore, that a better way to understand the popularity of the RE hypothesis is to recognize its role in rejuvenating and extending the monetarist view of macro-economics. In the 1970s, the hydraulic Keynesian school of thought, previously dominant, was unable to give an explanation for the serious failure of demand-management as regards stagflation. At the same time, in academic circles, it was thought that monetarism – mainly associated with Milton Friedman – had run out of new ideas: it had no theoretical developments, nothing new to say. Hence there was a void in macroeconomic policy and theory. It was just at this time that the RE hypothesis was incorporated into the monetarist frame of thought – and the void was filled. A whole new research programme emerged: new classical macroeconomics offers many important prescriptions to people interested in policy and normative issues; and it opens up many new developments for theoretical and empirical economists. (It also sits quite easily with the neo-classical view of economic man.)

We would argue, then, that RE is an example of how a theory is accepted *not* because of its plausibility or corroborated content (RE has little of either), but because of its normative implications and its intellectual interest.

A further point here is that the appraisal criterion proposed by Cross would seem to encourage rather than discourage the present emphasis in economics on highly technical positivist, empirical work to the detriment of a genuine understanding of the workings of the economy. The Lakatos criterion is drawn from the natural sciences. We suggest that human beings are qualitatively different from the phenomena studied by natural science. In particular, human beings' behaviour is not solely determined by precise laws, but is influenced by various factors, including personal choice, social values and habits. It is not clear therefore that social science should ape the methods of natural science: instead, it needs to find explanations of why people behave as they do. The methods of natural science are not enough for this. The criterion of corroborated content, however, emphasizes the relative accuracy of the predictions, to the detriment of the quality of the explanation and understanding gained.

Conclusion

It is the normative/prescriptive judgements that seem to us to lie at the heart of the differences between rival macroeconomic theories. The paper by Rod Cross helpfully points out the existence and persistence of these differences – despite much empirical work. His diagnosis of them is unsatisfactory, however. The proposed appraisal criterion of corroborated content is also weak: it bears no one-to-one relationship to truth; it will be overridden by normative choices between economic theories; and it encourages an unhelpful emphasis on natural science methods rather than on the understanding which social science should seek to gain.

Reply to Comments

ROD CROSS

In 'Monetarism and Duhem's Thesis' the question posed was, Are there 'rational' grounds for preferring one theory to another in economics? In what follows I respond briefly to the comments which my attempt to answer this question aroused.

Reply to Brian McCormick

Brian McCormick concludes that 'economists have nothing to gain from studying Duhem or Lakatos.' The argument is that economists are already aware of what is worth knowing in Duhem, and that what is in Lakatos is not worth knowing.

Taking Duhem first, if economists have long understood that it is not possible to refute single hypotheses – the one swallow noted by McCormick does not demonstrate that it is summer – this has not been apparent in the way economists have pursued their empirical work. That economists accept that what happens in one market depends on what is happening in other markets is one thing. This, however, does not imply that economists realize that there is no sure way of knowing which constituent hypothesis or hypotheses are at fault in the event of a theory – that is a conjunction of hypotheses – being in conflict with some piece of evidence. Nor does it imply that economists realize that there is no such thing as a crucial experiment in relation to a theory such as monetarism.

Empirical testing in economics is usually seen as being a job for econometrics. Most of the published econometric tests of hypotheses in economics do not even take account of the existence of alternatives to the hypotheses being tested, let alone admit that evidence can at most falsify conjunctions of hypotheses. There is much scope for the revision of auxiliary hypotheses should a theory be amended in an attempt to explain anomalous evidence. If reading Duhem helps to focus attention on the problem of appraising the amendments made to theories in such circumstances, then let economists read Duhem.

Turning to Lakatos, McCormick notes the problem of identifying theories or research programmes for appraisal. This problem exists whether or not Lakatosian appraisal criteria are employed Historians of thought, for example, expend considerable energy in debate about the theoretical positions which can most justifiably be attributed to particular authors. The issue of cross-fertilization amongst different theories or research programmes is also one that arises irrespective of whether economists pay attention to Lakatosian appraisal criteria. The supply-side Keynesian research programme outlined by McCormick appears to be consistent with most if not all observable states of the world; perhaps this helps to explain why this research programme has not attracted more attention.

Finally, and perhaps most importantly, McCormick argues that monetarism 'must still be deemed progressive' in spite of the theory's invocation of various kinds of 'shocks' not previously invoked to explain otherwise anomalous changes in unemployment, money holdings and exchange rates since 1973. An *ad hoc* hypothesis is one that serves to explain away otherwise anomalous evidence without generating any content other than with regard to the anomaly which is to be explained. In other words an *ad hoc* amendment makes a theory wise after the event at the cost of reducing the content of the theory, that is at the cost of immunizing the theory from vigorous empirical criticism. It is not the fact that monetarism has invoked 'shocks' which matters *per se*: 'shocks' to the rate of monetary expansion, of course, are central to the way monetarism explains economic phenomena. It is rather the fact that monetarism has invoked certain non-monetary 'shocks' in a selective manner which is important. Take the oil price hikes of 1973–4 and 1979–80, for example. It seems eminently reasonable for monetarism to invoke such 'shocks' to explain, *inter alia*, the otherwise unexplained upward shifts in unemployment until we recall that substantial oil price hikes also occurred in 1947–8, 1953, 1956–7, 1968–9 and 1970–1; it must be explained why these were not 'shocks'. Furthermore we are not told why the reductions in oil prices which have followed such hikes have not led, *inter alia*, to unemployment being lower than monetarism would otherwise predict. If economists do not understand what is wrong with *ad hoc* amendments to theories, let them read Lakatos.

Reply to Andrew Hartropp and David Heathfield

Andrew Hartropp and David Heathfield (HH from now on) suggest that I do not advocate the comparison of empirical content of rival macroeconomic theories. This is not my position, as can be gathered from my discussion under the sub-heading *The Lakatos Criterion*. The comparison of the empirical content of rival theories is not an easy task, given that the term content covers a wide variety of implications which a theory might hold: implications can be novel and true, novel and false, novel and not yet tested, known and true, known and false and so on. My position is that it is both possible and important to compare the empirical content of rival theories. My comparison of the empirical content of monetarism in relation to that of rival theories may not be particularly convincing, but that is another matter. The relevant section of my paper concludes as follows. 'Thus the new classical macroeconomics has successfully gained ground on monetarism through predicting novel facts, but shares much of the degeneracy associated with the response of the monetarist theory to the adverse evidence which has emerged since the early 1970s.'

A second point raised by HH is that it is important to define the hard core statements of a theory or research programme such as monetarism. My argument is that it is unnecessary to do so in order to identify a theory for appraisal. The counter-argument of HH is that identifying hard core statements leads to 'a better understanding of what monetarism is . . . [and] hints about the importance in macroeconomics of value-judgements concerning the role of government in the economy.' Any improved understanding of monetarism is likely to be gained at the expense of stimulating rather arid debates about what is in the hard core and what is not: for example, the 'surprises' version of the Phillips curve which has been incorporated into monetarism over the last decade or so involves agents being influenced by their perception of nominal variables and so is inconsistent with the third hard core statement identified by HH. If the hard core statements identified by HH hint at value-judgements concerning the role of government, the hints do not seem to be very obvious: for example, in the long run we are all dead, governments do not last so long, so why not have governments take action to alter real variables in the intervening period?

The third issue raised by HH relates to the role of normative criteria in theory appraisal. The fact that I discuss only evidential criteria for theory appraisal does not imply that I 'reject normative criteria'. Silence is silence – my paper was not an essay on the Humean guillotine, nor was it an essay on the influence of academic theories on programmes of political action. History does not show anything in itself, it is interpretations or assertions regarding historical events that attempt to demonstrate certain things. Economists, of course, have their own preferences about the way the world should be structured, as do those working in the physical sciences. This does not imply that evidential appraisal criteria 'will probably be overridden by the much stronger pressures from prescriptive values'; the phrase 'much stronger' simply begs the question. For what it is worth I think that value-judgements may have some importance in determining allegiances to different theories, but not in arguments about the relative merits of competing theories.

A fourth issue raised by HH is one of the relationship between corroborated content and truth. Evidential appraisal permits the attribution of falsity to the statements made by theories, not the attribution of truth. It seems that HH want more to be said about the evidential support for theories than can be said. The main concern expressed by HH with the criterion of corroborated content is that it does not encompass the normative criteria which they deem to be important in theory appraisal as practised by economists. The only example of this offered by HH is not convincing. I do not see how the emergence of the new classical macroeconomics (NCM) research programme at a time when monetarism 'had run out of new ideas' indicates the importance of normative criteria in theory appraisal. If normative criteria were important in the emergence of the new classical macroeconomics, HH do not spell out what this line of influence was. A more obvious interpretation sees the NCM as an almost classic example of a new research programme: novel facts were predicted, the observational foundations of existing theories were challenged, ways of explaining the empirical successes of other theories were suggested. Seen in such a light the subsequent evolution of content in the NCM can be compared with that of other theories. Would the invocation of normative criteria to explain the emergence and evolution of the NCM encourage 'a genuine understanding of the workings of the economy', whatever such an understanding might be? Let the Humean guillotine stand.

A Reply to Terence Gorman (see chapter 11)

Gorman has the wrong end of the stick. My discussion of econometric methods was concerned with '. . . the econometric methods usually employed . . .' (Cross p. 90) in appraisals of hypotheses in macroeconomics, not with best econometric practice. I took pains to point out that '. . . it would be grossly misleading to suggest that all econometric appraisals of hypotheses are tarred by the same brush . . .' (Cross p. 93). Gorman seems to think that I would have economists dispense with econometric methods of theory appraisal. I do not advocate any such thing. All that I say is that existing '. . . econometric appraisals of hypotheses have not succeeded in providing clear means of arbitrating in such major disputes as that between monetarism and Keynesian theories . . .' (Cross p. 94). I refer approvingly to the critique of the econometric practices usually employed to be found in Leamer (1978) and Davidson and Hendry (1981), and also refer the reader to the discussion of problems in the logic of statistical inference to be found in Horwich (1982), Dorling (1979), Glymour (1980), Rosenkrantz (1977) and Giere (1979). Gorman is surely acquainted with the distinction between good and bad econometric practice. For most of his discussion, however, Gorman appears to bar the monster of bad econometric practice from his discussion by taking it to be not econometrics. The only reference to deviations from good econometric practice is contained in the phrase '. . . econometricians often misuse significance tests . . .' (Gorman p. 262). Perhaps only econometricians, such as

Gorman, are allowed to say such things, and not non-econometricians, such as myself.

The substantive point, however, is that bad econometric practice is more common than good econometric practice in published appraisals of hypotheses in economics. Those who would deny that this is the case might care to apply a litmus paper test to the tests employed: list the number of articles which contain an account of the power of the tests employed as well as the size or significance levels, and those which do not. My assertion is that there is a low ratio of the former to the latter. Least-squares estimation procedures as far as I am aware, yield powerful tests only when certain very restrictive conditions hold, such as that there are no sign restrictions on the parameters involved. The main point is that the power of the test is not often discussed. Maximum likelihood estimation procedures yield tests which are not necessarily the uniformly most powerful tests, though uniformly most powerful tests, if they exist, are maximum likelihood tests (see Hacking 1965, p.94). Again the main point is that such nuances regarding the power of tests are not often taken into account in published econometric appraisals of hypotheses. I am not an econometrician, but do not see how Gorman's charge that I am '. . . extraordinarily misinformed about . . . the existing methodology of econometrics' holds water if we are referring to commonly adopted econometric practices.

Terence Gorman's further charge that I am '. . . almost equally misinformed about statistics in general' would be more convincing if he displayed a clear understanding of the work of statisticians such as R.A. Fisher, one of the founding fathers of modern statistics. I am not a statistician, but am aware that what Gorman says about Fisher (Gorman pp. 262–3) is misleading, at the very least. Gorman says that he cannot '. . . think of a single example . . .' (Gorman p. 263) in which Fisherian significance tests have not contained an account of the hypotheses being tested in competition with the null hypothesis. But '. . . the principle that there could be no statistical test of an hypothesis without reference to rival hypotheses . . . met with many denials from Fisher' (Hacking 1965, p.81). If Gorman were to read, or re-read, Fisher's final work on the foundations of statistical inference (Fisher 1956) he would find many forceful denials of the necessity or usefulness of testing statistical hypotheses with reference to rival hypotheses, as advocated by Neyman and Pearson. Fisher highly valued the *t*-test, invented by W.S. Gossett, and widely used in econometric appraisals of hypotheses. The irony is that Gossett, '. . . a practical statistician working for Guinness, the brewers . . . urges that it is not merely low likelihood which matters, but rather the ratio of the likelihood' (Hacking 1965, p. 83). Thus here is an example of a practical man, much admired by Fisher, who sees the relevance of testing hypotheses with reference to rival hypotheses, as denied by Fisher. On this subject I would prefer my ignorance of statistics to Gorman's knowledge.

For reasons of space, I can do no more than react briefly to Gorman's other comments on my paper. First, I made few references to specific empirical studies because I had already referred to the relevant empirical studies elsewhere (Cross 1982a, 1982b).

Second, the widely used econometric tests of hypotheses deal with only limited aspects of the appraisal problem arising from the conjointness of the hypotheses being tested. Of course, the conventional econometric tests can, and sometimes do, take account of hypotheses involving more than one explanatory variable, variables which are simultaneously determined and so on. What such tests do not take account of is the wide latitude that exists for revision of the hypotheses which constitute a particular theory should anomalous observations occur. In other words the widely used tests do not tell us much as to whether the amendments made to constituent hypotheses have increased the content of the theory, or merely patched up the theory to provide an *ad hoc* explanation of the anomalous observations. The model encompassing strategy presented by David Hendry (1983, pp.214–16) is precisely an attempt to outline stringent evaluation procedures for econometric hypotheses which allow tests to discriminate between progressive and degenerate problem-shifts in econometric models.

Third, the probability concepts employed in the usual econometric tests do not allow for the preferences we might have for bold hypotheses which have high content. Bold hypotheses might be defined as being non *ad hoc*; as having surprising implications; as having novel implications; as being able to pass severe tests; as being able to account for diverse bodies of evidence; as being able to cope with paradoxes of confirmation; and so on.

The Bayesian approach to statistical inference may or may not be the most useful way to account for the preference we might have for bold hypotheses (see Leamer 1978). The point again is that econometric tests which take account of such preferences are not the ones usually employed.

Fourth, provided that we discount *ad hoc* amendments to the hypotheses which constitute a theory and that we use diverse bodies of evidence, there are instances in which tests of the qualitative implications of theories can constitute severe tests. Take the replacement ratio hypothesis for instance – the argument that increases in the ratio of unemployment compensation to wages lead to higher unemployment. Consider the case where this hypothesis is embedded in the new classical macroeconomics. As far as I am aware, the new classical macroeconomics does not contain an alternative, non *ad hoc*, account of why unemployment remained high in the later 1920s and later 1930s in inter-war Britain (see Daniel Benjamin and Levis Kochin 1979). The replacement ratio was certainly no lower in the period from the late 1940s to the mid-1960s than it was in inter-war Britain (see David Metcalf *et al.* 1982), yet the 'equilibrium' rate of unemployment was dramatically lower in the post-war period in question. Does the new classical macroeconomics contain other non *ad hoc* hypotheses which could account for the lower equilibrium rate of unemployment in this post-war period? I would answer no – trade unions were if anything more 'active' in this post-war period, there are no obvious signs of a fall in the rate of 'black' economic activity, and so on – and so would see this qualitative test as being a reasonably severe test of a new classical theory containing the replacement ratio hypothesis. I would agree that more severe tests are preferable, and that, other things being equal, quantitative tests are more severe tests (the tests employed in David Hendry 1983 provide one such example). But if the quantitative tests are of the type often employed, i.e. tests simply of whether the specification of a hypothesis fits a limited body of pre-searched data which does not cover a diverse range of experience, then it is possible for qualitative tests to be more severe tests. The phrase I used was that '. . . it is not obvious that it is more productive to test quantitative versions of qualitative hypotheses rather than to test the qualitative hypotheses themselves' (Cross p. 93). Earlier in the paper I had already mentioned that more severe quantitative tests would be preferable, other things being equal: the point is that other things are not equal if we look at common econometric practice.

I find Gorman's remarks on the problems arising from preliminary specification searches which are not incorporated into final tests most stimulating and instructive. Methodological discussion in economics suffers from a lack of dialogue between methodology specialists and econometricians: the former often ignore econometrics, or talk about econometrics in a superficial manner; the latter sometimes ignore the broader methodological questions associated with theory appraisal. Gorman's discussion provides a valuable contribution to the opening up of such a dialogue.

In his reply to these comments Gorman places the answer 'yes' into my mouth as a response to a question of the type 'have you stopped beating econometrics?' My own answer would be, 'no, I have not been engaged in the activity'.

My task was to write on monetarism. This involved appraising the merits of monetarism compared to other theories. I argued the case for using the appraisal criterion of corroborated empirical content in this task. The employment of such a criterion involves certain problems when the relevant empirical literature is dominated by exercises in the econometric confirmation of hypotheses over limited bodies of data. This unsatisfactory feature of much empirical work in economics was pointed out with clarity by Edward Leamer, as indicated earlier. I also pointed to some other problems with the econometric methods employed in the literature which might explain why '. . . econometric appraisals of hypotheses have not succeeded in providing clear means of arbitrating in such major disputes as that between monetarism and Keynesian theories ...' (Cross p. 94).

I stand by what I said about econometrics in the context of the paper in the same way as I stand by what I said about the Irish international rugby XV in an Edinburgh bar a few months later – that they had won the Triple Crown playing boring, ten-man rugby. Presumably Terence Gorman would have taken this remark to mean that all Irish people are boring and put to use only ten men; or that all international rugby games are won by sides playing boring, ten-man rugby. Such implications do not follow. Similarly the implication that econometrics does not have a useful role to play in theory appraisal does not follow from what I said in the paper. Gorman's dogs may not like silence, but at least they should recognize such a state of affairs: how else would they be aware of their own noise?.

5

Homo Economicus and the Labour Market

DAVID MARSDEN

Introduction

Historically, the development of the market for labour is relatively recent, being associated with the spread of wage labour. In
eighteenth-century Britain, outside agriculture, the commonest
form of labour was that of the independent artisan, and in many
parts of Western Europe the widespread development of wage
labour is a twentieth-century phenomenon. In the late nineteenth
century there were many intermediate forms of labour relationship in between the status of the independent artisan and that of
the dependent wage-earner. Often, entrepreneurs were not
employers, and relied upon various forms of subcontracting,
ranging from subcontracting to the foreman who would then
assemble a team of workers under his own control and paid by
him, to simple putting-out systems. In most Western countries,
the first large-scale employers were not commercial organizations
but the civil service, the army and the church. Yet despite the importance of the state and of other non-commercial organizations
as employers, and despite the relatively recent appearance of
wage labour, our prevailing theories of the labour market are
framed in terms of small-scale private sector employers. And,
from a methodological point of view, the causes of the development and functions of labour market institutions tend to be
sought in the working or failure of the competitive labour market
rather than elsewhere.

Outline of the Argument

The main argument of this chapter will be that the competitive
model of the labour market, which provides the basic paradigm

for labour-market theory, is typical of but one type of labour market, which statistically speaking may not be the most widespread form. This model depends upon the existence of transferable skills which may be used by many employers, but these are of limited generality, and mostly require the prior existence of labour-market institutions (such as craft apprenticeship provisions) in order to function. Hence the competitive labour market should be taken neither as an empirical generalization, nor as providing the basic model from which all other labour-market structures are derived. Instead, it should be treated as one institutional form among others, of which 'internal labour markets' are one of the most common.

Analysis of the role of institutions underlying different types of labour market requires fuller recognition of the action of collective bodies, be they work groups, firms, unions or employers' organizations, since these bodies establish and maintain the rules which regulate labour markets to a greater or lesser extent. Such bodies are subject to constraints which would not normally apply to individual utility maximizers and which lead to different patterns of behaviour. For example, the need to maintain the internal political cohesion of groups can lead to a concern with inequality which is neither the result of 'tastes' for different degrees of inequality, nor that of altriusm, as conceived within the framework of individual utility maximization.

Homo economicus as a rational utility-maximizing individual may provide an adequate model for the analysis of structureless competitive labour markets. Utility maximization is logically distinct from perfect competition but it derives much of its power from the assumption of competitive conditions (including competition under conditions of uncertainty or of costly information). Without the empirical generality of competitive labour markets, or the assumption of the logical priority of competition in theory construction, the usefulness of individualistic maximization is less clear.

Moreover, although the introduction of training costs, imperfect information and uncertainty enables us to develop a stylized model of many of the elements of labour-market structure, institutions and group behaviour to be discussed in this chapter, stylized facts should not be confused with empirical descriptions based on observation.

Finally, a central problem is the theoretical status of groups and their activity on the labour market. Homo Economicus is a perfect example of methodological individualism, and lacks culture, history and group affinity. The task for methodological individualism is to explain these in terms reducible to statements about interacting individuals and their individual preferences. The author does not share this view, and believes that the best way forward is to recognize the importance of the institutional structure of labour markets, and of action by organized groups, and to treat competitive labour markets as particular *institutional* phenomena, Homo economicus as a limiting case of individual action, and to recognize that while individual workers often have the freedom to break with groups they belong to, group membership itself is often not chosen as a means to some other end.

Competitive Labour Markets and Internal Labour Markets

The Competitive Labour Market and 'Homo Economicus'

One of the most important preconditions of competitive labour markets is that most jobs in different firms may be done by any number of workers with the appropriate skills. In the extreme case, in which labour is assumed homogeneous, all jobs are similar. More commonly, the labour market is seen as divided into a number of occupational labour markets, such that an electrician's job in one firm involves the use of the same skills as in another. In this model, skills are easily transferable from one firm to another, otherwise the achievement of equilibrium by means of movements of labour towards higher-paying firms is not possible.

In such a model of labour-market structure, it is natural that the content of rational choice by individual workers seeking to maximize their net advantages should focus on searching for information about advantages in other firms, maintaining the possibility of changing employer, and on obtaining access to different occupational labour markets by investment in education.

There are sections of the labour market in most countries which correspond to this picture. Among manual workers, unskilled labour can usually move fairly easily from one employer to another, and has fairly high rates of turnover. Certain types of skill are also fairly transferable. In Britain many craft skills sanctioned by an apprenticeship, such as those of electricians, or plumbers, have a fairly wide market consisting of a large number of potential employers. The same is true of skilled workers in construction and printing in the USA and several European countries, and of many skills in the artisan sector which is still of considerable importance, for example, in West Germany and France.

But there are also large areas of employment in which skills are not transferable, or are only partially so for technical or organizational reasons. Doeringer and Piore (1971) have argued that most production skills in American manufacturing industry are of this nature, being acquired informally on the job, skilled positions being reached by upgrading often on the basis of informal seniority rules.[1] Evidence for Britain indicates that a similar pattern of non-transferability applies in many sectors: the services, and industrial firms with a continuous-process production method, such as in coal-mining, steel or chemicals. Many occupations in these sectors are organized into 'internal labour markets' within the firm, in which access to more skilled jobs is by upgrading of existing employees instead of by direct recruitment from the local labour market, as in the case of craft skills.

Most neo-classical theorizing on labour markets is based on two types of labour market, that of unskilled and casual labour, and that of occupations with transferable skills, such as craft skills. Skill transferability provides a paradigm for the marginalist wage theory, and also underlies the continuous renegotiation aspect of neo-classical labour markets in which, as Commons suggested, the terms of the labour contract are renegotiated every minute of the day (as stressed by Alchian and Demsetz, 1972, in their neo-classical theory of the authority relationship).

Such diversity of labour-market types suggests that the theory of competitive labour markets is not an adequate generalization either for the teaching of economics or for use in other branches of economics.

Evidence on the Validity of the Competitive Model as a Generalized Model of the Labour Market

Evidence supporting the competitive model of the labour market is, at best, somewhat ambiguous. On the one hand, certain theories which derive from the competitive model, such as human capital theory relating earnings to investment in education and training, can claim a degree of empirical success, as can some of the studies relating labour mobility to changes in relative wages (Pissarides, 1978). On the other hand, studies of local labour markets, which have relied for the most part on data gathered directly from firms, provide a rather different picture. In Britain, Mackay *et al.*'s (1971) study of local labour markets found quite considerable differences in earnings for the same occupation between plants on the same local labour markets, which persisted over fairly long periods of time without any apparent tendency for labour to move to the higher paying firms. Robinson (1970) found similar evidence of wide variations in hourly earnings for the same occupation between firms on the same local labour market. Moreover, several of these occupations were of a kind that involved transferable skills for which the competitive model should be most likely to work.

In the United States, Parnes (1954), reviewing an earlier set of studies of labour mobility, found evidence of only a weak link between labour mobility and relative wages even among voluntary job changers. In a study of the Chicago labour market, Rees and Shultz (1970) found that length of service was among the strongest determinants of hourly earnings for both the manual and the non-manual occupations included in their sample. Rees and Shultz suggest that their findings are consistent with Becker's (1975) argument that length-of-service differentials arise from the accumulation of non-transferable 'specific' skills while working with a particular company. While this may be true, it nevertheless implies a view of the labour market which differs considerably from that of the competitive model.

In a French study of a sample of firms in the Marseilles area,[2] and of a separate sample of firms in the paper and cardboard industry, Daubigney, Fizaine and Silvestre (1971) found wide variations in hourly earnings for the same occupation between firms, but a high degree of consistency in the rank order of firms' pay levels in the different occupations. The information collected did not permit a comparison of net advantages.

Doubt on the competitive model, or more precisely on the allocative role of changes in relative wages, was also cast by the OECD's (1965) study of wages and labour mobility, which consisted of a wide-ranging review of existing studies, plus statistical work of its own. This consisted of year-to-year correlations between changes in industry wage levels and changes in employment between 1950 and 1960, the idea being to test whether changes in relative wages between industries were serving to allocate labour between industries.[3] It showed a positive correlation at the two-digit level in some countries, notably the United Kingdom and the United States, but very little relationship at the more disaggregated three-digit level. What evidence they found for a link between changes in relative wages and employment appeared to be equally consistent with the 'competitive model' as with the 'prosperity thesis' – that firms expanding their output and employment could afford to bargain away some of their potential profits. Some support for the 'prosperity thesis' was provided by the correlation the OECD found between changes in profits and changes in relative earnings for the USA, France, Canada and the UK, and when the earnings and employment data were adjusted for changes in profits, the relation between earnings and employment was further weakened. On the other hand, in a more recent study for the UK using quarterly data for 14 broad sectors on changes in relative wages and in employment shares, Pissarides (1978) found that changes in relative wages appeared to have a marked effect, and that changes in employment shares were more sensitive to changes in relative wages than to changes in vacancies. This study is not, however, necessarily inconsistent with the other studies mentioned so far because it is possible that the mobility registered was that of certain categories of labour only (e.g. unskilled, young workers and craftsmen). Moreover, it is possible that his findings, like those of the OECD, would be attenuated at the three-digit level.

One reason for the wider divergences of wage levels even within the same local labour market may be that only a limited section of the labour market conforms to the competitive model, and that many workers are tied into internal labour markets, and can only gain access to better paid jobs in other firms by entering the other firm at a lower level, taking an initial (and possibly permanent) cut in pay while they await upgrading.

Within the mainstream neo-classical framework, one might attribute such observations to worker ignorance of alternative jobs and their pay levels, and thus conclude that search costs were high. Indeed, a large number of authors have argued that there is a great deal of ignorance on wages in other firms. However, in a recent study, Blackburn and Mann (1979) have criticized many of the earlier studies for relying upon somewhat impressionistic interviews. Their study was based on workers in nine large firms in the Peterborough labour market, in which they both obtained detailed information on job characteristics and average earnings in the firms, and interviewed workers about their own firms and those of certain major employers. Blackburn and Mann's results differed from those of previous studies. On the whole, the workers were fairly accurate in their ranking of major employers by their average pay levels, and had some knowledge of employment conditions offered by the firms, albeit according to rough and ready indicators. While any generalization from a single study can only be tentative, it suggests that the pattern of fairly longstanding differences in average earnings between firms in the same local labour market may not be the result primarily of imperfect information among workers.

An important reason for the rather weak and ambiguous support for the competitive model, then, is that many workers are not able to change jobs for higher pay even if they want to. This is because they are frequently tied into career structures of one kind or another within company internal labour markets. This can apply to both manual and non-manual workers.

The Significance of Internal Labour Markets

Internal labour markets are one of the most important departures from the competitive model by virtue of the fragmentation on the demand side arising from the limited homogeneity of the jobs in different firms, from institutional rules governing access to these, or from management policy. All of these contribute to the existence of only limited markets for the skills they require, hence reducing opportunities for mobility between firms, and for competition between firms.

An internal labour market may be said to exist when an employer regularly fills certain vacancies by the redeployment or upgrading of existing staff rather than by direct recruitment from the local labour market. In such cases, the vacancy finally communicated to the local labour market may be quite different from that initially created within the firm. Several reasons have been put forward for the development of internal labour markets some of which attempt to maintain the methodological priority of the competitive labour market. This is true of Doeringer and Piore's attempts to link the development of internal labour markets to technology and training, and of Williamson's analysis of internal labour markets as institutions to overcome problems of imperfect information. Evidence from other research suggests that while the processes highlighted by these authors may be important, the logical priority accorded to competitive markets may be harder to maintain. In this section, it will be argued that while internal labour markets fulfil important economic functions and can to some extent be explained by the need to adapt skills to technologies used by individual companies and by market failures arising out of imperfect information, they also represent the presence of wider institutional and social influences upon the workings of the labour market.

Doeringer and Piore argue that many firms use production methods which require skills which are not widely available on employers' local labour markets, and that even when such methods are used, as they become adapted to individual employers' requirements, their corresponding skill requirements become more specific.[4] Hence, in such cases, employers have to develop many of the skills they need within the firm. Doeringer and Piore argue that such 'specificity' of production technologies gives rise to job specificity, and hence to the development of specific or non-transferable skills. Such skills, they argue, are typically acquired by informally organized on-the-job training. The most economical way of organizing the accumulation of the necessary skill or experience is by the arrangement of jobs into career structures such that workers can be upgraded through them, acquiring some of the skills required for the next job up the ladder as they go. Doeringer and Piore argue that behind the organization of such structures is a process of economic optimization such that the occurrence of internal labour markets is 'a logical development in a competitive labour market' (1971, p. 39). They also discuss the role of workplace custom, but it is treated as a reactive process which develops around structures which have already been established as a result of the demands of on-the-job training.

Without denying the importance of limited markets for particular types of training, Williamson (1975) shifts the stress to the role of imperfect information, thus relaxing one of the assumptions of perfect competition. Williamson starts from the same point as Doeringer and Piore, from 'technological specificity' and skill specificity. He argues that severe informational problems arise because workers already doing the job are better qualified for vacancies than any external applicant (giving rise to relations of monopoly and monopsony) and because they can control the transmission of knowledge to new recruits. Because jobs in internal labour markets are so varied, according to Williamson, it is difficult to codify them in abstract terms, and knowledge of the necessary skills is essentially practical knowledge. The severe information imbalance gives a strong short-term bargaining advantage, so employers develop internal labour markets in order to give such workers a longer-term interest in the firm. Thus a degree of job security is traded for greater co-operation in organizing work, and in training new recruits and those newly promoted or redeployed.

Both Doeringer and Piore and Williamson also stress the advantages arising from internal labour markets in terms of the easier screening of internal job applicants, and the better knowledge that internal applicants have of the job's characteristics.

As mentioned, Doeringer and Piore cast workplace rules, notably seniority rules in bidding for job vacancies within the firm, and in lay-off, in a subordinate and reinforcing role in comparison with technology and skill formation. Seniority rules play an important part in blue-collar work in the United States, but a more limited role in Western Europe outside certain industries such as steel. Nevertheless, there have been a number of recent collective agreements and pieces of legislation in Western Europe on the question of job security which would seem to reinforce existing internal labour markets. This is done in two ways: by increasing the cost to employers of making workers redundant, and by giving priority to measures which involve a high degree of adjustment by redeploying existing staff within the company. There have also been agreements, such as the West German rationalization agreements of the late 1960s, and legislation such as the 1972 West German Works Constitution Act and the 1977 Swedish Act on employee participation in decision-making (the MBL Act) which have increased employee influence over redeployment and retraining within the company. To some extent these developments have taken place first in those industries in which internal labour markets were already most developed, such as steel, and so would appear to lend some support to Doeringer and Piore's idea that the collectively bargained rules follow the affects of technological specificity rather than act independently of it; however, this is only partly true as subsequent agreements, and legislation, extended these provisions to other sectors.

The discussion so far has highlighted some of the economic functions of internal labour markets, but before moving on to a discussion of the role of technology *vis-à-vis* social institutions and returning to the general question of the logical priority of the competitive market, it is perhaps as well to return briefly to the earlier theme of the implications of internal labour markets for the competitive model, and to touch on the quantitative extent of internal labour markets.

The Implications of Internal Labour Markets for Labour Market Functioning

Perhaps the most important implication of the existence of internal labour markets for conventional market theory lies in the restricted scope for labour mobility between firms, and for wage competition between employers. For those sections of the labour force affected, this neutralizes the equalizing pressures of the labour market and leads to greater variation in earnings for workers doing similar jobs. Indeed, Guy Routh (1980) has argued that the growth of internal labour markets helps to explain the increased dispersion of earnings within occupations in Britain during the twentieth century, thus reconciling the narrowing of interoccupational differentials which took place with the absence of any corresponding reduction in the overall dispersion of earnings.

Secondly, time becomes a major factor in employers' manning decisions because of the long period that often elapses between recruitment and the moment when the worker is available to fill certain key vacancies within the firm. In British retail banking, 15 years is about the minimum time between the recruitment of school leavers and their first promotion into the managerial grade. In parts of the chemical industry, it is common for skilled process workers to take between 10 and 15 years to reach skilled jobs – which is not to say that such a long period is required to train them. In coal-mining, it is reckoned to take about six years before a new recruit can begin work on the coal face. This expectation, as much as the investment in non-transferable skills, makes large parts of an employer's labour force into a 'quasi-fixed factor' (Oi, 1962), reducing the responsiveness of the labour market to short-term changes in relative wages. Indeed, such factors could well contribute to the present coexistence of high rates of inflation with high and increasing rates of unemployment.

Thirdly, internal labour markets use different adjustment mechanisms to those of occupational and local labour markets. The supply of workers in a particular grade can be increased by raising the speed with which people move along career structures. Changing the mix of skills at any point within the organization may be possible by 'importing' certain skills from outside, but it may also be achieved by a mixture of redeployment and retraining. Indeed, in the present climate of high unemployment, there is increasing pressure from employees for the adoption of this kind of adjustment strategy. Internal adjustment processes are often more likely to be subject to a degree of joint regulation through collective bargaining or employee participation instead of unilateral employer decisions, hence introducing constraints on the way factors of production are combined within the enterprise ignored in competitive theory. This area of employee influence has expanded greatly in Western Europe in the last 15 years.

Fourthly, other things being equal, adjustment to small-scale cumulative technical change may be easier within internal labour markets than in conventional occupational markets of the kind envisaged within competitive theory. This is because piecemeal adaptation to such changes causes a gradual evolution in job contents and thus in the worker's portfolio of skills. Where such changes vary from firm to firm, workers with transferable skills may be unwilling to adapt themselves as such additional skills increase the non-transferable component of their skills, reducing the bargaining power they derive from their potential mobility. Moreover, workers with transferable skills are likely to be more sensitive about changes which might threaten their job territory. In contrast, internal market skills are already less transferable, so that the addition of an extra non-transferable component will not reduce the worker's potential mobility. Thus, while occupational labour markets for transferable skills are flexible in facilitating shifts of labour *between* firms, they may be less so for changes in job content *within* the enterprise. In contrast, internal labour markets are less flexible for inter-enterprise labour-force adjustments, but may be more flexible for intra-enterprise adjustments of job contents. This latter form of adjustment has been particularly important during the post-war period owing to the fairly even spread of productivity growth across all branches of manufacturing (Marsden, 1985).

Finally, internal labour markets weaken the link between individual jobs and rates of pay, contained in the notion that there is a 'rate for the job'. A notable feature of the internal labour markets within large Japanese firms, as Dore (1973) observed, is the absence of any concept of such a rate for the job. Within the lifetime employment system, in the large Japanese firms, pay is more strongly linked to a worker's age than his job, and there is great flexibility in deployment of labour between jobs within the company. Although many of the smaller firms in Japan work on a subcontracting basis to the large firms, and frequently bear the first impact of recession, they apparently seek to provide the same principles, as far as possible. As a result, it is common for younger people in more demanding and more senior jobs to be paid less than older workers in lower positions. Indeed, it would be hard to attach the worker's wage to his job on account of the diffuse boundaries around jobs within Japanese firms, which is such an important part of their flexibility of task allocation. Needless to say, large Japanese firms undertake most of their own training, and rely very little on the external labour market (see also Odagiri here).

There is some evidence of similar tendencies in other countries. The 'age-wage system', as would be expected, gives rise to steep age-earnings profiles. Comparing these in Japan, the US and some European countries, Suzuki (1976) found that the age-earnings profiles were steepest in Japan, followed by the United States and France.

In internal labour markets in Britain, job boundaries, especially for manual workers, appear to have remained sufficiently precise for rates to be attached to them, even though the worker may expect to progress through them in a particular order. Nevertheless, in retail banking and in white-collar internal labour markets, the automatic or semi-automatic annual increments of many incremental scales represent a step in this direction (see Marsden, 1982).

The pace of technical change may further weaken the link between rates of pay and particular jobs, leading towards a system of a rate for each individual, in exchange for increased flexibility in the deployment of labour within the firm. The need to face Japanese competition has already led a large number of firms in Britain and America to look closely at Japanese methods of personnel management, for example 'quality circles',[5] and at Japanese manning practices.

The Extent of Internal Labour Markets

Internal labour markets are well developed in certain sectors and for certain occupational groups and are more extensive in some countries than in others. Occupational labour markets also have their areas of dominance, as do unskilled and casual labour markets. Doeringer and Piore argued that they are fairly widespread for semi-skilled and skilled manual work in United States manufacturing industry. In Britain, as in West Germany, the apprenticeship system gives rise to a number of fairly transferable skills, but in both countries there are also a large number of process skills and firm- or industry-specific skills which are much less transferable (as confirmed by much lower levels of wastage, and smaller variations in wastage over the business cycle). In the services sector in Britain, particularly in financial services (retail banking and insurance), there are also well-developed internal labour markets. In France and Italy, where apprenticeships are much less used, there is evidence of greater reliance upon internal labour markets for manual skills in production industries than in either Britain or West Germany. Indeed, the extensiveness of internal labour markets in France led the French government to ask the CEREQ to undertake a major survey of conditions for access to a large number of jobs in order to develop a more suitable occupational classification for a number of purposes, including an improvement in state job-placement services. Moreover, the highly developed internal labour markets for men in the large firm sector in Japan represent at least one-third of Japanese employment.

The evidence reviewed so far indicates that although the competitive model may be appropriate to the analysis of certain occupational labour markets, different conditions prevail in large areas of the labour market which are not easily treated within that model. Nor are they easily treated within the framework of the traditional monopolistic and monopsonistic models, since these too relate to labour markets for distinct occupations (which is not to deny that important elements of monopoly and monopsony are present within internal labour markets).

The Competitive Labour Market as an Institutional Construct

Both Doeringer and Piore and Williamson take the competitive labour market as the natural starting point from which to explain the emergence of internal labour markets. In this way they are part of a wider movement within economics which Simon (1976) characterized as a shift in emphasis from substantive rationality, concerned with the analysis of different equilibrium positions, to procedural rationality, that is of the behaviour of economic actors particularly in response to certain forms of market failure, or to a relaxation of certain assumptions of competitive equilibrium. Within this movement, the neo-classical approach has been to retain individual profit- or income-maximization and, as far as possible, perfect competition as fundamental methodological principles. In some cases, such developments have sought to get back to an equilibrium framework, although in Doeringer and Piore's and Williamson's work, it is not clear quite how such a return can be achieved even if they can explain the emergence of internal labour markets out of competitive labour markets using basic neo-classical principles.

The key assumption in their explanation lies in the role of technology and its links with job structures. This is also a long-standing neo-classical view built into the production function. For Doeringer and Piore, technological specificity gives rise to job specificity, which through the cost advantages of on-the-job training gives rise to internal labour-market structures. Technology is seen as fairly independent of institutional and cultural factors, at least as between advanced capitalist countries, and it seems natural to suppose that similar problems thrown up by technology would lead to the adoption of similar solutions.

However, differences in internal labour-market structures between countries can be observed when technology is held constant. The strongest example is Dore's (1973) comparison between British and Japanese factories in the same industry in which the Japanese factories made use of a highly developed internal labour market, while the British ones made much greater use of skills recruited from the company's local labour market. The same kind of contrast can be made for many other industries. A comparison between French and West German manufacturing establishments which had been matched for size and product showed that the French companies made greater use of their internal labour markets for the development of skilled labour than their German counterparts (see Maurice, Sellier and Silvestre, 1978). Similarly, comparison between British and West German retail banks indicates a more extensive reliance upon internal labour markets by the British banks in contrast to those in West Germany, which are able to make use of the highly developed system of white-collar apprenticeships.

Once the link between production technology and labour-market organization has been broken, the scope for the recognition of institutional and social factors upon labour-market structure increases greatly, and the case for arguing that competitive occupational labour markets are themselves the result of, and dependent upon, a strong institutional underpinning becomes stronger. Hence the case for analysing labour-market organization as an outgrowth of competition becomes more dubious.

Most occupational labour markets are the subject of elaborate institutional regulations, without which they could not function. In craft occupations, which are based upon transferable skills, the degree of regulation of the content of training is extensive, as is the use of demarcation rules to define craft work and to restrict access to it within the enterprise in Britain. West German apprentice-trained skilled workers, if not defended by demarcation rules, nevertheless have extensive powers through the works council to regulate upgrading on the completion of successive levels of their training, in addition to the role of the state in determining the content of training and in the administration of examinations. Most of the professions have widely recognized and transferable skills, at least at the start of a person's career, and have elaborate systems to regulate entry and to define the technical knowledge required.

Group Rationality and the Dynamics of Labour Markets

Work Group Rationality and the Dynamics of Work Rules

So far the argument of this chapter has not touched upon individual rationality, and has focused on the extent to which labour-market structures differ from the structureless market of competitive theory. However, many of the work rules governing labour-market structures, and more generally the organization of work, are generated and maintained by the activity of groups rather than individuals. Even if one can show that individual workers' decisions to join groups correspond to rational calculation of their own individual interests, the existence of a group creates new possibility for action, but at the same time imposes new constraints. Its rationality differs from that of the individual because of the need to maintain group cohesion.

One of the best-known forms of non-individualistic rational action on the labour market is the regulation of workplace relations by informal rules or by 'custom and practice'. Customary regulation in labour markets has often been regarded as evidence of out-dated and irrational practices by workers, or as something which may affect labour markets in the short run, but which is likely to be worn away in the Marshallian long run by the working of competition and substitution. For this reason perhaps worker custom has not received a great deal of attention from economists, except as a form of restrictive practice or localized monopoly. Yet the removal or alteration of workers' customs and informal rules by employers has in many instances only been possible after very bitter labour conflicts, and often the new work practices have themselves subsequently become subject to customary regulation (as in the 'degeneration' or 'decay' or piecework systems).

Informal rules in the workplace originating from the workforce rather than management have been observed in a number of countries, although their extent varies. Such rules governing promotion up job ladders in the steel industry can be found in Britain, West Germany (Bosch and Lichte, 1981), and the United States (Doeringer and Piore, 1971; Stone, 1973), Crozier (1963) has found evidence of such rules in France but the country in which they have received most attention is Britain, in the form of 'custom and practice'. In a fascinating study, Brown (1973) documents the emergence of a small number of customary rules, the failure of certain other practices to acquire the force of precedent, and the role played by shop stewards in the regulation of workplace custom. He shows how customary rules can develop out of management errors (of commission or omission), decisions often made on the spur of the moment to settle a particular grievance, or a quick interpretation of a particular management practice in an unforeseen circumstance. Shop stewards were not themselves initiators of new custom (nor did they pose as such), but they played an important role in selecting which management actions, or changes in work practices would constitute precedents.[6]

This type of system develops best where jobs themselves tend to be defined by current practice (rather than formal description), much of the knowledge belongs to the work group, and managerial control is limited. Just as knowledge of the job belongs primarily to the work group (which has the power to refuse to pass it on to new recruits), so knowledge of precedent and custom is also the property of the work group, giving rise to a form of collective memory. The cohesion of such groups depends on three main factors: how much individual members gain from group membership; how effectively the group members punish those who go against its informal rules; and the 'psychic' benefits from group membership, and from solidarity. The first condition is met as the group enables the customary rules to be applied, and creates the potential for bargaining in their application and over changes in work practices. Thus, although these rules appear to be long-standing, and to bear the sanctity of precedent, the precedent may not be very old. The system can be quite flexible, and may be seen as a method of bargaining over questions of job content. When a foreman questions such a precedent, he is arguing that a particular practice constitutes a normal part of a person's job, and at the same time is arguing that no additional payment is required. When work groups or their stewards defend a precedent, they may be insisting on a narrow definition of a job content, restricting the scope of managerial authority in this area, and at the same time seeking additional payment for the flexibility. Hence the element of gain to individual members from adhering to group norms.

Secondly, punishments for infringing group norms are not uncommon. Examples of the more common ones are 'sending someone to Coventry' (not speaking to them) and the hiding of their tools.

In his analysis of the functioning of work-group norms in two establishments in France, Crozier stresses similar aspects of inter-group relations as a constraint on the rules which develop – again the limiting factor is to maintain solidarity among the work groups within an enterprise (which does not exclude a certain amount of seeking gains for one group at the expense of another).

Third, the group provides an important focus of loyalty and an identification of 'the opposition' for its members. This dual aspect of group identification was stressed by Touraine (1966), and it is doubtful whether such work groups could apply their informal rules effectively without such identification. Nor is management unaware of this. It has been common in Britain recently to stress the group identification with the company engendered among workers in large Japanese firms,[7] and to link this to the flexible attitude of Japanese workers to their job descriptions, and to the high standards of quality control (which is to do with motivation). One of British management's problems in Britain's adversarial pattern of industrial relations is that workers have tended to iden-tify with the other members of their immediate work group, and to see management, and sometimes other groups of workers also, as the adversary. If the Japanese system were simply a question of encouraging rational income maximizers to recognize that it was in their long-term interest that their company should be success-ful, it is hard to explain all the symbols of group membership such as the 'company song', or company involvement in such central areas of domestic life as marriage.

The fact that group factors act on the content and selection of work rules means that to some extent one is dealing with group rationality rather than rationality of individual economic agents. The influence of the group on the individual does not involve metaphysical transcendence, but generates different actions sub-ject to a different set of constraints and creates different means of action, such as through customary regulation.

In explaining the development of internal labour markets, Doeringer and Piore place at least equal stress on workplace cus-tom to that on non-transferable training and specific technology.

They argue that thinking in terms of custom, combined with informal on-the-job training, helps to generate the structures of job ladders associated with the internal labour markets they analysed. The case for group influence and group custom on internal markets is even stronger in the Japanese case (see Odagiri here). Two main conclusions may be drawn. First, custom in the workplace, whether relating to customary work practices or customary pay differentials, involves a great deal more than the sanctification of situations which in the past corresponded to economic optima, and which have since ceased to be so. Hence the view that custom may survive in the economic short term but will be undermined in the longer run by the forces of competition is only partly true. Clearly, there are cases in which long-standing customs have been undermined by more efficient practices in rival firms or industries, but these represent only part of the picture. Workplace custom is being continuously renewed by work-group action.

Second, custom depends upon the existence of fairly strong work groups. While it is important that individual members should benefit from them, these benefits also depend upon group cohesion, and relationships of coalition with and opposition to other groups. While the action of such groups in a large part aims at economic goals, and individual members work mostly in order to earn a living, it is doubtful that the action of such groups is reducible to individualistic choices and actions.

Collective Bargaining and Managerial Prerogative

Within labour economics, the firm is usually treated as being completely free to combine factors of production in response to external market signals, although unions may affect the choice of technique by altering relative factor prices.[8] This assumes unrestricted managerial prerogative within the firm, but many of the most significant developments in collective bargaining since the mid-1960s have involved increasing restrictions on this prerogative as consultation and bargaining rights have grown on questions of hiring, lay-offs, training and redeployment of staff. This has happened because tight labour-market conditions increased union power in the workplace, because of legislative changes, and because many companies now need workforce co-operation in order to restructure. This has tended to reinforce labour-market structure, although there is some evidence, notably in France (Freyssinet, 1981) but also in Britain and the United States, that employers have been attempting to reduce the coverage of internal labour markets, against strong opposition by the unions. But it also affects manning decisions. Hence one cannot presume that the same results will be achieved as if the employer decided alone.

In Britain work rules governing manning levels and job demarcation have a long history. By and large changes in these are achieved by negotiation, as was illustrated by Flanders's (1964) study of the Fawley negotiations in the 1960s. Despite talk of 'macho management', most of the current introduction of new technology in British industry depends upon extremely detailed negotiation of changes in working practices and manning levels.

While Britain may represent an extreme in the influence of collective bargaining over manpower management within the firm, similar processes are also important in other countries. In Italian industry, since the events of the Hot Autumn of 1969 there has been a very big increase both in union power and in the range of issues in the workplace subject to collective bargaining, with what has been described as a shift from "quantitative' demands (on wage levels) to 'qualitative' ones (on work organization and authority patterns). Despite the present crisis for workplace union institutions (the factory councils) brought about by the depth of the recession, bargaining over such questions continues to play an important role. Recent legislation in West Germany and France has also greatly increased the influence of worker participation over questions of training, changes in work organization, and recruitment and lay-off policies.

Some would argue that collective bargaining in this area is merely an institutional process, and does not bring about outcomes that differ from those of competitive theory. After all, one of the strengths of the theory is to show how less effective methods of organization can be eliminated in the long run by the working of product-market competition.

However, the growth of bargaining in such areas can influence the institutional structure of the labour market, and in several cases may lead to increased internalization of labour markets. But this bargaining is not confined to action through formal union channels, and particularly in Britain a major role continues to be played by work groups, despite high unemployment. In Britain, craft demarcations are maintained largely through union action, and in West Germany the whole process of apprenticeship training and subsequent training and their link with promotion are carefully followed by the works council. In both cases, bargaining helps to maintain the job and skill structures which ensure the survival of an occupational labour market for workers with a particular skill. Likewise, in France, much of workplace bargaining is focused around the working of the grade structure, and the question of regrading can be particularly sensitive since the possibility of obtaining an equally graded post in another firm is limited. Indeed, Shirai and Shimada (1978) have gone so far as to argue that the 'life-time' employment system in Japanese internal labour markets was insisted on by unions as a counterpart to flexible skills, because of their vigorous opposition to redundancies.

Bargaining within the firm can also help to form and to maintain internal labour markets, as can be seen in the present recession with the emphasis of many workplace bargainers upon retraining and redeployment within the enterprise as an alternative to redundancy. Redeployment and retraining of existing staff may also often be an alternative to lay-off followed by recruitment of other workers with other skills.

Such practices probably increase the cost to firms of labour-force adjustment, although they may often also push firms to adopt different methods of internal organization which may cause the labour market to function differently but not necessarily less efficiently. They may also lead employers to adopt different types of labour-market strategy in order to keep down labour costs, such as the use of subcontracting (as in Italy or in Japan), which in itself helps to differentiate sectors of the labour market.

Thus union influence can affect manpower adjustments within the firm, and can help to shape and maintain labour-market structure. This type of action falls outside the standard discussion of the impact of collective bargaining upon resource allocation through its effect upon relative factor prices. It involves both the action of groups in the form of both unions and workgroups, rather than individual utility maximizers, and action on procedural more than substantive norms, which do not seem to be easily described in terms of objectives that can be maximized.

Organization Within the Enterprise and Wage Structure

The internal organization of the firm influences not only the patterning of labour mobility, but also the structure of earnings. Lydall (1968) sought to explain certain aspects of wage structure by organizational rather than strictly labour market factors using a hierarchical model to explain the skewed upper tail of the dispersion of earnings when measured in their log form. To generate the desired Pareto distribution he used a simple hierarchical model in which each employee at each level of the managerial hierarchy had a given number of immediate subordinates, and in which pay at each grade was a fixed proportion of that of the grade below.

More recent case-study work confirms the influence of the hierarchical structure of organizations upon pay structure, but suggests that the relationship is more complex, notably because different types of hierarchical organization are to be found in different countries.

In a comparison of wage structure in matched pairs of French and German manufacturing establishments, Daubigney and Silvestre (1972) (see also Silvestre, 1974) found that the French firms both paid their white-collar and technical staff more relatively to their manual staff than did their West German counterparts, and also employed them in greater quantity. This result has no ready rationalization in terms of competitive labour-market theory, and subsequent research sought to compare the nature of the hierarchical organization of work in the two countries, and the influence of training systems and collective bargaining. This confirmed the first set of findings, and indicated differences between the two countries in the hierarchy of authority. Indeed, using this evidence, Brossard and Maurice (1974) argue that the literature on the sociology of organizations has paid insufficient attention to differences between societies, and has focused too much on variables such as technology whose influence might be expected to be uniform across all societies.

In the German firms, the authority hierarchy had fewer levels, and involved a great deal more delegation, in contrast to the

French firms where a greater number of levels was used, and people at lower levels had to refer up much more often (see Maurice, Sellier and Silvestre, 1978). The authors argued that the greater autonomy of skilled manual workers and foremen in Germany was in part the consequence of the strength of the German system of technical education, especially as concerns apprentices. The apprenticeship system in Germany provides German skilled workers with transferable skills, greater independence from their current employer, and a powerful position in the German industry-based unions. In contrast, in France, a much greater proportion of training, particularly for manual workers, is organized in-house, and apprenticeships play a relatively small part. Consequently, workers' skills are much more dependent on their current employers, and greater reliance is placed upon upgrading on the basis of selection by hierarchical superiors.

The greater internalization of skills and of the basis of authority in the French firms affects pay structure in two ways. First, it causes a bigger premium to be placed upon length of service in the French firms, reflecting increased experience and upgrading, and the need to create greater attachment of the worker to the firm. Second, it gives rise to bigger occupational pay differentials, used to reinforce status differences and thus the authority structure within the enterprise. In Germany managerial authority rests more on the technical competence of people at different hierarchical levels as validated by formal diplomas. The greater amount of upgrading in France means that bigger differentials are more easily tolerated.

Statistical work by Saunders and Marsden (1981) lends additional support to these observations, and indicates that similar processes are at work in Britain and Italy, the former tending towards the German, and the latter towards the French pattern. Subsequent fieldwork by Sorge and Warner, extending part of the France–Germany comparison at the establishment level to Britain, also reinforces the observations of Maurice, Sellier and Silvestre (1978; see also Maurice, Sorge and Warner, 1980).

Hence organizational factors within the firms, and certain other influences such as the organization of vocational training, appear to exert a marked influence upon company and aggregate wage structures independently of supply-and-demand relationships in the firm's external labour market. This supports Lydall's initial observations, and suggests the need for further research on differences in the internal organization of firms in different countries (and their potential influence upon the behaviour of labour markets, and economic performance).[9]

Collective Bargaining and Wage Structure

The analysis of union influence upon wage setting is usually confined to those problems which can be handled with the analytical tools of monopolistic bargaining. In some respects, Dunlop's (1944) pioneering work in suggesting a variety of maximands for trade union activity directed attention away from collective influence upon the structure of earnings, except as between union members and other workers. In particular, it ignored a range of normative pressures in the wage-setting process which go beyond individual utility maximizing.

Barbara Wootton (1955) suggested that people approached wage bargaining with two mostly incompatible norms, one of attaining a greater degree of equality ('doing something for the lower paid'), and the other of maintaining established pay relativities. The influence of such norms would probably be fairly small in the absence of collective bargaining, since they require collective organization to give identity to the groups involved and to express the norms. Moreover, unions may give individuals the feeling that their fellow workers will make an equivalent sacrifice, which they would not have if acting alone. On several occasions reductions of skill differentials appear to have been closely associated with union wage policy. One such occasion was the reduction in skill differentials in certain industries during and just after the first world war, and the absence of any successful move to restore them later. Turner (1952) argued that the main reason was that, owing to the great changes in patterns of work organization during the war, and the changes in training, the craft unions realized that they could best defend their members' position by opening up their membership to less skilled workers. To attract such workers, in the face of competition from other unions, the craft unions pressed for sliding-scale agreements which compensated for increases in the price index by fixed monetary payments, the same for all workers. Although there are a number of questions left unanswered, such as why a similar reduction in skill differentials should have occurred at the same time in the United States, France and Germany, a great strength of Turner's argument is that he is also able to explain, for Britain, why differentials declined in engineering, but not in the cotton industry.

Labour-market-based explanations of the changes in skill differentials have been put forward by Reder (1955) and by Oi (1962). Reder argued that the possibility of up- and down-grading of workers over the business cycle meant that in the upswing differentials narrowed because the supply of skilled workers increased more than that of the unskilled, and fell in the recession for the opposite reason. Note that Reder's explanation relies heavily upon bargaining arrangements in American industry. Oi based his argument on differential shifts in demand for skilled and unskilled workers, as employers laid off unskilled workers more heavily in recession on account of their greater investment in skilled workers. However, in Britain, the relationship between changes in skill differentials and changes in unemployment is poor (Routh, 1980), and even Reder admitted that the fit was not good for his data.

Another such occasion can be found in Italy in the 1970s when skill differentials were greatly reduced after the big increase in union strength of activity after the 'Hot Autumn' of 1969. Paolo Santi (1981) has argued that changes in union organization and ideology played an important part, and also helped to explain the greater extent of the reduction in differentials in engineering than in some other branches.

These provide two examples of the way in which collective bargaining can introduce normative concerns, unknown to Homo Economicus, into wage determination and cause them to exert pressure to alter wage structures.

The Diversity of Workers' Motivations and Orientations

Little attention has been given so far to workers' orientations and their patterns of motivation. Without discarding the assumption of rational action, which is an important heuristic principle, one can nevertheless recognize differences in the content of such action, and its relation to particular institutional contexts.

Although the discussion of labour mobility has generally focused on changes in relative wages,[10] the importance of non-monetary aspects of different jobs, such as their status, autonomy or physical working conditions in job choice, has long been recognized. Marshall's theory of 'net advantages' has subsequently been incorporated into the worker's utility function, and this method of analysis has achieved wide acceptance, provided that the tastes embodied in the utility function are reasonably stable. Becker's (1971) work on the theory of discrimination, as applied to employee discrimination, provides a very good illustration of the way the theory can be adapted to take account of non-monetary motivations, as does Lévy-Garboua's (1979) use of similar concepts of nepotism and discrimination in the analysis of earnings functions of workers with different social backgrounds.

Two main questions dominate this section. The first is the extent of, and the role played by, workers' non-monetary motivations, as detected in interviews, in job choice and other forms of labour-market behaviour. The second is whether workers' 'orientations' as identified in such studies are reducible to 'tastes' for particular kinds of activity.

The *Affluent Worker* study by Goldthorpe *et al.* (1968) analysed the attitudes of mainly blue-collar workers in three high-paying firms in Luton in the early 1960s. A considerable proportion of the workers in the sample had moved there for work. The prime aim of the study was to test the 'embourgeoisement' thesis, that highly paid manual workers in modern industries adopt 'middle-class' attitudes, and to examine worker orientations. The authors identified three main orientations, the 'instrumental', the 'bureaucratic', and the 'solidaristic'. In the first case, work is seen largely as a means to provide the money for non-work activities; in the second, work is seen more in terms of the organization's requirements with a greater emphasis upon career and responsibility; and in the third, workers attach primary importance to group solidarity and loyalty. Among the skilled and particularly among the semi-skilled manual workers in the sample, the authors argued that the 'instrumental' orientation was dominant, to the exclusion of the other two orientations. The study also indicated that, consistent with the findings of previous studies, the bureaucratic orientation was stronger among the white-collar workers.

By showing, for their sample of manual workers, a number of the social correlates of the 'instrumental orientation', notably family economic pressures, and by showing no correlation between instrumental and solidaristic orientations and different working conditions, Goldthorpe *et al.* were able to argue that the instrumental orientation was not a product of the workers' immediate working conditions, and hence that it was an element in job choice. In this respect their study lends some support to two assumptions underlying competitive-labour-market theory – first, that monetary motivation, for certain groups at least, is an important element in job choice, and secondly that such orientations appear to be fairly systematic and stable, therefore justifying the assumption of stable individual utility functions. However, the authors also point to the existence of other types of orientation which might have achieved greater prominence had the sample been drawn differently.

Of the three orientations described in the *Affluent Worker* study, the instrumental one is probably the most easily assimilated to homo economicus. It is also the orientation that is most independent of a worker's immediate work situation, and is most congruent with the structureless labour market of competitive theory. On the other hand, the bureaucratic orientation, found more frequently among white-collar workers, is more congruent with the hierarchical work of office work. Although such orientations are independent of a worker's immediate job, and thus may be influential in such activities as job choice, it could be argued that they represent rational strategies for workers faced with the different kinds of career structure available in sections of the labour market which are differently structured. In this respect, it is perhaps significant that among the more highly skilled manual workers (craftsmen) in the study as compared with the semi-skilled, the indicators of instrumentalism were less pronounced, and interest in and confidence of obtaining promotion, although not that strong, were nevertheless stronger than among the mass of semi-skilled workers. Expectations of promotion were, as one could expect, higher among the white-collar workers (Goldthorpe *et al.*, 1968, tables 2 and 6).

Seen in this way, the orientations are less sets of tastes expressing a hierarchy of preferences than strategies which take account of structural aspects of the labour market, and the way in which rewards can be obtained. The 'instrumental' orientation is adapted to labour-market conditions in which the range of jobs available gives little scope for further training or advancement, and in which scope for individual fulfilment in work is limited. In contrast, the bureaucratic orientation is likely to lead to promotion and increased income in a situation in which jobs are more tightly integrated into a hierarchy with possibilities of promotion from below. Failure to develop such an orientation in such an environment would be unlikely to lead to success. Hence, it could tentatively be argued that while such an analysis maintains the importance of rationality in interpreting workers' labour-market behaviour, rational action can take a different *content* depending upon the circumstances. However, evidence on this is limited.

Conclusions

Labour economics in recent years has experienced a rapid growth of interest in what Simon (1976) has described as 'procedural rationality' as opposed to 'substantive rationality'. In other words, there has been a shift of interest away from the analysis of equilibrium positions towards analysis of the way in which equilibria are achieved – and thus a shift of interest towards individual behaviour on labour markets and the development of institutions. The most important of these have arisen from problems of imperfect information and uncertainty which have generated theories of job search, labour-market signalling, discriminatory hiring practices, implicit contracts, a broader look at union services, and internal labour markets. To some extent, these theories have developed in response to a number of the weaknesses of the traditional competitive hypothesis dealt with in this paper. It is therefore appropriate to ask how far these theoretical developments go towards eliminating these weaknesses. They retain individual utility maximization and although they often drop the simple model of perfect competition the particular institutional forms are treated as a response in such markets to problems of information and uncertainty. Two conditions need to be met if the perfectly competitive model of the labour market is to be maintained. The first is to show that the institutional structures discussed in this paper may be explained as a form of procedural rationality. The second is to show that they contribute towards the attainment of the same kind of outcome as under the simple competitive model.

In the case of labour-market structure and of internal labour markets two approaches have been discussed. First, in Doeringer and Piore's early work (1971), much is made of non-transferable human capital and the need to create institutional structures within which it can be accumulated. It meets the first objective, of explaining their development in terms of individual optimization decisions, but its conclusions are very different from those of the competitive model.

The second approach to internal labour markets has been developed by Williamson (1975) seeking to explain the development of internal labour markets as a response to labour-market information problems, and bounded rationality in particular, in connection with specific skills. In this approach too, Williamson succeeds in developing an explanation of labour-market structure while retaining individual maximization, but the end result is again very different from the world of competitive labour markets. These two approaches to internal labour markets offer a solution to the problem of providing a model of procedural rationality, but do not take the second step of integrating this into a competitive equilibrium.

Both approaches raise an important methodological question as to the relation between the general and the particular. It has been common within economics to treat competitive markets and individual utility maximizing as 'general', and to treat the observed form of institutions as belonging to the realm of the 'particular'. Thus economics has tended to emphasize those aspects of labour market institutions which fulfil functions identified within economic theory (such as information economies) and to neglect the rest. All attempts at theory construction require analysis of observed data, and a high degree of simplification. But when the labour-market institutions, such as internal labour markets, are shaped for example by national training systems, it is more problematic to treat such processes as belonging to the realm of the particular. This becomes even more serious when the initial general model (of Doeringer and Piore, or of Williamson) is heavily influenced by the particular institutional structure of blue-collar labour markets in manufacturing in the United States.

Thus one is left with two alternatives. The first is to treat the structures in different countries as responses to similar underlying problems and to seek models which will generate such structures from an optimization approach to these problems. This is broadly the approach adopted in Doeringer and Piore, and Williamson, but this has failed to give a satisfactory account of different patterns of transferable and non-transferable training found in different countries.

The second is to recognize that competitive occupational labour markets are no less institutions than internal ones, and are no more natural to economic systems. The first alternative requires an explanation of the emergence of labour-market structures and institutions out of competitive labour markets (for example 'a logical development in a competitive market' in which enterprise-specific skills, on-the-job training, and custom are present, – Doeringer and Piore, 1971, p. 39). The second does not postulate the logical priority of competitive labour markets over other types. Their development is as much to be explained as that of internal labour markets, or other types. This approach clearly requires use of a range of research methods, and reference to findings from a range of disciplines.

One of the prime justifications for maintaining the principle of individualistic utility maximization in labour-market analysis is its role in perfect competition theory. Hence much of the argument of the first part of this chapter on the importance of social institutions in shaping labour-market structure, and the need to treat competitive labour markets themselves as institutional phenomena, implies a much more limited role of individualistic utility maximization in theory construction. This is not to say that the decisions of individual workers, employers and their representatives should be treated as irrational or non-rational, although on many occasions they may be, but rather that greater attention should be given to the institutional context of their decisions. As an example, it was suggested that the 'bureaucratic' orientation often found among white-collar workers could be seen as an adaptation to the type of choices open to them in their section of the labour market. Indeed, it is somewhat ironic that in economics we should still be placing such a heavy emphasis upon radical forms of methodological individualism as a basis for our theory of social interaction at a time when sociologists have sought to understand rational action within a context of meaningful action, and after Wittgenstein's private language argument has shown that meanings cannot be explained in purely individualistic terms.

The relativization of the competitive model calls for a relativization of econometric among other research methods, and for reference to evidence drawn from a range of disciplines. Statistical methods are likely to be of as great importance as case-study methods, but some of the most frequently used devices for operationalizing econometric models, notably that of assuming perfect competition, will have to be revised. This applies equally to the Doeringer and Piore/Williamson approach which maintains the logical priority of the competitive market, as to the approach which treats all labour-market structures as institutional phenomena. The use of data gathered within the methodological frameworks of related disciplines unfortunately cannot usually be made in an *ad hoc* fashion because of the degree of interdependence between theories and empirical data (although this can be overstated for practical purposes). Consequently, there is a need to articulate concepts drawn from different disciplines at the theoretical level before empirical work starts, which requires a greater willingness for specialists of different disciplines to collaborate, and to be ready to amend the theoretical assumptions made by each discipline in order for this articulation to take place.[11] I would argue that our use of 'Homo Economicus' in labour-market analysis has been one of the obstacles to a broader approach to the analysis of the interaction between labour markets and the institutions regulating them, and between labour markets and social structure particularly in different countries, but also within countries.[12]

Notes

I should like to thank Peter Wiles for asking many awkward questions and Bob Elliott for many searching comments on an earlier draft of this paper. Some of the themes in this chapter will be more fully explored in my forthcoming *The End of Economic Man?*, Harvester Press (1985).

[1] Their argument receives some support from the study by Rees and Shultz (1970) of workers in the Chicago labour market which found that length of service was the major factor accounting for the variation of earnings within the occupations they studied.

[2] The Marseilles sample included 15 large firms in several branches, but employing semi-skilled production workers, skilled production workers, maintenance mechanics, 'caristes', shorthand typists, draughtsmen and foremen.

[3] The OECD's method of correlating changes in relative wages and employment has aroused much criticism. It seems to have made the implicit assumption that the changes were generated by short-run shifts in industry labour-demand curves, and that the competitive hypothesis implied short-run upward-sloping industry labour-supply curves. The assumed lack of movement in industry labour-supply curves can be justified by the gradual nature of demographic changes, although it is perhaps harder to justify if labour mobility between industries is fairly rapid (i.e. shifts in response to wage changes can occur in less than one year, since the data relate to year-to-year changes), and to assume such a small degree of inter-industry mobility comes close to assuming the competitive hypothesis invalid from the outset. Hence one must have some reservations about the extent to which the OECD's correlations show that wages are not allocators of labour in the short run.

[4] The terms 'specific' and 'general' skills were borrowed by Doeringer and Piore from Becker (1975). General training he defined as training which increases a worker's marginal product in all other firms, while totally specific training increases the worker's marginal product only in the firm currently employing him. From this was derived the concept of "specificity' as concerns jobs and technology. For skills, the terms general and specific correspond to those of transferable and non-transferable skills.

[5] Quality circles bring together workers and lower levels of management to discuss improvements in productivity and quality of output. Frank discussion requires a high degree of mutual trust which underlies their success in Japan, but in Britain such moves are viewed with deep mistrust by workers and their union representatives who continue to see management in an adversarial role.

[6] This was done largely by reference to the effect upon other groups within the enterprise, out of the need to maintain solidarity between groups.

[7] In presenting his paper, Odagiri spoke of his impression from working in a Japanese company that the workers felt that they *were* the company. Dore has reported similar observations, arguing that the relationship between the company and its shareholders meant that management is freer to identify with other employees than is the case in Britain.

[8] Recent work by the 'Harvard School', notably Freeman and Medoff (1979), has sought to investigate the impact of unionization on productivity, pointing in particular to the increase in productivity that may result from the channelling of grievances by unions. See also Addison and Barnett (1982).

[9] Additional evidence pointing to the importance of organizational and social factors in determining the internal structure of firms may be found in two pieces of research. Oliver and Turton (1982) interviewed a number of British employers to discover what they meant by a 'skilled' worker, and found that at least as important as technical competence were the ability to learn new skills, willingness to be co-operative, and the ability to work without supervision. Formal qualifications, they found, played a relatively small part in their sample employers' replies. Blackburn and Mann (1979), looking at manual workers (excluding apprenticeship-trained craftsmen) in Peterborough, found that in their recruitment policies employers placed relatively little emphasis on formal or technical qualifications as compared with the ability to work with concentration, steadiness and discipline. This led them to argue that the skills required in internal labour markets were primarily social rather than technical, and that internal labour markets (for manual workers) were 'fundamentally an apprenticeship in co-operation' (chapter 4).

[10] It should be noted that a wide range of other measures is open to employers anxious to increase the size of their labour force. Among the most important of these are to reduce wastage, for example by rewarding longer service. Such measures avoid discriminatory pay increases and usually increase total labour costs less than raising the wage rate for all workers in a particular category (see for example Manpower Services Commission, 1978).

[11] The author has developed some ideas on the nature of difference types of articulation of concepts from sociology and industrial relations with those current in labour economics in Marsden, 1976.

[12] There is some parallel between the argument about markets as institutions in this chapter and the work of some of the business historians who have been seeking to explain the emergence of different patterns of company organization in different countries and at different times. Hannah (1980), for example, pointed out that vertical integration in large firms was less common and developed more slowly in Britain as compared with the United States in part because of the highly developed distribution market in Britain which made reliance upon co-ordination through markets a viable alternative to the establishment of managerial hierarchies (see also Chandler and Daems, 1980).

Comment

LOUIS LÉVY-GARBOUA

Several labour economists have looked at the potential contribution of a more 'sociological' approach to the understanding of the
impact of institutions such as trade union rules, and apparently
irrational (non-economic) behaviour. But this is based on a misconception. David Marsden's chapter is a very useful contribution
to the improvement of economic methodology in that it reveals
how this group of economists perceive the economic postulates of
rational behaviour and competitive markets. Its main points are
illustrated by the findings of well-known empirical studies of
labour markets that, for the major part, seemed to call for an extension of economic postulates. It is argued that economists
should recognize the importance and specificity of group rationality (as opposed to individual utility maximization), and of structures or institutional elements (as opposed to perfectly competitive markets characterized by implicit forms or organization).

To make my own contribution to interdisciplinary communication, I shall focus my comment, firstly, on relating more explicitly
the sociological concepts of rationality and competition used in
the text to their mainstream economic analogues, and secondly,
on using the 'new' economic approach (advocated by Becker,
1976, and a growing number of professionals), to explain the
emergence of institutional elements in labour markets.

Throughout Marsden's chapter, I cannot see any clear rejection
of the rational-behaviour assumption at the individual level. Provided we realize that rational behaviour under limited information and uncertainty does not look like the rational behaviour of
an omniscient man, Marsden seems to be in agreement with the
new economic approach. However, he shares the current
sociologists' misconceptions of the content and scope of the
economists' view of rationality, which is different from the
sociological one.

What sociologists usually mean by rational behaviour is purposeful action, i.e. behaviour consciously oriented towards definite goals and using adapted means. In the sociological tradition, the orientation-component of rationality has received more attention than the economic or efficiency-component (for proper justification of these two dimensions of rational behaviour, see Lévy-Garboua, 1981). Moreover, sociologists derive the orientation of an action like choosing a job from what people think or say they did. The study by Goldthorpe *et al.* (1968) reviewed by Marsden illustrates this methodology. In fact, Marsden's discussion of its results ends up by revealing the search for one's own pecuniary interest behind the apparent orientations or attitudes of workers. And he concludes that 'while such an analysis maintains the importance of rationality in interpreting workers' labour-market behaviour, rational action can take a different *content* depending upon the circumstances.' Actually, his discussion and surprise would not be understandable by a standard economist and this last phrase can only be understood by giving an economic meaning to the use of the word 'rationality' and a sociological meaning to the use of the words 'rational action'.

Another good illustration of the sociologist's misconception of what mainstream economists usually mean by rational behaviour is the distinction made by the former between individual rationality and group rationality. According to methodological individualism, there can be nothing like a 'rational group'. This position is also taken by neo-classical economists. It has the merit of standing on a sound physiological and psychological footing and, also, of allowing for the possibility that the aggregation of individual choices produce unexpected, and sometimes undesired, effects to members of the group. These 'perverse effects' of aggregation, upon which the French sociologist Raymond Boudon (1977) has thrown new light, were recognized long ago by mainstream economists. There is no need to introduce the *ad hoc* notion of group rationality to explain them. The assimilation of rational behaviour with an action consciously oriented towards a specific goal is the reason, I believe, why most sociologists still find this notion useful. Indeed, it is their only escape from stating that the outcome of rational behaviour can be at variance with individual orientations at the group or market level. In the case under study, the contradiction between individualistic and group rationality seems to be, when a sociological meaning is given to these words, that individuals are primarily concerned with their earnings while group rationality is oriented towards the maintenance of group cohesion. If we rule out the possibility of a 'rational group' for the reasons mentioned above, the contradiction vanishes, since the maintenance of group cohesion cannot be a final end, but simply the means for any individual member of the group to capture monopoly gains economically. Although the idea of group rationality has more magic appeal than that of co-operative behaviour the latter is methodologically superior. It avoids making the arbitrary and rather illogical assumption that individuals are torn by conflicting needs of group conformity on the one hand and group distinction on the other. Instead, with the single assumption that individuals seek to maximize their net earnings, the theory of collusive or co-operative behaviour shows that disciplinary rules and sanctions are needed to deter cheating and other opportunistic behaviour by the individual participants.

It is clearly true that occupational labour markets coexist with other types of labour market, the most important being perhaps internal labour markets. But I would certainly not go as far as Marsden in suggesting that the degree of competition is equal to one in the first instance and to zero in all the others. All sorts of competitive pressures operate in real-world internal and external labour markets, either directly or indirectly. However, competitive pressures are *shaped* by different patterns of 'costs of adjustment' and 'costs of co-operative behaviour' (we leave entry barriers aside in this discussion). Costs of adjustment can be viewed in a Marshallian framework as the sacrifice of the firm's having to bear higher short-run costs whenever its prior planning is contradicted by facts. Costs of co-operative behaviour are the costs of monitoring group members' behaviour and punishing those who are convicted of cheating. The so-called competitive model assumes that adjustment costs are nil and co-operation costs high enough to make co-operative behaviour impossible. When internal labour-market theorists emphasize specific training, transaction costs, information problems and collective action, they just recognize the possibility and relevance of competitive markets with positive adjustment costs and 'low' co-operation costs. But it is impossible to say whether external labour markets are 'more competitive' than internal labour markets.

They are simply different in nature. Marsden's confusion might be caused by his understanding that competition is strictly defined by the assumption of perfect competition delineated by Walrasian pure economic models. Although this definition is found in a number of textbooks, it is of limited usefulness in positive economics, at least for partial-equilibrium analysis. Only the broader concept of competition (common to natural and social sciences and related to scarcity) is relevant for justifying the assumption of rational behaviour (see, for instance, Alchian, 1950). Thus rejection of the perfectly competitive model implies no rejection of rationality, and the postulate of competition or rationality can and should, I believe, remain an essential feature (Marsden speaks of a 'logical priority') of the theory of labour markets.

Indeed, the assumption of rational behaviour or utility maximization has even more powerful implications when uncertainty and market imperfections are considered. Not only, in this case, can it be used to determine quantitative data such as prices and quantities but it can also be used to explain the emergence of qualitative things, say institutions or structures. The role of these institutions is to insure or protect individuals against various kinds of costly risk. Competitive supply (not perfect competition) will then lead to the emergence of the very institution which minimizes the expected cost of a specific risk. Labour mobility and the difficulty of evaluating individual value productivities create uncertainty for both the entrepreneur and the workers. Quits and lay-offs, or a mistaken assessment of the (actual or future) value of the marginal productivities of (actual or future) employees are the manifestations of those kinds of uncertainty. They are usually costly to one or more agents because of work specificity or because transacting, hiring, screening, monitoring and measuring use up economic resources. With this framework, for instance, seniority rules and promotion ladders would appear to be methods of reducing the expected cost of labour mobility and enhancing the returns to specific human investments while customary rules of the sort examined in the text (pp. 127–30) would be interpreted as ways to cope with technological changes and economize on the cost of a full re-evaluation of productivities whenever the content of jobs is changed. In all these cases, the occurrence of risk will cause undesirable costs of adjustment.

Unbounded competition is, from the producers' viewpoint, a subtler kind of risk, although it was recognized long ago by the prisoner's dilemma. Thus rigid union rules might be considered as an attempt by workers to reduce the expected loss of non-cooperative behaviour. The function of norms would be to economize on the costs of repeated collective action, while the function of 'constraints' (i.e. monitoring and punishment of free riders) would be to deter cheating.

This short and incomplete comment will serve its purpose if it convinces labour-market specialists that 'structures' in the workplace, whose profound effects are usually emphasized, are amenable to methodological individualism, and that perfect competition is by no means the last word in economics.

6

Further Reflections on the Invisible-Hand Theorem

DENNIS MUELLER

The fundamental behavioural assumption upon which virtually all economic analysis rests is that individuals pursue their own egoistic ends. This assumption leads to a rich variety of predictions about human behaviour in organizations and in markets that form the bulk of positive economic science.

The leap from positive to normative economics is usually accomplished by a wave of the invisible-hand theorem. The beauty of this theorem is to transform selfish individual behaviour into benevolent social outcomes. This beauty has captivated economists for more than 200 years.

The technical literature in economics has pointed out in some detail the rather restrictive assumptions which must be made for the normative implications of the theorem to hold: managers maximize profits (present value), atomistic price competition, free entry and exit, no externalities, etc. These assumptions may be regarded as the core of the neo-classical paradigm, for, not coincidentally, the same assumptions needed to derive the normative consequences of the theorem are typically the assumptions made in positive economic modeling. Empirical support for predictions of positive economics is often interpreted as confirming the validity of the neo-classical assumptions from which they follow. From here it is a short step to arguing that the normative implications of the invisible-hand theorem accompany *laissez-faire* economic policies.

Given this logical chain running from empirical support for the predictions of positive neo-classical economics to *laissez-faire* policy prescriptions, it is important to know just how solidly forged is the first link in the chain. How persuasive is the empirical evidence supporting the main pillars of neo-classical economics?

The literature is replete with wars and skirmishes over this or that assumption (prediction) of the neo-classical theory: Do managers maximize profit? Do they set price by equating marginal cost and marginal revenue? Do they invest by equating the marginal return on investment to the marginal cost of capital? Each time a debate over one of these or similar questions has occurred, the scenario has been about the same. One or two substantive papers or books appear presenting rather convincing case-study or more aggregative empirical evidence against a basic assumption or proposition in the neo-classical theory. A counterattack is launched challenging either the logic or the empiricism of the attackers. Further exchanges ensue and the debate peters out. Details of the debate fade, and the profession carries on as if the challenge to neo-classical theory had been successfully turned back, regardless of what the weight of evidence on either side was. Neo-classical economics reigns supreme, not because it refutes challenges to it, but because it ignores them.

A good case in point are the many debates over the marginalist price doctrine. Challenges to this hypothesis date back at least as far as the full-cost pricing hypothesis put forward in the 1930s. While the challengers have mustered a variety of types of evidence to support their case, perhaps none is so impressive as that derived from another field, namely the evidence on the shifting of the corporate income tax. One of the strongest predictions of neo-classical theory is that a profit-maximizing firm does not change price or quantity in response to a change in the tax applied to profits. Such a tax affects profits alone. As usual, a long debate over whether the tax is shifted or not has taken place. I think a fair reading of this debate must lead any impartial observer to the conclusion that *some not insubstantial* shifting of the corporate income tax occurs.[1] Since any shifting of this tax is inconsistent with the most basic of premises of neo-classical theory, a rethinking of this theory would seem in order. But, as usual, no rethinking has taken place. The evidence of corporate income tax has, as usual, been ignored, and most neo-classical price theorists today proceed as if no empirical evidence in conflict with their assumptions exists.

In a recent essay, Robin Marris and I (1980) sought to illustrate that a wide body of both theoretical and empirical evidence exists that challenges some of the basic propositions of neo-classical economics including its showpiece theorem, the invisible-hand theorem. We focused upon two assumptions often violated: that managers maximize profits, and that they compete by price. Instead, we argued, managers' pursuit of their own interests often leads to a sacrifice of profits for some other end, e.g. growth, and that much competition is of a non-price or 'rent-seeking' nature. It should be stressed that our quarrel in that paper and my point in this chapter is *not* that the methodology most economists employ in their day-to-day research is somehow fundamentally flawed. If what one means by neo-classical economics is the study of the implications of assuming that rational individuals maximize their respective utilities subject to certain constraints, then Marris and I are both neo-classical economists, and the bulk if not all of the literature we cite in that paper and I cite here is neo-classical economics. Our critique might then be regarded as against that subset of neo-classical economics, let us call it neo-classical economics squared, that equates utility maximization on the part of individuals with wealth maximization, and on the part of corporate managers with the maximization of the present value of the firm, and further assumes that the relevant markets are sufficiently competitive and sufficiently free of other imperfections so that something like the invisible-hand implications hold in most situations. What we sought to show was that a large body of theoretical and empirical evidence now exists, that is both within the broad neo-classical methodological framework just defined and indeed is largely the product of neo-classical economists of impeccable credentials, which nevertheless does not support the rather sanguine assumptions about the normative properties of corporate capitalism many economists seem to hold. In this chapter, I wish to illustrate the weight of these arguments by applying them to a specific market, namely the stock market.

The Stock Market and the Invisible Hand

If there is one market that one might hope would conform to the predictions of the invisible-hand theorem in a capitalist economy, it is the capital market. The stock market is an important segment of the capital market. On the face of it, the stock market appears to meet many of the neo-classical assumptions for the invisible-hand theorem: large numbers of buyers and sellers, free (inexpensive) entry and exit, no externalities. Indeed, the London and New York stock exchanges may be the closest facsimiles we have to the Walrasian markets assumed in some modern versions of the invisible-hand theorem. Thus it seems an appropriate market for applying our critique.

In examining the stock market, two functions which it serves must be distinguished: its traditional role as allocator of capital, and its more recently emphasized role as market for corporate control. I treat each separately.

The Stock Market as Capital Market

In the standard treatment, the value of a common share to an individual shareholder is the present discounted value of the future dividend stream from the share. The price an individual is willing to pay for a share reflects his expectations regarding future dividend payments which in turn are based on anticipated profit streams. Changes in the prices of shares reflect changes in market anticipations regarding profits or dividends, or both.

In the neo-classical theory of the firm, managers maximize the present value of the firm by investing to the point where the marginal return on investment equals the firm's cost of capital, which in turn equals the return the firm's shareholders can earn on shares of comparable risk of other firms (Modigliani and Miller, 1958). In equilibrium, the market value of a firm, MV, with current profits X expected to grow indefinitely at rate g, and risk characteristics leading to a market discount rate of i, is

$$MV = \int_0^\infty X e^{(g-i)t}\, dt = \frac{X}{i-g} \tag{1}$$

Firms with given risk characteristics (in a given risk class) have lower current profit to market value ratios, the higher their growth rates

$$i = \frac{X}{MV} + g \tag{2}$$

A rise in the potential growth rate of a company leads present-value-maximizing managers to increase capital investment, and increases the demand for its shares in the stock market causing the market value of the company to rise until (2) is again satisfied. In this way movements of capital in the stock market parallel real capital 'flows' across firms. Firms with high growth potential (high market values relative to current earnings) undertake more investment relative to current earnings than do low-growth-potential firms. This movement of capital across companies should tend to equilibrate rates of return across firms giving the kind of invisible-hand-theorem, efficient-allocation-of-capital result one expects from a perfectly competitive market.

It is important to note that this result is expected even if all stock trading is in previously issued shares so that no direct effect on real investment occurs through funds raised on newly issued shares. The 'flow' of capital from low-return to high-return firms occurs because managers maximize the present value of their firms by investing in only those projects promising returns above the cost of capital, just as the flow of capital in the stock market is driven by the utility-maximizing decisions of stockholders based on their expectations of the future returns from each stock.

Neither the assumptions about the behaviour of stockholders nor those about the behaviour of firms are consistent with the empirical evidence. I examine each in turn.

Stockholder behaviour. Several studies have found that the variance in returns on the portfolio of all common shares far exceeds that which can rationally be justified by subsequent swings in dividend payments.[2] Either shareholders are continually overestimating future swings in dividend payments by factors of four or five or more, or individuals are making their buy and sell decisions on the basis of considerations other than the anticipated future dividend and profit performance of companies.

What appears as anomalous behaviour in neo-clasical terms is perfectly consistent with rent-seeking activity on the part of individual shareholders. Individual buying and selling of securities is predicated on differences in expectations about future returns. Swings in market averages of 10 and 20 per cent in a matter of months are common, and far greater returns can probably be made predicting market turning-points than predicting a single firm's future profits. Appropriately, much information-gathering and trading revolves around trying to profit from market swings, rather than from changes in anticipated returns for individual companies. Even much information-gathering about individual firms is of a rent-seeking nature. To be the first to know that X will be acquired at a high premium can be individually very profitable, but competitive information-gathering to learn which firms will be acquired will not affect the pattern of merger activity. Information-gathering of this type, like information-gathering about swings in the market, is socially unproductive rent-seeking.[3] The gains of one investor are the losses of another, and all resources expended to bring about these transfers are socially wasted.

Note that what is involved here is not necessarily behaviour which is individually irrational, but behaviour which is collectively so. The question of whether individual participation in markets with relatively high risk-return characteristics is irrational, is more complex. To begin to answer it one must first divide 'individuals' into persons and institutions. The bulk of trading is by institutions, which is to say by managers charged with making trading decisions for others. A separation between ownership and control again exists and the possibility of managerial pursuit of their own interests at some loss to the owners of securities traded must exist. One anticipates that most portfolio managers will avoid the disapprobation of their clients if they avoid making decisions that *conspicuously* lower the wealth of their clients, e.g. being the only fund to enter a market that falls, or leave a market that rises. In contrast, entering a market that eventually falls can probably be reasonably defended to client criticism if it occurs when many other firms are entering the market amid rumours of a coming rise in market prices. Thus one anticipates that risk-averse portfolio managers enter and leave the market at the same time as most other institutional investors, leading to collective overreaction to whatever good or bad news generates beliefs about market changes, and exaggerating market swings, thereby producing the larger than warranted variances in market returns.

My guess is that most individual traders do not enter and leave the market with the same frequency as institutional traders. But the fact that there are large swings in stock-price averages means that large returns can be made by correctly predicting market peaks and troughs. Some individuals may try to 'beat the market' by entering at troughs and selling at peaks. On average the market must be winning this game or the risk–return figures would not be what they are. But even losers may choose to play again, believing next time that they really do see a turning point or simply that their luck has changed. Whether this type of behaviour is best described as individually rational or irrational, I regard as more of an issue about semantics. 'Playing the market' may be a utility-maximizing form of gambling engaged in by the upper-middle class, satisfying the same needs as playing the horses or the numbers. If it is, fine, but we should not presume that this activity has the socially beneficial externality of improving the allocation of capital in society.[4]

The empirical findings of Shiller and others that movements in stock and bond prices are too large to be explained by correctly anticipated future dividend and interest payment movements are quite recent. Follow-up research to account for this discrepancy between what is observed and what neo-classical economics asumes has just begun. The topic is thus a good one on which to test the arguments of this chapter. If research on this topic follows the same pattern as other research on empirical anomalies for neo-classical economics, attempts to rationalize these results will concentrate on introducing auxiliary assumptions that are compatible with an invisible-hand interpretation to the allocative role of the stock market, and this research will continue until either a sufficient number of additional assumptions are found that allow one to reconcile the observed price swings without abandoning the normative implications of the theorem, or the topic will be abandoned with the empirical issue unresolved. Hypotheses, like rent-seeking, that might explain the observed price swings but have less desirable normative implications will not be used to try and explain the results, unless all other alternatives fail, and probably not even then.

There is, of course, one area where the stock market plays a direct role in the allocation of capital, however: when investment is financed out of new stock issues.

Table 2 lists total plant and equipment outlays and the value of new common and preferred stock issues over the 1970s in the USA. New issues amounted to less than 10 per cent of the value of new plant and equipment. If half of this investment would have been undertaken with the help of some other source of funds (a cut in dividends, bond issues, bank borrowing), had the stock market not existed, then the existence of organized stock

TABLE 2   NEW PLANT AND EQUIPMENT EXPENDITURES, NEW ISSUES, TOTAL STOCK SALES, 1970–9 (BILLIONS OF DOLLARS)

Year	1970	1971	1972	1973	1974	1975	1976	1977	1978	1979	Total
Total plant+equipment expenditures	80	81	88	100	112	113	120	136	154	170	1154
New issues	8.6	14.0	13.1	11.0	6.7	10.9	11.1	11.9	10.7	12.2	109.7
Total common share sales	131	185	204	179	118	157	195	187	249	300	1905

Sources: 1979 Statistical Supplement to the Survey of Current Business, Survey of Current Business, March 1980.
    Economic Report of the President, 1979.
Plant and equipment expenditures are for manufacturing and non-manufacturing business.
Total shares and new issues figures are for common shares on all exchanges.

exchanges resulted in a net addition to capital stock of less than 5 per cent of all plant and equipment purchases per year.

Against these benefits must be set the costs of running the stock exchanges. Brokerage fees should roughly equal the direct costs of buying, selling and holding shares, and the other services brokerage firms provide. To these must be added the expenditures individuals make gathering information from other sources (*Barrons*, *Fortune*), and the value of their time spent studying the market and making trading decisions. On top of these must be added the costs of running investment trusts and other stock-purchasing institutions. If these costs exceed *in toto* 2.9 per cent of the value of each share traded, then the social costs of organizing trading in stocks exceed the total value of additional investment induced by the sale of new issues (half the value of new issues equals 2.9 per cent of the value of all shares traded). Clearly the amount of new investment that can be *directly attributed* to the buying and selling of common shares is too small to justify any claim that the stock market makes a significant contribution to the allocation of capital based on the capital investment induced in this way. Any claim that the stock market makes a substantial contribution to bringing about an efficient allocation of real capital must rest on the *indirect* effect the market has on investment through the implicit determination of the cost of capital for each firm, and on the assumption that managers make their investment decisions on the basis of these stock-market-determined costs of capital.

Managerial behaviour. In the neo-classical theory managers maximize stockholder welfare by investing up until the point where the marginal return on investment equals the cost of capital for their firm implied by the price–return performance of their common shares in the stock market. The flows of investment, which stock-price changes bring about in this way, lead to an equation across firms at least on the margin, in rates of return on investment. Neither part of this story is consistent with the empirical evidence.

Substantial differences in rates of return on capital have been found to exist and persist across industries (Fraumeni and Jorgenson, 1980) and firms (Mueller, 1977a). While these are average not marginal returns, the persistence of substantial differences in even average returns over long periods of time suggests some form of impediment to the flow of capital.

Baumol *et al.* (1970) observed extremely low marginal returns on ploughed-back cash-flows for large US corporations, suggesting an overinvestment out of internal cash-flows. Grabowski and I (1975) found that this over-investment was a characteristic of mature companies, i.e. those with perhaps large current cash flows but limited investment opportunities. Such over-investment cannot exist if companies behave as described in standard neo-classical theory. Companies with large internal cash-flows relative to the quantity of new investment that can be undertaken at rates of return in excess of the returns stockholders can earn elsewhere will, under neo-clasical theory, invest relatively little and pay high dividends (or buy back their own shares).

Over-investment is predicted by Marris's (1964) managerial theory in which managers seek to maximize the growth of their firm. But it need not exist for all companies. For those firms whose investment opportunities imply rapid growth rates to maximize stockholder welfare, managerial and stockholder interests coincide. For those firms whose investment opportunities imply low or even negative growth rates, the conflict between managerial and stockholder interests is likely to be severe, and it is for these firms that one expects to find the most dramatic evidence of over-investment. The empirical findings of low returns on capital for mature companies cited above are consistent with this prediction.

Managers who invest at rates of return below their shareholders' opportunity costs are unlikely to make heavy use of the equity market to finance this investment. The managerial theory predicts that capital-investment decisions are more closely related to the available internal fund flows of the firms than to some external measure of the cost of capital read from the stock market (Grabowski and Mueller, 1972). The determinants of investment is one of those topics, mentioned in the introduction to this chapter, that is recurrently the subject of debate in economics. The most recent occurrence of this debate occurred in the late 1960s, when Dale Jorgenson presented several papers developing and testing the neo-classical theory of investment. In the paper most relevant to the question at hand, Jorgenson and Siebert (1968) tested two variants of the neo-classical theory against its three leading competitors, including a cash-flow model, using a sample of fifteen companies. They claimed that the two neo-classical theories performed best, the cash-flow model worst. In a less well-known follow-up paper Elliott (1973) retested the various theories using both cross-section and time-series techniques on a sample of 184 firms. Elliott found for this much larger sample a reversal of the rankings. The cash-flow model was somewhat better than all others, the neo-classical model was the worst. Although to my knowledge no subsequent study has overturned Elliott's findings, they have had no visible impact on the profession's thinking with respect to the relevance of neo-classical theory in explaining either investment behaviour or the broader aspects of corporate behaviour encompassed in the neo-classical theory.

Another empirical finding, at odds with neo-classical theory, which has produced continuing debate in the literature is the seemingly 'irrational' preference of shareholders for dividends over retained earnings, the so-called bird-in-the-hand fallacy. It follows from the Modigliani–Miller theorems that *if the marginal return on capital is equal to the cost of capital*, shareholders should be indifferent between an extra dollar of dividends and an extra dollar of retained earnings, since a dollar of retained earnings reinvested at a return equal to the cost of capital produces a dollar of capital gains. Given the heavier taxation of dividends, retentions should even be more highly valued. Yet numerous studies have found an extra dollar of dividends to be more highly valued by shareholders than a dollar of retained earnings.

Friend and Puckett (1964) in an oft-cited paper set out to reconcile the evidence with the theory. This paper is worth examining because it reveals quite clearly just why neo-classical theory remains so invulnerable to empirical falsification. Friend and Puckett first estimate standard regressions of share price on per-share dividends and retained earnings for five industries. They find dividends significantly preferred to retentions in three of the five. They then re-estimate the equations several different ways, but never satisfactorily succeed in eliminating the perverse preference for dividends in two of the industries. In a third they on one occasion resort to throwing out three observations, even though inclusion of the observations provides a better statistical fit for the equation, since their inclusion does not provide an acceptable fit for the maintained hypothesis. In the end they are left with two, maybe three industries for which the data do not support the hypothesis. Nevertheless, they conclude that their efforts have succeeded in vindicating the Modigliani–Miller theory.

A higher evaluation of dividends than retentions is so at odds with neo-classical theory that the literature has followed in Friend and Puckett's footsteps, inventing auxiliary hypotheses to rationalize away the result (clientele effects, market-segmentation effects, information-content effects), and applying alternative econometric techniques to the data. In some cases the authors succeed in getting the unwanted market preference for dividends to disappear, in others not. None has considered examining the most obvious explanation for the finding, i.e. that the premises upon which the prediction rests, that managers equate marginal return on investment with the cost of capital, is false, since to question this premise would be to question one of the neo-classical pillars on which the whole exercise rests.

Grabowski and I (1975) estimated similar equations in the same study in which we estimated marginal returns on retained investment. We found that the 'irrational' preference for dividends occurred for the same companies, which had low marginal returns on investment. Dividends were not preferred to retentions for young firms with high returns on investment. The stock market exhibits a preference for greater dividends and lower retentions only for those mature companies whose investment opportunities are limited relative to their cash-flows, i.e. only for those mature companies earning low marginal returns on capital. This finding is precisely what one expects, when one recognizes that managers have some discretion to pursue their own goals, and that managers of mature firms are likely to use this discretion to enhance (maintain) the size of their firms at levels greater than those their shareholders desire.

The Stock Market as Corporate Control Market

In the modern neo-classical view of the corporation, managers are constrained to maximize the present value of their firms by the fear of outside takeover (Fama, 1980; Manne, 1965). Three implications follow directly from this assumption: (1) Firms that perform badly because their managers either are incompetent or pursue goals in conflict with present value maximization will be taken over. (2) These firms perform better after being taken over. (3) The acquiring companies and their shareholders should be rewarded for bringing about these efficiency improvements by higher profits and shareholder returns.

In my view, confirmation of the latter prediction is crucial to acceptance of the 'efficient market for corporate control' thesis, yet it has received the least attention and empirical support. Mergers are the largest, most conspicuous investment decisions managers make, with risks that are well known. If the market for corporate control does effectively constrain managers to maximize stockholder welfare, then the returns to stockholders of acquiring firms should be positive in these most visible managerial decisions. Yet the bulk of the empirical evidence suggests that stockholders of acquiring companies are either no better off, or somewhat worse off following an acquisition. Since I have reviewed this literature on two other occasions,[5] I shall focus here on but a few recent contributions, chosen because I believe they illustrate salient features of this vast literature that are most at odds with neo-classical theory.

In an oft-cited paper Dodd and Ruback (1977) estimate the returns to 172 bidding and target firms involved in tender offers between 1958 and 1974. Excess returns are measured as the residuals from a regression of a firm's monthly returns on the returns on the portfolio of all common shares. This latter equation is supposed to explain the normal movement in monthly returns for a given company. Figure 1 presents the cumulative residuals from the rate of return equations estimated by Dodd and Ruback for successful bidding firms.[6] Time in months is measured on the horizontal axis. The cumulative residuals should normally bob back and forth across the zero line. A sustained movement in one direction signals a re-evaluation of the companies' prospects by the market, presumably from the receipt of new information.

From these results Dodd and Ruback conclude that tender offers have a positive impact on the returns of bidding firms. One might then infer that the tender offers were made at point in time A, since A obviously signals a long and sustained upward re-evaluation of the bidding firms' shares. But A occurs 43 months prior to the tender offers. The bids are actually made much closer to the point in time when the series begins to decline. They occur

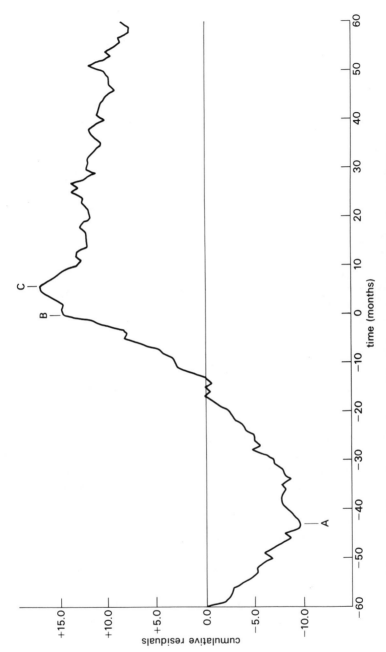

Figure 1 Plots of cumulative residuals for successful bidding firms, 1958–74

at B, six months before C. It would appear that the tender offers did not cause the single most important improvement in bidding firms' share performance occurring during the ten years surrounding the offers, namely that between A and C. On the contrary, if this upward movement is causally related to the tender offers at all, it would seem that it must have caused the offers rather than the reverse. If the tender offers set off any new trend, it is more likely the downward movement starting at C, roughly the point in time coincidentally when the market learns that the mergers will in fact take place.

In figure 2 I have added cumulative residual curves based on results by Mandelker (1974) for 241 acquiring firms involved in mergers between 1941 and 1962 and by Langetieg (1978) for 149 mergers between 1929 and 1969 to the Dodd and Ruback curve.[7] Since the Dodd–Ruback residuals are centred around the merger's announcement date, and the Mandelker and Langetieg residuals around the consummation date, we have displaced the residuals series of the latter two studies by six months, since most studies find that announcements precede consummations by six to seven months. Both the Mandelker and Langetieg cumulative residual curves exhibit the same long run-up to the merger's announcement date as the Dodd–Ruback figures. In all three cases this run-up stops around the time of the merger and is followed by a decline, precipitous in Langetieg's data, more gradual in Dodd and Ruback's and Mandelker's.

A decline in the rates of return of acquiring companies' shares was also observed in our cross-national comparison study (Mueller, 1980). In four countries (France, Holland, the UK and US) shareholders of acquiring firms earned significantly more than shareholders of non-acquiring, size- and industry-matched control group companies. This advantage steadily declined with time so that three years after the merger acquiring-firm shareholders were doing no better than the control group in France, Holland and the US, and were significantly worse off in the UK.

These results, and the others so far discussed, are mostly based on mergers taking place before the 1970s. Michael Firth (1979, 1980) examined 434 successful takeovers occurring in the UK between 1969 and 1975. Unlike the studies depicted above, Firth found but a small, insignificant rise in the returns of the bidding firms over the 48 months preceding the merger announcement.

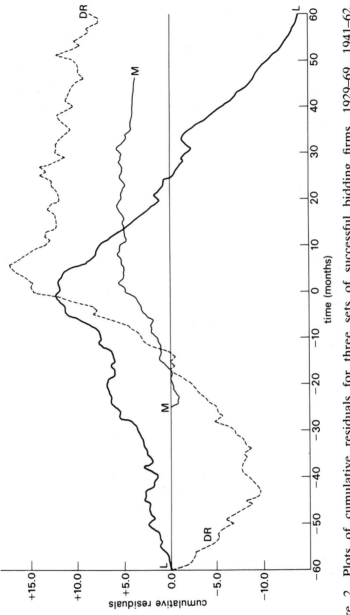

Figure 2 Plots of cumulative residuals for three sets of successful bidding firms, 1929–69, 1941–62 and 1958–74

He also found a significant *decline* in the returns to acquiring-firm shareholders at the time of announcement, but argued that the full drop occurred in a matter of *days* after the announcement, unlike what had been observed in the US.

Peter Dodd (1980) has also examined the share performance on a daily basis of 151 US firms making merger proposals from 1971 through to 1977. It is not possible to discern from his results whether a large run-up in the returns of the bidding firms occurred in the months preceding the announcements. A 7.22 per cent decline in the returns on the shares of the 71 companies that completed acquisitions did occur between ten days before the mergers were announced and ten days after they were completed. Thus both of these studies are consistent with those of the 1950s and 1960s in that acquiring-firm shareholders were worse off after the merger than before; the major apparent difference is that this result is substantiated in a matter of days in the 1970s rather than in the course of several months as in the earlier studies.

Despite this uniformly mediocre performance of the market for corporate control judged from the point of view of acquiring firm stockholders, most studies that claim to test the market-for-control hypothesis also claim that their results support it. This claim is based almost entirely on the gain to the acquired company's shareholders occurring at the time of merger. Dodd and Ruback (1977), for example, test the corporate-control hypothesis's prediction that the price of acquired-company shares rises at the time of acquisition against what they call a 'zero impact' hypothesis which they saddle with the silly prediction that a takeover can occur without there being a rise in the price of the target firm's shares. Since they observe a rise, they conclude there must be a positive impact, i.e. efficiency gain from the mergers.

Does the run-up in the target firm's share price at the time of acquisition signal a performance improvement that will follow the merger, or merely the fact that once the merger intentions of a management become known, whatever their motives, the acquirer must pay a premium for the target company's shares to complete the takeover? The answer to this important question cannot be gleaned from the existing literature. Several studies have observed a decline in the returns on target-firm shares in the months or even years preceding their acquisition.[8] A few studies have contradicted this finding (for example, Dodd and Ruback,

1977) but even if true, it does not tell us whether these firms became acquisition targets because they were performing badly *and* the acquiring firm's managers thought they would improve its performance, or that seeking to expand their own company the acquiring firm's managers chose to acquire a company whose market price was relatively low. Once again one's prior assumptions as to the motives of managers are crucial to how one views the evidence.

More persuasive support for the market-for-control hypothesis exists in the findings that target firms actually are performing, as measured say by real returns on assets, relatively poorly.[9] Nevertheless, these results have also been contradicted in some studies, particularly for the US.[10]

These considerations indicate the importance of establishing whether acquired companies do perform better following a merger. Testing for this is difficult, since the acquired firm is 'lost' in the merged company. In our cross-national study we compared changes in profitability of the combined companies over the three to five years following an acquisition to changes in profitability for matched control group firms, and the merging companies' industries for the comparable years. In three countries (Belgium, FRG and the UK) slight improvements were observed, in three slight deterioration (France, Holland and the US), and in Sweden no change. More relevant to the efficiency issue are comparisons of the changes in sales, since an improvement in efficiency should lead to a reduction in product price and an expansion of sales. In no country was an increase in the sales of merging companies observed following a merger compared to control group or industry averages. In Holland and the United States a significant decline in sales was recorded (see Mueller, 1980). Although declines in sales are consistent with neo-classical theory's predictions when market power rises following a merger, the lack of improvement in the profitability of merging companies in at least Holland and the US makes this rationalization implausible. Certainly it is hard to claim efficiency increases are evidenced by these results. Similar or more negative findings have been reported by other studies in the US and UK.[11] There just is not much uncontroverted evidence that mergers improve the efficiency of the companies merging.

One can argue that the three to five years of experience after a merger is too short a time-span to observe the effects of a merger in operating performance, and that stockmarket values should be used to predict future performance. Surprisingly few studies have computed the effect of a merger on the combined market values of the two merging companies. Of the five studies of acquiring-company performance discussed above, only Firth makes this calculation. He finds that the net effect of the merger on the two firms' market values is negative. Table 3 presents figures for the five studies.[12] The percentage returns to acquired-firm shareholders are all large and highly significant. The percentage returns to acquiring-firm shareholders are all negative, smaller in absolute value and sometimes insignificant. In comparing the two, however, it must be kept in mind that acquiring companies are much larger than the firms they acquire. In my study of the US they were ten times larger on average. If this relative size difference were true of the mergers in these studies, then the losses to acquiring shareholders in all cases would exceed the gains to the acquired-firm shareholders, and the combined effects would at best be insignificantly different from zero.

TABLE 3   GAINS TO ACQUIRING- AND ACQUIRED-
COMPANY SHAREHOLDERS

Study	Acquiring	Acquired
Dodd and Ruback (1977)	−3.08	27.55
Mandelker (1974)	−1.50	12.1
Langetieg (1978)	−1.61	12.92
Dodd (1980)	−7.22	33.96
Firth (1980)	−1140.2	1103.6

Figures for Firth are in £ (millions), for all other studies percentage changes in shareholder wealth. Changes are measured from month (day) preceding announcement of takeover to last point in time following announcement reported. Announcements are assumed to precede mergers by six months.

While the evidence in table 3 does not present a very convincing case for the market-for-control hypothesis, it is surprisingly consistent with the managerial thesis. The managers of a firm whose shares have experienced a long run-up in value above their normal level is likely to have both more discretion to undertake an unprofitable merger and more wherewithal to finance it. The

dramatic improvements in acquiring-company returns preceding
mergers depicted in figure 2 are explainable by the managerial
theory, while they have been totally ignored by the corporate-
control hypothesists. Similar reasoning explains why large upswings in the stock market typically lead to merger waves. To
explain this correlation by the corporate-control hypothesis, one
must assume that inefficient managerial performance is particularly apparent in stock market upswings, and becomes immediately concealed when the market collapses.

As noted above, the managerial theory of investment is a cash-
flow theory of investment. The recent US experience, in a depressed stock market, of mergers being financed out of cash-flows
by firms with relatively large cash-flows also seems more easily reconcilable with the managerial theory (Schwartz, 1980). The most
vivid example has been large acquisitions at very high premiums
by oil companies following the OPEC price increases. Did the
formation of OPEC improve the capability of oil company
managers to manage assets in other industries? Did it suddenly
reveal inefficiencies of other managers that were previously concealed? Or has OPEC simply generated so much cash that oil
company managers decided to acquire other companies rather
than 'give it away' to their shareholders?

While the managerial theory does not predict that *all* mergers
are unprofitable, since there is no reason to expect a growth-
maximizing management to pass up a profitable merger opportunity if it sees it, the theory is consistent with the observation
that some mergers are unprofitable. The results reviewed above
suggest that the fraction of all mergers that are uniquely
explained by the theory may be quite large.

Before closing this subsection, it is germane to the argument to
mention another explanation of mergers advanced with regard to
recent mergers. In the depressed stock market of the 1970s many
firms were selling at prices below the book values of their assets.
It is then argued that it is cheaper to acquire a given bundle of
assets as an ongoing firm than to put it together as new plant and
equipment. True. But the neo-classical theory teaches us that the
market value of a firm is the market's evaluation of the firm's
future profits. If managers maximize stockholder welfare, and if
they will not improve the profitability of the target firm after a
merger, one of two additional assumptions must be°made to

explain mergers by low market to book (valuation) ratios. Either the market has underestimated the future profits of target companies, or acquiring-company managers have overestimated them. Now one can never distinguish empirically the hypothesis that managers meant to improve stockholder welfare but made a mistake from the hypothesis that they correctly pursued a goal conflicting with stockholder interests. So the latter assumption offers no predictive superiority over the managerial thesis.[13] If the first assumption is correct, mergers become another example of inefficient rent-seeking. All the gains to the acquiring firm from finding undervalued firms become losses to the shareholders selling out (Grossman and Hart, 1981). The managerial theory offers the simpler explanation for these mergers, that neither the market nor the acquiring-company managers are making a mistake in evaluating the future profits of the target companies. The buying firm's management, seeking assets rather than profits, acquires companies with low market to book values, since as assets these firms are 'undervalued', even when the present value of their future profit stream is correctly valued by the market.

Summary and Conclusions

Neo-classical economics has obtained much good mileage out of the asumption that individuals pursue their own ends. When carefully applied, this behavioural assumption and the analytic tools of economics can yield important insights into the collective behaviour of individuals, and neo-classical economics' showpiece normative proposition, the invisible-hand theorem, can be a useful guide for public policy. Uncritical acceptance of the assumptions of the neo-classical theory in some situations can lead to both bad positive economics and misguided normative policy recommendations.

A good example of this is the paper by Peter Dodd entitled 'Merger Proposals, Management Discretion, and Stockholder Wealth', to which reference has already been made. As the title suggests, Dodd's alleged objective in this paper is to see whether managers involved in takeover bids use their discretion in ways that reduce stockholder wealth. But the entire focus is on the behaviour of the target firm's management, presumably because

Dodd assumes that the managers of the acquiring firms have no discretion to pursue any goal other than stockholder welfare, because of the evidence in favour of the market-for-control hypothesis he and Ruback claim. Thus the relevance of the 7.22 per cent decline in the wealth of the acquiring firm's stockholders to the purported topic of the paper totally escapes Dodd. He merely notes in passing that 'The negative abnormal returns to stockholders of bidding firms is puzzling. It is an obvious area for future research.' But these negative returns are puzzling only to someone with an unshakeable belief in the assumptions of neo-classical economics, and future research is unlikely to shed any light on this puzzle if it is undertaken and interpreted with the neo-classical blinders Dodd obviously wears.

More generally I fear that the blind adherence to the neo-classical paradigm of most economists has crippled their ability to understand and analyse the modern, corporate economy and recommend policies that will lift it out of its current rather awful predicament. That there is a 'crisis in economics' has often been commented upon by leading economists in recent years. Usually what is referred to is our inability to explain macro-phenomena like unemployment, inflation, the simultaneous existence of both; or to explain the failures of Keynesian economics, monetarist economics, supply-side economics. But a 'crisis in micro-economics' of equal proportions exists today, a crisis largely ignored, perhaps because, microeconomics being what it is, most observers see but a part of the gap between prediction and fact, perhaps because most observers are wearing their neo-classical blinders.

Over the last two decades there have been more than 20,000 mergers in the United States and a proportionally higher number in the United Kingdom. A reading of the mainstream economics literature would lead one to believe that the bulk of these were motivated to remove bad managers and improve the flow of capital in the economy. A reading of the conclusions of most empirical studies of mergers would lead one to believe that mergers had indeed had this effect. Yet after a generation of unprecedented efficiency-enhancing merger activity, both the US and UK economies were at a standstill, each had lost ground in world product markets, productivity increases had ground to a halt.

Correlation does not imply causality, of course (think how bad things would be had there not been all those mergers), and the main cause for today's shoddy economic performance in the West is usually alleged to be the rise in the price of petroleum. But it has been ten years since the first major oil-price increase, and one of the virtues of the market economy is supposed to be its ability to adjust to such shocks. Why has capital not flowed in response to the oil-price change to re-establish an equilibrium at a higher level of economic efficiency than we observe today?

The oil-price rise in 1973 is the kind of shock to an economic system that often makes comparisons of the predictions of competing theories easy. In concluding this essay I present such a brief comparison.

One assumes that the initial impact of the dramatic oil-price increase of 1973 was to shift the marginal return on investment schedules for many firms far to the left. Investment in technologies that required relatively large oil inputs, or that manufactured complements to oil, like automobiles, became much less profitable. Of course, investment in technologies that substituted for oil would become more profitable, but for such a large price dislocation as occurred in 1973 it is doubtful that such technologies could have been sitting on the shelf to make a smooth transition possible. Thus, particularly taking into account the importance of the automobile in the US economy, one expects in aggregate a leftward shift in the marginal return on investment schedule.

Assuming that the cost of capital was not immediately affected, neo-classical theory predicts a sharp fall in investment and a dramatic increase in dividends, since current profit flows did not fall much. Given the latter, the managerial theory predicts no fall in investment, no increase in dividends, and a dramatic decline in the returns on investment as management continues to plough back current cash-flows into technologies that have now become unprofitable, and that is exactly what occurred.

A glance back at table 2 indicates a steady growth in plant and equipment expenditures over the 1970s. Estimates of marginal returns on capital for a sample of 187 firms over this period have been made by Brainard, Shoven and Weiss (1980).

Comparison of the internal rate of return for the cash-out and constant-capital assumptions is also informative . . . Through 1969 the internal rate of the constant-capital case is always above the internal rate for the cash-out case. That is, the present value of the typical firm is higher if it remains in business and replaces capital as it wears out. From 1973 on, the internal rate is higher for the cash-out case – according to our calculations new investment is on average unprofitable at the discount rate implied in the valuation of existing capital. (p. 477)

In fact, the real rate of return hovers around zero after 1973 (p. 477).

Not only did management not respond to the oil-price shock by increasing dividends, they sharply cut them (Hall, 1980, p. 507). Not surprisingly given all of this, Brainard, Shoven and Weiss observe shareholders preferring dividends to retained earnings. 'It may not be too fanciful to suggest that this reflects the market's preference for receiving cash over investment in physical capital, which is perceived, on average, to be an unattractive use of funds' (p. 500). The point that something appears to be amiss between neo-classical theory and the Brainard–Shoven–Weiss findings is raised by Robert Hall:

> If management had whimsically cut dividends, market value would not have changed, finance theory tells us, or value might have risen, because of the adverse tax treatment of dividends. Indeed, finance theory tell us that dividends ought to be zero on stocks held by owners with higher tax rates on dividends than on capital gains.
> Instead of welcoming the cut in dividend payouts, stock market has reacted as if management did not go far enough . . . (p. 507)

Neither Hall nor Brainard *et al.* attempt to unravel the paradoxes for neo-classical theory which the performance of these firms during the 1970s raises. They are left dangling as puzzles to be pursued by other scholars in future research. But, if the past is prologue, future research will not explain them. It will either rationalize them away by inventing a sufficient number of auxiliary hypotheses to add to the basic neo-classical assumptions so that the core theory, as now fortified, can be claimed to be consistent with the evidence; or, as more typically happens, they will simply be ignored.

Notes

This paper benefited from comments by several participants at the conference out of which this volume grew. Special thanks are due to Oliver Hart and Peter Wiles, whose incisive comments greatly improved the exposition at several points.

[1] For a summary of the debate through 1970 and references, see Frederick D. Sebold (1970).

[2] Robert Shiller (1981), and Stephan LeRoy and Richard Porter (forthcoming). The same is true of bondholders (Shiller, 1979).

[3] Information-gathering of this type is what Grossman and Hart (1981) refer to as *acquisitional*. Allocational information-gathering by takeover raiders seeking to discover inefficiently managed firms can improve social welfare. This type of merger is discussed in the next section.

[4] It is perhaps worth noting, also, that there are many more kinds of inefficiencies one can associate with the functioning of the stock market than those discussed here, owing to the crucial role of information in this market. Joseph Stiglitz (1981) in his recent survey of stock market inefficiencies devotes *one sentence* in 16 pages to the inefficiencies focused upon here. But if Stiglitz's emphasis is correct, the stock market is still a very inefficient market indeed.

[5] See literature surveyed in Hogarty (1970), Steiner (1975), Mueller (1977b, 1981), and Fisher and Lande (1982).

[6] I calculated these by adding the monthly averages Dodd and Ruback report in their table 2. My cumulative totals differ trivially from theirs.

[7] Langetieg presents separate plots for acquiring firms up to the month of the merger, and for the consolidated firm starting with that month. My figure is a crude splicing of his two figures (p. 380). The curve for Mandelker is a plot of the figures in his table 1 (pp. 313–14).

[8] See Mandelker (1974), Smiley (1976), Langetieg (1978), Kummer and Hoffmeister (1978), and Franks, Broyles and Hecht (1977).

[9] The most impressive results here are for the UK (Singh, 1971; Kuehn, 1975). In our cross-national comparison, acquired firms had lower profitability than their size-matched control group firms and/or than their industries in Belgium, FRG, France and the UK.

[10] See Boyle (1970) and Mueller (1980). Acquired companies were also no less profitable than their control groups in Holland and Sweden in our cross-national comparison.

[11] For a review of earlier US evidence see Mueller (1977b). For the UK see Meeks (1977) and Cowling *et al.* (1979).

[12] The figures for Mandelker are based on the 167 acquisitions for which data on both the acquiring and acquired firms are reported (tables 5 and 6, pp. 319, 320). Unfortunately, these data cover only 20 months following the acquisition, cutting off some of the downward trend in acquiring-company returns, and thus underestimate the loss to acquiring-firm shareholders.

[13] In fact, it turns the corporate-control thesis on its head. Bad (predicting) managers acquire firms run by good managers.

Comment

OLIVER HART

In Dennis Mueller's stimulating and provocative chapter, he argues that 'neo-classical economics reigns supreme, not because it refutes challenges to it, but because it ignores them.' The particular challenges Mueller has in mind are empirical. Implicit in his argument is the idea that economists stick to the neo-classical paradigm because it provides them, through the invisible-hand theorem, with support for that most attractive state (at least to some) – *laissez-faire*.

As I have emphasized in my comments on chapter 2 by Robert Neild, I do not accept the view that the majority of neo-classical economists believe the assumptions underlying the invisible-hand theorem – perfect competition, absence of externalities, complete markets, etc. – to be realistic (by the way, free entry and exit is not required for this theorem). Instead I think that those who advocate *laissez-faire* do so not because they believe it is likely to work particularly well in practice, but rather because it seems superior to the alternatives, e.g. planning. I think that most economists retain the neo-classical methodology for rather different reasons, and I will indicate some of these below.

First, however, I would like to consider Mueller's empirical challenges. The first of these concerns the debate over marginal cost versus full-cost pricing. He notes that one of the strongest predictions of neo-classical theory is that a profit-maximizing firm does not change prices or quantity in response to a change in the tax applied to profits. On the other hand, the empirical evidence, Mueller argues, shows clearly that a not insubstantial shifting of the corporate income tax occurs. Can these two observations be reconciled? I think the answer is yes. The neo-classical proposition about non-shiftability applies only to a tax which is levied on pure profit, i.e. profit net of *all* costs, including payments to capital. However, as most recent work has shown, corporation income tax does not satisfy this requirement. Reasons for this include (1) the fact that equity payments, in contrast to debt payments, are only partially tax deductible; (2) the existence of accelerated depreciaton; (3) the fact that the tax system is not indexed (see, for example, King, 1977). Of course, it may be that, even taking such distortions into account, the shifting that occurs exceeds that which would be predicted by the theory. This is, however, a more difficult claim to test than the one suggested by Mueller.

The rest of his challenges (both theoretical and empirical) are with reference to the stock market. Some of these are concerned with the behaviour of shareholders, and others with the behaviour of firms. With reference to shareholders, Mueller cites evidence due to Shiller, and LeRoy and Porter, which, he claims, shows that investors are either continually overestimating future swings in dividend payments by factors of four or five or more, or are selling and buying on the basis of considerations other than the companies' anticipated dividend and profit performance. He goes on to suggest that such behaviour, which is anomalous in neo-classical terms, is consistent with what he describes as rent-seeking activities. This apparently refers to the attempt by individuals to profit from predicting market swings, i.e. from out-guessing the market.

Shiller, and LeRoy and Porter, are concerned with whether the observed volatility of share or bond prices is consistent with the idea that the price of a security should equal the expected net present value of future dividend or interest payments. They find that it is not. This is an interesting conclusion, but it does not necessarily follow from this that individual investors are behaving irrationally in the neo-classical sense. The Shiller/LeRoy and Porter work is a joint test of expected utility-maximising behaviour by investors; rational expectations; and the present value relation; and it could be, for example, the last of these which is incorrect. In fact in a more recent paper, Grossman and Shiller (1981) have shown that some of the volatility in share prices can be explained by certain sorts of investor risk-aversion. Thus it may not be necessary (or even helpful) to introduce rent-seeking activities to explain this phenomenon. (Note that rent-seeking activities are not, as Mueller suggests, non-neoclassical in nature. They are consistent with both rational behaviour and rational expectations. On this see Grossman and Stiglitz (1980).)

Mueller goes on to carry out a crude cost-benefit calculation of the stock market. He has already decided that the benefits to investors are very low since their behaviour is essentially irrational (or is a form of upper-middle-class gambling). As I have indicated, I do not think that the evidence suggests this at all. Mueller then goes on to argue that since only a small fraction of new investment is financed by the flotation of equity, the *direct* benefits to firms from the stock market are also very low. In view of the transaction costs from running the market (e.g. brokerage fees), he concludes that 'any claim that the stock market makes a substantial contribution to bringing about an efficient allocation of real capital must rest on the *indirect* effect which the market has on investment through the implicit determination of the cost of capital for each firm . . .' Reading between the lines, I feel that Mueller is suggesting that this indirect effect is unlikely to be large enough in reality to make the stock market socially productive. But he provides no evidence to justify this. An effect can be very large even if it is indirect!

So far I have discussed a small, but controversial, part of Mueller's paper. The bulk of the paper is in fact devoted to an analysis of managerial behaviour. Here I think that Mueller is on considerably firmer ground when he argues that there are a number of phenomena which seem at odds with neo-classical theory. The two principal ones are dividend behaviour and merger activities.

According to the Modigliani–Miller (henceforth M–M) theorem, the value of a firm depends on the real investment it undertakes, but not on how this investment is financed. In particular, whether the firm uses internal funds, issues bonds or floats new equity should have no effect on its valuation (the theorem makes certain quite strong assumptions, e.g. the absence of bankruptcy and taxes). Professor Mueller argues that this theorem is not consistent with the evidence of Friend and Puckett among others, which suggests that shareholders prefer an extra pound of dividends to an extra pound of retained earnings. One point which Mueller does not emphasize is that the irrelevance of financial decisions is only true when real investment is held fixed. That is, it does not follow from M–M that investors will be indifferent between 50 dividends and 70 retained earnings on the one hand, and 70 dividends and 50 retained earnings on the other, if in the latter case the level of investment is lower (because only internal funds are being used).

The role of dividends and retentions has in fact been the subject of much recent (neo-classical) theoretical and empirical work, and I was a bit surprised that Mueller does not refer to this. The basic issue that recent work has focused on is why firms pay dividends at all (see Gordon and Malkiel, 1982). Given that capital gains are taxed at a lower rate than dividends, firms, if they want to maximize market value, should pay no dividends and buy back shares if investment is less than current earnings. We do not, however, observe such behaviour (buying back shares is effectively illegal in the UK but not in the US). A number of attempts have been made to explain the importance of dividends in terms of their signalling effect, but none has been entirely successful. So the dividend puzzle remains.

Mueller seems to think that this puzzle can easily be explained using the managerial theory of the firm. I do not agree. I do not see why managers who wish to pursue growth would pass up the opportunity to increase their firm's market value, *given* a particular investment plan. Managerial theory might tell us something about the choice of investment plan, but this is another matter and seems to have nothing to do with the M–M financial-irrelevance proposition or with the dividend puzzle.

In the final part of his chapter, Mueller considers merger activity. He argues that the evidence shows that bidding firms generally embark on a merger after a period of sustained increase in their share price, but that once the merger is announced their share price falls. This seems to be inconsistent with neo-classical theory which suggests that managers should only undertake actions which increase share price. I entirely agree with Mueller about the puzzling nature of this observation. It seems to me, however, that it *may* be possible to explain the sustained increase in share price prior to the merger in one of two ways. First, in a world of asymmetric information, credit markets will be imperfect for adverse-selection and moral-hazard reasons. Therefore retained earnings will be an important source of investment finance. The sustained increase in share price may reflect increased earnings, which in turn give the firm the funds to undertake a merger. Secondly, high earnings may be a signal, say, about the ability of management. Managers who have done well in the past may therefore find it easier to get capital in the future, i.e. higher past earnings may reduce the current cost of capital, leading to more investment. (For an example of a signalling model, see Ross (1977).)

If this sounds like a cash-flow theory of investment, that is because it is. Unlike Mueller, however, I am not prepared simply to assume such a theory. I believe that it is important to show that this theory is consistent with self-interested, maximizing behaviour by individuals (subject to certain informational constraints). This has not yet been done, although recent advances in the economics of information suggest that it may be possible to do it in the future.

The fall in share price when the merger is announced I think will be harder to explain. But again I believe the way forward is to refine neo-classical theory rather than to abandon it. Mueller instead wants to substitute managerial theory. It is certainly true that to a managerial theorist the post-announcement fall in share price is easy to explain, since according to this theory the merger is carried out for the benefit of management not shareholders. What is unsatisfactory about this is that it is never explained how managers can get away with pursuing their own goals in this fashion. After all shareholders do have some control over managers and directors through voting, proxy fights, etc. Moreover, they can use incentive schemes (e.g. stock options) to reward managers, so as to bring managerial preferences in line with their own. Finally, managers who systematically mismanage a firm are subject to the threat of a takeover bid (something strongly emphasized in Marris's early managerial work).

The question for a neo-classical is why these mechanisms do not prevent management from carrying out mergers which are against the interest of shareholders. For example, if mergers generally reduce market value, it would seem that considerable profit could be made by taking over companies and rewriting their corporate charters so as to prohibit (or make extremely difficult) any further mergers (as I understand it, such a provision in the corporate charter would be feasible if the company were registered in Delaware). Why do we not see this happen? Is it only because it is not generally recognized that mergers reduce the share price of the bidding firm? In the long run, when this is generally recognized, will we see the prohibition of mergers?

These are questions which managerial theorists rarely ask. But to a neo-classical they are fundamental. To put it another way, to a neo-classical the managerial theory is not a theory at all, since it does not make clear what the informational and other constraints are which allow managers to carry out mergers (or to pursue growth), when this is contrary to the interest of shareholders. The recent (neo-classical) literature on the principal–agent problem has identified cases where, due to asymmetric information, shareholders are unable, even with the use of incentive schemes, to get managers to act on their behalf (see, for example, Holmstrom, 1979). However, while I think this literature provides the best hope for the managerial theory, we are still some way from having proper foundations for such a theory.

Unfortunately, I have not the space to discuss the numerous other observations which Mueller makes or implies. Let me just note that I do not find it particularly surprising that mergers often reduce the sales of the merging companies. After all, mergers may take place simply to increase monopoly power, in which case the merging companies will restrict output and increase price. I see nothing non-neoclassical about that.

In conclusion, I would like to return to the question of why the neo-classical approach has survived in spite of the various empirical challenges to it. I do not share Mueller's view that this is because neo-classicals have a vested interest in the invisible-hand theorem. Nor do I think that neo-classicals deliberately ignore these challenges. Rather I think the reason is that there is at this point no satisfactory alternative to neo-classical theory. Mueller complains that neo-classical economics often rationalizes the empirical puzzles away by inventing a sufficient number of auxiliary hypotheses to make core theory consistent with the evidence. But this is just the process of normal science (see Kuhn, 1970). Only when a real alternative to neo-classical theory becomes available can economists be expected to abandon it. I am surprised that Mueller does not recognize this.

7

The Firm as a Collection of Human Resources

HIROYUKI ODAGIRI

> When men have become used to working in a particular firm or
> with a particular group of other men in a firm, they become indi-
> vidually and as a group more valuable to the firm in that the
> services they can render are enhanced by their knowledge of their
> fellow-workers, of the methods of the firm, and of the best way of
> doing things in the particular set of circumstances in which they are
> working. (Penrose, 1959, p. 52)

It has been a quarter century since Edith Penrose wrote her
famous article (1955) and book (1959), which stressed the need to
regard 'the firm as a collection of productive resources' (1959, p.
24). Her thesis that 'the production of these services (required for
the making of expansion plans) requires time, and this limits the
scope of a firm's expansion plans at any given time' (1955, p. 535)
is now widely known. Several attempts at mathematical formulation have been made, most succinctly Uzawa's (1969) 'Penrose
Curve', but to me it appears that the consequences of reviewing
the firm as such a collection have not been fully examined. An effort is made in this chapter, without pretending to be comprehensive, to suggest some of what should be done in this direction.

The Importance of Human Resources

Penrose spoke of two productive resources: physical resources
and human resources. Of these I consider human resources most
essential and indispensable to the firm. We can in fact find the following statement by Penrose herself: 'There is one type of productive services which, by its very nature, is available to a firm in
only limited amounts. This is the service of personnel, in particular,

of management, with experience within the firm' (1955, p. 534). This accords with the belief among businessmen that the efficient use of human resources and their development are the key for the success of the firms, where the belief is most common in Japanese management but is becoming more and more so in American management as well: see Ouchi, 1981, and Peters and Waterman, 1982.

The importance of human resources largely stems from the fact that knowledge in its most broad sense, including skills and experiences, has become more and more important in our society. In knowledge we find three salient features. First, it is embodied in individual workers (from blue-collar workers to management staffs) so that the loss of a worker immediately causes the loss of knowledge to the firm. Second, it is more or less specific to each worker and to each firm, for one cannot have exactly the same background, training and experience as another inside or outside the company. Third, it is a capital stock accumulable only through time by investment, such as education and training, and gaining experiences.

Thus 'individuals with experience within a given group cannot be hired from outside the group, and it takes time for them to achieve the requisite experience' (Penrose, 1959, p. 47), and human resources are much more often a constraint in undertaking a new project than are financial and physical resources, namely capital. In fact one can think of a firm without capital – a singer may be a good example – but not a firm without a human being. More appropriately, therefore, a firm might be regarded as a collection of specific human resources, in which human resources employ physical and financial resources to achieve their goals, as opposed to the neo-classical presumption that capital employs labour.

These characteristics of knowledge imply that every worker is different from all the others and is to a considerable extent indispensable to the firm, and that the knowledge a worker has accumulated can be of full value only when working with the same firm (Penrose, 1959, p. 54). The first implies a monopolistic element for the worker and the second implies a monopolistic element for the firm, suggesting a bilaterally monopolistic element with each pair of worker and firm. As any microeconomics textbook would point out, in such a situation the equilibrium is indeterminate and dependent on the relative bargaining power, institutional setting, social custom, and so forth.[1]

There is one obvious consequence, nevertheless: continuous employment is mutually beneficial. Only by continuously working in the same company can a worker fully utilize his/her knowledge and be motivated to accumulate it. Only by continuously employing a worker can a firm derive the highest productivity out of him/her, maintaining an efficient production or management team. Lifetime employment has thus become a perfectly rational arrangement in making best use of human resources, benefiting both employees and employers. It should not be interpreted solely on the basis of a historical convention, of corporate paternalism or an insurance arrangement to guarantee income to the workers who are supposed to be more risk averse than corporate owners.[2]

These arguments also imply that if the firm needs to fill a vacant or new position, an efficient operation may be most smoothly maintained by promoting or transferring to the position one of its own employees, for such a person most likely possesses 'intimate knowledge of the resources, structure, history, operations, and personnel of the firm' (Penrose, 1959, p. 54). Internal promotion thus becomes the norm for the filling of vacancies at a higher rank, and the use of what Doeringer and Piore named the internal labour market 'within which the pricing and allocation of labour is governed by a set of administrative rules and procedures' (Doeringer and Piore, 1971, pp. 1–2) prevails, leaving the external labour market(s) to those who are seeking new jobs or who have left or been dismissed from their old jobs (namely, only at the port of entry and exit, using the terms in Doeringer and Piore).[3]

These phenomena, unfortunately, have never received due attention in the orthodox neo-classical theory, but they have grave implications for many aspects of the theory, such as the motive and behaviour of the firm, education and training, efficiency and welfare, and productivity and growth. To investigate all these is certainly beyond my capacity: only two will be discussed here.[4]

The Motive of the Firm

The neo-classical theory has presumed that the owners, namely stockholders, in a joint-stock company, by providing financial resources, possess the ultimate control of the firm and can hire or dismiss whatever and however much labour they want through the external labour market(s). The latter presumption has been questioned already. In reality each worker is endowed with specific knowledge and cannot be replaced with an outside worker without a loss in productivity. As a consequence, with or without trade unions, the employees tend to possess a degree of power which the owners cannot neglect.

The first half of the neo-classical presumption, namely that the controlling power rests with the owners, has already been challenged by many writers, most notably by Marris (1964). Not only has the ownership been so dispersed that no owner possesses sufficient power, not only are proxy fights too costly and risky to undertake, but also the punishment in the form of a takeover raid inflicted on a firm with a low market value is too infrequent and imperfect (particularly in countries other than the United States and the United Kingdom). These arguments are now well known and should need no further explanation.[5]

Therefore, neither of the neo-classical presumptions can be justified and there is no *a priori* reason to believe that the firm should maximize the interests of the owners subject to the market-determined level of the interests of the employees, where these two interests are normally measured by, respectively, the profits and the wages (in static analyses) or the market value of the firm and the lifetime income of a worker (in dynamic analyses). The employees would certainly demand more than what they will be able to get in the external market, since they know that they are valuable to the firm. Furthermore, given that the managers nowadays – from the chairman and the president to, say, the middle management – have usually worked for a long time in the firm gradually climbing up the promotion ladder,[6] and given that their stock-ownership of their own company is typically small, they tend to feel themselves more akin to the employees than to the owners. To them the employees are the in-group whereas most of the stockholders are unknown investors who simply own their share of the company as a part of a portfolio.

Thus, at least for the big corporation, I believe it more appropriate to depict its behaviour as maximizing the employees' interests subject to a certain minimum level of the owners' interests.[7]

An analysis along this line has been made in Odagiri (1982b) and is briefly summarized here (see also Aoki, 1982).[8]

The analysis incorporates lifetime employment and internal promotion in a simple generation-overlapping model in which a worker works for two periods in a firm with two ranks. Any worker is hired at the beginning of the first period as a rank 1 worker, may or may not be promoted to rank 2 at the beginning of the second period, and retires at the end of the second period. The probability of promotion is assumed to be common to every worker, and not dependent on any of his/her personal characteristics, and is shown to be a function of two variables, the rate of expansion of the employment of the firm, and the span of control, namely the number of subordinates whom a higher-rank worker supervises. The faster the firm expands or the smaller the span is, the more higher-rank positions are created in the future, thereby increasing the promotion probability. We assume the span of control to be fixed for technological or sociological reasons.

The expected lifetime utility of an employee then depends positively on the wages at the two ranks and the rate of corporate growth which determines promotability, as well as the worker's rate of discount and his/her risk attitudes.

The market value of the firm also depends on these two variables. Obviously, higher wages imply smaller profits and hence a smaller value. The effect of the growth rate is twofold. Faster growth, on the one hand, implies larger profits in the future and hence a higher value. On the other hand, faster growth is attained only with a heavier burden of investment which reduces the net cash-flow and hence the value. Because the marginal cost of investment tends to increase as the rate of growth becomes larger for exactly the reason put forward by Penrose, as quoted on p. 190, the negative effect likely becomes dominant as the growth rate increases.

The result is diagrammatically presented in figure 3. The horizontal axis measures the rate of growth of the firm and the vertical axis the wage rate or wage steepness (see note 8). The curves labelled U_i ($i = 1 \ldots 5$) denote the indifference curves for the employees with a larger i corresponding to a higher level of utility. The curves labelled v_i denote the combinations of the two variables that yield constant market values, which may be called the stockholders' indifference curves, with a larger i corresponding

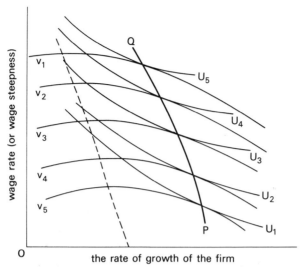

Figure 3   The stockholder–employee bargaining model

to a larger market value. The latter curves are upward sloping for small growth rates, but reach peaks the locus of which is given by the broken line, and afterward are downward sloping due to the Penrose effect mentioned above. The bold line PQ is the locus of tangency between the two sets of the indifference curves and may be called the Pareto-optimal or contract curve.

There are two notable findings. First, the contract curve always lies on the right of the broken curve. Note that the latter is the locus of the growth rates that the firm should choose if it is to maximize the market value subject to given wages; hence, we find that our firm chooses a higher growth rate than the value-maximizing firm provided that the wages given to the latter equal those chosen by the former. This lends support to the claim by Marris (1964) and Odagiri (1981) that because of the desire for promotion the firm tends to pursue growth more than is presumed in the neo-classical theory. Another proposition derivable here is that value maximization with wages given is not Pareto optimal because it neglects the contribution of growth to worker's welfare. That is, for instance, decreasing wages and increasing the growth rate along the v curve from the point on the dotted line makes the employees better off while keeping the stockholders indifferent.

Second, the contract curve is downward sloping, which implies that as the capital market constraint weakens and/or the employees gain more power, the firm tends to choose higher wages but a lower growth rate. Although this appears rather contradictory to the growth-maximization hypothesis, three hitherto ignored factors may work in the opposite direction. The first is the difference in information requirement between the two variables; that is, the stockholders will more easily discover excessive wage payments than excessive investment because the list of available investment projects with their costs and returns is rarely known to them. The second is the difficulty in attaining consensus among the employees. Because faster growth benefits almost all the employees through increased promotability, it may be more agreeable than wage changes which affect income distribution. The third is the point raised by Galbraith (1967) with his famous concept of 'technostructure'; that is, decisions are made through group decision-making with the participation of a large number of employees (probably most white-collars and quite a few blue-collars). In this group decision-making, individual staffs may find the extent of investment more influenceable than their pay. All these considerations suggest faster corporate growth with more employee power, working against the implication of the negatively sloped contract curve.

The importance of growth was also discussed by Penrose from a somewhat different viewpoint. In the statement quoted on p. 190, she argues that as individual workers accumulate more experiences with the firm, the services they can render are enhanced. Moreover, 'many of the productive services created through an increase in knowledge that occurs as a result of experience gained in the operation of the firm as time passes will remain unused if the firm fails to expand . . . A more complete use of the services of individuals is supposed to be made possible by promotion in rank, but this will eventually require enlargement of the firm's activities' (Penrose, 1959, p. 54). This argument of hers appears so obvious that I see no need to elaborate further.

This section presented an employee-welfare-maximization model showing that the firm tends to seek faster growth to create more opportunities to promote than has been presumed in the neo-classical theory, supporting the simpler growth-maximization hypothesis, and that the wage rates are also endogenously determined so that more employee power tends to result in larger wages. This latter view has not been incorporated in the growth-maximization theory, notwithstanding the neo-classical theory. However, only with this view can one explain the recent findings that the wage rate is positively correlated with market concentration, market share, and/or entry barriers,[9] since no such relation should be observed if wages are entirely determined in external labour markets.

The analysis here also suggests that if an unanticipated recession takes place with a reduction in the firm's value added, the firm is likely to respond not only with smaller profits and smaller dividends but also with smaller wage payments, for the capital market constraint may not be lowered as much as the value added. In other words, the risk of income fluctuation is likely to be shared by the employees as well. The Japanese practice of bonus payments comes to mind as a typical example. For instance, the end-of-year bonus was observed to decrease compared to the year before in 1975 when the adverse impact of the oil crisis was most serious and the profit rate recorded its lowest value. I have no room here to elaborate on this issue, but its importance as a consequence of our regarding the firm as a collection of human resources should be emphasized.

Intrafirm Competition and Efficiency

With the prevalence of lifetime employment, an important task to the firm as well as to the economy is to maintain, in those workers with little fear of dismissal, the incentive to work hard and invest in the accumulation of knowledge and skills. That is to say, if a worker expects dismissal is unlikely even if his/her poor performance is revealed, how can we expect him/her to work hard? A key to this question lies in separating intrafirm competition (namely competition among the employees for promotion) from market competition (namely competition in external labour market(s) among those seeking jobs). Thus, even if the latter is absent, competition could still be intense in the former sense. In fact, to me, this seems to explain at least partly why the country best known for the practice of lifetime employment, that is Japan, could achieve the highest increase in labour productivity among the major countries.[10]

In the last section, the probability of promotion was assumed common to all candidates. In reality, of course, it depends on the ability, effort and performance of individual workers. Consequently workers will be tempted to work hard and increase their ability and knowledge so as to increase their expectation of promotability. Given the span of control and the rate of growth of the firm, however, the number of promotable posts is fixed (see p. 194) and actually the promotion probability to the individual worker is only based on his/her relative ranking in comparison to fellow workers.

Lazear and Rosen called this scheme 'rank-order tournaments' and showed that under certain conditions 'wages based upon rank induce the same efficient allocation of resources as an incentive reward scheme based on individual output levels' (Lazear and Rosen, 1981, p. 841). Even though their analysis is based on a static analysis without the inter-temporal nature inherent in promotion as discussed in the previous section, and risk aversion and asymmetricity among candidates may produce difficulties, their result shows that intrafirm competition can be as effective as market competition in attaining Pareto efficiency. In fact the first may even be superior, because 'it might be less costly to observe relative position than to measure the level of each worker's output directly' (1981, p. 863).

The effectiveness of such intrafirm competition depends on the institutional arrangement concerning promotion. In one extreme we can think of a promotion scheme purely based on performance, as dealt with by Lazear and Rosen. In the other extreme we can think of a promotion scheme based solely on characteristics unrelated to performance, most commonly age and/or the length of service within the firm, which is referred to as seniority. If seniority is the only criterion, then promotability is independent of one's effort or knowledge and no incentive takes place to work hard and acquire knowledge. Hence, where the firm's promotion scheme lies between these two polar cases, that is, how much the promotion decisions are based on performance and how much on seniority, determines how much effort workers are willing to make.

Another relevant consideration is the range of candidates. That is, if a vacant post may be filled not necessarily by its direct subordinate but possibly by any suitable candidate in whichever department, the former has to prove him-/herself better than not only his/her colleagues in the department but every candidate company-wide. In fact if he/she could prove him-/herself superior, then he/she might be promoted to any vacant post (at the appropriate rank) not confined to his/her department, implying a higher promotability and more incentive for hard work and knowledge acquisition.

In order to make such wide selection of candidates viable, it is essential that the worker possesses a broad range of knowledge and skills. That is, the worker should not possess knowledge only related to a particular job but that related to a wide variety of jobs in the firm. In short, the knowledge should be firm-specific rather than job-specific. Such firm-specific knowledge (and skills) may be partly acquired by a series of conscious educational and training programmes which many Japanese companies in fact offer. However, probably more important is to have workers experience a wider variety of jobs by transferring them from one job to another. Hence it is desirable that the management has more freedom and willingness to transfer workers across jobs and departments.

How important seniority is in promotion decision and how widespread are transfers across jobs are questions which have not been studied enough, let alone internationally compared. Out of the limited number of such studies two are referred to here, both related to Japan. The first evidence was provided by Koike (1977), who found that through a Japan–US comparison of blue-collar workers in a few industries, the American factories are stricter in applying the seniority rule in promotion and the Japanese management has more discretion as to where to promote or transfer a worker.[11]

The second is Reitsperger's (1982) study of four companies in the United Kingdom: two of them are Japanese-owned; one American-owned; and one British-owned. He found that in Japanese-controlled firms 'the maintenance of a high degree of transferability of labour horizontally across jobs and departmental and craft boundaries, as well as vertically across different hierarchical levels, was considered as crucial' (pp. 11–12), and to achieve this end maintaining a single-union representation was considered to be of top priority, whereas the other two firms allowed the representation by multiple unions. Not surprisingly, the two Japanese-owned companies exhibited a higher labour productivity than the other two.

These two sets of evidence both suggest that Japanese firms, relative to American or British firms, succeeded in maintaining intrafirm competition with a less rigid seniority rule in promotion[12] and wider across-job transferability. It should be added that the latter, by providing workers with wider skills, contributed to maintaining productivity particularly during the time of rapid technical progress when skills pertinent only to one job rapidly become obsolete. This also makes it easier for the firm to introduce a new and more efficient production process because those workers who are not needed under the new process may be easily transferred to other jobs in the firm. That Japanese automobile manufacturers introduced industrial robots earlier than their American and European counterparts is no accident.

We have argued the importance of intrafirm competition to maintain efficiency. To the extent that competition leads to efficiency, it accords with the doctrine of the Invisible Hand (or the principle of competition, or the fundamental theorem of welfare economics, or what have you). If this doctrine may be regarded as the philosophical backbone of neo-classical economics, then our argument agrees with the neo-classical stand and we may say that Japan's economy is more neo-classical than most other major economies. Emphasized, however, is that the neo-classical theory presumed competition in *external* markets but that sort of competition is of little relevance to those modern large-scale firms where specific skills have become overwhelmingly important. It is not market competition but intrafirm competition that works there.

Synthesis

This chapter proposed to regard the firm as a collection of human resources, namely of workers embodied with diverse but specific knowledge, and considered the two consequences, one on the motivation of the firm and the other on the role of intrafirm competition. An effort to synthesize these two consequences, albeit a preliminary one, may be worthwhile.

In the previous section, the extent of intrafirm competition has been treated as if it is a given institution. Partly this is so because a firm adopts a certain rule more or less following the others in the economy, namely what Doeringer and Piore called the 'custom'. Yet it is a provision on which employees are supposedly able to exert their influence through collective bargaining. That is, *ceteris paribus*, they will demand a stricter seniority rule and a less intense intrafirm competition in pursuit of an easier and more comfortable working life. This is particularly so because intrafirm competition after all resembles a zero-sum game with fixed probability of promotion, given the control span and the rate of expansion (see Odagiri, 1982b, section 6, for a formal analysis).

In this argument, *ceteris paribus* means that the employee income is invariant. For the individual worker this is a natural assumption. However, for the employees as a whole it is not natural, since less intrafirm competition may result in less productivity and consequently a smaller fund from which the employees obtain their income in the manner analysed above in the section on the firm's motive. Hence their income may be reduced. This trade-off is depicted in figure 4.

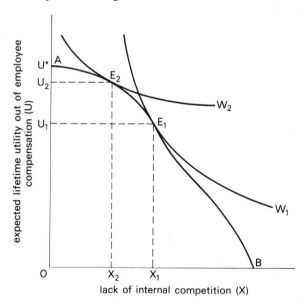

Figure 4   The case of endogenous intrafirm intensity of competition

Here the vertical axis measures the expected lifetime utility of a worker, U, as defined on p. 194 and the horizontal axis measures the extent of the lack of intrafirm competition, X; that is, further left implies more intense competition, however this is measured. Assuming a minimum market value to be given (without much justification, admittedly), we can draw a downward-sloping curve AB showing the level of employee utility corresponding to each level of the extent of competition. For instance, point A shows that with the most intense intrafirm competition the employees can attain U^*.

The utility level mentioned so far has taken into account the effect of risk associated with promotion in the manner of von Neumann and Morgenstern, but not the effect of the intensity of competition. Consider a utility function of the form, W (U,X), with both marginal utilities being positive because a larger X implies less competition and an easier life. If the employees as a whole can be supposed to make a deliberate decision to maximize their utility, then given an indifference curve W_1, they will choose the point E_1. Or if they do not much care about the competition, then the indifference curve will be like W_2 with the point E_2 being chosen.

We have speculated that intrafirm competition is more intense in Japan; can we say that Japanese workers have indifference curves more like W_2 than W_1 and have deliberately chosen a point more like E_2 than E_1? I do not have an answer. It is probably too neo-classical indeed to suppose that all economic matters are determined through optimization. Possibly the difficulty in obtaining a consensus among heterogeneous employees and the free-rider problem (a lazy worker, giving up hopes of promotion, nonetheless supports more competition in the hope of receiving a higher income generated by others working harder) are so serious that such decision is not practicable. For instance, if a consensus among employees cannot be reached, a prisoner's dilemma situation may arise with a result such that E_1 is realized despite the workers' indifference curves being more like W_2 than W_1.[13]

At any rate, it is not difficult to suppose that a social institution, such as the extent of intrafirm competition considered here, changes after a long gestation period as a result of interaction between economic forces and social custom in its broadest sense. Probably it is not just to attribute it entirely to economic rationality, nor is it permitted to treat it as completely exogenous to the economic system.

Postscript on Methodological Issues

I proposed in this chapter a new view of the nature and working of a modern large-scale firm which would criticize the naive neo-classical theory of the firm, as taught in the standard micro economic textbooks: that the owners of the capital fully control the firm, hiring from external labour markets a desired number of workers of desired quality. By no means does this imply that I disregard the neo-classical methodology as a whole. On the contrary, I have actually followed the neo-classical methodology in the following respects: first, the analysis was confined to orthodox economic motives; second, a constrained optimization technique was used; and third, for those institutions such as lifetime employment an economic justification was sought.

Consider the view that individuals, given certain constraints, seek to attain better economic conditions (not necessariy maximizing utility or wealth) and some interaction and/or adjustment among them takes place in the system (be it on markets or wherever, and be it converging to an equilibrium or not). If this view may be called neo-classical in a generalized sense then my analysis in this chapter is in this sense neo-classical despite its criticism of the 'textbook' neo-classical theory. In fact I believe that at this stage of the evolution of economic theory, one can avoid unnecessary logical error, controversy and confusion and make a greater contribution to our understanding of economic systems with the use of the 'generalized' neo-classical methodology. For, first, the 'generalized' neo-classical approach facilitates an analysis with the logical rigour not found in other branches of social science and I believe this should be maintained as much as possible. Second, the neo-classical theory doubtless stands as the most popular paradigm in economics now and I believe it helpful to present any new theory in a comparable manner.[14]

With this standpoint I have sought to give an economic rationale for the international differences in economic institutions and behaviour. Thus, although I certainly agree that Japan is as different from other developed countries as Germany is different from the United Kingdom and the United States, I rather avoid the view that Japan is special. Since this thinking seems to contrast with another recent study of the Japanese economy by

Morishima (1982), a few remarks are perhaps worthwhile. In his view, 'a remarkably idiosyncratic ethos prevails in Japanese society, and as a result of these ethical feelings Japanese capitalism has to a considerable extent deviated from the typical free enterprise system' (1982, p. VIII). Thus he explains Japan's 'success' (his quotation marks) as well as the lifetime employment system and the seniority system in terms of the idiosyncratic ethos of Japanese society – most importantly, Confucianism reformed in a Japanese way. This leads him to assert that 'it is therefore not surprising to find that Japanese capitalism was – and still is – nationalistic, paternalistic and anti-individualistic' (p. 18).

To me, however, it appears doubtful if such a view can explain many recent findings such as that (1) the lifetime-employment system is found in other countries as well (see Hall, 1982, and Main, 1982), (2) even in Japanese companies *de facto* dismissal has been observed, particularly following the oil crisis, (3) the seniority rule is also found in other countries, and it is even more important in some US jobs (see Koike, 1977), (4) labour mobility in Japan is much lower than in the United States or the United Kingdom for young workers and workers whose service with pre-vious employers was short; otherwise however the rate does not differ much across countries (see Ono, 1981), (5) the Japanese management system has also worked overseas (see Reitsperger, 1982), and (6) some of what the management does in the 'excel-lent' American companies is surprisingly similar to what is usually attributed to the Japanese management (see Ouchi, 1981, and Peters and Waterman, 1982).

These facts seem to suggest, contrary to Morishima's argu-ment, that Japan is not so different as to prevent comparative analysis with Western countries. I believe furthermore that an effort towards such analysis not only helps to find the common logic behind superficially different economic affairs, but also makes it easier for other countries to learn from the Japanese experience if these countries regard it as a success. It is with this in mind that I am seeking a theory of the firm not in accord with the 'textbook' neo-classical theory but yet on the same methodological ground as the 'generalized' neo-classical theory, so that the theory is applicable to industrialized economies, be they oriental or Western, and yet able to explain differences among them.

Notes

[1] On the basis of field observations, Doeringer and Piore (1971, p. 90) concluded that 'the rules governing internal allocation . . . sometimes narrow the range of feasible wages left by the traditional neo-classical constraints, but, except in unusual cases, individual wage rates remain indeterminate.'

[2] Akerlof and Miyazaki (1980), as an extension of the implicit-contract theory, justified the fixed-wage full-employment contract on this ground. A similar argument was given by Koizumi (1979) justifying what he called the stable-wage–stable-employment contract. Both assumed homogeneous unskilled labour in the traditional manner.

[3] For the superiority of the internal market structure scheme as a contractual mode over other schemes such as contingent claims contract, see also Williamson, Wachter and Harris (1975).

[4] Note that the arguments here do not deviate much from conventional economic analyses in that they are confined to economic motives and employ an optimization technique. We will return to this methodological issue in the last section.

[5] See Odagiri (1981), chapters 1 and 2. Grossman and Hart (1980) raised the free-rider problem – each shareholder not responding to a tender offer in expectation of a price rise following the completion of the takeover – as one of the reasons for infrequent takeovers.

[6] The study by Fiegehen (1981, p. 35) of 94 British companies reveals that 'senior staff spend on average about 15.5 years with their company as a member of its senior staff, not including service in less responsible positions.'

[7] Odagiri (1981, chapter 2) discusses the determination of this minimum level.

[8] As far as the qualitative results are concerned, it may appear irrelevant whether the employees' interests are maximized or the owners' interests are maximized, because maximizing A subject to a minimum value of B is mathematically equivalent to maximizing B subject to a minimum value of A. However, in an employee-welfare-maximization model (EWM) an appropriate measure of the employees' interests is the interests of an *incumbent* employee, whereas in a stockholder-welfare-maximization model (SWM) it is the interests of a potential *new* employee. These two interests are not identical; hence the two maximization problems yield different results even qualitatively. In fact, it turns out that between the two wage variables, the wage rate at the lower rank and the wage ratio across the two hierarchical ranks, the former tends to be fixed in EWM and the latter in SWM. For the detail see Odagiri (1982b).

[9] See Haworth and Reuther (1978) and Long and Link (1983) for American results and Nakao (1980) for a Japanese result. The former two found that the effect of concentration stayed significant even when the extent of unionization was controlled, implying that collective bargaining alone cannot explain the wage differential.

[10] I hasten to add, however, that lifetime employment in Japan is nowhere legally guaranteed, with *de facto* dismissal having been observed in the past even among big corporations. Also, many firms hire part-time and/or temporary workers along with regular workers. Still, a Japanese worker tends to assume that he/she will be able to work with the company until compulsory retirement.

[11] The concluding chapter of Koike's book is translated into English (Koike, 1978). Odagiri (1982a, subsection III.2) refers to Koike's findings in more detail.

[12] It is to be noted that the seniority rule is by no means absent in Japanese companies. As a matter of fact, seniority is one of the most frequently mentioned requirements for promotion and promoting a young worker over a number of older workers with longer services, probably not uncommon among American executives, is quite exceptional. However, the Japanese management subtly differentiates the speed of promotion among the employees so that the more able will be rewarded but at the same time the less able will not become desperate either.

[13] Thus a single, comprehensive and powerful trade union, because of its ability to foresee matters in a company-wide perspective and to obtain a consensus among the employees, can result in a more intense intrafirm competition (and a larger worker utility), in contrast to the view of Freeman and Medoff (1979) that unionism contributes to the seniority rule. We are not going to discuss the impact of trade unions on the problems discussed in this paper but it may well be very complicated, as this example illustrates.

[14] Also see Odagiri (1981, pp. 4–5). This does not mean that I wholeheartedly believe in the 'generalized' neo-classical approach. In particular, because I aim to analyse the motivation and behaviour of people working in an organization called the firm, its confinement to economic motives is unsatisfactory. McGregor's (1960) theory Y and Ouchi's (1981) theory Z are examples of how an investigation of non-economic motives yielded a new and perhaps more realistic principle of organization. For instance, the latter stressed the role of 'the organizational culture' that 'consists of a set of symbols, ceremonies, and myths that communicate the underlying values and beliefs of that organization to its employees' (Ouchi, 1981, p. 41).

Comment

OLIVER HART

Hiroyuki Odagiri's chapter addresses three aspects of the firm which he believes have not received sufficient attention in neo-classical economics. The first is the idea that workers acquire firm-specific skills, which means that workers and firms will have long-term relationships (the locking-in effect). The second is the idea that given dispersed ownership the controlling power in modern corporations lies with managers rather than with owners. The third is that, given the locking-in effect, competition between workers within the firm will be a more important influence on effort and productivity than competition between workers in different firms.

I very much agree with Odagiri about the importance of these issues. I also think that they have not received as much attention as they might in the neo-classical literature. This situation is, however, changing. With the development of new areas, e.g. the economics of information and incentives and the principal–agent problem, the tools are now available to tackle some of these issues, and I expect them to be the focus of a great deal of work in the future.

Let me turn to some of Odagiri's more specific points. First, he argues that the existence of locking-in effects will mean that workers and firms will, once their relationship is underway, be in a position of bilateral monopoly. In such a situation, Odagiri argues, the equilibrium is indeterminate and dependent on relative bargaining power, the institutional setting, etc. I do not agree with him about this. The existence of firm-specific skills does not lead inevitably to bilateral monopoly. The reason is that it is quite possible for the firm and workers, recognizing that they will have a long relationship together, to agree in advance on how wages and employment will be determined during this relationship. They can do this by writing a binding (contingent) contract at the starting date of their relationship (sometimes this contract may be implicit rather than explicit). Since there is no bilateral monopoly at the starting date, it is not unreasonable to suppose that this contract is determined on a competitive basis.

Thus I believe that many of the issues arising from the existence of firm-specific skills can be analysed using standard neo-classical methodology. In fact the large, recent literature on implicit contracts takes precisely this approach (see, for example, Azariadis, 1975).

Odagiri next considers the question of who runs modern corporations. His view is that it is management, rather than the shareholders. He then goes on to argue that 'since managers have usually worked for a long time in the firm gradually climbing up the promotion ladder . . . they tend to feel themselves more akin to the employees than to the owners.' Odagiri concludes that it is more appropriate to depict the behaviour of a large corporation in terms of maximizing the employees' interests subject to a certain minimum level of the owners' interests, rather than in terms of maximizing profit or net market value.

There are two issues here. First, do managers act on behalf of shareholders? Secondly, if they do not, what do they do? I agree with Odagiri that management does not generally act on behalf of shareholders. This has in fact been the subject of much recent neo-classical analysis (see, for example, Holmstrom, 1979). However, it is a very large step from this to the conclusion that management acts on behalf of the average employee. One glance at British industrial relations would suggest that this cannot generally be the case.

Moreover, even if one accepts Odagiri's objective function for the firm, it is very unclear why this should lead to substantially different conclusions about firm behaviour from the usual ones. If firms and workers sign contracts as suggested above, it would be natural to assume that each firm maximizes (net) market value subject to the constraint that the contract provides each worker with at least as much as he could get elsewhere (say, by signing a contract with another firm). How does this formulation differ (except possibly in distributional terms) from assuming that the firm maximizes the workers' interests subject to a minimum level of market value? The answer is that it does not, a point Odagiri himself recognizes in note 8. He argues, however, that the two formulations will no longer be the same once a distinction is made between the interests of incumbent employees and new employees. This may be so, but it is impossible to be sure until a formal model distinguishing explicitly between the interests of incumbent employees and new employees is developed. There is no such model in Odagiri's chapter.

Thus I do not see any difference between Odagiri's model, as it stands, and the usual neo-classical one. How then does he get the result that his firms will choose a higher growth rate than neo-classical firms? The answer is that in his model some workers are promoted over time, thereby receiving higher wages. The higher the firm's growth rate, the higher is the probability of promotion. This biases the firm towards high growth.

Unfortunately, this result seems to depend entirely on the assumption that senior workers get paid more than junior workers. But why? In Odagiri's model there seems to be no reason for this at all. There are in particular no explicit incentive problems which might cause the firm to use promotion as a reward for good service. Given this and the fact that there is some uncertainty about whether a particular worker will be promoted, it is always optimal for the firm to insure workers by offering them a constant wage path. But this of course leads to firms choosing the same growth rate as in the neo-classical model.

Let me turn to the third strand of Odagiri's chapter: the importance of intra-firm competition. Here I find myself very much in agreement with the sentiments he expresses. If a firm wants to encourage its workers to work hard, and if it cannot monitor their work directly, it should reward them according to some incentive scheme. This scheme will make their remuneration depend on their own output (assuming this can be observed), and also, as long as different workers face correlated environments, on the outputs of other workers. Part of the reward from working hard may come from promotion, part simply from an increase in wages. Note, however, that an incentive scheme based only on relative rankings within the firm, and not on the absolute performance of a worker, will be suboptimal. I therefore do not understand why Odagiri restricts his attention to relative performance schemes.

Odagiri refers to a relative performance incentive scheme as intrafirm competition. He distinguishes it from the usual sort of external competition through the market. I think that the distinction between these two is both interesting and important. However, I see nothing non-neoclassical about this distinction. As Odagiri notes, relative performance incentive schemes have been analysed recently by neo-classical economists such as Lazear and Rosen. In fact the whole question of what mechanisms are available to a principal (e.g. the owners or managers of a firm) to get an agent (e.g. the managers or workers of a firm) to do what the principal wants has been the subject of intense study in the neo-classical literature in the last few years.

My conclusion, then, is that the interests and concerns of Odagiri are shared very much by many neo-classical economists. I think that he recognizes this when he describes himself as a 'generalized' neo-classical. If some of the questions he raises have not traditionally received the attention they deserve, this is, I think, because the tools to analyse them have only recently become available. With the various advances in incentive theory and the principal–agent problem which have occurred in the last few years, however, I expect these questions to be a central focus of neo-classical economics in the future.

8

Whatever Happened to the Full-Cost Principle (UK)?

PETER WILES

It is very much like questioning the umpire's decision when this writer writes this chapter. Was not his own book (1961), largely devoted to this subject, the last pale flower of the Oxford School? Two editions, some favourable reviews: what are these to the verdict of history? Nevertheless, among the 'extremely worried' party referred to in the preface there was a firm decision to write under this title and no one else was willing. So here is a brief and biased account of matters *quorum pars minima fui*, before the Soviet Union went to my head.[1]

In 1933 Robinson and Chamberlin made an immense theoretical step forward: they incorporated imperfect competition and monopoly into marginalism in a rigorous and convincing way. But, first, they failed altogether with oligopoly, which remains today one of the most menacing skeletons in the cupboard of economic theory; secondly the factual input into their discovery was minimal; and thirdly its factual output (or predictive value) and policy consequences were equally minimal. As I put it in 1961 (pp. 1–3):

> In 1894 Philip Wicksteed published his *Co-ordination of the Laws of Distribution*. In place of the triform Ricardian schema, with the differential law of rent, the competitive law of interest and profit (to give names which Ricardo himself did not use), and the Iron Law of Wages, there was to be the single law of marginal productivity. The hiring and firing of all factors of production could be described by one theoretical proposition only, and in the same terms. This brilliant success has never since – so far as welfare economics is concerned – been subject to question. Even imperfect competition has not essentially modified it, while collective bargaining has touched it not at all.

In 1933 it seemed that the same fortunate result had been achieved for the price and output policy of the firm. In her *Economics of Imperfect Competition* (p. 4) Mrs Robinson said: 'Now no sooner had Mr Sraffa released the analysis of monopoly from its uncomfortable pen in a chapter in the middle of the book than it immediately swallowed up the competitive analysis without the smallest effort. The whole scheme of analysis, composed of just the same elements as before, could now be arranged in a perfectly uniform manner.' Marginal cost (m.c.) = marginal revenue (m.r.) is to be the sovereign rule. The Nigerian cocoa-grower, the Leicester hosier, the U.S. Steel Corporation and the Swiss Federal Railways are brothers under the skin. Differing legal organization and differing capacities to keep accounts cause no difference in policy. Changes in the elasticity of demand or the number of competitors merely produce interesting special cases.

Or is this to misrepresent the founders of the new theory? Perhaps they made no such claims? They did and yet they did not. Their sentences were usually in the indicative mood, and so could be understood as generalizations about reality. The theory of imperfect competition is rightly claimed to be the reaction of economists to the reality of modern industry, and a highly abstract selection of facts about modern industry is indeed to be found within its pages. But the facts were not seriously studied at all, and the generalizations were based on singularly little empirical research and subjected to surprisingly little qualification. Surely social scientists could not be presenting in these terms an important *factual* discovery. Nor were they: the authors were really presenting a *logical* discovery. But they were guilty of not making this point clear, even to themselves. The indicative mood has a fatal attraction: it is so much easier to say 'the entrepreneur does' than 'if my premises hold the entrepreneur would'.[2]

How could so great a fault have been committed? Nearly all economists commit it nearly all the time. The founders of imperfect competition theory erred in company with their forebears and their successors. The persistent source of this error is of course the confusion of normative and analytical with descriptive economics. In order best to allocate scarce resources between competing ends it is necessary that entrepreneurs should equate m.c. with price; and this they will in fact do if (i) demand is perfectly elastic, (ii) they know what their marginal cost is, (iii) they wish to maximize their money profits, and (iv) the price and output combination chosen touches the demand curve, i.e. there are no queues. The theory of imperfect competition is the reaction of welfare economists to the information that condition (i) does not hold in practice. The concept of marginal revenue is evolved, which differs from price when demand is less than perfectly elastic. Conditions (ii) and (iii) are assumed still to hold, and it follows that m.c. always equals marginal revenue, which in its turn can equal price as a limiting condition. It is pointed out that the failure in the new conditions to equate m.c. with price is a derogation from consumer's sovereignty and the best allocation of resources. Granted all the assumptions this is perfectly true. Even if we do not grant them, it is important and interesting.

But this, the quite legitimate content of the doctrine of imperfect competition, is purely hypothetical. Factual content there is none, for assumption (ii) is almost wholly untrue and (iii) very often untrue; and while it is a move towards reality to admit that demand may not be perfectly elastic it is a move away again to posit a known marginal revenue, a known elasticity or a known demand curve. Also (iv) is a tacit assumption we must make explicit and often reject. The service rendered to descriptive economics by this theoretical revolution was that it awakened interest in a quite new subject, the price and output policy of the individual firm: *some* precise statement having for the first time been made on the subject, economists began to check it with the facts. It is not sufficiently realized that the descriptive micro-economics of the entrepreneur only began with imperfect competition; before then we studied industries, not firms. Thus Birck[3] and Taussig (1919) writing immediately before 'imperfect competition', treat the marginal cost of an industry as the average cost of the marginal firm.

The disservice rendered has already been hinted at: first it was supposed that the new theory had some correspondence to facts, and secondly it was assumed that there must exist some single general rule adequately describing entrepreneurial behaviour. Now this assumption has only to be clearly stated to be seen to be most doubtful. There is not one simple rule about men in love or men in politics or men in lunatic asylums: how then could there be one about men in business? In fact there is not; price and output policies are as various as political programmes and mating approaches. The unity of the law of price and output must be broken up, and the more modest aim accepted of making such unrelated generalizations about parts of the field as the facts happen to warrant. The task of this book is to do precisely that. Where Wicksteed was fortunate enough to demolish a spurious diversity and substitute a simple unity my less popular task is to crumble a harmonious and beautiful whole into tedious little fragments.

In 1938–9 empirical research by means of visits and questionnaires was not yet taboo; one was even encouraged to test economic theories in this way. No one had yet conned us into the belief that 'Revealed preference' and the regression analysis of official macro-statistics were alpha and omega. The new 'victory' of imperfect competition stimulated interest in the individual price and output policy of entrepreneurs for the first time since Marshall. Reporting on their work Hall and Hitch said in 1938:

> If it is desired to illustrate the position of equilibrium geometrically, this may be done for the typical case where oligopoly elements are present by the use of a kinked demand curve, the kink occurring at the point where the price, fixed on the 'full-cost' principle, actually stands. Above this point the curve is elastic, because an increase in price will not be followed (or so it is feared) by competitors, who will be glad to take any extra sales. Below the point the demand is much less elastic because a reduction in the price charged will be followed eventually by competitors who would otherwise lose business. If this is the character of the demand curve it follows that over a wide range of marginal costs the existing price is the most profitable. It also follows that, with given costs, this price is most profitable over a wide range of possible fluctuations of the demand curve, since wherever the demand curve may be the kink will occur at the same price . . .
>
> These considerations seem to vitiate any attempts to analyse normal entrepreneurial behaviour in the short period in terms of marginal curves. They also make it impossible to assume that wages in the short run will bear any close relation to the marginal product (or marginal revenue) of the labour employed. (1951, pp. 116, 124)

The 'Principle of Substitution' is, of course, not invalidated. The ratio

$$\frac{\text{marginal cost of factor}}{\text{marginal product of factor}}$$

will tend to be the same for all factors. (It is interesting that Jackson (1982) takes up the same position. No doubt only long-run substitution is referred to.)

Thus Hall and Hitch felt bound on the whole to defend, not attack, the latest theory: since MC is low and constant a sufficient gap between MR and AR will see us all to rights: MR = MC but AR > AC. AR is *thought of as* average direct cost plus a margin;

but in reality it arises from the quantity sold and the demand curve. I was – and am – unable to agree with them:

> Alas for *a priori* reasoning! the facts are quite otherwise. First, however tempting this explanation it is simply not the case that true m.c. (p.a.)[4] is low and constant. Secondly, perfectly elastic demand is by no means uncommon. Perfectly elastic demand curves face small firms in industries where their large rivals exercise price leadership; they face firms producing for the government; they face firms in cartels or subject to gentlemen's agreements; they face the 'full cost perfect polypolists' of Ch. 6, sec. 1.[5] In all these cases demand, though variable, is *always* perfectly elastic to the firm; i.e. price = m.r. both immediately and ultimately, whatever the reigning level of that price may be. The only qualification is that in a few of the above cases there is an absolute stop to the demand curve at a certain point, i.e. where the production quota is fulfilled. Such quotas reign in government contracts and in some (but only some) cartels, so the qualification is very partial. Yet empirical research into cost data and price fixing shows no difference at all between firms faced with such demand curves and others.* (1961, p. 6)

There remains, that is, much to explain, and marginalism cannot so easily escape its conflict with fact.

What Lee (1983) calls the 'second wave' of the full principle was mainly in the hands of Philip Andrews. It remained for him (1949) to assert a contradiction between this research and marginalism. Secretary to the original research team, Andrews became much more emotionally involved than Hall or Hitch. A hater of marginalism and abstract analysis, he became also an early and prescient warrior on the methodological front. His writings were strongly condemnatory of much economics that the present writer is inclined to defend.[6] Not always temperate or rigorous, he was judged an unsuccessful defender of his point of view (Robinson, 1950; Kahn, 1952, p. 122).

---

* I have little direct evidence for this statement, and rely mainly on commonsense, and the entire absence in any of the sources of any connection between the elasticity of demand and the full cost principle. Some evidence is given in Ch. 6, sec. 1, and the point is implicit in Mr. Hague's article (*Review of Economic Studies*, no. 41): on p. 147 he tells us that most of the entrepreneurs he visited seemed to think the demand for their products was infinitely elastic, and on pp. 150–1 he relates that they almost all used the full cost principle [footnote in original].

Yet surely when all is said and done Andrews was mostly right and the imperfect competition people mostly wrong. He must be reckoned along with Mueller (see chapter 6) and Krzyzaniak and Musgrave (1963; see Mueller p. 160) among the bringers-up of contrary factual evidence that the theoretical Establishment has swept under the rug. I list the points he would surely have made had he lived to attend the New College conference (may his shade forgive me my self-appointed mediumship):

(1) The language of price-setting among price-makers is by no means that of marginalism. This fact imposes on us modesty and caution at least, as we try to discover whether they actually do what they say.

(2) The neo-classical methodology has grown to a diseased hypertrophy in which mathematical innovation outranks empirical understanding.

(3) Our first step must always be to state commonsensically what we have observed 'out there'.

(4) It is not enough to say that transaction costs are high, and this explains why prices are sticky. They are also sticky for moral reasons: overcharging is morally condemned. It is also not customary.

(5) Rightly or wrongly firms really do infer from the stability of average direct cost a low and stable marginal cost, so price-setting is mainly the setting of gross profit rates.

(6) But this is *not* the rationalization of something they 'really' do, but don't talk about: the judgement of price and output as a combination, in accordance with the demand curve. For the demand curve is simply unknown. What businessmen do is what they say they do: fix the price and then sell and/or produce the quantity demanded – *l'on s'engage et puis l'on voit.*

(7) Discounts from the price thus fixed are granted *occasionally*: they are not common enough to undermine the above account. In particular rising demand very seldom generates positive discounts.[7]

(8) Of course perfect competition and 'primitive higgles' are exceptions to all this.

So in Andrews' view entrepreneurs in manufacturing and retailing are not *homines economici* – point (4); nor even rational-point (5). Times change, and I doubt whether (4) at any rate has survived perpetual inflation and the decline of public morality. But Sir Roy Harrod, who was much involved with this research, did draw at that time the same conclusion (1939, pp. 8–10). A moral rule of pricing is likely to hold if:

(1) 'there is a clear apprehension that general adherence to it will be of general advantage';

(2) there is doubt as to where private profit lies, i.e. 'some alternative line of action should not obviously be to the private interest of a considerable number of individuals on the system';

(3) prices are under individual control, not perfect competition: 'for the manufacturer [and shop keeper: PJDW] the crucial decision is when he quotes a price'.

I feel that in slump conditions this qualified statement of weak morality is more convincing than neo-classical reductionism, but suggest that the very forces that have substituted Lucas's vertical, 'rational-expectations'-dominated supply curve for Keynes's horizontal one based on 'money illusion' have also cut the moral element out of pricing.[8]

Now the full-cost principle absorbs very easily the notions of transaction costs and 'satisficing' in face of an information shortage;[9] and the notion of *cost inflation* that these render possible. Not so neo-classical economics. It cannot accept the precondition that prices will normally be lower than their profit-maximizing level, and many of its exponents flatly deny the existence of cost inflation. They seem not to realize that thereby they deprive themselves of the right to say, as financial columnists often do, that retail prices must begin to rise again next month because many recent wholesale price increases are 'in the pipeline'. Indeed it is curious how seldom monetarists write indignant letters on this score to the financial press.

Yet we need not stray very far from orthodoxy to show how plausible it is for prices to be normally low enough to accommodate small (marginal) cost increases without output change. For the price-maker always finds it expensive and difficult to inform himself of the profit-maximizing level, so since he is an ordinary

human being he tends somewhat toward the price with the
maximin profit instead, *and that involves lower prices and more
output* than the orthodox maximum. This point is not certain, and
should not detain us too long. It depends on the normal curvature
of the average total cost curve (figure 5), and the possibility of a
somewhat improbable fall in demand pushing us up its steeper
part, i.e. covering our fixed costs with little output. AR_2 is the
original state of the market. The high fluctuation AR_3 is discounted, but the low fluctuation AR_1 matters to us because of our
risk aversion. We worry about the 'worst-case' profit, and
maximize it. And the low price maximin $>$ the orthodox price

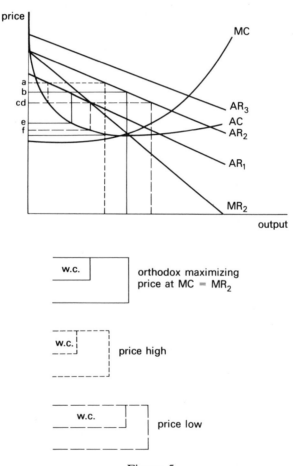

Figure 5

maximin in all cases where $\Delta AR/\Delta Q \leqslant \Delta AC/\Delta Q$, and in many cases where this is not so. Thus in figure 6 the three 'worst-case' profits are 'blown up'. If ab = de the lower of the two rectangles is larger; and though bc > ef this may still be so.

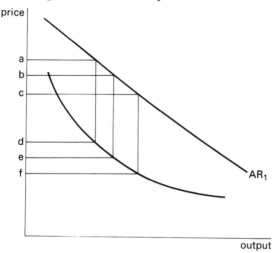

Figure 6

That AC curves have the shape shown, and that most people avoid risk I take to be empirically proven. However, the positions and shapes of normal AR curves have not been proven. It therefore remains merely plausible that *administered prices, chosen under the maximin principle, are 'too' low*. But if they are it is always possible to raise them when a higher cost of some kind raises the AC curve a little. Or as Hall and Hitch put it (1951, p. 125): 'Prices so fixed have a tendency to be stable. They will be changed if there is a significant change in wage or raw material costs, but not in response to moderate or temporary shifts in demand.' They thus prepared our minds to understand cost inflation before it existed.

Cost inflation can operate, of course, in the total absence of demand inflation. Its larger social causes do not here concern us, though the neo-classical failure to look them in the eye constitutes yet another methodological sin. What we have tried to show is that not only can it resist hostile monetary conditions but it also follows from a general tendency for price administrators to be less than *homines economici*.

When there is demand deflation there is more competition and behaviour becomes more orthodox.[10] But it must go on a very long time before cost inflation actually stops, and it seems that on balance administered prices are always 'too' high, since the perfectly competitive markets are always ahead – just as in demand inflation the latter always lead the opposite movement.

Yet again we see the temptation of a radical position versus the (to some) seductive notion of a moderate shift in, almost a sophisticated embellishment of, orthodoxy, as in the argument from maximins above. The writer however prefers, then and now, the radical position of Harrod, or indeed the bald statement that price administrators simply do adjust themselves more slowly, even over quite long periods. It is in no way clear which corresponds to the facts. But what became of the full cost principle is clear: it was swept under the carpet.

Of course, not everybody has wielded this guilty broom. An honourable exception is Koutsoyiannis (1975). In her microeconomics textbook she devotes two detailed and fair minded chapters to the problem, and includes the slightly different US tradition of Gardiner Means and Robert Gordon. These emphasize the administered price as such, never mind its relation to costs or indeed why it is administered at all; and grossly overemphasize the role of large oligopolists. Another exception is Okun (1981, chapter 4 and p. 223), and another of course is Lee himself, whose chapter follows.

Again Jackson's textbook (1982, pp. 234–5 and 270) gives a straight, brief, unblushing account on full-cost lines; and no other account in all his 714 pages. His object is to be practical and he is a professor of business economics. In his kind of department the retreat from empiricism is of course inadmissible. The concept of marginal cost enters only into the chapter on efficiency and input substitution (p. 279). He must be faulted for omitting agricultural pricing, and for not really facing the issue of his unorthodoxy, as does Koutsoyiannis. Samuelson on the other hand (1976) gives a long and orthodoxly marginalist account. His sole reference to this matter (pp. 508–10) gives the first-year student reader the strong impression that the whole issue is one of interpretation not fact, and confuses the maximization of profit with the payment of *some* attention to it – a common neo-classical ploy, by the way, when forced to debate the issue. Not a trace of doubt, then, sullies his text. His object is to write the best orthodox textbook, and he surely has. He has the virtue of consistency, which we see is not the 'hobgoblin of little minds' alone. The disarray within our discipline is nowhere more marked, or more disgraceful. Is it seriously denied that this is a flat contradiction on a central issue? How can it be that it *does not seem to have mattered* in the great world that we did not agree?

Notes

[1] I owe much, however to Frederic Lee, whose chapter follows.

[2] Mrs Robinson does this much less than her co-founder Prof. Chamberlin (*Theory of Monopolistic Competition*). She calls profit maximization as 'assumption' (p. 16), and herself a 'tool-maker' (p. 1). Prof. Chamberlin is interested in description, and not in the 'welfare' implications of his doctrine. Compare his illuminating article in the *Economic Journal*, 1952 [footnote in original].

[3] (1922) pp. 189–91 and Ch. 15.

[4] 'Partial adaptation' was my phrase for a lack of physical change in the fixed factors of production, whether over a long or a short period.

[5] 'Full cost perfect polypolists' was my name for, notably, the textile industry, which faced a perfectly competitive price it did not set, but still used the full cost language, and was unclear about its marginal cost.

[6] And so he condemned me too (orally)! Our personal relations were not good – a regular feature of any duopoly. This is yet another reason to take my account *cum grano salis*.

[7] A most striking case of this has been well studied by Bourguinat (1977, p. 24 and elsewhere). French, and no doubt other, exporters of manufactured goods do not on the whole raise their franc prices when the franc is devalued for what they think will be a long time, if (1) they have the habit of invoicing in francs; so the foreigner benefits from the devaluation. But if (2) they are invoicing in foreign currency they keep the price in that currency stable instead, and so they themselves benefit. If on the contrary the franc appreciates for what they think will be a long time they still keep the price stable in the currency of invoicing. There were 150 firms but, alas, only 65 respondents. These results have been further confirmed in 1982 (Bourguinat, letter of 28 December 1983). These were three exporters of raw materials: they invoiced in dollars.

[8] Sir Austin Robinson lays much weight, then and now, on his experience at Cambridge University Press. But a seller of books is a speculative monopolist of each issue he brings out. He sets a price on a batch of articles in which he has no competitors. He is thus like a speculative builder or a landscape artist, charging what the traffic will bear. The fact that he produces batches does not bring him under the full-cost principle. Cf. Wiles, 1961, p. 125.

[9] Which we owe, of course, in their fuller statement, to Herbert Simon and to no one at Oxford. Note how Hutchison has emphasized these points in chapter 1.

[10] Thus my counter to Robinson's formidable argument (p. 222) is that rational action has indeed greater survival value, and that is why we resort to it when survival is at stake. But we feel uncomfortable with it and blur its hard edges when we can.

Comment

AUSTIN ROBINSON

Like Peter Wiles I belong to the generation that some 45 years ago was concerned with the work of the Oxford School embodied in what we ordinarily called the Hall–Hitch report and in my own case in its criticism. I did not then accept its conclusions. I do not now accept its conclusions. But this was not because their field investigations conflicted with our particular Cambridge theoretical preconceptions. It was because their field investigations conflicted with our field investigations. We doubted the universality of their conclusions. We remained profoundly doubtful that irrational action in fact had greater survival value in a normally competitive system than rational action.

Looking back at the arguments of those days I am glad that serious discussion is belatedly coming back to these issues. But I think it is misguided to start from the assumption that one party in those arguments of 45 years ago was right and the other was wrong. It seems to me very much more probable that either both of us were wrong, or that both were partly right and partly wrong.

It is best, as I see it, to start with a reappraisal of Hall–Hitch. I cannot wholly distinguish after all these years my thinking of those days from its subsequent development. But most of what I shall have to say represents my contemporary thinking of those days.

The basic issue is how producers in different manufacturing activities respond to a change in demand. The first question that one needs to ask is why the Oxford researchers in the 1930s should have been surprised at the comparative stability of industrial prices and regarded it as something abnormal and requiring explanation. Had there been such changes of demand that a response in the form of a considerable adjustment of price would have been expected? If not, is this no more than another example of a group of theoretical economists trying to provide an ingenious explanation of a non-fact?

If one looks back at the period 1929 to 1935 unemotionally and with the aid of statistical data to which most of us did not have quick access at the time, it is surprising how far what emerges differs from the folk mythology of that period. The deep depression of those years was very limited in its extent and very largely confined to a small number of industries, only a few of them in the more strictly manufacturing factory sector. The indices of production, and even the censuses of production of 1930 and 1935, are in too broad categories to bring out the full story. It is easier to get this from employment data.

It will be seen in table 4 that if one excludes coal-mining, ship-building and ship-operating, iron and steel, the building and the textile industries, employment fell comparatively little, and almost throughout the period was increasing rather than diminishing.

TABLE 4   NUMBER OF INSURED WORKERS IN EMPLOYMENT ('000s)

	1929	1930	1932	1934	1936
All industries	10,921	10,334	9889	10,796	11,685
of whom:					
Coal-mining	872	767	613	650	662
Ship-building, marine engineering and shipping services	330	300	214	224	266
Iron and steel	163	138	96	139	158
Textiles: cotton	475	312	372	348	354
wool	201	178	170	174	198
jute	35	20	8	9	22
silk and artificial fibres	68	60	56	63	70
Building	754	717	620	685	902
Total of above	2898	2492	2149	2292	2632
All others	8023	7842	7740	8504	9053
All others (1929 = 100)	100.0	97.7	86.5	106.0	112.8

During this period, a number of industries showed no decline at all, or only a short pause during 1930–2 followed by steady growth. Electrical engineering, automobile production, scientific instruments and photography, book printing and publishing were all expanding steadily and in some cases rapidly. Almost all the industries studied in Hall–Hitch were, apart from a few textile firms, in the group covered by 'all others' in table 4. The saga of the great depression, as it concerns manufacturing industries, is almost wholly the story of coal, shipbuilding and, more temporarily, iron and steel and building. Looked at more objectively, it was a period of structural redeployment from obsolete and no longer competitive nineteenth-century activities to those of a modern economy of that period. Over the seven years 1929–36, a little more than one million workers were redeployed into the industries whose price policy is under discussion (it is of course regrettable that they could not expand more rapidly to absorb the large numbers of unemployed). We are not discussing a failure to cut prices in the face of declining demand.

The second fact that needs to be established is whether it was or was not true that industrial prices were stable. This is more difficult to establish. The price data for the 1930s are sadly inadequate. In general terms the wholesale index of manufactured articles fell from 100 in 1930 to 93.5 in 1933 and thereafter slowly recovered. In the retail price index, the clothing component fell from 100 in 1929 to 86.2 in 1932; the figure for other items (excluding food, rent, clothing, fuel and light) fell from 100 in 1929 to 95.8 in 1932. One can get more from the unit values of exports. Between 1929 and 1931 there were declines of over 20 per cent for almost all textiles; declines of 15 to 20 per cent for most iron and steel products and some chemicals. For a few other manufactures the unit value fell significantly (including automobiles where this was the period of the introduction of the mass-produced car). For machine tools the value per ton rose (one suspects because of a higher-quality product mix). In general it is true to say that labour-intensive manufactures, in which raw material input was small, remained fairly stable in price. But the evidence is very inadequate because there is no indicator of the volume of exports for most such products.

There is, that is to say, evidence that manufactured products varied in price over this period substantially less than prices of food and raw materials. But within manufactures there were very considerable differences which need to be explained. In particular there were significant differences between the textile industries, the iron and steel industry and shipbuilding on the one hand and the industries described as 'all others' in an earlier paragraph. Hall–Hitch is gravely misleading in suggesting that all manufacturing industry was behaving alike.

If one is interested in more recent times, a few minutes with table 18.4 in the United Kingdom Annual Abstract of Statistics, showing the differences between prices of manufactures in 1975 and 1980, will leave any reader very doubtful whether all the relative differences are to be explained by costs of inputs and productivity.

Before we can proceed to discuss Hall–Hitch properly it is necessary to consider the question set out above: how do producers in different activities respond to a change in demand and particularly a decline in demand?

This was the problem that Richard Kahn had set himself in his fellowship thesis for King's College, Cambridge. We all of us in Cambridge knew the essentials of his results. But he had not published them so that we could quote them; they are only now belatedly being published. And apart from his work, others of us were engaged in trying to push the thinking further and to extend it from the answers that were appropriate to the cotton industry (on which Kahn's work was largely based) to other activities with different forms of organization. I lectured on this at the time.

If a firm was faced by declining demand, there were essentially four questions that needed to be asked and answered:

(1) Should one close down completely or continue to operate?

(2) Should one close down partially or continue to operate?

(3) What minimum price does it pay one to accept?

(4) If one introduces a new product what minimum price does it pay one to accept?

Kahn's general answer was, of course, that one should disregard all fixed costs and make the decision in terms of marginal variable costs. But the precise interpretation of this needed to be worked out.

The practical answers to these various questions depend in part, for instance, on the forms of organization. Is the firm a single-plant firm or a multiple-plant firm? Is the middle management of a plant of a multiple-plant firm a fixed cost, or can it be sacked if the plant is shut down? Is the firm a single-product producer or is it a multi-product producer? If it closes down one operation does it close down the whole operation? If it is a multi-plant multi-product operation, is each plant producing one single homogeneous product, or several products? Is it or is it not technically possible to reduce the rate of output of the operation? Is it physically and financially possible or impossible to stock a large part of an annual output? And how is production organized? Is it, as was and still is most common, batch production? What is the batch-specific fixed cost of starting up a batch? Or is one's plant a continuous-flow production operation, the hourly and weekly rate of which is predetermined by technical conditions? (It will be realized that the Hall–Hitch diagrams and analysis appear to be discussing a single-plant firm with continuous-flow production.)

The point at which it pays to close down was one of the things we were examining with the help of evidence about iron and steel, shipbuilding and other activities. For ship-operating we had data regarding costs of laying-up (a minimum crew of two or three was necessary), costs of recommissioning and so on. Unless the operating loss exceeded the lay-up cost, it paid you to go on operating. Similarly for iron and steel, we knew the closed-down costs and the very considerable reopening costs, if, as was probable, you had to reline furnaces. Again it paid you to accept these losses below variable costs.

But in practice how long you could hold on within the limits of your available resources quite largely depended on whether medium-term fixed costs had to be met from reserves or whether they could be met in part by continued operation of some of the other activities of the firm, if it was a multi-plant or multi-product organization. One shipping line for which we had data was laying up individual ships, but others continued to cover most of head-office costs.

In this Comment I cannot possibly attempt to fill the whole matrix of possible forms of organization, possible types of product and their different effects on policy. Certain things, however, became clear. If one takes at one extreme a single plant firm with a single product which cannot be partially shut down which is operating in a competitive framework, it will go on producing its full output so long as it does not pay better to close down completely; and if, as in agriculture or fishing, partial shut-down is technically impossible and the family labour has little or no opportunity cost, production will continue and very low prices will be necessary to clear the market. Cotton-spinning and iron and steel came very near to the same situation.

At the other end of the spectrum, with a multi-plant, multi-product firm, it will pay it to concentrate output, close down one or more plants completely, sack some middle management if medium-term prospects are poor, possibly make standard products for stock (depending on stock-holding costs). It will shade its prices, if demand is believed to be elastic, provided that they cover variable costs.

When one is thinking about the type of industry in which mutli-product firms predominate one must always have in mind the time and work that is required to change prices. Most such firms produce a catalogue once a year and are reluctant to change prices over a shorter interval. Publishers, of course, work in this way. In 1951, when the Korean War raw-materials price boom sent paper prices rocketing I argued on the finance committee of the Cambridge University Press that we were selling stock at far below variable cost, and we must revise prices. I was told that it would take six months to do this. No doubt it can be done more quickly now. But a multi-product firm cannot do it overnight. Prices are ordinarily fixed for a year and not for today's output.

And because this is true, I am sceptical about the universal validity of the kinked demand curve that plays such an important part in Hall–Hitch analysis. A firm may, it is true, say to itself, 'If I cut prices others will cut prices and I shall not increase my share in the market.' But it may equally say one or other of two alternative things: 'Even if I don't increase my share in the market, it would pay us all to have lower prices and expand the total market'; or, 'I suspect that others are going to start cutting prices, I cannot afford to be undersold for the next year ahead until I can revise all my prices.' (The first assumption leads, of course, to almost the same pricing policy as that of a monopoly.) If there is in the industry a price-leader, as suggested by Hall and Hitch, he may make the first of these assumptions and cut on the assumption that others will cut; he may hope that he will increase rather than diminish his share in the market. At the Cambridge University Press I succeeded in 1951 in deliberately price-leading the Oxford

University Press upwards in respect of bible prices in which we had a duopoly, though they were much the larger. The price-leader does not need to be the largest firm.

It is additionally necessary to ask whether, if you close down one product which is making a loss, it does or does not pay you to replace it with another product, rather than close down altogether. To this question the answer is more complex. If the new product can be produced with already existing and available capital and that capital equipment has no other possible use the answer is, of course, that you disregard the 'water under the bridge' expenditure on that capital; you measure the variable costs, price at what the market will bear and make such contribution as that permits to fixed cost. But if the fixed capital equipment has alternative uses, you must charge to the new product the opportunity cost of the capital. And if there are additional product-specific fixed costs for the new product, those must be taken into account in calculating whether it does or does not pay you to introduce the product.

It is very relevant to have in mind that in most of the industries that Hall–Hitch was investigating the firms are multi-product firms, and in some cases multi-plant firms. The normal life of a product may ordinarily be taken to be four to five years. Thus in any year about a quarter of all products have to be replaced. The important decisions are decisions as to whether some new product should or should not be introduced. For every such decision, if the firm is a multi-product firm, one needs to know:

(1) What are the direct variable costs?

(2) What is the product-specific investment required?

(3) Over what volume of sales can that product-specific investment be amortized?

(4) What is the opportunity cost of existing capital involved?

(5) What is the opportunity cost (if any) of the management involved?

(6) What is the product-specific introduction cost (advertising, etc.) of the product?

What I have set out above bears a very close resemblance to what might be regarded as a full-cost pricing operation. But it differs in one very important respect. It seeks to measure the opportunity cost of the capital and management and not the historical cost.

I myself believe that all of this is too sophisticated for Hall–Hitch and Andrews to have seen at that time. And if, as I suspect, they got most of their information from the cost-accountants of firms, I am not sure that the accountants would themselves have known exactly how their calculations were used by management when it came to a decision.

First of all, important elements in the fixed overhead costs are very far from unambiguous. The period over which you depreciate machinery is as short as the tax authorities will permit (though the time when certain things must be replaced plays a part), and it is not a precise parameter. The profit margin is largely a matter of what the traffic will bear and what will make it as easy as possible to raise more capital if you have to, or enable you to get along without having to go to the market. I have very clear memories on the Cambridge University Press in the 1950s of an inquiry into our competitiveness which ended in a recalculation of our overheads, depreciation rates and the rest. This in effect meant that our overheads in costing a book represented in reality the opportunity cost of our equipment and organization rather than a strict historic cost. I know that various firms have similarly revised and readjusted their estimated overheads.

Such a calculation has an additional value for the price-fixing operation. If your overheads are in fact adjusted to indicate what addition to direct costs will permit you to be competitive, a costing calculation for a new product so made will in fact give you the cost at which a competitor might be expected to produce a rival product. It helps one to judge what price the market will bear – a very necessary element in one's pricing decision.

But if I may go back to the whole process, the crucial decision in the great majority of manufacturing firms as it affects prices is whether or not and at what price each of a series of new products shall be introduced to replace products which are becoming obsolete. Of course, the crude evidence before the group which has to make the decision includes the cost accountant's calculations of product-specific investment, variable costs and the like and an allowance for general overheads. All of this is related to certain assumptions of sales over a period of time. But the final decision of the group is not determined by simple arithmetic.

If the firm is short of work evidence shows that it may be decided to go ahead even if the price that the market will bear does not fully cover the 'normal' overheads. In the case of publishing, moreover, one always has before one alternative costings and unit costs for two or three alternative numbers of copies. There is discussion of probable sales at alternative prices. (This is the normal practice for example of the British Academy publications committee on which I have recently been serving as well as of the Cambridge University Press.) There is in effect a marginal calculation. If there is shortage of work, a product may be accepted with possibly optimistic views of probable sales and a slightly lower price.

There were in the 1930s, and still are, other ways in which a firm which supposedly relied on full-cost pricing in fact adjusted to the state of the market. It needs to be asked whether full-cost pricing is or is not supposed to extend over the whole range of activities of the firm. Most multi-product firms in the 1930s (and I believe now) had some steady 'bread and butter' line of business which, when things were slack, they could and did make for stock, to keep things going. In some cases, especially in the automobile industry, they would seek subcontracts. In the case of the Cambridge University Press, Walter Lewis, the head of the printing house, would come to our Tuesday meeting, find out what new manuscripts we had for him and go off each Thursday to London to collect as many manuscripts as he needed from the publishers for whom he was prepared to work. Those manuscripts and the bargains he made were not full-cost priced, though he would normally hope to do better than cover direct costs. This was our way of clearing the market.

If I may try to sum up, the process of short-term price–fixing is very much more complex than the discussion in Hall–Hitch suggests. It is only to a very small extent dictated by the extent of monopoly in the particular industry. I do not find the attempts to distinguish between oligopoly and monopolistic competition very illuminating. It is vastly more important to concern oneself with the range of products of the firm, the problems of product life, the opportunity costs of the fixed capital and management in terms of alternative activities, the technical possibilities or impossibilities of switching capacity to other products, the technical and financial possibilities or impossibilities of stock-building and stock-reduction, the opportunities or lack of opportunities for filling capacity by sub-contracting, the intervals of price-determination.

If one takes account of all these factors, one does not need to assume, as it seemed to us in Cambridge, that Hall–Hitch and Andrews were succeeding in showing that firms were acting irrationally. We were, it is true, shocked at being told that rational behaviour, as exemplified by balancing marginal cost against marginal revenue, was less desirable than irrational behaviour. But our main conclusion was that the investigation was somewhat naive. It failed to take account of the very wide differences between different types of manufacturing industries. It tried to establish a universality. It neglected the differences between what was happening in the severely depressed industries and what was happening in the prosperous and still expanding industries.

Let me sum this up. In 1939, Cambridge like Oxford was profoundly worried about industrial pricing theory. I regret that the coming of the war and the diversion of most of us to other and more urgent problems cut short what should have been the beginning of a valuable attempt to discover and present a serious analysis of short-term and medium-term pricing in all its varieties. One has only to glance at the contemptible nonsense that is represented by the discussion of these problems in almost any textbook of economics to feel regret that others have not sooner picked up the threads of our work in the 1930s.

Then, as indeed now, the elementary texts of economics were ridiculously oversimplified. They expounded pricing theories which made assumptions about industrial structures and industrial procedures which were not stated and were not realistic. Our thinking in Cambridge was more concerned with the consequences for pricing of industrial structures; we had increasing difficulty in attaching meaning to the concept of an industry and to multi-firm perfect competition. Such an industry as printing and publishing divided not only into printers and publishers, and those that did both, but also into educational publishers, novel publishers and other groups. When one came to ask who was really competing with whom, the number was often reduced to four or five and oligopoly theory and assumptions about how one's few and well-known competitors would react became of central importance.

We knew full-cost pricing ideas primarily through Hall–Hitch and the writings of Andrews. We were not yet fully familiar with the refinements of Peter Wiles. But we were in any case sceptical of conclusions drawn from geometry. I myself had always in mind the scathing comments of Pigou (the arch-misogynist) regarding 'young women who drew curves and said "therefore"'. We were drilled in the duty to define always the assumptions that underlay the curve. We were well aware of the properties of the kinked demand curve (we had helped to invent it). But we did not regard the underlying assumptions as universal or even general. The assumptions were obviously inconsistent with any form of price-leadership and we believed (and I still believe) that that is far more common than is usually assumed.

In other words we believed that industrial price-formation was a complex process, with many factors of short and long periods, of types of industrial structure, of product lives and quality competition, of the numbers of closely competitive firms all involved. The heroic assumptions of full-cost pricing seemed to us as far from the truth as the oversimplifications of the textbooks.

I remain unrepentantly of the opinion that a new attempt at understanding and presenting the processes of industrial pricing should begin afresh with a *tabula rasa* and not handicap itself with the oversimplifications of the earlier and unrefined concepts of full-cost pricing.

9

Whatever Happened to the Full-Cost Principle (USA)?

FREDERIC LEE

What happened to the full-cost principle is an interesting question; however, a simple answer to it does not exist. On the one hand, the full-cost principle (FCP) has undergone continual theoretical development since 1939 (Lee, 1983, chapters 6, 7 and 8; and Lee, 1984a). Moreover, it has been absorbed into the post-Keynesian paradigm as part of the theoretical foundation of its price theory (Eichner, 1976 and 1978). Finally, it has been subject to over 50 empirical investigations over its 40 years and has played an integral part in analysing national and world-wide inflation. Thus it could be concluded that the FCP is very much alive and well. On the other hand, the suggestion has substance if it refers to its position *vis-à-vis* neo-classical price theory. That is, the early developers of the FCP saw it as a broad and sustained attack on marginalism, a view initially accepted by many orthodox economists. But by the mid-1950s, the principle was viewed as being completely compatible with neo-classical price theory in general and marginalism in particular. Consequently the FCP ceased to be of interest to most economists, and they no longer awarded it special attention. It is this change in the perception of the FCP which lies at the basis of the question 'Whatever happened to the FCP?', and which I shall try to answer in terms of the American experience.

Marginalist Controversy 1946–52[1]

In 1946, Lester's well-known critique of the marginal productivity theory of wages and published.[1] Using the article's empirical evidence as a backdrop, Lester developed two critical arguments of marginalism. His most developed argument was that marginalist tools were not sufficiently developed for businessmen to use them in their work. Consequently, it was rational for them to use rule-of-thumb procedures that were devoid of marginalist attributes. His second and less developed argument was that marginalism was inherently incapable of explaining business behaviour. That is, businessmen did not think or behave in marginalist terms, in part because the firm's cost structure was not compatible with marginalism. Therefore if economists were to explain, say, the wage–employment relationships for the individual firm, a new theory would need to be developed.

Quickly following Lester's article was a counter-reply by Machlup. In a carefully designed article, he argued that Lester's second argument was invalid because he incorrectly understood marginalism. Maintaining that marginalism was only designed to explain changes in employment, prices and output resulting from a change in the firm's environment, Machlup concluded that it could not be criticized for failing to be used in the determination of a given price, output and wage rate (Machlup, 1946 and 1967). Against Lester's first argument Machlup maintained that marginalism was implicitly used in practice. Using the analogy of an automobile driver, he argued that firms need not consciously realize that they use marginalist tools when reacting to changes in their environment or to establish definite numerical estimates of marginal costs, marginal revenue and price elasticity of demand when reacting to these changes. Hence, the rule-of-thumb procedures used by businessmen were, contrary to appearances, grounded in marginalism. To substantiate this argument, Machlup showed that the 'anti-marginalism' evidence presented by Lester and by Hall and Hitch could be interpreted as completely supporting marginalism.

The impact of Machlup's article on the marginalist controversy was twofold. First, it made the FCP, as opposed to wage-rate determination, the focal point of the controversy. Secondly, because the participants viewed marginalism as a box of tools that were not market-structure specific, Machlup's second argument appeared to promote the view that marginalism needed to be interpreted in a more realistic manner. Hence, the controversy became much narrower in focus and only addressed the problem of the realism, applicability and compatibility of the marginalist tools in explaining business behaviour, and thus became more of a groping towards a unified, coherent explanation of full-cost pricing which showed that full-cost pricing was consistent with neo-classical price theory in general and marginalism in particular.

Following Machlup's article, the marginalist controversy split into two different arguments. One argument was principally concerned with the realism and applicability of the marginalist tools and concepts to explaining business behaviour. Because businessmen were largely ignorant and uncertain about their economic environment, they were unable to obtain the information needed for marginalist decision-making; consequently they employed pricing policies and procedures which made the most of their limited information (and entrepreneurial ability). Moreover, because businessmen viewed their firm as a going concern, short-period profit maximization would not be adopted as a policy since it would lead to the firm's demise in the long period. Therefore it was argued that the businessmen formalized the pricing policies and procedures into the rule-of-thumb FCP and that businessmen pursued objectives other than profit maximization, such as satisficing[2] (Oliver, 1947; Gordon, 1948; Fellner, 1948; and Katona, 1951). However, the implication of this conclusion was that the marginalist (hence neo-classical) tools and concepts could not adequately explain business behaviour. Thus to reconcile the FCP with orthodox theory it was argued that the existing tools and concepts needed to be reshaped. The end result of this argument was the rise of a more generalized neo-classical price theory – including behavioural and managerial theories of the firm – which subsumed the FCP as a special case (Horowitz, 1967; Yeung, 1969; Eichner, 1976; and Cyert and Pottinger, 1979).

The second argument saw the conflict between the FCP and marginalism as primarily a theoretical problem. That is, while the empirical data supporting the FCP were not disputed, the anti-marginalist theoretical interpretation given it was. However, to show that the FCP and marginalism were compatible, it had to be shown that the full-cost price was theoretically identical to the marginalist price. Proving this required that the cost and mark-up constituents of the full-cost pricing procedure be compatible with their marginalist counterparts. In the case of costs, it was argued that if average direct costs of production were constant with respect to different flow rates of output, it would coincide with marginal costs. As for the mark-up, it was argued that if it included demand considerations and was sufficiently flexible, it could stand as a proxy for the price elasticity of demand. Therefore, if the two conditions were fulfilled, the businessman would in fact be equating marginal cost and revenue when using his full-cost pricing procedure to set his price. This theoretical argument was adopted by economists in America and widely propagated via textbooks and articles. The argument's acceptance was in part due to its elegance, to the emergence of empirical cost studies showing constant marginal cost, and to numerous references to demand considerations embodied in the mark-up (Apel, 1948; Bain, 1948; Scitovsky, 1951; and Samuelson, 1951a). The argument's acceptance was also in part due to Heflebower's article 'Full Cost, Cost Changes, and Prices' (1955) which in effect argued that full-cost pricing was the practical businessman's approach to implementing marginal analysis.[3] Thus by the end of 1952 this aspect of the marginalist controversy came to an end since there existed no conflicting issues between full-cost pricing and marginalism.[4]

The Aftermath: Maintaining Neo-classical Orthodoxy

The outcome of the marginalist controversy was that economists viewed the FCP as being completely compatible with neo-classical price theory and thus ceased to award it special attention. Moreover, this viewpoint has been maintained since then. This, in part, was and is due to the fact that after 1952 the marginalist rationalization of the FCP was widely disseminated among economists via microeconomic and industrial organization textbooks. In fact, there was an immediate noticeable shift in many textbooks – such as Samuelson's text *Economics* and Due's text *Intermediate Economic Analysis* – from a weak marginalist rationalization of the FCP to a very strong one in which the mark-up was interpreted in terms of price elasticity of demand.[5] As a result, subsequent professional discussions of the FCP assumed without question the marginalist interpretation and thus viewed it as marginalism in a different language (e.g. Ferguson, 1957; Schere, 1970).

There also exists a different set of reasons for the continuation of this viewpoint. Beginning in the 1940s, American economists have, in a somewhat systematic manner, excluded non-neoclassical modes of economic theorizing from the domain of economic knowledge, either by 'marginalizing' the modes of theorizing or simply by ostracizing them. Included in this purge was Keynes/Kalecki's short-period theory of unemployment and a whole series of theories of the business cycle. In the case of FCP, the purging process not only gave rise to the marginalist controversy, but also generated an intellectual xenophobic reaction to any non-neoclassical interpretation of the FCP.

On the one hand, domestic non-neoclassical (or non-marginalist) developments of the FCP were either severely criticized or ignored. For example, Eiteman (1949), R. Robinson (1961 and 1978) and Williams (1967) discussed and developed the FCP, but since their mode of analysis was in part either non-neoclassical or specifically non-marginalist, their work has virtually been ignored.[6] Another example is Markham's very deprecating remarks (1954) on a paper by Heflebower in which he presented a sympathetic and somewhat non-neoclassical interpretation of the FCP.[7]

On the other hand, 'foreign' interpretations of the FCP were blocked from entering the US. For example, P.W.S. Andrews's analysis and development of the FCP was virtually unheard of in the US, in spite of his books and articles being cited and reviewed in American journals (Irving, 1978). For a case in point, Robinson had not heard of Andrews during his graduate days at MIT; so when writing the first draft of his 1961 article, he did not mention him. However, after being told of Andrew's work, Robinson cited him in the article's final draft. (Interestingly enough, a MIT faculty member told Robinson that he had weakened it by dragging in Andrews, since his stuff was nonsense (Robinson, 1981).) A further example concerns Sylos-Labini's (1962) work with the FCP. Because of the dynamic approach he adopted to the study of economics, Sylos-Labini became quite dissatisfied with the orthodox theory of prices. In his search for something better, he discovered Andrews's *Manufacturing Business* (1949) and the volume *Oxford Studies in the Price Mechanism* (Andrews and Wilson, 1951). Combining these discoveries with his reading of cost accounting books, Kalecki and

Harrod, he developed an integrated account of price determination and price variation that revolved around the determination of the costing margin and the FCP (Sylos-Labini, 1982). Although Sylos-Labini's analysis incorporated some aspects of neo-classical price theory, it clearly presented the FCP in a positive and non-marginalist manner. But when Modigliani (1958) introduced it into the US, the non-marginalist (non-neoclassical) aspects of the FCP were replaced with a strictly marginalist interpretation, with the result that the neo-classical/marginalist interpretation of the FCP remained unchallenged.

With non-neoclassical (non-marginalist) interpretations of the FCP excluded from the domain of economic knowledge, many additional arguments supporting the consistency between the FCP and neo-classical price theory were developed. For example, Baumol (1959) and Marris (1964) demonstrated that the FCP could be reconciled with a generalized marginalist model while Cyert and March (1956 and 1963) argued that it was consistent with their behavioural theory of the firm. As a result, interest in the FCP as a broad and sustained attack on neo-classical price theory and in particular on marginalism for all practical purposes disappeared in the US. So the answer to the question with which we began this chapter can be stated very simply: 'The full-cost-principle? Isn't that simply a businessman's description of pricing which we [neo-classical economists] handle quite easily with our theories?

Notes

[1] For a more detailed discussion of the marginalist controversy, see Lee, 1984b.

[2] In the following quote, Scitovsky succinctly captures the above argument as it was seen by the economists involved: 'As to full cost pricing, my reaction at the time was to regard it as a confirmation of my suspicion that the practical obstacles to empirically calculating marginal cost (especially in a multi-product firm) were insurmountable, and that average direct costs were a kind of best approximation to the calculation of marginal cost. The addition to average direct costs of a percentage margin to cover overheads and an allowance for profit seemed like a good rule of thumb for estimating the profit-maximizing mark-up. In other words, I tended to ignore or slur over the oligopoly case and to regard pricing by adding a mark-up to estimated average direct costs as profit-maximizing behavior under real-life circumstances, given the businessman's inability to estimate the two quantities dear to the economist's heart: marginal cost and price elasticity of demand' (Scitovsky, 1982).

[3] This was the conclusion that M. Adelman arrived at when reading Heflebower's paper: 'The moral of the Heflebower paper, it seems to me, was that business executives go

through a somewhat round-about procedure to do what they would do more directly if they had a lot of information they don't have' (Adelman, 1982).

[4] Ruggles sums up the impact of Heflebower's paper in the following manner: 'In effect, Heflebower gave the game away and from then on no issues were seen to exist. Full cost pricing was seen as the practical businessman's approach to implementing "true marginal analysis"' (Ruggles, 1981).

[5] Compare Samuelson, 1951a and 1955, with Samuelson, 1958 and 1964; and compare Due, 1950, with Due, 1956.

[6] Less than five entries occur under their names in the *Social Science Citation Index* for the years 1965–82.

[7] Markham made the following remark about Heflebower's paper: 'Unfortunately, however, through his analysis Heflebower mostly disregards the analytical tools of orthodox value theory and appears to rely heavily upon something bearing close resemblance to the principle of cost-plus pricing – a strange skeleton to find in Heflebower's closet considering the fact that he was assigned the task of burying this corpse at the Princeton meetings in June, 1952' (Markham, 1954).

10

What to Teach to Undergraduates

GUY ROUTH

I

'There is a whole tribe of nags,' my wife remarked, 'who make it their business to tell everyone else where they went wrong.' This in response to the criticisms with which I have attempted to assail my fellow teachers of economics for the last 25 years. So far, their immunizing stratagems have proved effective against the strictures of people who speak with much more authority than I – presidents of economic associations, of Section F of the British Association, Richard T. Ely Lecturers.

One reason is that the nags have been soloists, whereas the established schools perform in massed choirs. They follow their ritual formulae – invisible hand, *laissez-faire*, perfect and imperfect competition, general equilibrium; marginalist, monetarist, post-Keynesian, neo-Marxist – whereas the nags are more inclined to echo Proudhon's reply to Marx: 'By all means let us work together to discover the laws of society, the ways in which these laws are realized and the process by which we are able to discover them. But, for God's sake, when we have demolished all *a priori* dogmas, do not let us think of indoctrinating the people in our turn.' So the schools prefer to remain in Egypt, thinking up ways to make bricks without straw, rather than follow a path into the wilderness that is sure to be arduous and may or may not lead to the Promised Land.

In this chapter I present the thesis that it need not be nearly so arduous or uncertain as many fear, that it is a practical path that all who will may follow, provided that enough people elect to do so.

II

Despite the fact that the critics have not acted in collusion, there is a gratifying degree of consensus in their recommendations for reform. I offer the following summary:

(1) Doctrines must be drawn from empirical studies, in terms of which hypotheses should be formulated and tested.

(2) Studies of the present require a historical base that helps to explain the growth, change and decay to which economies are subject.

(3) Disciplinary boundaries must be relaxed so that behavioural studies of households, organizations and governments may be conducted and interpreted.

These guidelines suggest also what to avoid: the belief that economic variables determine themselves and each other without human intervention; that it is possible to explain the workings of the world by process of deduction from axioms or assumptions arrived at *a priori*; that economists, unlike biologists, are exempt from the wearisome task of examining what the organisms that constitute their subject-matter actually do.

Great changes at the 'adult' end of the subject require great changes in what is taught to beginners, for one may discern a sort of Darwinian process at work: learned professors indulge in abstraction; this is communicated down the hierarchy and students adopt it as protective colouration; those survive best who can outdo their teachers. So, unreal assumptions are not relaxed – their unreality is intensified and camouflaged by mathematics. As Terence Hutchison remarks in his chapter, 'No fruitful way has emerged of gradually relaxing the certainty assumption step by step, or of getting from the first approximation to a second approximation significantly less distant from the real world.'

III

As everybody knows, there are many practical questions involved in the design of a curriculum. The constituent subjects must be adequately documented; books must be readily available and up to date; the teacher must know what he or she is supposed to teach, the student what he or she is supposed to learn; the subjects should be readily examinable, with a fair degree of consensus pertaining to the distinction of right from wrong. The curriculum now proposed meets these requirements. It is designed to comprise the economics content of a first honours degree in economics. In addition, there would be whatever non-economic subjects were prescribed by the department or school concerned.

It incorporates those important advances, not yet included in the textbooks, in the study of consumer behaviour, organizations, pay and industrial relations, finance and banking, that economists ignore at their peril.

(1) *Economic and social history* Pre-capitalist societies: hunters and gatherers; herdsmen and cultivators; city states and empires; ancient India; classical Greece; the Romans; the Mogul Empire; the feudal system. The rise of capitalism: from feudalism to despotism; the great explorations; the downfall of absolutism and the rise of the bourgeoisie; the industrial revolution; imperialism; the divestment of colonial empires. Similarity and diversity in national development; varieties of capitalism.

Homo sapiens spent two million years as hunter-gatherer, ten thousand as herdsman and cultivator. It is in hunting and gathering that the human mind has developed, so a study of these societies gives insight into the nature of man. Existing remnants display systems for conflict-avoidance, and work assiduously at the social conditioning of their members – devices essential for their survival. The next generation of economists might be able to teach this subject themselves; the present generation will have to call in archaeologists, social anthropologists and historians. There is a voluminous and fascinating literature.

(2) *Economic statistics; national and company accounts* Economic variables as measures of the effects of decision-making; through them, inter-connections are sought and economic performance gauged. National accounts: presentation in coherent fashion of the elements of specified economies; taxonomy and the meaning of economic categories. Devices for the measurement of change, dispersion, correlation and significance. Company accounts: profit and loss accounts and balance sheets.

Not many economists would quarrel with the idea that national accounting is important. It presents the 'wiring-diagram' upon which macroeconomics is based. A knowledge of business accounting is also necessary (see Neild, p. 45 above). Students must acquire the ability to read statistical tables with facility. Regular statistical workshops are as important as work in the lab for natural scientists. Here, movements in the economy are monitored, directions determined, turning-points identified, explanations sought. It will be found that these movements are not neat and determinate, but often clumsy and untidy, their causes in the group psychology of millions of decision-makers.

Statistics are effective for falsifying hypotheses, but only part of the process necessary to establish them. The categories of the national accounts must themselves be analysed, for similar proportional changes in different periods may have contradictory meanings. Of course, all that glitters is not gold in company accounts either, and students must be made aware how they may be manipulated to give different appearances to the same events.

There are interesting experiments in progress in the teaching of statistics. At Keele the economists have a statistics course integrated with economic studies. It deals with modelling, data collection and statistical analysis and ends with a project designed and executed by each student requiring the use of the Keele computer. Dudley Jackson has devised a similar system at the University of Aston and has designed a textbook for this purpose (1982).

It is commonly claimed that a discipline should have a 'hard core': a coherent body of necessary and difficult principles shared by all its branches. To some extent this is an unproven educational dogma which, obviously, could not govern politics, psychology, sociology or history. To this extent its use by orthodox economists is merely self-serving and carries no conviction: it is their idea of keeping the whole discipline respectable. Insofar as a hard core is really necessary, statistics and accountancy provide it.

(3) *Social and analytic history of economic thought* The history of economic thought can be of great interest when, as Wesley Clair Mitchell remarked, one begins to take the mental operations of the theorists as the problem. This requires the interpretation of economic doctrines in terms of the social and political history of the time, and the application to them of the philosophy of science, as demonstrated by various chapters in this volume, and by Mark Blaug (1980), and Terence Hutchison (1938 and 1953).

A purely 'internalist' (see p. 296) view of how economics has developed, as if in some triumphal progress from darkness to light, is very common amongst students and, since it is quite untrue, must not be taught. There are large differences between economists on basic issues. They should be emphasized, not glossed over. Sociologists, we note, are more honest: they let their differences 'all hang out' in elementary courses, where economists tend to say, like quarrelling parents, 'pas devant les enfants'. But students are not children. They find the greatest difficulty in assessing the practical significance of economic theorems but must be encouraged to try to do so. Static states, mysteriously divorced from time, or dynamic ones in which change is instantly communicated, strain the powers of the mind. If the diagrams of elementary economics are essentially pedagogic instruments, as Sraffa argued, 'somewhat like the study of the classics', what are they supposed to teach? They are, of course, based on eighteenth-century illuminism and natural law, and this historical fact is important.

For the argument that the casual influences of the real world masked a divinely designed utopia was propounded in the days when royal despots and their agents interfered intolerably with the endeavours of entrepreneurs to grow rich. But once the despots had been disposed of, the economists interested themselves in refuting the socialists. With hindsight, their efforts appear to have been misdirected and Wicksell mistaken when he identified the labour theory of value as a 'terrible weapon against the existing order' (1901, p. 28).

(4) *Production* Structure, growth, size and organization of firms; managerial decision processes; managerial motivations, organizations, bureaucracy; price, production and sales strategy; extra-market operations; conflict and co-operation within and between firms; mergers, seizures, asset-stripping; transnational operations. Technology: mass production, technical organization, automation, innovation; research and development; technological competition; choice of techniques; ergonomics; pollution.

It is here, perhaps above all, that our courses are deficient. The giant corporations are the most conspicuous feature of world capitalism; business enterprises have common features, whatever their size, because they are shaped by common socio-institutional factors. But the giants differ from one another in important respects and must be studied individually. Managers display a common psychology, but styles may show significant differences, while sometimes the personality-cult breaks out with interesting results. There is now a thriving literature based on empirical studies, including the work of Marris, Mueller and Odagiri reported in this volume, and the pioneering work of Thomas Wilson, Philip Andrews and the other members of the Oxford Economists' Research Group (Andrews and Wilson, 1951).

(5) *Consumer behaviour*   The socio-economics of households and their cultural–historical base; customary, habitual, contractual and problem-solving behaviour; emulation, judgement and choice; discretionary expenditure. Fashion-makers and fashion-takers; tastes and choice; time preference; instability and turning-points of consumer spending; market research. The distributive trades: rise of supermarkets, hypermarkets, chain-stores, discount houses, cash-and-carry: their buying and selling strategy, power and influence. Advertising: persuaders, manipulators, want-creators; sales resistance. The work and findings of consumer associations.

George Katona spent many years in the Survey Research Center of the University of Michigan in the systematic study of consumer behaviour. The literature, with its empirical studies, is now abundant. Some of the most conspicuous economic changes manifest themselves in the distribution of power between manufacturers and retailers, with consumer movements and official consumer protection growing in parallel.

(6) *Income and work*   Occupational and industrial distribution of the work force; psychology of work; training; unemployment, social security and the work ethic; job design and work study. Convention, emulation, custom and practice in earnings and rates of pay; industrial relations, collective bargaining, trade unions; job evaluation and internal pay structures; pay and inflation. The distribution of wealth; households and individual earners; determinants of unearned income.

There is a high degree of indeterminacy in rates of pay now as in Adam Smith's day when he observed 'different prices being often paid at the same place and for the same sort of labour'. Fortunately there is today much empirical work that reveals some of the curious social processes involved. In his contribution to this volume (chapter 5), David Marsden illuminates the present state of the subject.

(7) *Banking and finance*   Banking services; financial institutions as intermediaries between lenders and borrowers and as creators of credit; money and its measures; insurance; pension and investment funds and their management; building societies; the stock market; merchant banking; takeovers; foreign exchange; central banking.

This encompasses the most staid and the most flamboyant of capitalist activities. The Radcliffe Committee removed some of the veils; the Wilson Committee continued the process; various Congressional committees have done the same for the United States. But to gain insight into the ramifications of the financial scene students should study one or two cases in depth, from the files of the Department of Trade or the Securities and Exchange Commission.

(8) *Political economics*   Public finance; public policy and attempts at the management of the economy; taxation and social services; trade and protection; government participation in business affairs; health and education; military–industrial complexes; consumer protection.

The OECD countries offer interesting contrasts in public consumption: unemployment insurance, health services, education, housing. On attempts to manage the economy, the OECD, the President's Council of Economic Advisors, the Federal Reserve Board, the Treasury and the Bank of England produce material in high volume.

(9) *Alternatives to capitalism*   Planning in the Soviet Union, Hungary, France. The Soviet and the Hungarian industrial enterprise. The Yugoslav economy and society. Third World countries and their attempts at intermediate or independent strategies. Worker and consumer co-operatives: amongst many failures, some manifest successes – Mondragon, Migros, National Carriers, People Express, as well as the longer-established co-operative societies.

We are confronted by cultural, social, behavioural and motivational differences, variations of Leibenstein's X-efficiency. The 'dynamic' growth models of the 1940s and 1950s are of little help, while no one really pretends that the neo-classical paradigm applies.

IV

Of course I do not present the above outline as definitive, but as a sensible division of the essential subject-matter of economics. The approach is on the whole more important than the content. At the end of their course students would have a high level of economic understanding, free from the trained incapacity that is a by-product of immersion in orthodoxy. They would be able to enter government, industry or research without the painful readjustment at present required for understanding real economic affairs.

It will be observed that I have not suggested separate rubrics for foreign trade or agricultural economics. Some departments might like to do so. Nor have I separated macro from micro-economics, on the ground that to explain the one you have very soon to enter the other, macro being merely one way of keeping the score.

Robert F. Hoxie, in the first year of this century, designed a curriculum that has some remarkable similarities to the one outlined above (Hoxie, 1901).[1] He stressed the need for empirical research to be conducted by the students themselves as part of the learning process. In North America, sandwich courses, which are growing in popularity, perform this function; they are employed with good effect, too, in Britain, for example at Brunel. To be effective, they require on the university side teachers versed in the realities of business and thus able to help their students to systematize the data to which they are exposed.

Students are in any case in a good position to co-operate in research projects, for investigations conducted in teams enable them to accumulate enough information to make tentative generalizations and to compare notes and impressions. The lessons learnt remain in their memory long after those from lecture rooms are lost in the mists of time. The transition would be greatly facilitated if a group of universities co-operated in trying out a common curriculum, and common research projects whose findings would before long constitute a useful pool of knowledge.

Papers in the learned journals often contain a prediction or two for supporters to confirm or adversaries to refute. To this practice, I conform. I predict that the mentality of marginalists is such that they will resist any radical attempt to meet the criticisms contained in volumes such as this. Instead, they prefer to restore equilibrium to the classroom by marginal adjustments: a footnote here, an addendum there, so that the integrity of lecture-notes and textbooks is preserved. My contention is that this need no longer restrain those amongst the teachers who feel the need for reorientation, the confrontation of *real* problems concerning *real* people, and the rejection of those immunizing strategems described sixty years ago by Sraffa, that are applied when someone openly expresses his doubts, and when, 'to prevent the scandal spreading, he is promptly silenced, frequently with some concessions and partial admission of his objections, which, naturally, the theory had implicitly taken into account' (Sraffa, 1926, p. 181). I suggest that, for those who accept the need, the proposals contained in this chapter present a practical method to escape the intellectual tyranny of the past.

Note

[1] I am grateful to Professor Leslie Fishman for having brought Hoxie's work to my attention.

Comment

MORRIS PERLMAN

Guy Routh censures the established schools for preferring to remain in Egypt rather than follow the prophet into the wilderness bound for a promised land. As a member of at least one of the 'schools' (given his list, it would be difficult not to belong), let me make my position clear. A journey into the wilderness does not frighten me. It can be exhilarating. If the invitation were extended for the pleasure of the journey, I might accept. But it is not. It is extended for the destination, the promised land. Many, if not all, prophets hold out such a carrot, and many such have I seen. But, alas, more often than not when the promised land is approached it turns into a chimera.

I shall evaluate Routh's proposals and criticisms with these questions in mind: what is the promised land implied by them, and is it attainable or worth attaining? However, to drop the prophetic language so beloved by critics of orthodoxies, there is a more important point. I believe that the general methodological attitudes underlying the proposals are not conducive either to transmit to the student any of the insights acquired by economists over the years or to train him to extend those insights.

Before looking at the detailed curriculum offered by Routh, I will consider his second section, where we are told of the recommendations about which there is a consensus among the critics and by implication the major sins to be avoided if these are followed. Three propositions are offered as a summary of the critics' consensus (p. 241). The first is that 'Doctrines must be drawn from empirical studies, in terms of which hypotheses should be formulated and tested . . . [This will avoid] the belief that it is possible to explain the working of the world by process of deduction from axioms or assumptions derived *a priori*.'

Hypotheses consist of some set of assumptions or general statements (assumed laws, assumptions about rational behaviour, etc.) conjoined with a set of particulars (for example initial conditions). These are used to explain the phenomenon under consideration. Without getting into the inductive–deductive debate in the philosophy of science, it is not at all clear how these general statements can be logically deduced from empirical studies. When Routh criticizes 'assumptions derived *a priori*', he surely does not mean *a priori* in the sense of an analytical statement, nor the Kantian synthetic *a priori*. He presumably means the type of assumptions made in orthodox economics about the behaviour of various groups; for example, the assumption that firms attempt to maximize profits. His criticism seems to be directed against the deductive method in general, against making general law-like statements from which consequences are deduced. Or, possibly, he is arguing against making such law-like statements without first looking at the data. He seems to believe that if such statements can be made, they can only be made by induction. These interpretations of his criticism here are reinforced by similar criticisms he has made elsewhere where he approvingly quotes what one can only call naive inductionists. For example, he quotes Richard Jones that 'if we wish to make ourselves acquainted with the economy . . . I really know but of one way to attain our object, and that is to look and see. We must get comprehensive views of facts, that we may arrive at principles which are truly comprehensive.' Routh then adds, 'What a splendid banner under which economic science might have advanced, "Look and see"' (1975, pp. 7–8). This, however, leaves two important questions unanswered: What do I look at? And how do I see?

I am not just being difficult. As we shall see, throughout Routh's proposals and criticisms there are many assumptions that serve as law-like statements, and cannot be derived from just looking and seeing. I, of course, do not object to that. But I would like to know why my assumptions are not permitted, while those of the critics are. It is hard not to avoid the feeling that it is all right to make grand assumptions about the effects of history on phenomena (p. 247), about the importance of social and political factors on the hypothesizing process itself (p. 243) and things of that sort, but it is not permitted to make small assumptions about, say, profit maximizing or revenue maximizing and things of that sort.

Let me now turn to the curriculum offered by Routh. The menu he offers to the student is very wide-ranging indeed, from *haute cuisine* to beans on toast. They should study hunters and gatherers for insight into the nature of man, and company accounts for insight into how they can be fiddled.

Part 1 of the curriculum, 'Economic and social history', covers a fascinating range of topics. If this is the wilderness into which I am invited to roam for the pleasure of the journey, I will go gladly. But here again the carrot is dangled in front of my nose, suggesting that I undertake the journey to achieve another promised land. Hunters and gatherers are to be studied because 'It is in hunting and gathering that the human mind has developed, so a study of these societies gives insight into the nature of man.' To say the very least, the question of the nature of man is a very big one. Philosophers, artists, social scientists, more recently socio-biologists, have all attempted to elucidate the nature of man. If the purpose of studying hunters and gatherers is to throw light on the nature of man, it is legitimate to ask whether this particular promised land is not attainable more easily by some other means.

Possibly reading Dostoevsky is a more enjoyable and more fruitful way of gaining some understanding about the nature of man than studying hunters and gatherers. But more important than the question of how best to understand the nature of man is another: Do we need to understand the nature of man before we can say anything useful about at least some economic phenomena? Do we want students to come out with the belief that without knowing the nature of man they cannot say anything useful about what determines the price of fish? Do we have to know everything before we can understand anything?

The reason for raising these questions is that in reading Routh's chapter, and possibly I am reading into it more than was intended, I get a feeling of anomaly. On the one hand there is the theme that understanding certain economic phenomena is extremely difficult. Uncertainty and our problems in understanding behaviour under uncertainty pose great problems. Because of the varieties of styles of individual managers in firms, and therefore presumably the varieties of possible responses to changes in the economic environment, it is difficult to generalize about the behaviour of firms. Because of these difficulties, we are urged to move to the study of grand problems, the nature of man, the role of history and culture. There is a kind of global optimism combined with local pessimism. By studying hunters and gatherers we shall get an insight into the nature of man. By studying history, we shall achieve understanding of the growth, change and decay of economies. By crossing disciplinary boundaries and studying archaeology, social anthropology and history, we shall acquire the knowledge we seek. Yet to understand the giant corporations, we are told we must study each one individually because every manager is different. This of course means that we can never achieve understanding of their behaviour.

Part 2 of Routh's curriculum covers statistics. He states that 'regular statistical workshops are as important as work in the lab for the natural scientists. Here movements in the economy are monitored . . . explanations sought.' I only wish to stress one point here. When scientists enter their labs they do so with hypotheses. Often they build giant labs to test some existing hypothesis.

For the statistical workshop to be of any use students have to enter it with preconceived ideas, with hypotheses, and leave it either pleasantly surprised or disappointed. If they do find that the movements they are considering 'are not neat and determinate . . . but clumsy and untidy', this might be because they have the wrong hypothesis rather than because the movements are caused by 'the group psychology of millions of decision-makers.'

In this part Routh tells us that the claim that a discipline should have a 'hard core' 'is an unproven educational dogma . . . its use by orthodox economists is merely self-serving . . . it is their idea of keeping the whole discipline respectable. Insofar as a hard core is really necessary, statistics and accountancy provide it.' I assume that he is using the term 'hard core' in the sense of Lakatos (1970), who used it for a research programme rather than for a discipline as a whole. But, be that as it may, the statement that statistics and accounting should be the 'hard core' of economics is surely a misunderstanding of the concept and its function.[2]

The 'hard core' represents a set of assumptions, hypotheses or principles which are assumed to be true as long as the particular research programme is maintained. These are used to generate auxiliary hypotheses, and are protected from anomalies by changes in these hypotheses or in the assumed initial conditions.

The purpose of such principles is twofold. First, it is to pick out from all the facts pertaining to a particular phenomenon those that are relevant for an explanation. Statistics are after all only the data of the phenomenon to be explained, for example the price level, and of the variables that are to be used as an explanation, for example the money supply, or the price of oil, or whatever. But what principles are used to select either the phenomenon that is considered as needing an explanation, or the variables that are to be looked at for an explanation? Should the students in their statistical workshop examine the statistics on sunspots, or the distribution of the population by hair colour, to explain the movements in national income? 'Look and see' is useful advice, but some hypotheses are necessary to tell us what to look at.

The second function of a 'hard core' is 'self-serving', but not quite in the way used by Routh. The 'hard core' or rather the protective belt surrounding it serves to maintain the research programme against anomalies which always exist, and if allowed to threaten the 'hard core' might lead to the abandoning of the programme too early (for an elaboration of this see Lakatos, 1970, p. 135). Of course, Routh may want to argue that the research programme of orthodox economics is degenerative, and so it and its 'hard core' should be abandoned. Instead he may want to replace it by a different research programme with a different 'hard core' which will be just as much protected and just as self-serving as was the old one. A perfect example of this is given by Routh himself in the next part, where he considers the research programme of the history of economic thought.

In part 3 we are told that 'The history of economic thought can be of great interest when . . . one begins to take the mental operations of the theorists as the problem. This requires the interpretation of the economic doctrines in terms of the social and political history of the time.' I strongly disagree. The history of economic thought is profoundly interesting because many of those who contributed to economics were profound theorists of economics. Moreover, some of their theories have not been incorporated into present theorizing, and this has often occurred in the past. Thus, quite often in economics, theories have to be rediscovered rather than developed, modified and extended. By posing the mental operation of the theorist as the problem rather than the theories, the historian of thought contributes to this problem of the continual need for rediscovery.

However, be that as it may, the particular statement I have quoted above raises a point I have mentioned before. In part 1 Routh warned us against the evils of *a priori* theorizing. Here we are told that to understand the mental processes of the theorist requires 'the interpretation of economic doctrines in terms of the social and political history of the time'. This is surely grand *a priori* theorizing, which is not at all immediately obvious. Moreover, it is easily refutable unless drastically modified by various legitimate and possibly illegitimate *ad hocery*. The proposition that the quantity of money affects prices has been debated for the last two hundred years or so. It is not as though at some point in history all or even most theorists were monetarists, and at some other point they were not.

Moreover, Routh himself has claimed that he has refuted the proposition that social and political phenomena affect mental processes. In his study of the development of economic ideas over the past three hundred years or so, he concludes, 'Thus it is that the hereditary characteristics of economic thought are much more pronounced than the environmental: the environment has gone through various transformations; the thought, in its methodology and ideology has changed hardly at all' (Routh, 1975, p. 295). Yet he is willing to maintain the 'hard core' of *his* research programme, namely that social and political factors affect mental processes. To protect this 'hard core' he will presumably have to differentiate between mental processes that involve methodology and ideology, and other kinds.

If the mental operations of the theorists are the objects of study, there are many alternative hypotheses to explain mental processes. A Freudian may hypothesize that the relationship with parents is of crucial importance to the operation of mental processes. Possibly if we want to understand Ricardo (rather than his theories), we should consider his difficult relationship with his father. Smith's relationship with his mother was also suspicious, from the psychoanalytic point of view.

If one does take the mental operations of the theorists as the problem to be studied in the history of economic thought, surely one should approach it with the same awareness of the assumptions made, the same regard for alternative hypotheses, and the same attempt at validation or otherwise as is or should be taken when one is hypothesizing about the behaviour of the firm. We shall then presumably find that some theorists fit our hypothesis and others do not. Those cases which do not fit our hypothesis we put aside as anomalies, and if too many of those occur we shall have to reconsider our theories. Grand theories should not be exempted from the same requirements that apply to more mundane theories, and students should not be led to believe that the grander the theory, the more protected it is from critical analysis.

On p. 244 Routh makes an aside about the diagrams used in economics and asks 'what are they supposed to teach?' He then gives us a hypothesis, which he calls 'a historical fact', that they are based on 'eighteenth-century illuminism and natural law'. Their purpose, as far as I can understand this difficult passage, was to promote the idea that 'the real world masked a divinely designed utopia'. Though how this hypothesis can explain why there are no diagrams in Smith or Ricardo or Mill puzzles me. I believe the reason for the use of diagrams is much simpler and their purpose less devious. Economics, whether orthodox or otherwise, deals with quite complex interrelationships, often involving many variables considered simultaneously. Any tool that might help the student understand these interrelationships, whether it be diagrams, or even, dare I say, mathematics, should not be thrown away. It is true that some people become so enamoured with their tools that they forget what they were designed for. But because there are some who devote their lives to polishing and sharpening their chisels, surely the rest of us do not have to use our fingernails to gouge wood. It is true that diagrams and mathematics can be used to obfuscate as much as to clarify. But it should be remembered that words can and have been used for this purpose just as effectively.

In part 4 of his curriculum, Routh tells us that 'business enterprises have common features whatever their size because they are shaped by common socio-institutional factors. But the giants differ from one another in important respects and must be studied individually. Managers may display a common psychology but styles may show significant differences . . .' This quote raises two questions, or possibly different aspects of the same question. In some sense, all individuals are unique. For some purposes this uniqueness cannot be ignored. Because everybody's fingerprints are different, they can be used in identification. In some other sense, we all have something in common. After all, in a previous part we are urged by Routh to pursue studies which will give us an insight into human nature, and that presumably is something that is common to us all because we are human. The problem before us as economists is to try to understand and explain economic phenomena. If it were true that with respect to the phenomena we are trying to explain the uniqueness of individual actors is so important that without this specific knowledge we cannot say anything about them, then we should renounce any claims to understanding. Unless we can postulate (reasonably correctly) that with respect to the phenomena we are considering, there is enough in common that we can say something useful even if we ignore those aspects which make us unique, we have no hope in making any general statements which can have any interest.

Therefore we have to ask for what questions is the uniqueness of the styles of managers and therefore the differences among enterprises important? Consider some of the questions that may interest an economist, for which we have to know something about enterprises. Will a tax on corporations affect their output or prices? Will a tariff affect the location of multinationals? Under what conditions will we observe price discrimination? This list is of course not exhaustive. For the behaviour that will determine an answer to these questions, are the common features of enterprises important, or are the differences in style of different managers important? If the latter is true, then before answering any of the above questions we would need to know all the individual particulars of all managers. And of course any change of personnel would mean a change in our answers. But why then study the giants individually? How many of them should the student be asked to study, and for what purpose? What questions are being asked, and why are the answers important?

In the second section of the paper Routh is critical of abstractions, something that 'learned professors indulge in . . . and students adopt . . . as protective colouration'. The seed sown in that section will be reaped by the student in this one.

Surely knowledge is the ability to generalize, to discover what is common in phenomena which on the surface appear different, or for that matter to distinguish phenomena which on the surface appear to be the same. If everything is unique, we can at best describe a limited number of phenomena. We can list them, and that is all. We cannot say we understand them.

A feather and a stone are different for some questions. I would rather have the former fall on my head than the latter. But it was the discovery that for some quite important questions the differences could be ignored and abstracted from that great progress in physics occurred.

But of course in this area, as in others I discussed previously, the critics indulge in the same process which they criticize. Routh does tell us that 'business enterprises have common features . . . because they are shaped by common socio-institutional factors'. I assume that this revelation is interesting, because we can say something more about business enterprises by taking account of these common features. Otherwise, the statement is of no interest at all. Presumably because of lack of space, we are here not told what these common features are, nor what we can say about enterprises when we do take them into account. But if we were to deduce something from these common features, we would be abstracting from all those other features which make them unique.

In the other parts of the curriculum Routh lists an immense number of topics in 'Consumer behaviour', 'Income and work', 'Banking and finance', 'Political economics', and 'Alternatives to capitalism'. The stress here again is on the particular rather than the general, the descriptive rather than the theoretical. To cite just a few examples, Routh tells us that the Radcliffe Committee 'removed some of the veils' (from banking and finance). The views of the Radcliffe Committee represent one side of a theoretical debate which has been going on for at least two hundred years. The student let loose on this report without a reasonable grounding in the theoretical issues involved in this controversy will come out with generalized confusion, or what is worse, with the illusion of understanding.

We are told that 'On attempts to manage the economy, the OECD, the President's Council of Economic Advisors, the Federal Reserve Board, the Treasury and the Bank of England produce material in high volume.' The implication seems to be that this is what the student should read to understand the issues involved in the problems of managing an economy. On the contrary, I believe that such an approach will only provide the student with garbled and often inconsistent versions of theories which happened to be popular or expedient at the time and place the reports were written.

In the final section we are told that 'At the end of the course students would have a high level of economic understanding . . . They would be able to enter government, industry or research without the painful readjustment at present required for understanding real economic affairs.' For the various reasons mentioned throughout this chapter, my conclusion is quite different. I believe that if the curriculum offered by Routh is followed, students will come out only with a dangerous illusion of understanding. On the one hand, they will feel competent in making grand theories about human nature, about the importance of socio-economic factors, about the importance of history, and be under the illusion that in doing so they understand something. However, most such statements are too vague and gradiose to provide any detailed understanding at all. On the other hand, they will have acquired an immense amount of particulars which by the logic of the approach itself will become obsolete very quickly. In between these extremes they will have nothing. The approach will dull their critical faculties. Most grand theories are too unspecific to be approached critically, and particulars are not subject to criticism.

I believe that the 'painful readjustment' students have to make when they leave university is to learn how to operate in the 'real world', not how to understand it. This painful readjustment they will have to make whatever they are taught. The often complicated details of the occupations they enter will not and cannot be taught at university. For that, only on-the-job training is feasible. If they leave the course believing they 'know', then, yes, they will be disappointed, whether they have been taught orthodox or unorthodox economics. In both cases the world will soon provide them with many anomalies to challenge their knowledge, unless, that is, they are taught in such a way that nothing is an anomaly and nothing challenges their claim to knowledge.

Let me conclude by stressing one point. Because I am critical of the approach suggested by Routh, that does not mean that I would defend all that is currently on offer. Economists and teachers of economics, both orthodox and otherwise, should be more modest in their claim to understanding. We are making tentative hypotheses about quite complex behaviour. They should be testable and tested, but that is not easy. That is why alternative hypotheses can coexist over long periods. The student should learn that the hypotheses we are interested in are those that have implications about observable behaviour. He should learn to distinguish among those that do and those that do not. The latter he should place in the realm of metaphysics. As a first step in this process, the student must learn how to draw out from any hypotheses the implications for what will be observable: what he expects to see and what he would be surprised to see in the 'real world', if that hypothesis is correct. That is not easy, does not come naturally, and has to be taught.

At the end of his course I do not expect the student to have a 'high level of economic understanding' of 'real economic affairs'. I do not claim to possess that; how can I expect it from my students? At best, they should come out with a little understanding of some aspects of the economy, a lot of unsolved problems, and some critical framework to grapple with these problems if they want to continue the search for understanding.

Notes

1 I would like to thank Peter Wiles for helpful comments. Needless to say, he does not necessarily agree with anything contained in the paper.
2 The following comments, possibly with minor changes in emphasis, are, I believe, valid even if Routh is here referring to what is sometimes called an 'educational hard core'; a body of knowledge considered necessary for students to understand a subject and communicate with other practitioners.

11

Towards a Better
Economic Methodology?

TERENCE GORMAN

Prologue

As you will see in the opening footnote, my brief was to write about the papers read *to the conference* on which this book is based. It was entitled *Towards a Better Economic Methodology*. I added the '?' to signal my doubts about its success in its proclaimed role. That the editors should call the book *Economics in Disarray* instead suggests that they have come to share those doubts. It also describes the contents much better: a sweet disarray, nevertheless, reflecting their agreeable permissiveness as organizers.

1 Introduction

Peter Wiles tells me that this conference sprang from the Presidential Addresses in which Henry Phelps Brown, Phyllis Deane, Kenneth Galbraith, Nicholas Kaldor, Wassily Leontief and David Worswick criticized the way in which our subject has been developing. Having discussed them[1] with a group of like-minded colleagues, he decided we need to know more about what has gone wrong in particular fields, and how to teach our successors to do better. They secured the support of the Royal Economic Society for a conference on the condition that each paper would be followed by a neo-classical discussant. The Council assumed, I take it, that the papers themselves would be critical of neo-classicism. Many organizers would have brought this about by assigning specific targets to specific contributors and insisting that they stick to them; and in doing so would have lost the best and wrung only perfunctory performances from the others. Peter, it seems to me, chose people he knew to share his general views, and allowed them to get on with the job as they thought best, knowing that appropriate asides on perfect competition and rational expectations, for instance, and on history, would come naturally.

The result is a much better read than most conference volumes.

Of course such permissiveness has its costs, too. None of the speakers scheduled[2] to tell us about *Macroeconomic Flaws in the Theory of the Firm* had anything to say about macroeconomics, for instance, and there was very little about methodology in a conference dedicated to that subject. Most surprisingly to me, only one speaker discussed econometrics, which is, after all, the existing methodology of economics, tailored for the subject, and taught as such to graduate students almost everywhere. How can one say that another is 'better' without comparing it with this incumbent, as Rod Cross alone attempted? I found it less surprising that he should apparently know next to nothing about the subject, or rather, a lot, almost all of it wrong. He is clearly highly intelligent and articulate. That Peter Wiles could see for himself; but how was Peter, as innocent of mathematics as a babe, to tell whether contributors knew what the econometricians had been up to, or anyone else who used mathematics for that matter? How indeed would any who could float into his ken.[3] In fact they did not; so that his allies, fighting unseen enemies, mostly missed them in the dark.[4] That does not make the book any the less enjoyable, but it does reduce its value as propaganda.

It is as if Samuel Johnson had had no idea what the Whig dogs had been up to and nobody to tell him. His reports would have been almost as entertaining; but not much help to the Tories, at least among the tolerably informed.

The relative absence of econometrics as a target is another matter, and turns out to have a simple explanation: Peter's group just decided to rule it out. Some of them, I presume, rather approved of econometrics, and seem to have missed that fact that dropping it left their Hamlet without a Prince. I will suggest below that the resulting scarcity of methodological discussion worried Peter, and that he tried to do something about it.

Should you find my style annoyingly informal, *do not read on.* It is so by design and meant to signal the fact that in what I have to say, is based mainly on my own personal experience and cogitations, and not on scholarly research. Hence my use of first names, for instance.

If you do read on, you will be assailed by an army of I's, reflecting the fact that I am the economist I know best. If I thought x at time t, the chances are that others did so, too. Writing as an amateur, to a deadline, in rural Cork, it will often be the best evidence at my disposal, and not bad evidence either. I am proud of my amateur status, believing economics to have become too professional a discipline rather than a way of thinking.

A word about organization. In Section 2 I will discuss what the methodologists *said at the conference*;[5] in Section 3, the economists; in Section 4, the historians of thought, each time concentrating on the most important paper, as I read it. In Section 5, I turn to what seems to me, and I believe to Peter Wiles, the crux of the matter: how should we go about teaching the next generation to do better?[6]

2 Rod Cross on Econometricans

As I said before, only Rod Cross discussed methodology in an organized way *at the conference*.[7] I am going to have some harsh things to say about *Monetarism and Duhem's Thesis*, so let me make it clear at the outset that it is a beautiful piece of work: clear, honest and incisive. That it should also be dramatically wrong on a number of important points, as I believe, is no crime, specially as he may well have been trailing his coat for the professional econometricians whom he must surely have expected in the audience.[8]

First the facts as I see them. Rod Cross realized that, to prove an alternative 'better', he had to compare it with econometrics. I agree with him that, though econometricians often misuse significance tests, 'it would be grossly misleading to suggest that all econometric appraisals of hypotheses are tarred by the same brush. Not all econometric studies amount to an inane application of Fisherian significance tests to presearched data' and that 'Davidson and Hendry (1981)',[9] in particular, does not. With one possible exception everything else he says seems to me not only to be wrong, but directly opposite to the facts, unless his words are given very strained meanings indeed, which I would not like to ascribe to so clear a writer as Rod Cross; the exception, if right, a strength rather than, as he implies, a weakness in econometrics compared with the alternatives.

Remember in considering what follows that the adjective 'Fisherian' is important, that, 'as [Rod Cross] understand[s] it, Fisherian significance tests are the orthodox means of testing for the significance of behavioural relationships in econometrics[10] and that 'as far as [he is] aware most econometric tests ignore Type II errors',[11] as if econometric theorists were not forever discussing the power of their tests against particular alternatives and classes of alternatives, and were not practitioners really rather well informed about the tests to apply.[12] Having done so turn to his section entitled *Econometrics* which begins on page 93 and contains a list of his main criticisms:

'First, the Fisherian significance tests often involved do not contain an account of the hypothesis being tested in competition with the null hypothesis.'

I personally cannot think of a single example in which this has been so *in econometrics*.[13] Commonly one tests whether a single coefficient in a complete model is zero; or, say, not positive; against the alternative that is not zero; or positive; spelling both out in boring detail. If this is unFisherian, all econometrics is.

'Second, such tests do not capture the conjointness of hypothesis testing.'

In fact it is to the explicit realization of this conjointness that econometrics[14] above all else owes its birth, as a reading of Trygve Haavelmo's classic *Probability Approach in Econometrics* or the more detailed Cowles Commissions Monographs edited by Koopmans, and Hood and Koopmans, let alone any elementary textbook on econometrics, would have made clear.[15]

'Third, econometric methods of testing hypotheses are too permissive in allowing specification searches for best fitting relationships.' This is the doubtful case I mentioned. Perhaps he is talking about data mining, a *practice* against which econometric methodologists thunder, perhaps about maximum likelihood and likelihood ratio tests. His use of the word 'method' rather suggests the latter. If so he is quite wrong: they take full account of the search involved. If the former, as the phrase 'specification searches' suggests, he is right, but has put his finger on a relative strength of econometrics, not a relative weakness.

What to do about data mining – preliminary search *not incorporated in the final test* – is not clear. If one is to 'learn from the data' in a freewheeling way, as those who advocate history as the model presumably, and I think rightly, wish, one cannot restrict oneself to what can be formally modelled at the outset. On the other hand one is bound to come across something which fits the facts to hand if one tries long enough. In principle one should probably spell out in detail all the ideas which have gone through one's mind, and all the preliminary analyses one has tried, in each particular piece of research. The editors of the two journals with which I have some personal knowledge – *Econometrica* and the *Review of Economic Studies* – considered insisting that all empirical articles should be accompanied by such statements, to be made available on demand, but dropped the idea as impracticable – apart from anything else they would have been quite incomprehensible to the readers unless spelled out at unbearable length, and probably even then. Historians may imagine what it would be like to list all the information they might have used but did not, and all the ways they might have arranged it. I doubt whether the *Decline and Fall* would have been written under those conditions.

One compromise, often urged by econometricians, and often practised, is to publish predictions, another is to test the model on separate data. The problem with the former is that it comes to testing the model as a whole, rather than separate components; with the latter, the shortage of data: though the growing practice of trying out something which worked in America, for instance, on British or other data, mitigates that to some degree; another sometimes advocated and occasionally practised is to model the search procedure itself in a rough and ready way, and take account of it in one's tests.

Any intelligent open-minded researcher faced by limited information and wishing to learn from experience, faces this dificulty whatever his methodology. The difference between econometricians and every other group known to me is that they have thought seriously about it, attempt to do something about it, and take account of it informally when reading each other's work. Who else does any of these things?

'Fourth, econometric techniques employ probability concepts that do not allow for the preferences we might have, for example for bold hypotheses which have high content but low probability.'

Where to begin? Most econometricians reject the idea of the probability of a hypothesis, and having read a fair amount about it, I can see their point.[16] They cannot therefore summarize their preferences between hypotheses in terms of prior probabilities. Their revealed preferences seem to me strongly to be for 'bold hypotheses'. After all, it is such that makes one's name. Moreover they are favoured by the significance tests to which Rod Cross objects.[17]

Bayesians sometimes do give bold hypotheses high prior probabilities.[18]

'Fifth, most economic theories yield only sign restrictions on, rather than quantitative relationships between, the relationships between economic phenomena: it is not obvious that it is more productive to test quantitative versions of qualitative hypotheses rather than to test the qualitative hypotheses themselves'.

As someone who has worked on qualitative economics, all I can say to him is – just try. He has forgotten his central, Duhem, thesis that one must pay regard to the rest of the model in attempting to test any one relationship. All the indirect interactions it gives rise to commonly have to go in the same direction as the original direct effect for such a simple test as he seems to suggest to be feasible, even in a world of certainty, and that puts very strong constraints on the model. That qualitative hypotheses scarcely ever yield even qualitative conclusions is just one of the reasons why the main aim of econometric research is to add specific content to initially general, and hence rather empty, theories. Would the other contributors not welcome more rather than less of this?[19]

Rod Cross goes on to Appraisals of Monetarism, Hydraulic Keynesian Theory, and Disequilibrium Keynesian Theory, 'illustrat[ing] how the Lakatos criterion of corroborated content at least provides a framework which permits some of the reasons of good sense we might employ in theory appraisal to be taken into account'. It is very well written, and, as far as I can judge, reflects careful reading of some of the most important theoretical papers but there is not a single reference to any empirical work in the field. The facts directly known to him apparently speak for themselves and that without reference to the rest of the economy, and despite his insistence that 'tests [should] capture the conjointness of hypothesis testing'.

Let me repeat: Rod Cross has written a clear and highly entertaining paper, which reflects a great deal of hard work. He wrote so well on a subject about which he seemed to know so little, that I took him for a philosopher. In fact he was trained as an economist. It is the zeal of a convert, I take it, that blinded him to what econometricians do, not lack of information.

Let us turn for the moment from what was said about econometrics at the conference to the thing itself.

Above all, perhaps, economics is the subject whose practitioners have faced the fact that perfect experiments are impossible, and tried to take explicit account of it in their work. A succession of able econometricians have faced a succession of particular problems, at first in isolation, and then jointly, and have established a wide variety of results, which have found their ways into the textbooks in a tolerably recognizable form, and are really rather competently applied by many young economists.[20] The continued vitality of the theorists is shown in the transformation they are working in the analysis of social surveys, for instance, now that they have become important in empirical economics; of the practitioners, that their application of these new methods of the *Gary Income Maintenance Experiment* has just won Jerry Hausman and David Wise, for instance, the Ragnar Frisch Medal mentioned on page 272.[21]

I am relieved to see from his reply that Rod Cross would not have us throw all this away without a hint of a viable alternative, as I had thought.

That he might only be attacking 'bad econometric practice' was a hypothesis to which I had given serious consideration. It seemed to me to be rejected by the evidence. That in favour is quoted in my second paragraph. The first sentence, which he quotes in his reply, seemed to me to be qualified quite markedly by the second: 'Not all econometric studies amount to an inane application of Fisherian significance tests to presearched data' which he does not. As against this, he had nowhere referred to 'bad practice', contrasted practice with theory or suggested that the numerous particular criticisms which he spells out clearly and precisely in his well-organized paper, referred only to misapplications of econometric methods. More fundamentally, his paper would have lost much of its point were it to have been interpreted largely as an appeal for existing methods to be better used. To have done so, as it seemed to me, would have been to insult an intelligent man writing on a subject which appeared to move him deeply.

Many such people have minds teeming with conflicting ideas. 'If they are to get anything down they have to choose among the many notions crowding their minds, leaving out the doubts, side considerations, and remote references.[22] Perhaps that is what happened here.

In any case I am glad to have given Rod Cross the opportunity to put the matter straight.

He goes on to say that 'bad econometric practice is more common than good in published appraisals of hypotheses in economics' and to quote as proof the fact that few applied econometricians publish the power of their tests. Now the power of a test is, in general, a *function* of all the parameters in the model. Even small models commonly contain a dozen or more parameters; and his commitment to Duhem's thesis would seem to commit him to large models which often contain many hundreds. Just how are functions of half a dozen parameters, let alone hundreds, to be presented in understandable form? By that 'litmus test' almost all applied econometrics is certainly bad; almost all saints would be too were we to apply equally stringent and inappropriate tests to them. Luckily it does not matter much: econometric methodologists have been assiduous in discovering the properties of their tests, whose properties are commonly understood by readers of their own generation: as for the rest of us, we would be even more thoroughly confused were they to spell them out for us – Rod Cross, by the look of it, as much as anybody.

Where did all that leave Peter Wiles? Rather worried, I think, by the scarcity of methodology in a conference in principle devoted to the subject. Hence, I take it, the title of Terence Hutchison's contribution *to the conference, Our Methodological Crisis*, and the opening sentences of its first (original version), third and fourth paragraphs: 'To start with I am obliged to point out that the title of this paper originated not with me, but with Professor Wiles, though I am perfectly willing to adopt, and take responsibility for it. Anyhow, for over ten years, a crisis in economics, and in economic policy, and in economic theory, has been widely discussed'; 'however, among the various aspects of this crisis, something describable as a methodological crisis may be discerned'; and 'this methodological crisis centres on the extremely simplified assumption regarding *knowledge, expectations and uncertainty* – or *certainty* – first explicitly deployed by Ricardo'. He then goes on to repeat the phrase I have italicized, or slight variants of it, eighteen times in the twenty-two doubly-spaced typed pages he circulated, apparently without realizing that econometricians might have done anything about the way in which expectations are adjusted, lags vary, and regimes change, or that mathematical economists, and more particularly game theorists, have had anything to say on the subject.[23]

What Terence did, like everyone else, was to write about what then interested him: trading insults with Joan Robinson and with his Model of a Modern Economic Theorist. He does it very well. I, for instance, cannot begin to compete; it is foolish of me even to try!

A highly entertaining performance then, but even less use as propaganda than Rod Cross's.

3 Dennis Mueller and Others on Economists

Being interested in what had gone wrong in individual fields, and how to put it right, the organizers devoted half their sessions to particular topics in economics. In the event, Hiroyuki Odagiri and David Marsden talked about internal labour markets, and Dennis Mueller about the capital market. Hiroyuki Odagiri argues that the Japanese version of the former – lifetime employment – goes with intense internal competition for promotion, combined, of course, with the absence of direct competition between similar people in different firms, after the point of entry. Superficially such competition might seem to go against the Japanese spirit of management by consensus of which we have all heard, but the experience of the Economics Department in the LSE in the seventies suggest not. As long as promotion is, and is seen to be, carried out fairly, carefully, and on recognized principles, intense competition seems to be consistent with good, cooperative, relationships. The long term is another matter.

Interestingly enough he does not take up either of these points, as more mathematical economists would have been tempted to, nor give any evidence for his claim, as econometricians would have. David Marsden's contribution is an interesting survey of the literature on the internal labour market in America and Europe. His lack of mathematics, I imagine, has kept him, too, ignorant of the more mathematical discussions of implicit contracts and of the relations between principals and agents, of what the game theorists have been up to in general, and of the econometric literature, but he is quite right in my opinion in suggesting that more labour economists should pay attention to the industrial sociologists, though what he himself has to say about their work does not go much further than what one finds in the posh Sundays, nor than Hiroyuki Odagiri's from mainstream economics.

Dennis Mueller's essay on the Stock Exchange as a market for corporate control[24] is in a different class, densely packed with information, cognisant of the econometric literature[25] ably argued, and above all dealing with problems central to our understanding of the capitalist system and how it is developing. I imagine that Oliver Hart will have taken him up on the theoretical points at issue, so I will concentrate on the more empirical.

Berle and Mean's great book has been famous since its publication; Burnham's *Managerial Revolution* was one of the first Penguins, which had such an impact when they came out; Sargant Florence was forever telling us in Birmingham, in particular, that directors almost always know how much their firms produced, hardly ever what profits they earned. That managers have interests of their own, probably tied up with the size of their firms,[26] has been commonplace among economists ever since I can remember. Nowadays it is a leading theme in the principal–agent literature, and among the Virginians,[27] for instance. All this is, I am sure, as well known to Dennis Mueller as to most modern economists, and in no way detracts from the value of his research, except as propaganda.

The early British take-over bidders were entrepreneurs, as one would expect, rather than Muellerian managers, or so I believe: Charles Clore looking for underdeveloped sites; Isaac Wolfson, as he told the seminar we ran for Birmingham managers in the late fifties, for able young men[28] whom he could deploy throughout Great Universal Stores. Of course these were dynamic entrepreneurs, bent on growth, and needing to expand their organizations. Nevertheless the managers they sought were potential competitors for the top posts with those already there.

Activities which bulk as large in the public consciousness as those take-overs did, come, in my judgement, to have many functions. All sorts of people turn to them as possible solutions of their own particular problems: the experts from whom they seek advice are, I would guess, apt to agree, and not only from self interest: to a cobbler there is nothing like leather.[29]

In any case, perfectly ordinary boards of directors were soon making take-over bids. To succeed they needed to persuade target shareholders to sell, and for that, the help of financial experts. Anybody who thought about such matters – and what economist who read the newspapers did not? – must have suspected that these active participants would do well at the expense of the onlookers: the shareholders in the bidding, and the top managers in the target company. I certainly claim to have, and to have discussed the matter with others who expressed no surprise, so that I was not at all surprised myself when the statistics to which Dennis Mueller refers, began to come out. It seemed clear that senior managers, who effectively write their own contracts as a group, would soon learn how to defend their own incomes at least. The open question was: how would the market react once operators in general began to understand what was happening?

Here I think Dennis Mueller may have gone wrong.

As he says, 'the managerial theory of investment is a cash flow theory of investment', and it is the resulting stocks of cash which seem to finance his take-overs. However take-overs in Britain at least seem[30] typically to take the form of share exchanges, which have tax advantages, so that both predator and prey have reasons to keep the prices of their shares as high as possible. Given that there are also tax advantages in buying shares indirectly through undistributed profits, rather than directly through commonly relatively highly taxed dividends, the shareholders in question may even gain from otherwise inefficient take-overs.[31]

This is a distinguished piece of work nevertheless, which any economic journal should have been happy to publish. There is all the difference in the world between daydreams and hard research. From the organizer's point of view, however, it is rather a pity that these are the sort of daydreams which occurred over thirty or more years to a perfectly ordinary quantitative economist, specifically chosen as a neo-classic,[32] who has never written on finance, bought a share, or even sat on his College's investment committee. To whom have they not? The Whig dogs have escaped once more.[33]

4 Michio Morishima on the Role of Mathematics

If Peter Wiles felt he could bank on anybody, it must have been Michio Morishima: a highly distinguished mathematical economist, President of the Econometric Society in his early forties, and a senior member of the Cultural Order of Japan, he has come to have more and more doubts about many applications of mathematics to economics, has recently written studies of Marx and Walras, and an enthralling general history of Japan, leading up to an explanation of its current economic success. Surely he could be relied upon to produce a paper at once splendid intellectually and ideologically highly acceptable?

However it came about, Michio agreed to talk on 'Good and Bad Uses of Mathematics'[34] He must soon have realized that it was as impossible task. Almost any branch of mathematics can prove useful in economics, according to the topic attacked and the quality of the author; or arid and confusing, when used by someone sufficiently unskilled or self-important. Michio could hardly go through paper after paper, saying 'this was good, because the author was able and knew what he was about; this bad because he was a bumptious fool'. Being Michio nevertheless, he kept to his promise, and the strain shows.

The bad use of mathematics is commendably typified by Paul Samuelson's Substitution Theorem, and by the fact that Kenneth Arrow's and Frank Hahn's *General Competitive Analysis*. 'in particular is poor in term of empirical content despite its being a volume in a Mathematical Economics Text series, whose stated aim is expressed in the claim that: 'students of mathematical economics and econometrics have . . . difficulties [one of which] is that the theoretical and empirical writings often make little reference to each other. The main object of this series is to overcome these difficulties. Most of the books are concerned with specific topics in economic theory, but *they relate the theory to relevant* work (MM's italics)" '. I can well believe that Kenneth Arrow and Frank Hahn did not do so and that the publishers, overjoyed at being offered a book on this subject by such distinguished authors, did not call their attention to the fact. Like Peter Wiles and equally wisely, in my opinion, they allowed their authors[35] to do what they wanted to do, and were rewarded with a highly successful book.

Michio comes back to the same point later when he quotes the report of a committee composed of Paul Samuelson, Tjalling Koopmans and Richard Stone which recommended an increase in the proportion of empirical studies of economic behaviour and technological structure in *Econometrica* in 1954. The difficulty about that was that writers like to be widely read; and writers of good empirical papers are readily publishable in journals much more widely read than *Econometrica*.[36] The editors considered dropping their standards for such papers, or permitting them to jump the then lengthy queue: the former would have lost them the few good empirical papers they were getting, the latter was held to offend against abstract principles of justice. The Econometric Society has since founded a biennial Ragnar Frisch Medal for applied and empirical papers published in *Econometrica*, the first three winners of which are highly impressive. Dennis Sargan had proposed in 1972 that we publish three journals, like the Royal Statistical Society, one each on economic and econometric theory and one applied, which would be sold singly relatively expensively, but of which members would get two rela-tively cheaply. It seemed clear[37] that most would take the applied journal and one other, and that it would also have a considerable circulation on its own, and so have been attractive to authors, but he ran into the same, almost religious objection: econometrics, in the wide sense, is a holy trinity, not to be divided, however much the economics of divided labour have in fact led to its being so.

It is a commendable ideal nevertheless, however unrealistic, whether voiced by Paul Samuelson, Tjalling Koopmans, Richard Stone, Kenneth Arrow, Frank Hahn, Jack Johnston, Frank Fisher or Michio Morishima; as it is for him to disdain to confound prin-ciple with bad practice by criticizing less able economists.[38]

Michio goes on 'despite this, twenty seven years later *F.H. Hahn was forced* – [TG's italics] to recognize that theorists all over the world have become aware that anything based on this mock-up [i.e. general competitive analysis] is unlikely to fly'. So far from being *forced to recognize* this, Frank Hahn has been a thorough bore on the subject ever since January 1949 at least. Even his picturesque and fantastic overstatement began to pall on me by February 1949 or thereabouts, and my only consolation for his exile in Cambridge is that I am freed from his monologues on the subject. I envy Michio the fact that he was apparently spared them. To have doubts about one's work, but to get on with it, realizing that it is important to get individual things straight, is a good thing nevertheless.

It is important in economics, then, as in every branch of thought, to know what implies what. It is from the solid basis of such knowledge that one can make imaginative leaps into the unknown. In his criticism of Paul Samuelson's Substitution Theorem, Michio seems to me to have forgotten this. One does not need to believe that there is perfect competition between single product firms operating under constant returns, and only one non-produced means of production, to find it useful to know that they[39] imply Leontief's fixed coefficients, particularly since the theorem called out for, and soon led to, generalizations, as mathematical theorems are apt to.

This as I understand it, was also Walras's assumption: possibly he needed it because he was not a very good mathematician? In any case, I do not think that his work is at the centre of Michio's paper as an example of the good use of mathematics, but because what interested him at the time was whether Walras was 'concerned with realistic utopia, . . . nowhere to be found in the actual world . . . ideally perfect in certain respects, and yet composed of realistic psychological and material ingredients' as Jaffé argues, or had as 'his ultimate aim . . . to construct a model by the use of which we can imagine how the capitalist system works'. I do not for the life of me see why he should not have been concerned with both. Michio Morishima is not only abnormally clearsighted, he is also an abnormally clear and prolific writer. It comes naturally to him, as I imagine, to assume that others have distinct, clear, thoughts in their minds, which they put down with similar ease and clarity. Not so. Many people in my belief are prolific thinkers, but less adept than he on paper. If they are to get anything at all down they have to choose among the many notions crowding in their minds, leaving out the doubts, side considerations, and remote references. For all I know Léon Walras may have been one such: he would not have had to be particularly bad case to have been a Morishima–Walras at one time, and a Jaffé-Walras at another, or, indeed, both at once. Frank Hahn's refrain is an example of a similar phenomenon. Consistency is a very minor virtue in my book compared with imagination, fertility and open-mindedness.

Like several others, Michio's cure for our 'methodological crisis' is that we should pay more regard to history and institutions. He must have noticed that he, the mathematical economist, was the only person present to have written a general history, and that Sir John Hicks wrote an influential, fluid, *Theory of Economic History* but seems to think of these as isolated examples, and knowledge of mathematics to go with a lack of interest is history in general or at least unwillingness to bear it in mind when thinking about economic matters.

Michio chose me as his discussant, and his examples of a historical work are from Kenneth Arrow, Frank Hahn and Paul Samuelson. Let me quote those four in rebuttal, therefore, *to avoid any question of selection bias*, once again relying on personal experience.

You cannot talk to Kenneth Arrow for three minutes when he is in the right mood without hearing about the Wars of the Roses, the reason why the Land Grant Act was passed in 1859, or the Second Bank of the United States; Paul Samuelson, the same squared! Frank Hahn is an expert on the building of English Cathedrals, on which he plans an economic hisory.[40] As for myself, here is a sober statistic: *neglecting journals* I own almost exactly the same number of volumes of history as of economics, have read them more diligently, and quote them more frequently in discussing economic matters.

Here is another story. I tried to set up a joint degree in Economics and Economic History at the LSE in the mid-seventies as a counterweight to the intellectual dominance of the more mathematical students. Try as I might I could not persuade any of my non-quantitative colleagues to take part. Meghnad Desai and David Hendry on the other hand were enthusiastic. I nevertheless continued to insist that the students should not be allowed to present mathematics or statistics beyond the minimum required of all economists, and accordingly assumed in their other courses.

The first pair graduated just before I left. They were rather good. Jane Brockliss just missed a First; Mary Morgan[41] did not. Both, it transpired, had done very well in Mathematics in their A levels. Of those I have mentioned, only Michio himself and John Hicks have published books on history to the best of my knowledge. However, Paul Samuelson's pieces on current policy seem to me informed by his reading of history, as does Kenneth Arrow's decision to study organizations as institutions.[42] Frank Hahn, as I said, plans a book on the economics of medieval cathedral building. Meghnad Desai has published well-regarded articles in economic history. As for myself, teaching has bulked much larger in my life than publication, and has been pickled in history: *even my research has largely been directed to the end of flexible modelling, to make it possible for practitioners to choose models appropriate to the data at their disposal* as Michio urges.[43]

How does all this come about?

Competent mathematicians have several well-trodden roads laid out before them, into life as professional mathematicians, scientists, engineers, statisticians, computer experts, systems analysts, or actuaries. It takes a conscious decision to do anything else. The most important proximate cause, in Britain at least, of their deciding to enter economics, in my experience, has been having combined mathematics with history at school.[44] Once they have taken up economics, mathematics saves them so much time in learning its formal structure, studying econometrics, and even reading work in applied economics, that they can continue to pursue their interest in history, which they do with a clear conscience, because they naturally regard it as relevant to their work as economists. Paul David and Bob Fogel are examples of much the same sort of thing happening in economic history.

Whatever the reason, there are proportionally many more history buffs among quantitative economists than in the profession as a whole, at least among those I know. Michio Morishima and John Hicks are not at all the isolated special cases Michio seems to take them to be, but leading examples of a large genus. If we are to have more history in economics, as I too believe we should, we need to recruit more, not fewer, mathematicians.

Michio's paper was announced as 'Good and Bad Uses of Mathematics' but that he read contained the important qualification 'with Special Reference to General Equilibrium Analysis'.

Relatively few mathematical economists worked on general equilibrium even at the peak, though they included some of the ablest, with Michio Morishima himself well to the fore, together with Kenneth Arrow, Frank Hahn, and, earlier, Paul Samuelson. Nowadays young mathematical economists tend far more to game theory, which they use to elucidate a wide variety of particular problems, commonly arising out of the practicalities of living together: legal liability rules, principals and agents, implicit contracts, patent races, auctions, enlightened self-interest . . . all of which are necessarily missed in Michio's discussion, but which seem very much the sort of thing which his fellow critics would welcome. In doing so, of course, they go well outside the traditional confines of economics. As more mathematically-minded students enter the other social sciences, we can hope to see valuable links being forged between them. Already economists, political scientists, sociobiologists, anthropologists[45] and, for all I know, psychologists find a common meeting ground in game theory.[46]

To get more economists to know more about the other social sciences, as David Marsden in particular, and in my opinion rightly, wishes, we again need more mathematicians, not fewer. I am sure Michio Morishima thinks that too. Why otherwise would he have asked Kenneth Binmore – the Professor of *Mathematics* at the the LSE – to organize the Workshop in Theoretical Economics in the International Centre for Economics and Related Disciplines, leading to its becoming one of the most important centres of game theory in the world? As he says, he, I, and, I add, a great number of other mathematically inclined economists, have much in common.

Meanwhile this particular breed of Whig dog has escaped too.

That being so, I would like to register my own particular complaint about the effect of mathematics on economics: as a censor which has led to our being unwilling to publish our ideas until they can state them rigorously and prove their validity. It is important that we should know just what we know so that we can build on sure foundations, but unfettered imagination and innovative unproven ideas are also important. In minding our Ps and Qs, we tend to forget that there are other letters in the alphabet. Economics has become a collection of theorems rather than a habit of thought. It is to his immunity[47] from this infection that we owe Peter Wiles's magnificent *Economic Institutions Compared.*

The better the mathematician, commonly the less he is affected by this, because the less daunting the technicalities to him.[48]

Nevertheless, the infection came from mathematics in the first place.

5 How Should we Teach Economics?

Anybody who feels that the current state of economics is as bad as Peter Wiles and his colleagues do, and that this is harmful to society, has to try to do something about the way it is taught. I believe that they were wrong in asking '*what* to teach?'[49] since it is to the notion that there is a Platonic ideal curriculum, against which actual curricula should be judged, that we owe our depressing sameness. Economists, as a whole, are scale models of each other in my opinion. When two of comparable quality are talking to one another it is almost a matter of chance which says what. We need to be able to understand each other, but each should bring his own contribution to the feast.

As it happens I personally did quite a lot of research in the early sixties, on 'the teaching of the social sciences in Britain' for the *Weltwirtschaftliches Archiv.*[50] More to the point, I was in Birmingham in the early fifties when we designed our new degree in the social sciences. I believe it to have been a marvellous degree, and the process by which it was designed exactly right. Once more, do not be scandalized by the instrusive I's in what follows, here due to the fact that I am my own best witness of these events.

The Faculty of Commerce in Birmingham was the oldest school of management in the English-speaking world, or so we claimed.[51] It was designed by Ashley, the economic historian, from scratch. As to disciplines, it was based mainly on economics,[52] economic history, law, statistics and accounting; but it was the method of teaching and examining which counted. His great legacies[53] were the Commerce Conference, to which we trouped on Saturday mornings to hear an undergraduate discuss a serious piece of work done during the long vacation; the Current Economic Problems paper, for which there was no formal preparation,[54] so that students had to read the *Economist* and like publications assiduously, and think seriously about what they read; and the similar General Paper, which dealt with social and cultural matters, but offered candidates a very wide choice of topic.

Philip Sargant Florence, driven from Cambridge, I understand, for being interested in facts[55] and in the other social sciences, had introduced social administration in the thirties, and sociology and politics in the forties. About 1950 he was succeeded as Dean of the renamed Faculty of Commerce and *Social Science* by Gilbert Walker, who ruled through a Tutorial Board composed of all the teachers in the faculty, whose decisions were rubber stamped by the faculty board: an innovation which so enraged the engineering professors that it ultimately led to a counter-revolution. For the moment, however, the young ruled, under the demagogic deanery of Gilbert Walker, and set about designing a new degree in the social sciences, to go with the title of the faculty, not in the tutorial board, but in the Ashley Society, an academic dining club with the same members.

This was, I believe, a stroke of genius. It made the design of the new degree an academic matter, not one of competing departmental interests.

We decided at the outset that everybody should be given a smattering of ·all the social sciences in their first year, and be thrown into sufficiently active contact later to learn from each other by osmosis. The first year was therefore compulsory: economics, economic history, politics, sociology, social psychology and statistics.[56] How to pull all that together? We did not do it by laying down syllabuses, but left it in the first year to their tutors whom they met in pairs each week. Since none of us had been lucky enough to have taken such a degree, that meant a good deal of reading of each other's subjects. Above all it meant that tutors had to be willing to make fools of themselves and be seen by their pupils to do so. Most of us thought that all to the good then, and I still do now. Best of all, perhaps, it made the students willing to risk mistakes, and try out new ideas.

In the second and third years the main rules were that no individual should present more than four of his eight papers in any one discipline, that he should present an extended essay[57] ranking as a ninth, and the General paper, almost as a tenth; and that teaching in the final year should where possible be by seminars, to which the extended essays in particular would be read. Since each was commonly attended by people with different outside interests, that is statistics for instance, by sociologists and social psychologists as well as economists, this generated useful criticisms which everyone could understand because they had learned each other's language, and general way of looking at society, in the first year. Most, as it happened, presented papers in at least three disciplines in their finals, but that was less important.

Of course we used other devices too. In particular the second and third year tutorials, now fortnightly in pairs, continued to be used largely for integration. I personally tended to use history and current problems, occasionally philosophy, as the matrices for discussion between pupils from different disciplines. David Eversley used to take the entire first year to Coalbrookdale at the outset, in principle to show how all the social sciences were needed to throw light on what happened there, though I imagine that he, too, took care that the Whig dogs did not come out of it too well. That, incidentally, was a further advantage of the scheme: one could teach one's own subject wholeheartedly, not underlining the ifs and buts, knowing that one's colleagues would do that for one.

What about the teachers? We already had the Ashley Society in which to discuss general papers in the social sciences. It was soon supplemented by the Economic, the Economic History, and then the Sociology Clubs. Frank Hahn and I commonly went to them all, the other young economists quite often; others tended to keep to their own clubs and the Ashley Society, though Chelly Halsey and Jose Klein sometimes came to Economic History. I do not think that it was by accident that it was the economists, and the more mathematically minded in general,[58] who most commonly ventured outside their own fields. We also ran a workshop on Decisions one year in which most of the young teachers took part. In the long run it affected my thinking a good deal. I do not know about the others. Like mutual gift giving, it strengthened our social bonds.

This sort of thing depends on a small, enthusiastic group. In 1956 we had the counter-revolution, carried out while Gilbert Walker was in hospital with a detached retina. In the event the young fought back rather well, and the faculty remained fairly democratic, but much of the spirit had gone, and several who

might have stayed in such a marvellous place, had already left
even before the expansion of the sixties had really got under
way.[59] I think that a little more, rather under the counter,
specialization has become possible. All the same Birmingham remains a rather special sort of place, as you will discover if you in-
terview one of its graduates, and give him opportunities to bring
wide general knowledge of the social sciences to bear, as well as
detailed technical skills in his own particular fields.

How successful was it? Very, in my experience. My own
tutorials, for second year students, were a joy to me for the vigour
and informed good humour with which students with different interests discussed each other's work, as were the third year seminars in statistics. Those extended essays with which I was personally associated were good too, and quite as closely related to the
'facts' as Michio could wish. Nor was this at the cost of professional skill. Harry Johnson and Austin Robinson as external
examiners independently protested at the standards expected of
the economists, and, when the Royal Statistical Society published
a report on the 'Supply and Demand for Statisticians' in 1959, I
was able to point out to Professor Pearson that more of our
graduates had taken up teaching in the field in British universities
than from any of the departments he had listed. As to numbers, I
believe that rather over a third of the 120+ entrants to the faculty
were entering this course by 1961, when I left, which was, of
course, before the real expansion. However that does not tell the
whole story. Those reading for the other degrees, mainly in Commerce and in Social Administration, were greatly affected by
what was going on, attending the same lectures and, more importantly, seminars and tutorials; and, in the case of Commerce,
spreading their interests quite as widely.

Could such a degree be developed nowadays? I suspect that
most universities, and their social science departments, are too
large. If one has enough close colleagues to absorb one's social
and intellectual energies, they tend to do so. Informal social con-
tacts with others tend to be sacrificed; without them the shared
values, knowledge and enthusiasms on which such joint enterprises depend, do not come into existence. You must remember
that all sorts of people have to know when courses are changed,
for instance, which is much better done by informal chats in the
Common Room. A concept of the general interest has to be kept

alive, too, and strong enough to override departmental interests.

Joint degrees such as that in Economics and Economic History at the LSE I mentioned in Section 3 are another matter: all they need is one or two enthusiasts on each side, and a little cooperation from their colleagues. Yet the research I did in the sixties suggests that they commonly fail. The reasons mentioned were the same everywhere. The teachers commonly concentrated on their specialities; the joint honours students felt outsiders almost everywhere. They also found it difficult to relate what they learned in the two departments. Anomie, then, and lack of integration, are what one has to guard against. Here are a few wise words for anyone thinking of having a go:

(1) Anomie: how one gets around that depends on the teaching methods used in particular institutions, which tend to be sacrosanct. One good general idea is to allow the students very few choices,[60] so that they remain together as a group. If classes of 10–20 students, for instance, associated with particular lecture courses are commonly used, there is a lot to be said for aiming at an intake of 10–20, and forming them into classes on their own.

(2) The second great dificulty is relating the two sides of the curriculum to each other. Since the teachers mainly engaged will commonly not be too well informed, they have to be willing to appear stupid. Given that, the classes referred to in (1) can be diverted to serve the cause of integration as well as technical training. Tutorials are good for this, too.

(3) In my experience supervised projects, preferably interdisciplinary and preferably in small groups, followed by workshops, are both good in themselves, and good integrators. In the ten years or so that I organized the projects and workshops in mathematical economics and econometrics at the LSE I never had any difficulty recruiting supervisors from the department as a whole;[61] and the workshops never failed to be lively and enjoyable. It is a marvellous way of learning about sources too and about the importance and illusiveness of facts. Interestingly enough, those were the aspects of their experience which these young quantitative economists best enjoyed discussing and comparing notes about.

Let us look at that programme for a moment. It was effectively a joint degree in mathematics, economics, and statistics, and was notably successful despite violating my first two precepts. This was because the mathematicians, mathematical economists, econometricians and statisticians at the LSE talked to each other, got on well together, and shared common values. In other words, the situation was much as it was in Birmingham in the fifties. Even the numbers engaged were similar. Now this was at the London School of *Economics*, and the mathematicians and statisticians accordingly got some of their best students from among the economists. More importantly, they were not locked away in the different faculty. Nevertheless mathematically inclined people in different departments quite often talk to each other, and share common values, in other universities too, so that our experience may be of some general interest.

First, the general principles. As much of the mathematics and statistics as possible were taught in the first year, so that they could be used in the economic courses throughout. This motivated the students, gave them practice in applying what they learned, and made them able to digest economics and econometrics quickly and efficiently from the start. That was the first principle. The second was that we set out to teach ordinary economics, using mathematics and statistics where they seemed useful, not mathematical economics conceived as a subject in its own right,[62] and the third that the students presented projects, almost always empirical, adequately supervised, and read to, and vociferously discussed in, special workshops. This not only provided an excellent introduction to sources, but an insight into what economic research was about, and a better understanding of its implications. Because we had quite a lot of students, we were able to run courses at two levels of mathematical sophistication, the more sophisticated commonly read a second mathematical course in their first year, and one each in mathematics and statistics in their second, so that most of their work was in mathematics, statistics or economics, a good deal of it in applied economics; but the less mathematical, whose courses incidentally were also available to most other groups of economists and popular among them, were able to spend almost half their second and third years working on subjects other than these three – more, I ·believe, than any other group[63] were allowed to do outside their single specialist subject, and almost twice as much as the political scientists, who were forever talking about general education, allowed theirs. This was possible because their mathematics and statistics helped them to digest economics, both pure and applied, quickly.

Having observed the provenance of our first batch of economist/ economic historians I drew up programmes for mathematically inclined geographers and historians who might feel inclined to combine them with economics, within this degree, with the aid of people in those departments who promised to help with the teaching. I left almost immediately afterwards, and do not know what happened to them. But the point was that mathematics and statistics, taught early to appropriately talented students, can so simplify economics for them as to allow more, not less, time for related subjects.

The mathematical economics and econometrics seminars played much the same role among the teachers at the LSE as the various academic clubs at Birmingham. People from both sides commonly attended both, as indeed did most of the younger members of the department from time to time, and some of the historians, mathematicians and statisticians. If the department had an intellectual centre, this was it. I am told that that is so no more; the mathematical economists have even arranged their workshop to clash with the econometrics seminar. I am also told that the numbers reading for the joint degree in mathematical economics and econometrics have fallen. In the circumstances, I am not surprised, and would not be surprised were the programmes for geographers and historians within it never to have got off the ground.

The problem about all such programmes is that they need at least one enthusiast, whom the students can consult and complain to, who is willing to spend time talking to teachers about what they are doing, and how it chimes in with what the others are, and even chivvying them occasionally. I was the busybody at the LSE. This sort of thing requires constant, quite hard, work, not an occasional sermon. It is therefore apt to collapse when one or two enthusiasts leave – a point to remember when setting up such programmes, or deciding whom to promote.

A word now about graduate work. As the reader may have gathered, my personal *bête noire* is the American graduate school, based on the idea that there is a unique way of producing professional economists. Under Harry Johnson's influence, as I understand, our ESRC began to insist on this sort of thing here, in the late sixties; it relaxed in the mid seventies, letting at least two or three flowers bloom. I understand that it has tightened up once more. Were they to relax again, we might have more variety. Graduates can probably look after themselves more easily, and cope with a medley of relatively unrelated courses by people who do not work very closely together. Were the SSRC to make that easier, we might ultimately have a greater variety of programmes for undergraduates too – though not, I very much hope, anything along the lines suggested at this conference.

Notes

I am notably ignorant of methodology in general, though I used to know something about econometrics. That Peter Wiles is nevertheless publishing this paper in this volume is due to a series of misunderstandings. When I happily agreed to talk on Michio Morishima's paper, I did not realize that it would be on a subject of which I know so little; when I talked to it, that the proceedings would be published; when, on hearing that they would and I suggested I discuss the conference in general, I had not read, or heard, the other papers. Should you find it worth reading nevertheless, thank Meghnad Desai, Jim Mirrlees, John Muellbauer and David Rowan who read it in a great hurry and checked my Irish exuberance; Frank Hahn and Marion O'Brien who encouraged me not to kill it outright; and David Hendry who looked over my econometrics.

It was originally presented in the guise of a detective story: the mystery to be explained being how the collection came to be at once so much more readable than most conference volumes; and so little to do with its ostensible subject – at least in my view – and so ineffective as propaganda. At Peter's suggestion I have played it down in this version, while keeping it as a connecting thread.

[1] Peter did not actually list the Presidents in question, and Phyllis Deane's address may seem to have been inappropriately recent. However, she was a member of his group, so imagine that they saw it in draft. I imagine that Joan Robinson's Ely lecture influenced them too.

[2] In *the conference programme,* which is what matters for my argument. Peter tells me that he has changed the title in the table of contents of this book. It was I who pointed the peculiarity out to him: further evidence for my hypothesis of benign neglect?

[3] Those who read mathematics tend to write in it too, at least by Peter's standards, and hence, I presume, be unread by him. Peter tells me that Guy Routh helped him to choose speakers: I imagine from what I have read of his work that he is almost equally innocent of mathematics. Perhaps he was the permissive one? I certainly did not find Peter a permissive *editor*: It was only my immense respect for him as the author of *Economic Institutions Compared* which prevented my dropping out long ago.

[4] Obviously Michio Morishima is an exception, though even he seems to suggest that general equilibrium theorizing engages the energies of many more mathematical economists than I believe.

[5] This excludes Mark Blaug's scholarly review of *Beyond Positivism*, and Peter Wiles's stimulating and enjoyable *Epilogue*, and allows me to cover all I need of the rest in the space available to me.

[6] Peter says 'what' not 'how'; there they and I disagree.

[7] Mark Blaug's admirable paper was not presented at the conference.

[8] Not only would the title of the conference seem to imply it; Peter Wiles's colleagues at the LSE included 'James Davidson *et al* – '*al*' being David Hendry, Jim Durbin, Andrew Harvey, Steven Pudney and Dennis Sargan – the best group of econometricians in the world, many would argue.

[9] Cross, p. 94.

[10] Ibid.

[11] Cross, p. 91.

[12] Though they are too apt to use the same conventional significance levels however much evidence they have at their disposal. If this is all Rod Cross meant he could have said it in 19 words.

[13] Obviously individual readers may disagree with the account, or find it inadequately thought out. The important thing is that it is laid out for them to inspect. Note that Rod Cross ignores the words '*in econometrics*' in his reply.

[14] Individual readers may disagree with the remainder of the model being discussed, or think it inadequately thought out, but, once again, it is laid out for their inspection.

[15] Textbooks in econometrics tend to be remarkably up to date in my experience.

[16] Personal probability is easy to justify, given extreme rationality and free computation, but that merely gives you the calculus. How different people would agree to the same probabilities is quite another matter, that they should be truly objective, yet a step further. Savage regards standard procedures as effectively a way of compromising such difficulties.

[17] For myself, I would give more weight to ease of understanding; and the capacity to yield results which can be filed easily in one's mind for quick reference.

[18] By giving point masses of prior probability at desired points, for instance. I realise that Rod Cross would disapprove.

[19] That he should not discuss estimation at all is to me the most surprising thing about Rod Cross's paper.

[20] This may sound faint praise, but it is not intended as such. Having had cause to read a good deal of empirical work by other social scientists and run workshops for economists beginning their theses, I can vouch for the notably superior technical standards of the latter.

[21] That Jerry Hausman is as distinguished a theoretical as an applied econometrician is further evidence of the healthy state of econometrics, where such dual roles are common.

[22] See my comments on Michio Morishima on Jaffé, pp. 273–4.

[23] Three other particulars bear me out in the belief that Peter was worried at the lack of methodological discussion: the copy of Mark Blaug's scholarly review of Bruce Caldwell's 'Beyond Positivism: Economic Methodology in the Twentieth Century' from the *Wall Street Review of Books* which is included in this volume, though it was not given in the conference: my suspicions that his ready agreement to my writing about the conference in general rather than on Walras alone reflected in part an expectation that I would have something to say about econometrics at least, if not about methodology in general: and his own highly entertaining essay into the field. That it is also haphazard and higgledy piggledy is further evidence that it was written at the last minute, when he realized just how few of the papers bore on the theoretical subject of his conference. Jim Mirrlees has persuaded me that I should not say things like this without giving an example. Here is one:. Peter blames the state we are in on the fear of the young for the old at one point, and of the old for the young at another. Both may be true: but surely

he would have brought them together in some way if that is what he meant. Peter told me in December that he had removed this feature, and suggested I comment on another. Since he did not send me his new version, I will not venture to guess what other interesting contrasts he had removed, or introduced, but one thing I will say. The author of *Economic Institutions Compared* would have no difficulty in writing a highly enjoyable, and valuable, *Epilogue* to a series of essays though, of course, his innocence of mathematics is likely to have hidden the Whig enemy from him as effectively as it has from most of his contributors.

[24] This is the core of his paper: he disposes of the Stock Exchange very effectively at the outset as a market for investment funds, though not, I think, as a barometer of credit-worthiness for the bankers.

[25] He has had to be pretty elliptic to pack so much in; I have interpreted what he says in such cases in what seems to me the most favourable way.

[26.] To which pay and prestige are often linked.

[27] Though the latter, of course, are more interested in bureaucrats than managers.

[28] Held back by somnolent seniors whom he pensioned off. Another entrepreneur told the Oxford Economic Research Group the same about his firm a little later.

[29] I do not think that Robin Marris and his associates have investigated this possibility: perhaps they share the professional single-mindedness which to me is the besetting sin of much modern economics.

[30] John Flemming tells me that there are no hard statistics, but that most take-over bids at least have this as an option because of the tax advantages. Perhaps they do not accrue to the institutions. If so 'typically' may be too strong a word.

[31] This field is full of conundrums. Think of the investment trusts in the seventies. Perhaps the most important criticism of Dennis Mueller's paper is that he totally neglects the central one – why are dividends paid at all, given their tax disadvantages? – despite its obvious bearing on his subject. I do not take this up in the text because I assume Oliver Hart will have.

[32] By order of the Council of the Royal Economic Society. See the Introduction.

[33] I really should have discussed Professor Neild's recycled address to the Business Economists here. After all, it was the keynote speech. However Peter Wiles, justifiably fearing that I might be tempted to discourtesy, suggested that I should not. I will therefore confine myself to saying, in the decent obscurity of a footnote, that the Whig dogs seem to me to have escaped his fire too.

[34] According to the conference programme.

[35] That they themselves were the editors involved, with Jack Johnston, is further evidence of their good sense. One may talk pompous nonsense on committees; but writing a book is a serious matter.

[36] Applied research is more often published in book form, too, than theory, and in specialist journals.

[37] I happened to be president at the time and was bombarded by complaints from econometric theorists that they were being squeezed out of *Econometrica* by unreadable mathematical economics, from mathematical economists in like terms about econo-metrics. Both said that they would welcome more applied work.

[38] Michio is quite wrong in believing that I ever thought otherwise; a writer of his distinc-tion does not confound principle with practice.

[39] And with strict quasi-concavity, to be pedantic.

[40] Or so he told me soon after retiring to the fens.

[41] Who is preparing with David Hendry a history of economic theory.

[42] If you do not believe me, read *The Limits of Organisation*.

[43] So that they can look at the facts first, as Michio would like, and also take account of the fact that they are not the facts which they would have liked to theorize about.

[44] I do not know that I agree with Michio that it is better to recruit mathematicians who have studied history rather than science. I believe we need more variety, and scientists

have also something to tell us. Those who joined the econometric programme at the LSE had quite a lot.

[45] I am indebted to my colleague, Clyde Mitchell, for this information.

[46] It may not last of course. The common use of linear methods, and of statistical techniques, provided similar meeting grounds in the fifties.

[47] Not acquired, but natural. Like the 'true born [non-mathematical] Englishman' he is, he has ignored 'all temptations to belong to other nations' from the beginning. Hence his quirky originality.

[48] This was notable among candidates for tenure and promotion in the LSE in the seventies, for instance.

[49] As David Rowan has pointed out to me this is really to do with the design of teaching programmes rather than actual teaching which, above all, depends upon the specific abilities of the teachers involved. However it is not about what to teach.

[50] I did not write it up, much less publish it, but I did work hard, visiting quite a few universities; discussing the problems with their teachers, and carrying out a postal survey of all higher educational establishments known to me in the field. Slightly earlier I had visited several universities to find out what they had been doing about education for management, and did a lot of external examining when it was taken more seriously than now.

[51] Founded in the early nineteen hundreds. I believe Joseph Camberlain chose Ashley as a tariff reformer.

[52] Initially, I believe finance and, of course, commerce, reflecting Ashley's low opinion of the economics of his time.

[53] I may be imputing too much of what existed when I came to Birmingham in January 1949 to Ashley.

[54] Students learned industrial economics from Philip Sargant Florence, who was Professor of Commerce, but that was the only applied course for the generality of students, who were otherwise taught only Economic Principles, to be applied by themselves. Of course most, presumably, read papers on current problems to their tutors.

[55] Perhaps an overpicturesque legend.

[56] The great absentee was social anthropology but that was partly compensated for by the Mason lectures which attracted a different highly distinguished anthropologist to Birmingham for several weeks most years.

[57] It replaced the Commerce Conference Paper I referred to above, a year or two later. To my shame I opposed it as a universal requirement. Specially promising students were allowed to present more serious extended essays, replacing one of their ordinary papers as well. Some of these, in particular, were very good indeed, much better than a good deal of published work, in my opinion.

[58] Frank Hahn and I among the economists, Chelly Halsey and Jose Klein among the others.

[59] Including the four mentioned in note 58.

[60] There can be long lists of choices under one or two headings, but the rest should be bankers, common for everyone, at least in the early stages.

[61] Admittedly the LSE was lucky in having many teachers interested in theory, who did applied work, and knew their data. Such teachers commonly have many small problems they would like looked into: keen young undergraduates do it much better than bored professional research workers, in my experience. Admittedly these particular students were rather good too.

[62] When Frank Hahn introduced a mathematical treatment of economics into the first year: he promised that he would cover everything *then* in the mainstream course. We kept to that promise, though Michio later modified the mainstream course markedly. The more sophisticated mathematical options in the third year were called Mathematical Economics, but that was to distinguish them from the somewhat less mathematical course traditionally called Economics Treated Mathematically.

63 Except the joint honours schools, whose candidates had to take *all* their papers in the two disciplines involved. I included both Economic Statistics and Econometric Methods in economics here.

Reply to Replies

Contrary to Michio's beliefs,[1] I have always: (a) honoured him for attacking mathematical economics in its ablest exponents; (b) known that Kenneth Arrow and Frank Hahn were among their own editors; (c) wished mathematicians to enter economics from a variety of backgrounds, including science and engineering as well as history; and (d) tried to devise flexible models to permit economists to take account of 'facts', institutions and the views of other social scientists when setting about their own work.

I, (a) know of no econometrician who is 'Fisherian' in Rod Cross's[2] sense; (b) would never have guessed the rich variety of meanings encompassed in the simple word 'bold'; (c) dropped all reference to his views on probability when I discovered, long ago, that he was not a philosopher.

Notes

[1] Remarks and references: (a) a principle which could have led to his attacking his own work; MM p. 44. (b) TG footnote 35 and list at bottom of p. 272; MM p. 74. (c) TG footnote 44, MM bottom of p. 75. (d) TG p. 275; MM p. 76.
[2] References: (a) RC p. 115–16; TG mid p. 263 and footnote 13. (b) RC bottom p. 116; TG p. 265 and footnotes M, 18. (c) RC. p. 115.

A Reply to Gorman

PETER WILES

It is a rare pleasure to be able to include Terence Gorman's piece. Let me spare the reader an account of its difficult birth. Let him in turn forgive me for having ridden Terence on so loose a snaffle. Methodology, after all, is about personalities. That he has illustrated this point, but within the bounds of courtesy as loosely set by the editor, is perhaps his major achievement.

In an atmosphere charged now with personality, even though devoid of malice, I am entitled to a bit of personal reaction.[1] First I observe that methodology's capacity to rouse people is due to its moral foundation; it is about how people ought to be. It generates with great rapidity a confessional atmosphere, and so it should. That it did not, at our conference, generate also acrimony, I record but cannot explain. Anyway Terence is a moral man – clearly so. In emphasizing his teaching over that polar opposite, his theoretical activity, he has given us an *apologia pro vita sua*.

That particular dead language puts me in mind of the fabulous Terentius Magnus (his Roman, not his barbarian, name), the tribal leader of the fierce Mathematici, who conquered the Roman province of Economia, was made a consul and married the Emperor's niece. Satisfied, he enjoyed his new patrimony but briefly, for lo, here on his heels came the utterly barbarous Factalegentes, with whom he had shamefully flirted when he too was on the wrong side of the *Limes*. Living in the stupor of victorious luxury, he is at first reluctant to recognize the seriousness of the situation. Eventually, he pulls himself together and tries to rouse the effete natives of Economia (the autochthonous Tautologoi) by reminding them of their intermarriage with his tribe. We are one people now, he cries desperately, we never carried off your fat Nobel prizes, we never put you to the torture of the dreaded Equilibrium Generale, I am your natural leader, out there is the enemy, they are Monophysites, they do not believe in the duality of theory and fact,[2] our civilization is at stake. But the new invaders, with their coarse manners, low brows, and shaggy ponies, guided over the passes by a ruffianly Japanese turncoat, press on, they want their place in the sun. The Vestal Margins are taken out and averaged, while the Oracle of Ratex falls silent. Between the two enemy peoples they make at first no distinction, but later they come rather to respect the Mathematici, who fight well. They intermarry, and then they both turn their odium methodologicum onto the effete Tautologoi, and trample them into the sands – those shifting sands that, rule who may, are the sole foundation for buildings in the province of Economia.

For econometrics is, most unfortunately, not the methodology of economists. It is not even the methodology of econometricians. Some readers who know me may suspect the adverb 'unfortunately' to be hypocrisy. This is not so. I was the first to edit and publish a work of Sovietological econometrics (Niwa 1971). In Wiles 1979–80, I welcome econometric testing whole-heartedly – as being the Trojan horse within the ramparts of Chicago. My life's work within Sovietology has been to lay the arithmetical foundations for others' work along these lines. This is not to say that I approve of the methodology of econometrics as a whole! Merely, the establishment and testing by arithmetical methods of the arithmetical values of parameters seems to me to be a wholly worthwhile activity.

But this is not enough. The notion that there ought to be models, 'endogenously' confined to economic events, is simply a trade-union restrictive practice. There is of course usually no reason for overall models at all, let alone for such as exclude 'exogenous' political or sociological events. It seems to me that econometricians (who make frequent incursions into Sovietology, as they should), behave much like, and only slightly better than, economists. I can confirm to the hilt something resembling Cross' complaints from thirteen years of experience. Econometricians do not respect fact, they do not look at institutional data, they do treat their own wild assumptions as facts, they do show a perverse reluctance to abandon them because of their computational convenience, their elegance or their conformity to this or that traditional *economic* theory. The magnificent testing apparatus is hardly ever used on unorthodox theories.

I draw particular attention to the econometric treatment of expectations. These are now conventionally called rational expectations, and econometricians are astounded, even uncomprehending, when I query the adjective. Yet expectations certainly are not known, and clearly may not be rational. The idea of rational expectations seems to be that the population of some capitalist country had, in some past pre-Lucasian period, a Lucasian econometric model, which they did in fact use to form their expectations. I am proud to have prevented the appointment of a candidate who used that ploy: and was shocked to hear a respected professor of econometrics (not Terence) defend him on the ground that this was the 'permitted paradigm' (sic). This ploy seems to me to be a straightforward intellectual disgrace.

It was not, however, astounding to meet a Polish econometrician who used the ploy for Poland in the admittedly partly post-Lucasian period 1970–80. But does Joe Pajestka read Lucas (1972), even after he is published?! Again, econometricians persist – inside Poland even Polish econometricians persist – in supposing that there is a Communist trade cycle: a series of economically endogenous and fairly regular fluctuations in macro-magnitudes. No logical protest, no factual refutation seems to be able to dislodge this fallacy.[3]

In the field of income distribution, where I have also worked, they persist in seeking some single magical number, arrived at by a sophisticated formula, that can capture the whole complexity of a distribution. But of course no single number can do all this work. Thus Gini's average (as we should all learn to call it, since the word 'coefficient' is only there to intimidate us) neglects the all-important extremes and is virtually useless for policy purposes in comparison with an array of quantile ratios (Wiles 1974, pp. 7–12). 'What you want,' a distinguished econometrician once said to me in a seminar, 'is to find a single number that sums all that up'. 'Speak,' I replied, 'for yourself, Terence'.

It is clear to me that Terence Gorman does not live on my sublunary level, and he does not know what econometricians do. Indeed he seems not to be interested in such a question: witness his inability here to detect methodological discussion in the guise of factual complaints about economists' behaviour. Thus he pays no attention to how Mueller, in his very large experience of them, says economists who specialize in his field react to his non-profit maximizing enterprises. He thinks it enough to say that he personally is not surprised by Mueller's findings and has read the – wholly non neo-classical – basic works himself. All he has demonstrated is his own unorthodoxy, good sense and wide interest (generated in his days as a Birmingham *mafioso*), and alas his more recently developed remoteness from the economic scene. It is appropriate to wonder again at that transformation. Above all his whole claim that 'econometrics is the methodology of economics' runs counter to elementary factual observation. If any one, it is Friedman (1953) who has laid down the most widely used methods.

This latter is exactly Neild's complaint, and this factual influence of our *actual* methodology on ourselves, and through us on the outside world seems to be beyond Terence's intellectual horizon. For I did and do think (*pace* his note 33) that Neild's paper touches on the essence of our book – and had to fight to get it included! It is precisely on neoclassicism taken to an extreme (general equilibrium theory) that monetarism rests. Therefore that theory is responsible for millions of unemployed.

What econometricians ought to do Terence in part knows well and says authoritatively, and in part, considering his own reverence for elegance and disrespect for fact, does not know. This book, however, is mainly about what people do.

Notes

[1] One correction on a 'point of order': note 23. I never told Terence that I had removed, and I have not in fact removed, the apparent contradiction between my claims that young economists are afraid of old ones (who brandish SRPs at them and sit on promotion committees), and that old ones are afraid of the young ones (who are technically better equipped). Both points are true. The result is a 'delicate balance of terror', and a spiralling 'arms race' in economic methodology.

[2] Their unity is described as 'pompous nonsense' in note 35.

[3] Strictly the fallacy is that the initial upturn is dictated by either the Gosplan or economic events, as opposed to a voting shift in the Politburo. Thereafter the course of the fluctuation is indeed heavily endogenous (cf. Wiles 1982). This reminds me to acknowledge wisdom wherever it is found. Towards the end of section 3 Terence points out that the spread of mathematics increases the quantity of interdisciplinary work. He is very right: it even aids détente. Communist mathematical economics is virtually indistinguishable from capitalist – no compliment, of course, is implied to anybody.

Epilogue:
The Role of Theory

PETER WILES

> It would be no answer to me to say that men were ignorant of the
> best and cheapest way of conducting their business and paying
> their debts, because *that is a question of fact not of science*, and
> might be urged against almost every proposition in Political
> Economy. (David Ricardo, letter to Thomas Malthus, 22 October
> 1811. Works, Vol. vi, p. 64) [my italics]

My role as editor casts me as, in the language of the preface,
'extremely worried'. Here is my personal attempt to extract the
essence of that point of view; in the light of what was said (in the
first three sections of this chapter); and for the rest to indicate the
main lacunae in the book as a whole – for there was no space to
make out the whole indictment at length. The rule against thun-
derous generalities is still observed – but by being too briefly particular about several different things.

Our Disrespect for Fact

The main thing that is wrong with economics is its disrespect for
fact. This book can be justly summed up in that one sentence.[1]

This disrespect shows up in many ways: failure to gather
primary data; straightforward neglect of the established results of
factual research when someone else, whom we cannot prevent,
has gathered them (Mueller here); use of axioms (p. 308); excessive honour for 'absolute', self-generating theory (p. 308–11);
persistence in believing worn-out paradigms (this whole book);
preference for algebra over arithmetic; interest in puzzles not
problems (e.g. general equilibrium and not the full-cost principle); use of 'stylized facts', (i.e. convenient half-truths – p. 311).

Ideology

There is one other, even less creditable, form of disrespect for facts, which afflicts not all of us but a good number: ideological bias. At the conference, politely, too little was said about ideology, and I have written elsewhere about it at length (1979–80). This passage must therefore be brief, however overriding the importance of the subject.

An ideology is much more anti-scientific than a mere paradigm. It is a connected group of propositions, some of them seemingly factual, that (1) appear to explain a very great deal, (2) have a heavy normative content, (3) carry a strong emotional charge. Mainstream economics originated in, and has in its Chicago-monetarist form reverted to, the *laissez-faire*/individualist/capitalist/anti-state ideology. This was and is a faith, capable of inspiring millions. A constituent part used to be the promise of universal peace (with the demise of Mercantilism) and substantial income equalization (with the final liquidation of 'feudal' privilege). But the rise of Communism has obscured the goal of peace and the rise of 'unprivileged' capitalist millionaires, precisely as a result of *laissez-faire* plus inheritance, has rendered equality an unassimilable element. The faith is now conservative, and so marginally less persuasive.

Ordinary working economists, especially of the younger generation, have no time, when working for tenure, to lift their noses above the grindstone, and so little idea of the articles of this faith. Many do not subscribe to even a majority of them. But others do; and all, by using the methodology and so liberating the theoreticians from the facts, are willy-nilly participants in this vast modern movement of ideas. For in the stratosphere a new minuet is being danced by shimmering concepts, most of them old, to be sure, but all in glorious new algebraical raiment.

Let me enumerate these concepts (with my own comments in square brackets):

Laissez-faire, or the state is your enemy and competition in fact works everywhere it is allowed to;
only one thing must your enemy do for you: control the quantity of money;
this stops inflation, and that is all it does, because:

unemployment is voluntary and so beyond control [i.e. money doesn't matter!];

anyway unemployment is mainly search [which is a form of value added like a commercial traveller's work];

general equilibrium is a good thing, and must be sought;

the market, even many interconnected markets, are stable if left alone;

externalities are small;

monopolies don't matter if private because they are all very weak; indeed the state virtually creates them [it is therefore bad manners to say much about trade unions];

competition is thus for practical purposes perfect;

optimal resource allocation matters passionately [and increases wealth more than fuller employment or higher investment];

taxes, which nourish your enemy, also diminish production [because the supply curve of labour is positively sloped];

therefore public services must be cut;

anyway almost all public services can in fact be efficiently privatized;

income and wealth distribution between persons are unimportant subjects [i.e. justice is justice in exchange: the factors of production should get out what they put in];

crime, education and having children are everyday human activities, therefore part of microeconomics [*homo economicus sum: humani nihil a me alienum puto*].

'Practical men,' one might conclude, 'who believe themselves to be quite exempt from any intellectual influences, are usually the slaves' of some living economist. The intellectual whirligig has accelerated.

An ideology needs methodological protection; people must be persuaded to wear blinkers so that they cannot see the fundamental factual flaws but may pursue instead minor developments from the given set of doctrines, according to the SRP (see note 6). Such a protective methodology may be deliberately adopted (e.g. Platonism by the Gnostics, Hegelianism by the Marxists), or it can be honestly stumbled upon: and this was the case of Ricardo. But once it is in place it acts to preserve the ideology and so becomes a part of it.

Keynesians, being on the whole less ideological, are also more prepared to throw Ricardo over. But his methodology is powerful, their own master's trumpet had a most uncertain sound (see pp. 303 and 305), and their emancipation has been very slow. This is in no small part due to the great *law of sunk intellectual capital*: what has been learned in youth will be taught in age.

Our Uniqueness in the History of Science

The state of modern economics taxes past breaking point the imaginations and the various doctrines of the best historians of science. These scholars, however, are among the least historical of historians. Each of them seems to have his Procrustean law(s) of scientific history, to which the actual course of intellectual events among those fallible human beings who constitute the community responsible for a discipline, must fit or be fitted. But in fact the actual course of the history of a science fits none of these preconceptions. Without going too far afield, we shall stick in what follows to the two most recent giants, Kuhn and Lakatos.

Scientists are human beings; therefore they behave badly. Scientists live in history; therefore their badness varies. The history of science is history; therefore it should describe both disaster and triumph, both bad men like Schmoller[2] and good men like Barrow.[3] *It is perfectly possible for a science to be sick*, and ours is now.

The concept of a sick discipline (I shall use this weaker and less loaded word) will seem far-fetched and unnecessary. But this is only because historians of science have grossly neglected this possibility since they concentrate on the logical, 'internal'[4] development of bodies of knowledge, and on ultimate success, which must certainly be logical, and 'internal' as defined. But this concentration leads them to neglect the frequent doldrums, when nothing much happens, mainly because of some 'external' factor.

The history of science is written by people who feel themselves inferior to scientists; therefore it is favourable to them. Thus both Kuhn's paradigm[5] and Lakatos's 'scientific research programme' (SRP)[6] *describe* scientific action. Their authors fail to say whether they are also *prescribing* it. The answer seems to be that they are – but they should not be. Science has no need of paradigms or SRPs. They are both concessions to human weaknesses in the scientific community, which substitute for truth habit, and for free enterprise the power of the old over the young. They are both inferior to Popper's 'falsificationism',[7] which is purely prescriptive and makes no such concessions.

We, the hard core of objectors, are 'extremely worried' by the pre-Popperian, nay the pre-Galilean, the absolutely scholastic, state of our methodology. We struggle hard to upgrade it, and now along come Kuhn, Lakatos and Feyerabend – or Hollis here – to tell us that anything goes. In the most important respect, post- and pre-Popperian are indistinguishable. Our particular sickness is opposition to falsification, i.e. disrespect for fact; and an almost religious reluctance to challenge existing paradigms. To the new laxist methodologists this is merely one of the many permissible ways of conducting a science. It is not surprising to find neo-classicists like Hart (here, p. 189) quote Kuhn in their own support.

The current state of studies in methodology leaves us without concepts to deal with the case of economics. Neo-classical theory is indeed a research programme, and a highly fertile, by no means exhausted, one. But it is a 'mathematical', not a 'scientific', research programme. It grows upon itself, an inverted pyramid of elegant and complicated entailments: each one – without sarcasm – worth tenure or promotion, but resting ultimately upon the single 'stylized fact' (i.e. half-truth, see p. 311): homo economicus. Fertility and degeneracy are not opposed: consider all the 'epicycles' developed to protect the original simple statements that the quantity of money is all-important, or that corporations maximize their profits, or that the sun and the planets all go round the earth.

I do not mean by this sickness the state of every discipline just before a paradigm change. It was not sick to believe in epicycles or phlogiston: those were honest errors. But Soviet biology was sick under Lysenko, for obvious reasons. Psychoanalysis, and to a lesser extent psychology in general, have for long resisted all tests, and are only now undergoing a painful but honourable self-criticism. For Freud, to take a famous psychologist almost at random, disrespect for fact was almost a methodology in itself. Still more to the point, German economics under Schmoller was sick – and this, to repeat, is described in every elementary history of economic thought. Sickness, in this context, is organized error.

Theory and the Social Structure of the Discipline

Secretly many economists ask themselves, ought I to worry about methodology? is it good for my career? consonant with my place in the intellectual pecking order? The answer is no. Would it not interfere with my grinding out of printable articles, even destroy my self-confidence? The answer is yes.

The reason is that the agreed elite of the discipline is happy enough with its methodology. It is difficult and exacting to learn: it sorts out the men from the boys easily, with no doubt and little effort. So the theoretical Establishment can continue to get papers published, award PhDs and apply successfully for research grants within the present conventions. The defence and elaboration of degenerating SRPs is most stimulating to publication!

Applied work by such people either uses their latest theoretical findings or is of some interest – never both. In either case it is of course good since these people are our best brains. The fact that the work they turn out is good even when they stray from the SRP and say something useful, is in an important way a misfortune. It serves to protect the neo-classical SRP, and makes it appear a generator of interesting propositions.[8]

It follows that while discussing methodology is a possible pas-time for the old and distinguished, Hahn is not wrong in saying (1973) that critics of abstraction and general-equilibrium theory 'cannot understand what the best minds in their subject are say-ing'. I am not opposed altogether to this claim, however arrogant it may seem. For if the truth itself is arrogant it must still be stated.

The corollary is that a systematic attack on neo-classicism from within the discipline, such as this book, is probably being con-ducted by inferior minds. Whom the cap fits, let him wear it. I shall at least try it on, speaking for myself alone. I am a very in-ferior mathematician, and always the one to protest at seminars that the blackboard be not rubbed clear yet awhile. I feel no superiority at all when arguing about neutral matters, e.g. on an administrative committee. But none of this makes it impossible that better minds than mine should be collectively pursuing some will o' the wisp which only they have the agility to keep up with, but which the mere accident of having become a Sovietologist at an early age enables me to see for what it is. After all the best minds of the Middle Ages were preoccupied with Scholasticism.

Controversy is good, the bandying of personalities however is discourteous and deservedly counter-productive. Yet the trouble is that our methodology, infinitely more than our politics, defines us. To quote myself:

> His methodology *defines* a scientist, an academic, any sort of intellectual . . . In sum, *le style c'est l'homme*. But what is style? Why, simply a short, obsolete word for methodology. (1979–80, p. 157)

It is, then, simply not possible to discuss this subject honestly without urging people to stop being who they are and become someone else. Methodology, unlike any proper science, is inescapably normative at bottom. It goes straight to the jugular of the scientist's own life-style, and says Thou Shalt Not.

It should not have to be added that no hint of corruption, conscious conspiracy or personal oppression is being made, because none would have the least basis in fact. Among honourable people *déformation professionnelle* has been enough.

The 'political sociology' of this matter has been so well expressed by Benjamin Ward that we need but quote him:

> Once one accepts the notion that a science is a social system, it is hard to avoid the prospect that there are instruments available to make it worth a scientist's while to do one thing and costly to do another. In the case of economics it is easy enough to see what the instruments are, though not quite so easy to get a feel for the extent to which they are applied in practice . . .
>
> First, and most obvious of all, an economist may choose his activities because of a primary desire to improve economic science . . .
>
> A second motivation may be simple ambition. An economist who wishes to get ahead is encouraged by the reward system to simulate as closely as possible the choices of a selfless scientist. This does not produce the same result, however. The careerist is likely to get into administration early in his career; he may try to team up with a 'selfless' or at least more competent type in order to raise the average quality of the work attributed to him. And perhaps most important, he is relatively more strongly oriented toward the ingenuity of his solutions and less toward genuine advancement of the science.

Despite these careerist possibilities, there is a surprisingly good match between intrinsically and extrinsically motivated behaviors in economics, and apparently in most normal science, as compared with many other social systems. The reason for this is that the censors who eliminate from professional consideration some work and who allocate praise among the acceptable studies, are themselves extremely competent. Indeed, they tend to be among the leaders of the profession . . .

The power inherent in this system of quality control within the economics profession is obviously very great. The discipline's censors occupy leading posts in economics departments at the major institutions, and their students and lesser confreres occupy similar posts at nearly all the universities that train new PhDs. The lion's share of appointment and dismissal power has been vested in the departments themselves at these institutions. Any economist with serious hopes of obtaining a tenured position in one of these departments will soon be made aware of the criteria by which he is to be judged. In a word, he is expected to become a normal economic scientist.

Of course it is not true, as the last paragraph may seem to imply, that this decision as to whether to become a normal science economist is made at the stage in his career at which the economist has obtained his last degree. For, as in all normal sciences, the entire academic program, beginning usually at the undergraduate level but certainly at the graduate, consists of indoctrination in the ideas and techniques of the science. As much as anything, this is a self-selection process. Those who do not accept the basic ideas of the science will not proceed very far with its study . . . Those who drop out of the system, at least in the author's experience, are not typically intellectual failures. Rather they are those who have become 'turned off,' and their most common complaint is lack of relevance, not difficulty. (Ward, 1972. pp. 28–30)

We must indeed go a little further than Ward:

There is a vicious spiral here. The young, knowing what is good for them, have learned everything better, and the old are afraid of them. Nor are these [appointments] committees merely conservative or out to protect their own intellectual capital; there is also a large element of convenience and time-saving. For the mastery of this very advanced and demanding methodology is an extremely convenient criterion for such committees. If a candidate possesses such mastery, meetings are shortened and controversy stilled. Everybody knows he has it; frauds are easily detected. This writer, on the other hand, does not have such mastery, but pleads regularly that an improved knowledge of the Polish language is an obvious priority over mathematics in his special case – a claim invariably treated as a joke, for some reason. Consequently, people like him cannot be so easily judged. Fraud is easier. Indeed, we can only be certain of the value of such candidates after they have aged – but that renders the whole academic career so uncertain that they abandon it. (Wiles, 1979–80, p. 169)

Defects common to all sciences must here be omitted. I think in particular of 'publish or perish'. Hundreds of thousands, perhaps millions, of people throughout the world are refused appointment or promotion unless they contrive to have something printed over their name. But of such a large number very many are, inevitably, mediocre, and ought to be teaching better instead – and being promoted for it. In any case the flood of articles and books is such that a scholar can read only an infinitesimal part of even the good stuff published in his field. Thus, taking a broad view of what is relevant and a narrow view of what is worth reading, and including accessible foreign languages, I read perhaps 1.3-thousandths of the annual output, and have read perhaps 2-thousandths of the stock, of Sovietological economics. Or again, the system of peer review before publication causes conservatism, above all methodological. But these are large topics often dealt with, and economics is not specially guilty.

There is vastly too little political sociology in Kuhn and Lakatos. Thus in Latsis's 1976 book, which is dedicated to Lakatos and handles also Kuhn at length, all references to 'people of power', unscrupulous propagandists, etc., concern outsiders. Why? What protects the morals of scientists and academics? Have they, within their own bailiwick, no power? Have they no personal imperfections?

A political sociology of Academe is not, it should be noted, the sociology of knowledge, but of ignorance. Science should be so conducted that there is no valid sociology of knowledge. Indeed this branch of learning, insofar as it is itself validly conducted, is about scientists' behaviour, not science. There are many errors, and there is indeed a sociology of their persistence. There is also the sociology of truth-avoidance: research into unimportant or uncontroversial matters, i.e. the acceptance of the SRPs of influential people. But there is not, strictly speaking, any sociology of knowledge at all, and the term is a misnomer. There may, above all, be facts scientists will not take into account, but there are none they should not. Obedience to the proper rules makes for a dull and trivial sociology of knowledge, so all scientists should aim to make it dull and trivial.

A Lakatosian SRP seems to be a dynamized Kuhnian paradigm with an attached methodology. The old are saying to the young, 'Here is our basic way of looking at the world, and here are the ways in which we think, conduct experiments, etc. A great deal remains to be discovered along these lines, which will prove us to have been genial, seminal, prescient. Do that, and we'll promote you.' In other words an SRP is an even worse straitjacket than a paradigm.

For all his refreshing scepticism, Imre Lakatos seems not to have understood this. It is quite one thing to use the concept of the SRP to understand the history of science; indeed as a behavioural generalization about scientists it is indispensable. But it is quite another to recommend it. Lakatosian SRPs, like Kuhnian paradigms, are simply bad scientific habits, except as guides to the mediocre. The best young people should never have such demands made upon them: just the contrary, they should be instructed to question everything.

But did not Apriorism Succeed in the Past?

First, Ricardo did indeed contribute 'rent' and 'comparative cost'; so he may be forgiven his pioneering errors on every single other matter. There have been two other, more remarkable successes of the *a priori* methodology: marginalism in 1871, Keynes in 1936.

These great successes of apriorism cannot be denied. But they are very exceptional in the history of science, and we have no reason to expect their repetition. Moreover, if we examine them with care they embody important new empirical content. Marginal utility does diminish: this is a fact, and it takes an economist somehow to dress it up as an *a priori* proposition.[9] Here we have one of the very few propositions in our discipline which is important for its consequences but simultaneously in accordance with reality. Yet with almost unanimous masochism we reject the bonanza and try to reduce diminishing marginal utility to a logical trick.

For the rest, the marginalist revolution was what we must call 'Occamical': it used Occam's Razor[10] on a number of superfluous theories, like the treatment of monopolistic prices as a separate case, and the tripartite laws of distribution. These special cases were like Ptolemy's epicycles, and the marginalist pioneers resembled Copernicus, who contributed few facts but substituted for all that a single grand logical simplicity.[11] It should therefore not surprise us that marginalism included massive new aprioristic errors: the downgrading of the supply curve, e.g. in Wicksteed and Menger.

Keynes's empirical *preoccupation* is there for all to see. But his empirical *content* is low. He made little detailed study of fact, and certainly used, nay misused, the *a priori* method. He was, again, far from 'Occamical': he shamelessly multiplied concepts. He also misused algebra, tricking himself into such a monstrosity as the instantaneous multiplier (Wiles, 1968, pp. 57–8). He based much of his General Theory on the confusion of *ex ante* and *ex post*, and could not make up his mind about the logical status of 'Saving = investment'. All these errors are so quintessentially Ricardian that we are apt to say he made no methodological changes. But that is not true: *he rejected the paradigm, and put no other in its place; and this is why the neo-classical counter-revolution has almost won.*

Facts Without Theories and Sciences Without Paradigms

Paradigms flourish, but are better dispensed with. The trouble with modern methodologists is that they seek only to understand, and never – by some private *déformation professionnelle* – to judge. Methodological laxism at work includes slipping graciously into the language of the 'natives' and using their concepts as if they were the only ones. Thus Hollis here (my comments in square brackets; my italics): 'Without a *dynamic model* [why not 'thorough empirical knowledge'?] of changes (such as have occurred in the last half-century), we do not know which *tautologies* [why not 'acceptable theories'? – for a theory cannot possibly be a tautology] of microtheory to apply in understanding the states of an economy' (p. 28). 'It is at present unclear, methodologically speaking, what is to be best *assumed* under the heading of 'knowledge'; and the *need to assume something*, where physics assumes nothing, should make us wonder whether a science of action is in the same line of work as a science of nature' (p. 28). But why assume anything? Economics is about facts, the same as physics; only the facts are much more difficult and labile. Untested assumptions are probably false. *All valid methodologies are one*, in the sense that the more complicated include the less (cf. Blaug here).

Methodologists are not responsible for scientific failures, say like the present world slump, of which monetarism is in the writer's opinion the main cause. As a purer economist he feels an aliquot part of the total guilt on his back. He could have turned back from the Soviet economy and devoted his time to the disproof of monetarism, but he preferred easy success. Rod Cross on the other hand is, for all his superior technique, more of a philosopher than an economist. Within these very pages he exemplifies the excessive tolerance of his trade: 'There is no falsification before the emergence of a better theory' – he quotes Lakatos and lets it stand.

But there is! We were promised stable prices and equally full employment through mere monetary restriction. But all the historical evidence was against this, and the promise was not fulfilled, just as many of us predicted. This simple fact, this empirical refutation of monetarism, does not prove some other theory right. A part of Keynesianism has indeed been falsified by the perpetual inflation in this country since 1968; but you do not have to be a Keynesian (nor do I feel myself so), or to have any positive theory whatever, in order to refute the main theses of monetarism. All you need to do is read the newspapers.

Or again (Cross in chapter 4), 'we are enjoined to prefer some theory T_1 to another theory T_2 if $C(T_1) > C(T_2)$ . . .' Very right, but where is the simpler proposition? – if T_2 persistently offends, even after adjustment, against some fact, just one fact, it must be rejected anyway. We should indeed prefer T_1 if it exists, *but it does not have to exist.* If you lose your way in Oxford because you are using a map of Cambridge, it is enough to explain your predicament to see that the map is indeed of Cambridge, and you will be ready humbly to ask your way. Buying a map of Oxford is a separate activity – and perhaps none is available.

'Facts not admitted unless accompanied by respectable hypotheses. Should the latter fail to satisfy the authorities, both will be requested to leave the premises immediately' (Haynes, 1980). This inverts the right order of science. It is a *nul homme sans seigneur* of the mind, subordinating the serfs of fact to the barons of theory. There is of course no requirement whatsoever that an observation should be comfortable or conformable. All it has to do is to be true, and it is for the mind to adapt itself.

It is not quite the same doctrine, but a similar attitude when Cross (p. 88) asserts that 'the facts themselves are theory-laden', and Hollis agrees. This seems to be excessively sophisticated and deeply misleading. *Primary* facts are not theory-laden at all. Thus in Cross's example either 'those not in jobs are not actively seeking work' or they are; and either those 'registered as seeking work' are telling the truth or they are not. These are not theoretical questions, though some theory may have suggested them. One can make a lot of trouble over the assertion 'he is lying' since 'his' state of mind is not a primary fact to any outside observer; but 'he is not telling the truth' is a fairly simple primary fact. Again an index of production is very far indeed from a primary fact, but the conformity or otherwise of its weights with standard statistical practice is such a fact. All these difficulties have been much exaggerated – no doubt in order to get away from Popper.

Another way to suppress facts is to have a paradigm. Now Keynes rejected homo economicus[12] and many other orthodox 'hypotheses inappropriate to the facts' (1936, p. 371) for a number of scattered empirical observations, not always soundly based: sticky wages; equilibrium with unemployment; a marginal propensity to save greater than the average; money illusion; 'animal spirits' as an explanation of investment, etc. Indeed these almost might as well be called assumptions. Above all he made little attempt to explain or co-ordinate them. Simultaneously he refused to incorporate, or to say that he had not incorporated, imperfect competition or administered prices. So, as is notorious, he left himself *without a microeconomic base, i.e. with no paradigm.* He saw that, taken seriously, the orthodox paradigm leads to monetarism.

A house built on sand . . . many have said. But what he said was not untrue. Though it was only casual empiricism it was empiricism, and so a much less sandy foundation than homo economicus. Yet instead of elaborating or correcting this base with more research we have gone back to our tidy and obsessive fantasy. Are wages sticky? – let us dream up contracts that no one actually signs. Is money illusion irrational? – never mind if it reflects people's actual state of mind (for a time)[13] let us substitute rational expectations which no one checks empirically. Are animal spirits[14] indeterminate? – let us invent half a dozen determinate theories of investment, all of them profit-maximizing and all of them wrong. Is unemployment a little large to seem voluntary?[14a] – let us invent 'search', and have the proletariat *cyclically* decide to give up their wages in order to spend their days looking for betterment opportunities they know aren't there.[15]

Keynes, then, pointed to the testing of our paradigm, but probably himself thought we could all rub along without one. We have taken up neither challenge, and must therefore be ranked close to the bottom among scientists. For unsatisfactory as Kuhnian paradigms and Lakatosian SRPs are as normative guides to science they are greatly superior to the neo-classical economics, since their hard-core, protected theories at least have survived one bout of direct empirical testing: the one that accompanied their birth. It is not so bad to declare holy that which once went through the fire. But the hard core of economics has never been through any fire.

This hard core should therefore now be tested to destruction. It is important to see that it may substantially survive, but that if and where it doesn't we shall have no paradigm. It is my personal belief that the survival will be *merely* substantial, and that no other paradigm as good will be thought up (and tested!). We shall then have a science with a *limping paradigm*. E.g. *homo* will not be *economicus* in respect of career choice, imperfect competitors will not maximize their profits when they set prices, trade union leaders will have irrational expectations, or no expectations, about future prices, etc., etc.; but meantime many parts of the neo-classical building will survive, like terrace housing part of which has survived bomb damage.

Let us avoid the 'laws of scientific history' since hitherto they have all been wrong. The revolution that *we* need *now* is 'anti-Occamical': *entia sunt multiplicanda, sed non praeter necessitatem.*

Gradations of Applicability of the Paradigm

The neo-classical holist will find such a situation intolerable, for he had rather be tidy than true. But I myself have always cheerfully habited such a structure; assuming notably, on vaguely empirical grounds, homo to be economicus in perfectly competitive markets. This enables me to switch in, when discussing peasants and stockbrokers, a whole circuit of neo-classical reasoning in contexts where its assumptions seem to be empirically true. There is no logical inconsistency, and a proper respect for fact, if I simultaneously reject the neo-classical analysis of oligopoly and monopoly, including the assumption that homo is economicus in these environments.

It is in this eclectic spirit that development economics and Sovietology have always proceeded. The neo-classical paradigm is so manifestly a bad fit that it is not even contemplated. Ward (1972, p. 10) notes how low such 'sub-disciplines' are on the social pecking order. This is not because they are not successful. On the contrary they are a great deal more successful. But the reason for their success is the same as the reason for their social inferiority: they don't stick to the paradigm or SRP. Our Establishment has evidently never heard of hybrid vigour.

Other 'options' are of even greater interest, and yet more disputable. 'Industrial' economists tend to apply the neo-classical paradigm, without question, to facts about capitalist industry. 'Business' economists never really specialized in economics, and study facts about capitalist industry without regard to the paradigm: e.g. Jackson, 1982. So they are more objective. If 'agricultural' economists study agriculture in poor countries, they come under 'development'; if in rich ones, they present a very interesting case. They have no reason to be dissatisfied with the neo-classical paradigm, since it has primarily been evolved with them in mind. So with a good conscience they assume perfect competition and profit maximization, use ordinary supply-and-demand diagrams, and forget about the managerial revolution. This happy but legitimate state of affairs extends to the Common Agricultural Policy of the EEC.

What Is Theory and What Ought It To Be?

There is no term more emotionally loaded and more definitionally vague than 'theory'. I do not know myself what it means, but note that it has been used, *inter alia*, as follows:

(1) a sentence in the indicative mood that is neither normative nor based on any observation, nor offered for testing, i.e. an assumption;
(2) a hypothesis, and so something to be immediately tested by observation;
(3) an abstraction;
(4) an axiom;
(5) a normative proposition; and even
(6) an empirically founded generalization (disliked by the speaker).

It can mean, of course, any non-self-contradictory combination of one or more than one of these types; and much else besides.

Let us set aside number 6 as a lexical misuse. Number 5 speaks for itself as something of different logical type. As to number 4, an axiom is only an assumption I forbid you to challenge. There is therefore no place for axioms in economics or in any would-be science.[16]

We are left with some combination of numbers 1 to 3. Each is defensible and useful in its place. In particular without *abstraction* from irrelevant detail science is impossible. It may even be necessary to abstract from things one suspects to be very important. All this amounts to *starting* any thought experiment with a *ceteris paribus* clause; and of course thought experiments are necessary where laboratories are impossible or too expensive. The clause must later be relaxed, just as laboratory conditions must be relaxed. But in economics the wrong things are often, nay usually, abstracted from; and the *ceteris paribus* clause often includes the very variable that should be the main object of research. A prime example of this is unemployment in the works of monetarists. Often indeed the *ceteris paribus* clause is never relaxed at all; so the theory remains dead letter – not that that stops people from believing it.

Good theory is the rightful aim of much science. The connotation only of the word is bad: undue compactness, apriorism, remoteness from observation, advanced methods for their own sake and intellectual superiority. A good theory is very useful, because it tells us a lot in a few words, even if it is difficult to understand. A bad theory contradicts some fact – but if it contains many propositions most of them will survive a few such contradictions

(Cross in chapter 4). There is however no way in which a proposition can be 'true in theory but false in practice.'

Good theory may not use advanced methods, indeed applied science may easily be forced by its circumstances well 'ahead' of theory. For *Occam's Razor applies also to methods*, and there is no contesting the truth of O'Brien (1975, pp. 90–1):

> The majority of the profession would be concerned then with developing the 'ground floor' of the theoretical structure so that in time it might be strong enough to bear some upper floors. This would be a fruitful exercise; at the moment only those who shoot from the ground floor ever seem to hit the target. In preparation for this lecture I read some of the reminiscences of economic advisers: and universally they seemed to have felt that it was the ground floor which was viable.[17] But strong support for such an argument can be gained from reading H.G. Johnson's inaugural lecture at LSE 'The Economic Approach to Social Questions' (1968). For here we find a virtuoso applying the tools of economic theory to social problems: and without exception we find him using only those to be found in the ground floor of the building (even though some of them are recent additions to that floor).

It is common to complain that the *prestige hierarchy* within the discipline (theory > application > history) is vicious. But that is the natural hierarchy within nearly all intellectual disciplines, since they normally do rest and always should rest on good theory. What is wrong with us is that *our* theory is bad: it throws no light on practical problems, it is sterile except of itself (which it reproduces like rabbits), it protects itself against being tested. To say this is not to be philistine or to shield one's own incompetence in advanced methods, or to lay down an anti-theoretical rule for the conduct of science in general. It is to take a historical and particular stand about the pathology of economic 'science' in 1983. The complaint is not against the intrinsic worthwhileness of all theory, but against that of the theory that we are supplied with, and against its dominance over other activities.

Moreover there are two items absent from the hierarchy: discovery and testing. In conformity with most methodologists, we say little here about discovery, since hunches – and it is hunches we need, not paradigms – cannot be legislated for. *Spiritus flat ubi vult*: methodology should no doubt be, but is not, about either factual or theoretical discovery.[18] But it is very much about testing. To test is not to apply, nor is it to theorize. The prestige hierarchy should begin with discovery and testing, while theory comes third. There is, after all, no shortage of ideas!

So if discovery must remain for us here a closed book, the same is not true of testing. This subject needs here one important methodological observation: it is not logically possible to test a new hypothesis without testing all one's old assumptions. For the test assembles: (1) the old assumptions (in their normal form of accepted theories), (2) the old facts that supported the old assumptions, and (3) the new hypothesis. It confronts *this whole complex* with (4) the new facts, the ascertainment of which constitutes the test. (1), (2), (3) and (4) are a logically interconnected whole. If, God willing, there is no contradiction anywhere, the new hypothesis *and the old assumptions* have not been falsified – and there is no reason to re-examine the old facts either. But if there is a contradiction we have only pragmatic reasons for rejecting the new hypothesis or re-examining the new facts rather than the old ones. The main thing is, they form a logical whole and something has to give. Every test of a conclusion also tests the premises.[19]

Turning now to applied economics, strictly to 'apply' is to accept the edicts of theory, and to use them to explain some phenomenon, or to give advice. This is indeed a junior activity, however honourable and demanding. But what is in common parlance called 'applied' often includes new, *ad hoc*, theoretical ideas, which may or may not be orthodox. For in the middle of some applied study one suddenly discovers the need for new theory, and has to develop it oneself (cf. Wiles, 1961, p. 105). Often the last people to go to are the professional theorists, who are very seldom interested in theorizing for a currently important problem, but rather in theorizing about other theories. Thus the applied economist is quite as likely to be theoretically original as the pure theorist. On the other hand his work is also often unexciting and backbreaking: the getting together of a lot of facts, hard to collect, and then their arrangement in ways suitable for the asking of 'relevant' questions. Bureaucratic, or entrepreneurial, skills become very important. Intuition plays as great a role as ever, but it is a different sort of intuition. Such skills should also be rewarded. Only one such economist (Simon Kuznets) ever received the Nobel Prize.

Yet the activity itself of theorizing is more fun, and an article on it is more quickly finished. Facts can be left to others or else 'stylized facts' (below) can be tailor-made to suit the theories.

A word on stylized facts, and similar phenomena. The notion that facts are somehow important in science cannot quite be shaken off. Economic theorists have developed four defensive reactions.

(1) They call their assumptions themselves 'stylized facts'. A stylized fact is what the theorist finds it convenient to believe that his favourite empiricist has probably established. Stylized facts tend to be untrue: e.g. the lognormality of income distribution; the constancy of the capital/output ratio. Their untruth is not surprising, since their *raison d'être* is to be convenient for a theory.

(2) Contrary facts are described as 'puzzling'. This word implies 'It's trivial, but even so we're working on it.' But actually 'we' are not working in good faith on the fact, but rather on the further sealing off of the theory.

(3) The new category of 'anecdote' has been invented. The 'anecdote' is a single, true, observation that has not yet been repeated under laboratory conditions. It is usually a fact thought to be characteristic, nay even statistically average, within its category, by the objector (such as the author; e.g. a price in a recondite but not very imperfect market). The objector ordinarily has neither time nor professional interest in seeing if his single fact is typical. It is difficult to see why it should not be, but the theorist tells him that his fact is only an anecdote. Yet the GNP itself is but the sum of a billion or so anecdotes. It suffices that the word is vaguely pejorative; no research need then be done.

(4) Contrary facts that have been sufficiently researched to graduate from anecdotes, and remain puzzling, can still be given the neo-classical brush-off. It is complained that they are 'not accompanied by respectable hypotheses', and they are simply forgotten.[20]

In one way or another, then, our theories are not developed in response to needs arising from the real world or from demands of empirical students thereof. They are developed 'internally', and even also incestuously, breeding on each other and not on such facts as even economists discover.

An intellectual discipline, especially one conducted at the taxpayer's expense, should be conducted in a balanced, publicly auditable way: not as some *féodalité*. If falsificationism is rigorously enforced, as Blaug here suggests, it *will* – and here I disagree with his blandness – lead to the 'wholesale rejection of research programmes'. It will therefore have financial consequences for certain kinds of person. It should also, incidentally, lead to an increase in total funding, since serious economic research is so very expensive.

'Pure' Theory

How useful, we are bound to ask, is *any* pure theory? Pure theory is not the same at all as pure science. In the latter one investigates some factual problem, say of astronomy or economic history, that one knows cannot affect life on earth directly. In the former the problem is set by logic alone, and has, by my definition, no immediate factual answer. The Marxian Transformation Problem is an excellent example, and another is the question how Walrasian theory can (in the artificially assumed absence of transaction costs) account for the existence of money.

When we remember that pure theorists must eat, and that their great talents might have been diverted, this becomes a substantial question of social opportunity cost. When one takes into account risk, i.e. the mere vulgar question of how probable it is that the theory will ever be 'profitable' at all, and applies also a futurity discount (since that profit will not immediately accrue), it is not obvious that pure theory is worth paying for in any science. If it is nevertheless done, either this must be for the respectable reason that some individual wishes to do it for interest's sake, *i.e. without payment*; or else the state has 'misspecified his bonus function'. We note that in wartime the production of pure theory virtually ceases.

I deny, then, the 'strong grounds in academic freedom for protecting serious academic interests which may, like pure mathematics, have no relevance or relation to any kind of real- world fruitfulness of policy making' that lead Hutchison (chapter 1,

p. 14) to allow scientists to play around without even the hope of a (1) serious or (2) useful outcome. I am saying *as a taxpayer* that the public funding of science should be more sceptical and more Philistine. What people do after hours with their already earned income is their own affair – and the recognition of *that* sufficiently preserves academic freedom.[21] Freedom is the absence of human restraints, not the presence of state subsidies.

Theory's Unfulfilled Promises

Hutchison (p. 15) speaks of 'the record of unfulfilled promises of eventual, real-world fruitfulness'. Our post-war history is littered with much heralded breakthroughs that led nowhere in the end; and surely, case by case, no one should have been surprised.

Thus I remember how at Oxford in the late 1940s people began to attach enormous importance to Pareto-optimality, and to pride themselves on the contribution to social questions that this concept could make. But Pareto-optimality accepts as given some initial income distribution in which it makes minimal changes: therefore it is distributively of no interest. Or in Routh's (unpublished) words:

> A Pareto-optimum is said to obtain when nothing more can be given to the hungry, the cold, the ragged and the homeless without incommoding the glutton, the miser, the usurer and the play-boy

– and of course, let us be fair, vice versa.

Moreover, the movement towards Pareto-optimality is itself seldom Pareto-optimal. Thus in figure 7 an initial position A corresponds to a certain division of income and product among the consumers and (indirectly) the producers of goods X and Y but, despite being short of the production-possibility frontier, cannot yield to the equilibrium B without violating Pareto-optimality. Nor even can position C, which is at least on the frontier, since those who prefer X lose to those who prefer Y – and, indirectly, so do the producers of X to the producers of Y.

Again many ordinary acts, such as the drawing up of the state budget, cannot possibly be Pareto-optimal. It is also extremely unlikely that any large change in a market situation could be so (indeed C→B above might be such a change) – and that includes

Peter Wiles

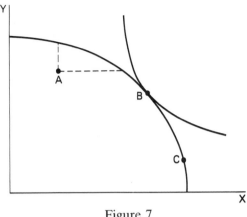

Figure 7

a long series of small changes under perfect competition, if they all go in one direction. To enforce the rule we must violate it. Moreover all this was just as obvious in 1949 as it is today. Yet so promising did this arid and abstract concept seem that welfare economics was narrowed down from its Pigovian connotation to just this small thing.

Another, much more trivial, example is 'factor-price equalization'. In 1948 Samuelson showed that free trade in goods could achieve this under very limiting assumptions. This was generally accepted at the time, e.g. in Oxford, to be a great intellectual event, and the race was on to relax these limitations and prove it more generally. The succession of attempts is beautifully described and the eventual failure of the enterprise is registered, by de Marchi (1976). But what if the attempts had succeeded? What is the policy result of proving that the relative wage-rates of three sorts of labour in five different countries will be equalized by free trade in commodities – provided, of course, that it does not result in complete specialization?! Is such equalization a great social goal? especially when we remember that this is the gross and not the net wage, and nothing whatever has been said about income-tax or household structure, so its distributive significance is minimal. Should we perhaps introduce protection in order to *avoid* such equalization? Such strategic questions were not posed at the outset of this scientific venture. The army of workers in this field were surely led by the

Noble Duke of York
[who] had ten thousand men.
He marched them up to the top of the hill
And he marched them down again.

The choice of SRPs needs a strong dose of common sense.

The Rejection of Subjective Evidence

Many have smiled at Cairnes's naïveté

> *The Economist starts with a knowledge of ultimate causes.* He is already, at the outset of his enterprise, in the position which the physicist only attains after ages of laborious research. If anyone doubts this, he has only to consider what the ultimate principles governing economic phenomena are . . . certain mental feelings and certain animal propensities in human beings; the physical conditions under which production takes place . . . (1875, p. 75; his italics)

He was naive, and especially about the use of 'physical conditions'. He was anti-mathematical yet simultaneously made apriorist noises – for the classical economists feared mathematization as the intrusion of empiricism! But on introspection was he actually wrong? Surely there *is* within each of us a fund of *empirical evidence* which we can, with caution, extract and use. Sometimes it confirms, sometimes it denies, homo economicus. It must of course be supplemented by *asking other people what they think.* One of the most curious features of our implicit methodology is the attitude that the economist or other researcher should not look into his own mind, because that is subjective; but he just might be permitted to look into other people's minds. Why? – for that is doubly subjective. Probably because if he interviews other minds he produces a statistic, and that excuses nearly anything. If he gives us a correlation coefficient we will forgive him the possibility that his sources were lying. The fact remains that if we look into our own mind there is *less* probability of error than if we ask someone else to look into his – and then copy down his answer wrongly (cf. Katona and Simon in Katona, 1979).

Of course it is nice to add the evidence from 'revealed preference', but too often we get bogged down in the immensity of the *ceteris paribus* clause, and sometimes also in technical econometric questions. There is not much to choose in practice between 'observed' and 'confessed' preference. The former avoids, to be sure, direct mendacity on the part of the observed; but it generates other and equal data-gathering problems.

Incidentally why is only an observed preference a revealed preference? – what else is a confessed preference? Jurisprudence is full to bursting with critiques of the value of confessions, and would ridicule the implication that they reveal nothing.

We are, then, constantly admonished to stick to observed preference. But to submit to this self-limitation is flatly to state that there is no true psychological school but behaviourism, and to throw out our sister social sciences' methodologies lock, stock and barrel. Behaviourism is not more scientific; it is never scientific to neglect data. It is not even more 'statistical', since of course introspection and interviewing both generate masses of quantifiable data.[22]

Similarly introspection is not *a priori* or Kantian. It was simply Kant's error to think so – if he did! Introspection does not reveal to us (or at least not to the writer) tremendous constraints like Kantian categories, but states of mind concerning quite vulgar matters, such as butter versus margarine. What is good for market research and investment intentions can hardly be inadmissible in other parts of economics. Diminishing marginal utility, to repeat, was originally established because it is an empirical fact based on introspection. Statistical observation, say by market researchers (what we here call observed preference), has many times confirmed it.

Our observed preference for 'observed preference' has, I believe, psychological origins. It is tough, mechanistic, inhuman, objective. *It makes us feel like natural scientists.* Now no doubt the latter have these qualities – nor are they misplaced in the study of non-human beings. But our best way to be like them would be to seek more facts, and to respect and empathize with the human beings we study, much as they do with inanimate matter. Simply to treat human beings as invariable physical objects is reductionism.[23]

Indeed among the most ideological words in our ideologically loaded discipline is the phrase 'price *mechanism*'. Inside a mechanism the units cannot express their individuality, learn, remember or combine. If they have any consciousness it is an epiphenomenon. The mechanism determines their behaviour altogether: they can only react. But inside a 'system' the units can do all these things. *Perfect competition is a mechanism, other market forms are systems.* The methodology of the natural sciences suffices for the former, and reductionism is genuinely in place, but in the other cases economics becomes a social science. To my knowledge, there is nothing like perfect competition in the other social sciences.[24]

Nay more, 'observed preference' supports the extremist position, that assumptions need not be tested, only conclusions. For we start from the ideological (or otherwise convenient) assumptions of homo economicus; we refuse to test them directly, by introspection, and we end up with empirical observations, to be sure, but observations very indirectly related to our sacred assumptions. These it is safe to test. They can always be reinterpreted if the results are embarrassing.

Homo Economicus, a Clinical View

In contrast with Hutchison's sole emphasis on expectations in chapter 1, I assert that homo economicus himself is often factually wrong and often right but misleading. I list first some cases of factual wrongness, with extreme brevity:

(1) The common practice of living a long time, dying at an unsurprising moment and yet leaving a great fortune; i.e. of not maximizing life-time consumption.[25] This is really only a very important case of:

(2) The gratuitous extension of family obligations beyond the 'anthropologically necessary': maintenance of able-bodied adult children, care of young cousins, nephews and nieces, etc. In Indian and Far Eastern cultures such behaviour *is* 'anthropologically necessary', so we must look at still further extensions of the family for instances of this same point. Moreover economics can in no way explain why these anthropological differences exist in the first place.

(3) Actions, including acts of consumption or leisure sacrifice, due to malice.[26] These, like (1) and (2), show man behaving not like a Leibnitian monad but like a human being, taking others' feelings into account.

(4) The failure of nearly everybody to engage in economic crime (theft, receipt of stolen goods, blackmail and bribery) even when it is safe.

(5) The failure of a large minority to engage in tax evasion, black production and black marketing, even when it is safe. But note here the many *national* differences, e.g. between Georgians and East Germans. Homo economicus further errs in having no nationality for religion (Wiles, 1981).

(6) Voting for left-wing parties when rich, or for right-wing parties when poor, even under *ceteris paribus* conditions such as the parties' similarity on foreign policy or constitutional issues.

(7) All *déformations professionnelles*, including Veblen's Instinct of Workmanship. Principal among these is the *technological snobbery* of Third World engineers, native or imported, who insist on inappropriate technology.[27]

(8) Working for charities at low or no pay (whereas giving to charities could genuinely be dismissed as a peculiar consumer taste).

(9) Corporate giving to charities contradicts corporate profit maximization; for corporations cannot consume, so corporatio economica must invest its surplus.

(10) Racial, sexual, political and religious discrimination when its victim is admitted to be of equal productivity or, as a consumer, to have equal effective demand – but not when there is good statistical reason to expect early retirement (e.g. of a woman marrying), or radical union leadership (e.g. by a communist). Such discrimination is really only a case of:

(11) 'Group rationality'. Cf. Marsden and Lévy-Garboua in chapter 5: let me only say that homo economicus could not indeed be guilty of such a thing, but since it undoubtedly exists it proves that men are not entirely rational. A good case of group rationality is profit-maximization by corporations (see p. 320).

(12) Price setting in imperfect markets, or at least a good deal of it (Wiles and Lee in chapters 8 and 9).

Many neo-classicists will admit that some of these items are indeed 'puzzling'. But they will reject most of them by availing themselves of the greatest of all neo-classical loopholes: calling an exception consumption instead of production. For example, an irrational 'means' item like racial discrimination at work becomes the 'ends' item of 'consuming' one's racial prejudices – and 'ends' are undiscussable to by the rules of the game.

I reject this altogether as a mere logical trick. We end up saying that men do what they like (which is vacuous) but are also acting neo-classically (which is false). Homo economicus started as selfish, materialistic and individualistic, through and through. He had a modest number of easily identifiable ends, and the means available were all distinct from them. It is scientifically useful that he remain so: an excellent heuristic (see note 6) device, which should never lie untried in any economic or quasi-economic practical situation – but quite likely to be factually wrong. Man has indeed tastes that it is not the economist's task to examine. Some of them – butter or margarine, income or leisure – present no philosophical problem, though they may be otherwise extremely important. Others – profit versus growth, individual versus group interest, career choice in general – are very grave problems. No talk of taste will cover up the unorthodox nature of these questions.

In this context, what is 'constrained' maximization? In his original and natural state homo economicus maximized unconstrainedly, except perhaps for the law – but in those days there were not many laws constraining economic behaviour, and it was commonly supposed that he would not respect a large body of detailed law.

Times have changed, and along with a vast development in the law many constraints have become standard in economic theory.

They are nearly all legal, traditional or ethical, which is as much as to say, they have been introduced in order to approach reality. Thus each one of them is a vote of no confidence by economic theorists in their one great basic assumption – a narrowing of the limits within which their work is useful, made by themselves. After all who would disagree that people maximize their profits or incomes *ceteris paribus*?! – or, it sometimes seems, *omnibus paribus*. Many constraints are 'epicycles'.

A heuristic that is *a priori* the only successful key to knowledge is no longer a heuristic but a shibboleth, and its product may easily be ignorance. If it never fails, some concealed definition, some cheating is at work. Many failures condemn a heuristic in one way, no failures in another. These things are useful tools and no more. The good scientist has as many heuristics as there are clubs in a golfer's bag.

A Division Amongst the Critics

But there are also merely apparent exceptions to the rule of homo economicus, which must be demoted to this rank after deeper analysis; and some of us prefer to emphasize these. The greatest of these is the *notion of corporatio economica. It does not follow from the strict neo-classical position that firms with more than one owner–manager maximize their profits.* The firm is a secondary construct and has no genuine or separate interest at all. If its pretended interests outweighed those of its managers and owners this would be a case of that very 'group rationality' that Lévy–Garboua rejects. A corporation with its own maximand is non-neoclassical.

It should not therefore be a matter for surprise that takeover bids are unprofitable (Mueller in chapter 6): they constitute growth, and therefore could merely serve the interests of individual managers in their own lifetime incomes. So far from contradicting the neo-classical economics, this is required by it: it would be a mystery if all takeover bids *were* profitable! – and this is Mueller's own position (p. 161). But such bids could also be a *déformation professionnelle* (point 7 on p. 318), and that really would be unorthodox. The paradox here is that modern neo-classicism, at least in its Chicago version, includes a deep prejudice in favour of *laissez-faire*, and it is this prejudice that Mueller has offended, as his choice of title indicates. From Adam Smith to John Stuart Mill and indeed Menger the classics would have been astounded. Just precisely the corporation was one of their *bêtes noires*: takeover bids would have made them apoplectic. *Laissez-faire* was an individualist doctrine until the 1850s, but it is now a capitalist, and indeed a trade-unionist, doctrine. Chicago has extended Adam Smith's blessings to these corporations, just when the individual requires the protection of the state against them.

Take the Japanese management's preference for lifetime employment and an internal labour market which it can control over an external one that would be dominated by non-company unions. This could be simply a recent and 'rational' social invention: an unsentimental profit-maximizing policy, not *yamato damashii* or feudal remnants at all. After all, from 1868 (the Meiji Restoration) to 1930 there were external labour markets, and lifetime employment was not a recognized ideal (Taira, 1970). But to read Taira more closely is to be persuaded that modern Japanese paternalism *is* in direct historical continuity with Tokugawa feudalism. Two threads are common: revulsion from class warfare and antagonistic relations between labour and capital, and deep unwillingness to accept a freely functioning labour market. These resulted in the twin problems of trade unionism and labour turnover. It is true that various solutions were tried, many of them silly or oppressive or impossible or all three. And it is true that the celebrated final solution adopted is superior to the Western capitalist solution. But none of this reduces its feudal origin or its Japanese eccentricity.

Homo economicus does not sing company songs or do callisthenics beside his machine. The Japanese worker is therefore different, and the attitudes of the government are also different. It is entirely possible that Japanese success is due to superior workers and government, while lifetime employment for managers, and their exclusive promotion from within, are a drag on productivity, much as Western capitalists (and universities) hold to be the case.

But one must admit with Odagiri (in chapter 7) that the management may well be taking a more neo-classical view. *Their* preference for internal labour markets, both for themselves and for their workers, could be recaptured for neo-classicism as a conscious attempt to maximize profits by manipulating everyone including national tradition; and Odagiri himself rightly hesitates to claim flatly special national circumstances. The same kind of argument can be used about the Japanese financial system (which is more dependent on industrial groups and less on banks) and the advantages of giving 'lifetime tenure' also to subcontractors (as opposed to their highly competitive treatment in the USA). But in all three cases one wonders how a different national character would react to such a monopolistic environment? The preference for internal labour markets is often condemned in the English-speaking world as 'labour-hoarding.'

Conclusion

What these two contributors really prove is the frightened con-servatism of the orthodox, their blind uninterest in new fact, in intellectual adventure. Their methodology is so constricting that they do not even recognize its occasional power, and have to be dragged, kicking and screaming, even towards new victories. Thus these apparent (or, better, perhaps only apparent) excep-tions tell us something else that is wrong with our discipline: its much vaunted heuristic is telescope and blinkers in one.

   In the historically unique pathology of economics in the year 1984, parts of our paradigm are false in various degrees. In par-ticular homo economicus, the keystone of the arch, is, say, 80 per cent true. But after all, as Routh points out (unpublished), Russian roulette gives you 83 per cent, and still it is inadvisable. Moreover that other 20 per cent is heaped up in a very non-random way, so that it is not at all enough to say, ah well, the average, or the marginal, or the representative, or the randomly selected, homo is always economicus. Notably administered prices are almost always *lower* than the most profitable price, so that it is very tolerable to raise them: hence cost inflation (Wiles in chapter 8). The 80 per cent general truth of the paradigm yields about 40 per cent truth in this particular case. It is as much as to say, if you play Russian roulette on Tuesday you're sure to die. And lapses from homo economicus can only be dis-covered empirically, like whether or not it's Tuesday.

So homo economicus is false in important respects. Yet it contributes greatly to the unique pathology of our discipline that we are still able profitably to export him to other disciplines, notably sociology (Lévy-Garboua, 1981) and demography[28] which in the past underused him. These exports have not in fact had, or deserved, great success.[29] But it remains undoubted that the neoclassical methodology has something to contribute outside economics, and we have radiated even from our sick bed. An SRP does not have to degenerate in all fields at the same time.

Triumph is premature. These minor peripheral successes abroad have not arrested the disease at home. For there is a sociology of, for instance, price-setting under imperfect competition, especially oligopoly. We too have much to learn, right within our 'hard core', from other disciplines and indeed from common sense.

The economist must make up his mind. He professes *either* the subject *or* the methodology that give him his name. Or, thirdly, there is the substantial overlap (we have just seen reason to accept the somewhat flattering implications of this word: the methodology is not only a partial failure within economics but a partial success outside it.) But if the economist chooses to range only within this overlap he must do so explicitly. Moreover the soil there has by now been overcropped.

Notes

[1] Too late for much notice, I record with intense pleasure the birth of the new experimental economics, cf. Smith 1982; also the same author's *Research in Experimental Economics* books.

[2] Gustav Schmoller, 1838–1917, who dominated the appointment and publication system in German departments of economics in his later years, and suppressed the marginalists. Schmoller is thus a protagonist in the *Methodenstreit*, and should be a very well-known character to any economist. It appears that contemporary neo-classicists have forgotten him in order to imitate him.

[3] Isaac Barrow, 1630–77, who in 1669 resigned his mathematics chair early in favour of the superior genius of Isaac Newton.

[4] 'Internal' means following the logic of what has already been agreed, or the new factual information that has recently been added – as opposed to such 'externalities' as scientific quarrels, political or commercial influence, or even, it appears, the ideologies of scientists.

[5] This word was introduced by Kuhn (1970). It had various meanings in that book, which the author only sorted out later (Kuhn, 1974). The definition here is a sentence or a few sentences *describing* the essence of some part of the natural or social order (e.g.

Ptolemy, Copernicus, Keynes, Friedman). A paradigm is positive, and neither normative nor axiomatic. It may or may not be ideologically loaded; if it is, its users will of course be intellectually and perhaps also otherwise unscrupulous in its defence.

6 A SRP is based on a paradigm, and consists in developing knowledge on that basis, i.e. *not in contradiction with it*. Its methodology contains a 'heuristic', a sentence in the imperative mood that instructs the researcher to apply a part of the paradigm: 'Find the minimum necessary number of epicycles,' 'Test for the effect of variations in the quantity of money.'

7 Absolute confirmation is never possible, because an observation (or even logical argument) can always turn up tomorrow that is entirely contrary to our hypothesis. The best we can do as scientists is try to falsify it with might and main. The securest status it can *ever* attain is that it has not yet been falsified.

8 A striking example of such applied work is Sen, 1981. The main result is quite empirical, and arithmetically based. It is at least plausible, possibly brilliant. High theory has nothing to do with it, and the small amount of advanced algebra in some of the appendices adds nothing.

9 The empirical character of the proposition is at once evident from the fact of exceptions. Drug addition leads to increasing marginal utility. The collector of a *set* of things experiences the same when his set approaches completion. I do not argue that all absolutely certain laws are non-empirical – far from it; only that all probable laws *are* empirical.

10 *Entia non sunt multiplicanda praeter necessitatem*: concepts must not be unnecessarily multiplied. It is a common fault of economic theorists to quote the first four words only, and so leave out the human judgement of necessity (Wiles, 1970). There is of course no virtue at all in reducing the number of concepts at the expense of understanding the phenomena. Taken strictly Occam's Razor is not a very important rule. It reminds us too strongly of the German joke: *Warum es einfach machen wenn es auch komplizierter geht?* – why do it simply when more complicated methods suffice?

11 It is not clear that Kuhn distinguishes the 'Occamical' from the 'factual' scientific revolutions, such as the abandonment of phlogiston in view of the discovery of oxygen. Cf. Kuhn, 1970, pp. 68–72. The beginner in methodology should also be warned that the planet's orbits are elliptical, so Copernicus, who insisted that they are circular, still had to use epicycles to reproduce the truth; only not so many.

12 Homo economicus offended the aesthetic element in him, derived from the philosopher G.E. Moore (Keynes, 1938; Schaefer and Schaefer, 1983).

13 It seems to me that it *was* true, but that persisting inflation has indeed slightly rationalized our expectations; and that this disaster, occurring 'out there' in the real world, lends to the Lucasian supply curve its true importance. It is quite enough for such a doctrine that we have developed *more* rational expectations.

14 Keynes once threw up his hands and suggested this explanation of capitalist investment. (1936, p. 161). It has never been empirically refuted.

14a Cf Lukas 1976 sec. VI for a very hesitant statement.

15 Incidentally why can't employed people call in at the labour exchange in their lunch hour, or read the paper in the evening? Search is a very important element in the monetarist SRP, with the ultimate, half-acknowledged aim of reducing involuntary unemployment to nothing, and substituting cyclical waves of unusually high 'search'.

16 Cf. Wiles, 1979–80, appendix. I had once the privilege of discussing axioms with an admiral in the Indian navy. The achievements of a great Indian theoretician, much given to their use, came up in conversation. 'X's economics', I said 'reminds me always of the Hindu cosmology: the universe is of course known to rest upon an elephant, but when you ask what the elephant is standing on, they say, a tortoise. This answer is hardly satisfactory.' 'Oh, no,' said the admiral at once, 'that tortoise is an avatar, so his own position supports him.'

[17] See especially Cairncross 1955, 1970. This was also a consistent theme in the writings of Ely Devons. (Note by O'Brien).

[18] For an up-to-date survey of the literature on creativity see Busse and Mansfield, 1980.

[19] It is not unfair, then, to call Friedman's methodology (Friedman, 1953) self-contradictory.

[20] See p. 304 above. Mueller in chapter 6 and the full-cost principle (chapters 8 and 9) both illustrate the neo-classical brush-off. It even happens to neo-classicists! Thus the 'welfare triangle' has been used by orthodox economists (Harberger, 1954; Schwartzman, 1960; Johnson 1970) to estimate the numerical proportion of the national income lost by sub-optimal resource allocation. It appears, unbelievably, to be under 2 per cent! Hardly anyone has ever taken any notice of these results, except the unacceptably unorthodox Leibenstein (1976, chapter 3).

[21] This view, to be sure, raises difficulties with very expensive scientific games, like astronomy. Astronomy is to the sciences as Grand Opera is to the arts – and both problems must be set aside here. However I may rightly be charged with an ignorant Philistine suspicion of astronomers and theoretical physicists. Let me only say that their methodology is *much* more empirical in the end – but they are in grave spiritual danger! On the other hand let the reader imagine himself a member of a natural-science grant-giving body in 1830: how much would and should he give Bolyai or Lobachevski?

[22] There are also statistical techniques for dealing with ordinal relations like 'more' and 'less': e.g. the coefficient of rank correlation.

[23] This is the claim that all phenomena in a more complicated universe of discourse can be explained by means of theories pertaining to a more simple one that underlies it.

[24] Moreover, economics abuts at many places on accountancy, the base of which is a set of tautologies – so at its core is not a science at all but a branch of mathematics. But the *inevitability* of these tautologies is deceptively like the mechanistic attributes of the natural sciences, and has fed our self-important illusions and our reductionism. Cf. Wiles, 1972.

[25] Which we are assumed to do by Modigliani and Brumberg, 1954. Cf. Wiles, 1977, p. 453. Many of these fortunes are bequeathed outside the nuclear family.

[26] Envy is a marginal case, for which we have no space.

[27] Cf. Hawrylyshyn, 1978 (factual references in footnote 1, p. 215); Stewart, 1974 (factual references pp. 35, 38); Timmer, 1975. Note however that this insistence is more likely to get its way in the public sector.

[28] Cf. the whole issue of the *Journal of Political Economy*. March–April 1973, Part II. There are also more theoretical matters like optimal voting systems and the Prisoner's Dilemma.

[29] I distinguish them from the re-exportation of multivariate analysis, which economics took from psychology and rebaptized econometrics, to criminology. This statistical technique has indeed effected a revolution there. As samples of a very large literature, cf. Heineke, 1978; Carr-Hill and Stern, 1981.

Bibliography

Addison, J.T. and Barnett, A.H. (1982) 'The Impact of Unions on Productivity', *British Journal of Industrial Relations*.

Adelman, M.A. (1982) Personal letter, 4 Feb. to Frederic Lee.

Akerlof, G.A. and Miyazaki, H. (1980) 'The Implicit Contract Theory of Unemployment Meets the Wage Bill Argument', *Review of Economic Studies*.

Alchian, A. (1950) 'Uncertainty, Evolution and Economic Theory', *Journal of Political Economy*.

Alchian, A. and Demsetz, H. (1972) 'Production, Information Costs, and Economic Organisation', *American Economic Review*.

Andrews, P.W.S. (1949) *Manufacturing Business*, London: Macmillan.

Andrews, P.W.S. and Wilson, T. (eds) (1951) *Oxford Studies in the Price Mechanism*, Oxford: Oxford University Press.

Aoki, M. (1982) 'Equilibrium Growth of the Hierarchical Firm: Shareholder–Employee Cooperative Game Approach', *American Economy Review*.

Apel, H. (1948) 'Marginal Cost Constancy and its Implications', *American Economic Review*, pp. 870–85.

Arrow, K. (1974) *The Limits of Organization*, New York: Warton.

Arrow, K.J. and Hahn, F.H. (1971) *General Competitive Analysis*, San Francisco: Holden-Day; Edinburgh: Oliver & Boyd.

Azariadis, C. (1975) 'Implicit Contracts and Underemployment Equilibrium', *Journal of Political Economy*.

Bain, J.S. (1948) *Pricing, Distribution and Employment*, New York: Henry Holt.

Barro, R. and Grossman, H. (1976) *Money, Employment and Inflation*, Cambridge: Cambridge University Press.

Baumol, W.J. (1959) *Business Behavior, Value and Growth*, New York: Macmillan.

Baumol, W.J., Heim, P., Malkiel, B.G. & Quandt, R.E. (1970) 'Earnings Retention, New Capital, and the Growth of the Firm' *Review of Economics and Statistics*.

Becker, G.S. (1971) *The Economics of Discrimination*, 2nd edn, Chicago: University of Chicago Press.

Becker, G.S. (1975) *Human Capital: A Theoretical and Empirical*

Analysis, With Special Reference to Education, Chicago: University of Chicago Press.

Becker, G.S. (1976) *The Economic Approach to Human Behavior,* Chicago: University of Chicago Press.

Bell, D. and Kristol, I. (eds) (1981) *The Crisis in Economic Theory,* New York: Basic Books.

Benjamin, Daniel K. and Kochin, Levis A. (1979) 'Searching for an Explanation of Unemployment in Interwar Britain', *Journal of Political Economy.*

Birck, L.V. (1922) *The Theory of Marginal Value,* London: LSE.

Blackburn, R.M. and Mann, M. (1979) *The Working Class in the Labour Market,* London: Macmillan.

Blaug, M. (1980) *Methodology of Economics,* Cambridge: Cambridge University Press.

Bosch, G. and Lichte, R. (1981) 'Die Funktionsweise informeller Senioritätsrechte (am Beispiel einer betrieblichen Fallstudie)', in Dohse *et al.,* below.

Boudon, R. 1977) *Effets pervers et ordre social,* Paris: PUF.

Bourguinat, H. (1977) *Le Flottement des Monnaies,* Paris: PUF.

Boyle, St.E., (1970) 'Pre-merger Growth and Profit Characteristics of Large Conglomerate Mergers in the United States 1948–1968', *St Johns Law Review,* special edn.

Brainard, W.C., Shoven, J.B. and Weiss, L. (1980) 'The Financial Valuation of the Return on Capital', *Brookings Paper on Economic Activity.*

Brittan, S. (1982) *How to End the 'Monetarist' Controversy,* 2nd edn, London: Institute of Economic Affairs.

Brossard, M., and Maurice, M. (1974) 'Existe-t-il un Modèle universel de l'organisation?', *Sociologie du Travail.*

Brown, J.N. (1982) in R.G. Ehrenberg, (ed.), *Research in Labour Economics,* Connectituct: JAI Press.

Brown, W. (1973) *Piecework Bargaining,* London: Heinemann.

Brunner, K. (1968) 'The Role of Money and Monetary Policy', *Federal Reserve Bank of St Louis Review.*

Busse, T.V. and Mansfield, R.S. (1980) 'Theories of the Creative Process', *Journal of Creative Behaviour.*

Cairncross, A. (1955) 'On Being an Economic Adviser', *Scottish Journal of Political Economy.*

Cairnes, J.E. (1874) *Some Leading Principles of Political Economy,* London.

Caldwell, B. (1982) *Beyond Positivism: Economic Methodology in the Twentieth Century,* London: Allen & Unwin.

Carr-Hill, R.A. and Stern, N.H. (1981) *Crime, the Police and Criminal Statistics,* London: Academic Press.

Chamberlin, E. (1935) The *Theory of Monopolistic Competition*, Cambridge, Mass.: Harvard University Press.

Chamberlin, E. (1952) 'Full Cost and Monopolistic Competition', *Economic Journal*.

Chandler, A.D. and Daems, H. (eds) (1980) *Managerial Hierarchies: Comparative Perspectives on the Rise of the Modern Industrial Enterprise*, Cambridge, Mass.: Harvard University Press.

Clower, R.W. (1965) The Keynesian Counter-Revolution: a Theoretical Appraisal', In F.H. Hahn and F.P.R. Brechling, (eds), *The Theory of Interest Rates*, London: Macmillan.

Coddington, A. (1976) 'Keynesian Economics: the Search for First Principles', *Journal of Economic Literature*.

Coddington, A. (1982) 'Deficient Foresight: a Troublesome Theme in Keynesian Economics', *American Economic Review*.

Cowling, K., Stoneman, P., Cubbin, J., Cable, J., Hall, G., Dornberger, S. and Dutton, P. (1979) *Mergers and Economic Performance*, Cambridge: Cambridge University Press.

Cross, R. (1982a) 'The Duhem–Quine Thesis, Lakatos and the Appraisal of Theories in Macroeconomics', *Economic Journal*.

Cross, R. (1982b) *Economic Theory and Policy in the U.K.*, Oxford: Martin Robertson.

Crozier, M. (1963) *Le Phénomène Bureaucratique*, Paris: Seuil.

Cyert, R.M. and March, J.G. (1956) 'Organizational Factors in the Theory of Oligopoly', *Quarterly Journal of Economics*. 70.

Cyert, R.M. and March J.G. (1963) *A Behavioral Theory of the Firm*, Englewood Cliffs, NJ: Prentice-Hall.

Cyert, R.M. and Pottinger, G. (1979) 'Toward a Better Microeconomic Theory', *Philosophy of Science*.

Daubigney, J.P., Fizaine, F. and Silvestre, J.J. (1971) 'Les différences de salaires entre entreprises', *Revenue Economique*.

Daubigney, J.P. and Silvestre, J.J. (1972) *Comparaison de l' hiérarchie des salaires entre l'Allemagne et la France*, Aix-en-Provence: Laboratoire d'Economie et de Sociologie du Travail.

Davidson, J.E.H. and Hendry, D.F. (1981) 'Interpreting Econometric Evidence', *European Economic Review*.

Davidson, P. (1981) 'Post-Keynesian Economics', in D. Bell and I. Kristol (eds) 'The Crisis in Economic Theory', *The Public Interest*, special edn.

Deane, P. (1983) 'The Scope and Method of Economic Science', *Economic Journal*, March, pp. 1–12.

Dodd, P. (1980) 'Merger Proposals, Management Discretion, and Stockholder Wealth', *Journal of Financial Economics*.

Dodd, P. and Ruback, R. (1977) 'Tender Offers and Stockholder Returns: An Empirical Analysis', *Journal of Financial Economics*.

Doeringer, P.B. and Piore, M.J. (1971) *Internal Labour Markets and Manpower Analysis*, Lexington, Mass.: Heath.

Dohse, K., Jürgens, U. and Russig, H. (eds) (1981) *Statussicherung im Industriebetueb: alternative Regelungsansätze im internationalen Vergleich*, Campus Verlag, Frankfurt and N. York.

Dore, R.P. (1973) *British Factory – Japanese Factory: The Origins of Diversity in Industrial Relations*, London: Allen & Unwin.

Dorling, J. (1979) 'Bayesian Personalism, the Methodology of Scientific Research Programmes and Duhem's Problem', *Studies in the History and Philosophy of Science*.

Due, J.F. (1950) *Intermediate Economic Analysis*, rev. edn, Holmewood, Ill.: Richard D. Irwin.

Due, J.F. (1956) *Intermediate Economic Analysis*, 3rd edn, Holmewood, Ill.: Richard D. Irwin.

Duhem, P. (1906) *The Aim and Structure of Physical Theory*, Princeton: Princeton University Press (edition reprinted, New York: Atheneum, 1981).

Dunlop, J.T. (1944) *Wage Determination Under Trade Unions*, London: Macmillan.

Eichner, A.S. (1976) *Megacorp and Oligopoly*, New York: Cambridge University Press.

Eichner, A.S. (1978) 'Review of P.W.S. Andrews and Elizabeth Brunner', *Studies in Pricing, Journal of Economic Literature*.

Eiteman, W.J. (1949) *Price Determination*, Bureau of Business Research, Ann Arbor: University of Michigan.

Elliott, J.W. (1973) 'Theories of Corporate Investment Behavior Revisited', *American Economic Review*.

Fama, E.J. (1980) 'Agency Problems and the Theory of the Firm', *Journal of Political Economy*.

Fellner, W. (1948) 'Average-Cost Pricing and the Theory of Uncertainty', *Journal of Political Economy*.

Ferguson, C.E. (1957) 'Static Models of Average-Cost Pricing', *Southern Economic Journal*.

Fiegehen, G.C. (1981) *Companies, Incentives and Senior Managers*, Oxford: Oxford University Press.

Firth, M. (1979) 'The Profitability of Takeovers and Mergers', *Economic Journal*.

Firth, M. (1980) 'Takeovers, Shareholder Returns, and the Theory of the Firm', *Quarterly Journal of Economics*.

Fisher, A.A. and Lande, R.H. (1982) 'Efficiency Considerations in Merger Enforcement', Federal Trade Commission, mimeo.

Fisher, R.A. (1935) *The Design of Experiments*, London: Oliver & Boyd.

Fisher, R.A. (1956) *Statistical Methods and Scientific Inference*, London: Oliver & Boyd.

Flanders, A. (1964) *The Fawley Productivity Agreements*, London: Faber.

Franks, J.R., Broyles, J.E. and Hecht, M.J. (1977) 'An Industry Study of the Profitability of Mergers in the United Kingdom', *Journal of Finance*.

Fraumeni, B.M., and Jorgenson, D.W. (1970) 'Rates of Return by Industrial Sector in the United States, 1948–1976', *American Economic Review*.

Freeman, R.B. and Medoff, J.L. (1979) 'The Two Faces of Unionism', *Public Interest*.

Frey, B. (1981) 'Schumpeter, Political Economist', in H. Frisch (ed.) *Schumpeterian Economics*.

Freyssinet, J. (1982) 'Politiques d'Emploi des Grands Groupes Français', P.U. de Grenoble.

Friedman, M. (1953) *Essays in Positive Economics*, Chicago: University of Chicago Press.

Friedman, M. (1956) 'The Quantity Theory of Money – A Restatement', in M. Friedman (ed.), *Studies in the Quantity Theory of Money*, Chicago: University of Chicago Press.

Friedman, M. (1968) 'The Role of Monetary Policy', *American Economic Review*.

Friedman, M. (1977) 'Nobel Lecture: Inflation and Unemployment', *Journal of Political Economy*.

Friend, I. and Puckett, M. (1964) 'Dividends and Stock Prices', *American Economic Review*.

Galbraith, J.K. (1967) *The New Industrial State*, Boston: Houghton Mifflin.

Galbraith, J.K. (1973) 'Power and the Useful Economist', *American Economic Review*, March.

Gardner, M. (1982) 'Predicting Novel Facts', *British Journal for the Philosophy of Science*.

Giere, R.N. (1979) 'Foundations of Probability and Statistical Inference', in P.D. Asquith and H.E. Kyburg Jr. (eds), *Current Research in the Philosophy of Science*, Michigan: Philosophy of Science Association.

Glymour, C. (1980) *Theory and Evidence*, Princeton: Princeton University Press.

Goldthorpe, J.H., Lockwood, D., Bechhofer, F. and Platt, J. (1968) *The Affluent Worker*, Cambridge: Cambridge University Press.

Gordon, R.A. (1948) 'Short-Period Price Determination in Theory and Practice', *American Economic Review*.

Gordon, R.J. (1981) 'Output Fluctuations and Gradual Price Adjustment', *Journal of Economic Literature*.

Gordon, R.J. and Malkiel, B. (1982) "Corporation Finance', in H. Aaron and J. Peckman (eds), *How Taxes Affect Economic Behaviour*, Washington DC: Brookings Institute.

Grabowski, H.G. and Mueller, D.C. (1972) 'Managerial and Stockholder Welfare Models of Firm Expenditure', *Review of Economics and Statistics*.

Grabowski, H.G. and Mueller, D.C. (1975) 'Life-Cycle Effects on Corporate Returns on Retentions', *Review of Economics and Statistics*.

Gregory, R.G. and Duncan, R.C. (1981) 'Segmented Labor Market Theories and the Australian Experience of Equal Pay for Women', *Journal of Post-Keynesian Economics*.

Grossman, S.J. and Hart, O.D. (1980) 'Takeover Bids, the Free-Rider Problem, and the Theory of Corporation', *Bell Journal*.

Grossman, S.J. and Hart, O.D. (1981) 'The Allocational Role of Takeover Bids in Situations of Asymmetric Information', *Journal of Finance*.

Grossman, S.J., and Schiller, R. (1981) *American Economic Review*.

Grossman, S.J. and Stiglitz, J. (1980) 'On the Impossibility of Informationally Efficient Markets', *American Economic Review*.

Haavelmo, T. (1944) 'Probability Approach in Econometrics', Special Supplement to *Econometrica*, July.

Hacking, Ian (1965) *Logic of Statistical Inference*, Cambridge: Cambridge University Press.

Hahn, F.H. (1973) 'The Winter of our Discontent', review of J. Kornai, *Anti-Equilibrium, Economica*.

Hahn, F.H. and Hollis, M. (1979) *Philosophy and Economic Theory*, Oxford: Oxford University Press.

Hahn, F.H. (1981a) 'General Equilibrium Theory', in D. Bell and I. Kristol (eds), *The Crisis in Economic Theory*, New York: Basic Books.

Hahn, F.H. (1981b) Review of M. Beenstock, *A Neoclassical Analysis of Macroeconomic Policy, Economic Journal*.

Hall, R.E. (1980) 'Comment', *Brookings Papers on Economic Activity* 2.

Hall, R.E. (1982) 'The Importance of Lifetime Jobs in the U.S. Economy', *American Economic Review*.

Hall, R.E. and Hitch C.J. (1938) 'Price Theory and Business Behaviour'. reprinted in P.W.S. Andrews and T. Wilson (eds), *Oxford Studies in the Price Mechanism*, Oxford: Oxford University Press, 1951.

Hamilton, J.D. (1983) 'Oil and the Macroeconomy since World War II', *Journal of Political Economy*.

Hannah, L. (1980) 'Visible and Invisible Hands in Great Britain', in A.D. Chandler and H. Daems (eds), *Managerial Hierarchies: Comparative Perspectives on the Rise of the Modern Industrial Enterprise*, Cambridge, Mass.: Harvard University Press.

Harberger, A.C. (1954) 'Monopoly and Resource Allocation', *American Economic Review*, pp. 77–87.

Harrod, R. (1939) 'Price and Cost in Entrepreneurs' Policy', *Oxford Economic Papers*.

Hausman, J. and Wise, D. (1979) 'Attrition Bias in Experimental and Panel Data: the Gary Income Maintenance Experiment', *Econometrica*, March.

Hawrylyshyn, O. (1978) 'Capital-Intensity Biases in Developing Country Technology Choice', *Journal of Development Economics*.

Hayek F.A. (1980) *1980's Unemployment and the Unions*, London: Institute of Economic Affairs.

Haynes, R. (1980) 'The Boggle Threshold'. *Encounter*.

Heathfield, D.F. and Hartropp, A.J. (1982) 'A Critique of Rational Expectations', mimeo, available from the authors.

Heflebower, R.B. (1955) 'Full Costs, Cost Changes, and Prices', in R.B. Heflebower, *Business Concentration and Price Policy*, Princeton: Princeton University Press.

Heineke, J.A. (ed.) (1978) *Economic Models of Criminal Behaviour*, Amsterdam: North Holland.

Hempel, C.G. (1945) 'Studies in the Logic of Confirmation', reprinted in C.G. Hempel, *Aspects of Scientific Explanation*, New York: Free Press, 1965.

Hendry, David A. (1983) 'Econometric Modelling: The "Consumption Function" in Retrospect', *Scottish Journal of Political Economy*.

Hicks, J.R. (1939) *Value and Capital*, Oxford: Clarendon Press.

Hicks, J.R. (1974) *The Crisis in Keynesian Economics*, Oxford: Blackwell.

Hicks, J.R. (1979a) *Causality in Economics*, Oxford: Blackwell.

Hicks, J.R. (1979b) 'The Formation of an Economist', *Banca Nazionale del Lavoro Quarterly Review*.

Hogarty, T.F. (1970) 'Profits from Merger: The Evidence of Fifty Years', *St Johns Law Review*.

Hollis, M. and Nell, E.J. (1975) *Rational Economic Man*, Cambridge: Cambridge University Press.

Holmstrom, B. (1979) 'Moral Hazard and Observability', *Bell Journal*.

Hood, W. and Koopmans T. (eds) (1953) *Studies in Econometric Methods*, New York.

Horowitz, I. (1967) 'The Advance of the Theory of the Firm: One Step Forward, One Step Back', *Quarterly Review of Economics and Business*.

Horwich, P. (1982) *Probability and Evidence*, Cambridge: Cambridge University Press.

Hoxie, R.F. (1901) 'On the Empirical Method of Economic Instruction', *Journal of Political Economy*.

Hutchison, T. (1938) *The Significance and Basic Postulates of Economic Theory*, (reprinted New York: Augustus M. Kelley, 1965).

Hutchison, T. (1953) *A Review of Economic Doctrines 1870–1929*, Oxford: Clarendon Press.

Hutchison, T. (1977) *Knowledge and Ignorance in Economics*, Oxford: Blackwell.

Hutchison, T. (1978) *On Revolutions and Progress in Economic Knowledge*, Cambridge, Cambridge University Press.

Hutchison, T.W. (1981) *The Politics and Philosophy of Economics*, Oxford: Blackwell.

Irving, J. (1978) 'P.W.S. Andrews and the Unsuccessful Revolution', DPhil Thesis, University of Wollongong.

Jackson, D. (1982) *Introduction to Economics: Theory and Data*, London: Macmillan.

Jaffé, W. (1980) 'Walras's Economics as Others See It', *Journal of Economic Literature*.

Johnson, H.G. (1958) 'The Gains from Freer Trade with Europe: An Estimate', *Manchester School*.

Johnson, H.G. (1968) 'The Economic Approach to Social Questions', *Economica*.

Johnson, H.G. (1973) 'The Monetary Approach to the Balance of Payments', in H.G. Johnson, *Further Essays in Monetary Economics*, London: Allen & Unwin.

Jorgenson, D.W. and Siebert, C.D. (1968) 'Theories of Corporate Investment Behavior', *American Economic Review*

Kahn, R.F. (1952) Review of P.W.S. Andrews and T. Wilson (eds) *Oxford Studies in the Price Mechanism, Economic Journal*, March.

Kaldor, N. (1972) 'Conflicts in National Economic Objectives', *Economic Journal*, March, pp. 1–16.

Kaldor, N. (1978) *Further Essays in Economic Theory*, London: Duckworth.

Katona, G. (1951) *Psychological Analysis of Economic Behavior*, New York: McGraw-Hill.

Katona, G. (1979) *The 1979 Founders Symposium Honoring George Katona*, Ann Arbor: Survey Research Center, University of Michigan.

Katouzian, H. (1980) *Ideology and Method in Economics*, London: Philip Allen.

Keynes, J.M. (1936) *The General Theory of Employment, Interest and Money*, Cambridge: Cambridge University Press.

Keynes, J.M. (1937) 'The General Theory: Fundamental Concepts and Ideas', *Quarterly Journal of Economics*.

Keynes, J.M. (1938) *My Early Beliefs*, London: Hart-Davis.

Keynes, J.M. (1972) *Essays in Biography*, in *The Collected Works of John Maynard Keynes*, London: Macmillan.

Keynes, J.M. (1973) *The General Theory and After*, in *The Collected Works of John Maynard Keynes*, 13, London: Macmillan.

King, M. (1977) *Public Policy and the Corporation*, London: Chapman and Hall.

Knight, F.H. (1921) *Risk, Uncertainty and Profit*, Boston: Houghton Miffin.

Koertge, N. (1979) 'The Problem of Appraising Scientific Theories', in P.D. Asquith and H.E. Kyburg Jr (eds), *Current Research in the Philosophy of Science*, Michigan: Philosophy of Science Association.

Koike, K. (1977) *Shokuba no Rodo Kumiai to Sanka* (Trade Unions and Participation in Factories: Japan–US Comparison of Industrial Relations), Tokyo: Toyo Keizai Shinposha.

Koike, K. (1978) 'Japan's Industrial Relations: Characteristics and Problems', *Japanese Economic Studies*.

Koizumi, S. (1979) 'Investment, Uncertainty and Wage-Employment Contract', Discussion Paper No. 19, Faculty of Economics, Osaka: Osaka University.

Koopmans, T. (ed.) (1950) *Statistical Inference in Dynamic Economic Models*, New York.

Kornai, J. (1971) *Anti-Equilibrium*, Budapest: Közgasdasagi es Jogi Könyvkiado.

Koutsoyiannis, A. (1979) *Modern Microeconomics*, 2nd edn, London: Macmillan.

Krzyzaniak, M. and Musgrave, R. (1963) *The Shifting of the Corporation Income Tax*, Baltimore: Johns Hopkins Press.

Kuehn, D. (1975) *Takeovers and the Theory of the Firm: An Empirical Analysis of the United Kingdom, 1957–1969*, London: Macmillan.

Kuhn, T. (1970) *The Structure of Scientific Revolutions*, 2nd edn, Chicago: University of Chicago Press.

Kuhn, T. (1974) 'Second Thoughts on Paradigms', in F. Suppe (ed.), *The Structure of Scientific Theories*, Urbana: University of Illinois Press.

Kummer, D.R., and Hoffmeister, J.R. (1978) 'Valuation Consequences of Cash Tender Offers', *Journal of Finance*.

Laidler, D.E.W. (1978) *The Demand for Money*, 2nd edn, London: Harper & Row.

Laidler, D.E.W. (1981) 'Monetarism: An Interpretation and an Assessment', *Economic Journal*.

Laidler, D.E.W. (1982) *Monetarist Perspectives*, Oxford: Philip Allan.

Lakatos, I. (1970) 'Methodology of Scientific Research Programmes', in I. Lakatos and A. Musgrave (eds), *Criticism and the Growth of Knowledge*, Cambridge: Cambridge University Press.

Lakatos, I. (1978) *Philosophical Papers*, I: *The Methodology of Scientific Research Programmes*, II: *Mathematics, Science and Epistemology*, in J. Worrall and G. Currie (eds), Cambridge: Cambridge University Press.

Langetieg, T.C. (1978) 'An Application of a Three-Factor Performance Index to Measure Stockholder Gains from Merger', *Journal of Financial Economics*.

Latsis, S.J. (ed.) (1976) *Method and Appraisal in Economics*, Cambridge: Cambridge University Press.

Lazear, E.P. and Rosen, S. (1981) 'Rank-Order Tournaments as Optimum Labor Contracts', *Journal of Political Economy*.

Leamer, E.A. (1978) *Specification Searches: Ad Hoc Inference with Non-Experimental Data*, New York: Wiley.

Lee, F.S. (1983) 'Full Cost Pricing: An Historical and Theoretical Analysis', D.Phil thesis, Rutgers University.

Lee, F.S. (1984a) 'Full Cost Pricing: A New Wine in a New Bottle', *Australian Economic Papers*.

Lee, F.S. (1984b) 'The Marginalist Controversy and the Demise of Full Cost Pricing', *Journal of Economic Issues*.

Leibenstein, H. (1976) *Beyond Economic Man*, Cambridge, Mass.: Harvard University Press.

Leontief, W.W. (1941) *The Structure of the American Economy 1919–1939*, New York: Oxford University Press.

Leontief, W.W. (1971) 'Theoretical Assumptions and Non-Observed Facts', *American Economic Review*, March.

LeRoy, S. and Porter, R. (forthcoming) 'The Present Value Relation: Tests Based on Implied Variance Bounds', *Econometrica*.

Leslie, C. (1879) 'The Known and the Unknown in the Economic World,' in C. Leslie, *Essays in Political and Moral Philosophy*,

Lester, R.A. (1946) 'Shortcomings of Marginal Analysis for Wage–Employment Problems', *American Economic Review*.

Lévy-Garboua, L. (1979) 'Education, origine sociale et distribution des gains', in J.C. Eicher and L. Lévy-Garboua (eds), *Economique de l'Education*, Paris: Economica.

Lévy-Garboua, L. (1981) 'L'Economique et le Rationnel', in *L'Année Sociologique*, Paris.

Long, J.E. and Link A.N. (1983) 'The Impact of Market Structure on Wages, Fringe Benefits, and Turnover', *Industrial and Labour Relations Review*.

Lucas, R.E. Jr (1972) 'Expectations and the Neutrality of Money', *Journal of Economic Theory*.

Lucas, R.E. Jr. (1976) 'Understanding Business Cycles', Paper for the Kiel Conference on 'Growth without Inflation', photo-copied.

Lydall, H. (1968) *The Structure of Earnings*, Oxford: Oxford University Press.

McGregor, D. (1960) *The Human Side of Enterprise*, New York: McGraw-Hill.

Machlup, F. (1946) 'Marginal Analysis and Empirical Research'. *American Economic Review*.

Machlup, F. (1967) 'Theories of the Firm: Marginalist, Behavioral, Managerial', *American Economic Review*.

Machlup, F. (1978) *Methodology of Economics and Other Social Sciences*, New York: Academic Press.

Mackay, D.I., Boddy, D., Brack, J., Diack, J.A. and Jones, N. (1971) *Labour Markets Under Different Employment Conditions*, London: Allen & Unwin.

Main, B.G.M. (1982) 'The Length of a Job in Great Britain', *Economica*.

Malinvaud, E. (1977) *The Theory of Unemployment Reconsidered*, Oxford: Blackwell.

Mandelker, G. (1974) 'Risk and Return: The Case of Merging Firms', *Journal of Financial Economics*.

Manne, G.H. (1965) 'Mergers and the Market for Corporate Control', *Journal of Political Economy*.

Manpower Services Commission (1978) *Labour Shortages and Manpower Policy*, Manpower Studies No. 1978/2, London: HMSO.

de Marchi, N. (1976) 'Anomaly and the Development of Economics, the case of the Leontief paradox', in Latsis (1976).

Markham, J.W. (1954) 'Industrial Pricing – Discussion', *American Economic Review*.

Marris, R. (1964) *The Economic Theory of 'Managerial' Capitalism*, London: Macmillan.

Marris, R. and Mueller, D.C. (1980) 'The Corporation, Competition, and the Invisible Hand Theorem', *Journal of Economic Literature*.

Marsden, D.W. (1976) *Critique de l'analyse économique des faits sociaux: le cas de la recherche sur le marché du travail*, Aix-en-Provence: Laboratoire d'Economie et de Sociologie du Travail.

Marsden, D.W. (1982) 'Career Structures and Training in Internal Labour Markets', *Manpower Studies*.

Marsden, D.W. (1985) 'Collective Bargaining and Industrial Adjustment in Britain, France, Italy and West Germany', in F. Duchêne and G. Shepherd (eds), *The Management of Industrial Change in Western Europe*, London: Frances Pinter forthcoming.

Matthews, R.C.O. (1968) 'Why Has Britain Had Full Employment Since the War?', *Economic Journal*.

Maurice, M., Sellier, F. and Silvestre, J.J. (1978) *La Production de la hiérarchie dans l'entreprise: recherche d'un effet sociétal France–Allemagne*, Aix-en-Province: Laboratoire d'Economie et de Sociologie du Travail (rev. and published as *Politique d'éducation et organisation industrielle*, Paris: PUF, 1982).

Maurice, M., Sorge, A. and Warner, M. (1979) 'Societal Differences in Organizing Manufacturing Units. A comparison of France, West Germany and Great Britain. International Institute of Management, Berlin, Paper I.I.M. 79–15.

Meade, J.E. (1981a) *Stagflation, I: Wage-Fixing*, London: Allen & Unwin.

Meade, J.E. (1981b) 'Monetarism: A Comment', *Economic Journal.*

Meckling, W.H. (1978) 'Comment', in J.M. Buchanan and R.E. Wagner (eds) *Fiscal Responsibility in Constitutional Democracy.*

Meeks, G. *(1977) Disappointing Marriage: A Study of the Gains from Merger*, Cambridge: Cambridge University Press.

Metcalf, David, Nickell, Steven J. and Floros, Nicos (1982) 'Still Searching for an Explanation of Unemployment in Interwar Britain?' *Journal of Political Economy.*

Middleton, R. (1981) 'The Constant Employment Budget Balance and British Budgetary Policy 1929–39', *Economic History Review.*

Minford, P. (1980) 'The Nature and Purpose of U.K. Macro-Economic Models', *Three Banks Review.*

Minford, P. and Peel, D. (1981) 'Is the Government's Economic Strategy on Course?' *Lloyds Bank Review.*

Mises, L. von (1949) *Human Action: A Treatise on Economics*, London: William Hodge.

Modigliani, F. (1958) 'New Developments on the Oligopoly Front', *Journal of Political Economy.*

Modigliani, F. and Brumberg, R. (1954) 'Utility Analysis and the Consumption Function' in K.K. Kurihara, *Post-Keynesian Economics*, London: George Allen and Unwin.

Modigliani, F. and Miller M.H. (1958) 'The Cost of Capital, Corporation Finance, and the Theory of Investment', *American Economic Review.*

Morishima, M. (1956) *Sangyō Renkan Ron Nyūmon* (Introduction to Input–Output Analysis), Tokyo: Sōbunsha.

Morishima, M. (1964) *Equilibrium, Stability and Growth*, Oxford: Clarendon Press.

Morishima, M. (1977) *Walras' Economics*, Cambridge: Cambridge University Press.

Morishima, M. (1980) 'W. Jaffé on Léon Walras: A Comment', *Journal of Economic Literature.*

Morishima, M. (1982) *Why Has Japan 'Succeeded'?*, Cambridge: Cambridge University Press.

Morrison, D.F. and Henkel, R.E. (1970) *The Significance Test Controversy*, Chicago: Aldine.

Mueller, D.C. (1977a) 'The Persistence of Profits Above the Norm', *Economica.*

Mueller, D.C. (1977b) 'The Effects of Conglomerate Mergers: A Survey of the Empirical Evidence', *Journal of Banking and Finance.*

Mueller, D.C. (ed.) (1980) *The Determinants and Effects of Mergers: An International Comparison*, Cambridge, Mass.: Oelgeschlager, Gunn & Hain.

Mueller, D.C. (1983) *The Determinants of Persistent Profits*, Washington DC, Federal Trade Commission.

Musgrave, A. (1981) 'Unreal Assumptions in Economic Theory: The F-Twist Untwisted', *Kyklos*, Fasc. 3.

Muth, J.F. (1961) 'Rational Expectations and the Theory of Price Movements', *Econometrica*.

Nakao, T. (1980) 'Wages and Market Power in Japan', *British Journal of Industrial Relations*.

Neumann, J. von, and Morgenstern, O. (1947) *Theory of Games and Economic Behaviour*, Princeton: Princeton University Press.

Neyman, J. and Pearson E.S. (1967) *Joint Statistical Papers*, Berkeley: University of California Press.

Niwa, H. (1971) 'An Econometric Analysis and Forecast of Soviet Economic Growth', in Peter Wiles (ed.), *The Prediction of Communist Economic Performance*, Cambridge: Cambridge University Press.

Nozick, R. (1982) 'The Meaning of Social Justice', *New York Times*.

O'Brien, D.P. (1975) 'Whither Economics?', *Economics*, Journal of the Economics Association.

Odagiri, H. (1981) *The Theory of Growth in a Corporate Economy*, Cambridge: Cambridge University Press.

Odagiri, H. (1982a) 'Antineoclassical Management Motivation in a Neoclassical Economy', *Kyklos*.

Odagiri, H. (1982b) 'Internal Promotion, Intrafirm Wage Structure and Corporate Growth', *Economic Studies Quarterly*.

OECD (1965) *Wages and Labour Mobility*, Paris: OECD.

Ogura, K. (1940) *Nihon no sūgaku* (The History of Japanese Mathematics), Tokyo: Iwanami Shoten.

Oi, W. (1962) 'Labor as a Quasi-Fixed Factor', *Journal of Political Economy*.

Okun, A.M. (1981) *Prices and Quantities*, Oxford: Blackwell.

Oliver, H.M. (1947) 'Marginal Theory and Business Behavior', *American Economic Review*.

Oliver, J.M. and Turton, J.R. (1982) 'Is There a Shortage of Skilled Labour?', *British Journal of Industrial Relations*.

Ono, A. (1981) *Nihon no Rodo Shijo* (The Labour Market in Japan), Tokyo: Toyo Keizai Shinposha.

Ouchi, W.G. (1981) *Theory Z*, Reading, Massachussetts: Addison-Wesley.

Parnes, H. (1954) *Research on Labor Mobility*, New York: Social Science Research Council.

Pearson, E. (1959) 'Report of the Committee on the Supply and Demand for Statistics', *Journal of Royal Statistical Society*, Series A, Part I.

Penrose, E.T. (1955) 'Limits to the Growth and Size of Firms', *American Economic Review*.

Penrose, E.T. (1959) *The Theory of the Growth of the Firm*, Oxford: Blackwell.

Peters, T.J. and Waterman, R.H. (1982) *In Search of Excellence*, New York: Harper and Row.

Phelps Brown, H. (1972) 'The Underdevelopment of Economics', *Economic Journal*.

Phelps Brown, H. (1980) 'The Radical Reflections of an Applied Economist', *Banca Nazionale del Lavoro Quarterly Review*.

Phillips, A.W. (1958) 'The Relationship Between Unemployment and the Rate of Change of Money Wage Rates in the U.K. 1861–1957', *Economica*.

Pigou, A.C. (1939) Presidential Address, *Economic Journal*.

Pissarides, C.A. (1978) 'The Role of Relative Wages and Excess Demand in the Sectoral Flow of Labour', *Review of Economic Studies*.

Poincaré, H. (1902) *La Science et l'hypothèse*, Paris: Flammarion.

Prest, A.R. (1983) 'Letter to a Young Economist', *Journal of Economic Affairs*.

Quine, W. van O. (1980) *From a Logical Point of View*, 2nd, rev. edn, Cambridge, Mass.: Harvard University Press.

Reder M.W. (1955) 'The Theory of Occupational Wage Differentials', *American Economic Review*.

Rees, A. and Schultz, G.P. (1970) *Workers and Wages in an Urban Labor Market*, Chicago: University of Chicago Press.

Reitsperger, W.D. (1982) 'Japanese Business Strategy and British Industrial Relations', mimeo; to be published in B. Wilpert and A. Sorge (eds), *International Yearbook of Organizational Democracy*, II: *International Perspectives on Organizational Democracy*, Sussex: Wiley.

Report of the Evaluative Committee for *Econometrica*, *Econometrica*, April 1954.

Ricardo, David (1951–73) *Works*, in Piero Sraffa (ed.) Cambridge: Cambridge University Press.

Robinson, D. (1970) 'External and Internal Labour Markets', in D. Robinson (ed.), *Local Labour Markets and Wage Structures*, Farnborough: Gower Press.

Robinson, E.A.G. (1950) Review of P.W.S. Andrews, *Manufacturing Business*, *Economic Journal*.

Robinson, J.V. (1933) *Economics of Imperfect Competition*, London: Macmillan.

Robinson, J. (1972) 'The Second Crisis of Economic Theory', *American Economic Review*, May, pp. 1–10.

Robinson, J.V. (1973) *Collected Economic Papers*, IV, Oxford: Blackwell.

Robinson, R. (1961) 'The Economics of Disequilibrium Price', *Quarterly Journal of Economics*.

Robinson, R. (1978) 'The Theory of Imperfect Markets Reconsidered', *Journal of Economic Issues*.

Robinson, R. (1981) Personal letter to Frederic Lee, 18 June.

Rosenkrantz, R.D. (1977) *Inference, Method and Decision*, Dordrecht, Holland: Reidel.

Ross, S. (1977) 'The Determination of Financial Structure: The Incentive-Signalling Approach', *Bell Journal*.

Routh, G. (1975) *The Origin of Economic Ideas*, London: Macmillan.

Routh, G. (1980) *Occupation and Pay in Great Britain 1906–1979*, London: Macmillan.

Ruggles, R. (1981) Personal letter to Frederic Lee, 9 Dec.

Russell, B. (1927) *The Analysis of Matter*, London: Kegan Paul, Trent, Trubner.

Samuelson, P.A. (1948) 'International Trade and the Equalization of Factor Prices,' *Economic Journal*.

Samuelson, P.A. (1951a) *Economics*, New York: McGraw-Hill. 3rd edn 1955, 4th 1958, 6th 1964, 10th 1976.

Samuelson P.A. (1951b) 'Abstract of a Theorem Concerning Substitutability in Open Leontief Models', in T.C. Koopmans, *Activity Analysis of Production and Allocation*, New York: Wiley.

Samuelson, P.A., Koopmans, T.C. and Stone, J.R.N. (1954) 'Report of the Evaluative Committee for Econometrica', *Econometrica*.

Santi, P. (1981) 'I differenziali retributivi occupazionali nell' industria italiana e la politica sindacale negli anni '70', *Rivista internazionale di scienze sociali*.

Saunders, C. and Marsden, D.W. (1981) *Pay Inequalities in the European Community*, London: Butterworths.

Savage, L. (1954) *Foundations of Statistics*, Dover Publications.

Schaefer, R. and Schaefer, D. (1983) 'The Political Philosophy of J.M. Keynes', *Public Interest*.

Schere, F. M. (1970) *Industrial Market Structure and Economic Performance*, Chicago: Rand McNally.

Schwartz, St. (1980) 'Micro-Determinants of Conglomerate Mergers', PhD dissertation, University of Maryland.

Schwartzman, D. (1960) 'The Burden of Monopoly', *Journal of Political Economy*.

Scitovsky, T. (1951) *Welfare and Competition*, Chicago: Richard D. Irwin.

Scitovsky, T. (1976) *The Joyless Economy: An Inquiry into Human Satisfaction and Consumer Dissatisfaction*, Oxford: Oxford University Press.

Scitovsky, T. (1982) Personal Letter, 18 Jan. to Frederic Lee.

Sebold, F.D. (1970) 'Short-Run Tax Response in a Utility-Maximization Framework', *National Tax Journal*.

Sen, A. (1981) *Poverty and Famines*, Oxford: Oxford University Press.

Senior, N.W. (1836) *An Outline of Political Economy*, (new edn 1951) Kelley.

Shiller, R.J. (1979) 'The Volatility of Long-Term Interest Rates and Expectations Models of the Term Structure', *Journal of Political Economy*.

Shiller, R.J. (1981) 'Do Stock Prices Move Too Much to be Justified by Subsequent Changes in Dividends?', *American Economic Review*.

Shirai, T. and Shimada, H. (1979) 'Japan', in J.T. Dunlop and W. Galenson (eds), *Labor in the Twentieth Century*, New York: Academic Press.

Silvestre, J.J. (1974) 'Industrial Wage Differentials: A Two-Country Comparison', *International Labour Review*.

Simon, H. (1976) 'From Substantive to Procedural Rationality', in S.J. Latsis (ed.), *Method and Appraisal in Economics*, Cambridge: Cambridge University Press.

Simon, H. and Katona, G. (1979), see Katona (1979).

Singh, A. (1971) *Take-Overs: Their Relevance to the Stockmarket and the Theory of the Firm*, Cambridge: Cambridge University Press.

Smiley, R. (1976) 'Tender Offers, Transactions Costs and the Theory of the Firm', *Review of Economics and Statistics*.

Smith, V.L. (1982) 'Microeconomic Systems as an Experimental Science', *American Economic Review*.

Smith, V.L. (ed.) (1983, 1984) *Research in Experimental Economics*, London: JAI Press.

Sraffa, Piero (1926) 'The Laws of Returns under Competititve Conditions', *Economic Journal*. Reprinted in *Readings in Price Theory*, London: Allen & Unwin (1953).

Steiner, P.O. (1975) *Mergers: Motives, Effects, Policies*, Ann Arbor: University of Michigan.

Stern, N.H. (1981) see Carr-Hill and Stern.

Stewart, F. (1974) 'Technology and Employment in LDCs', *World Development*.

Stewart, I.M.T. (1979) *Reasoning and Method in Economics*, London: McGraw-Hill.

Stiglitz, J.E. (1981) 'Pareto Optimality and Competition', *Journal of Finance*.

Stone, K. (1973) 'The Origins of Job Structures in the Steel Industry', in R.C. Edwards, M. Reich and D.M. Gordon (eds), *Labor Market Segmentation*, Lexington: Heath.

Suzuki, H. (1976) 'Age, Seniority and Wages', *International Labour Review*.

Sylos-Labini, P. (1962) *Oligopoly and Technical Progress*, Cambridge, Mass.: Harvard University Press.

Sylos-Labini, P. (1982) Personal letter, 10 Jan to Frederic Lee.

Taira, K. (1970) *Economic Development and the Labor Market in Japan*, New York: Columbia University Press.

Taussig, F.W. (1919) 'Price Fixing as seen by a Price Fixer', *Quarterly Journal of Economics*.

Timmer, C.P. (1975) *The Choice of Technology in Developing Countries*, Boston: Harvard University Press.

Tobin, J. (1982) 'The Meaning of Social Justice', *New York Times*.

Tomonaga, S. (1979) *Butsurigaku wa ika ni shite Tsukurareta ka* (The Creation of Physics), I, Tokyo: Iwanami Shoten.

Touraine, A. (1966) *La Conscience ouvrière*, Paris: Seuil.

Turner, H.A. (1952) 'Trade Unions, Differentials and the Levelling of Wages', *Manchester School*.

Tylecote, A. (1981) *The Causes of Inflation*, London: Macmillan.

Uzawa, H. (1969) Time Preference and the Penrose Effect in a Two-Class Model of Economic Growth', *Journal of Political Economy*.

Wald, A. (1950) *Statistical Decision Functions*, New York: Wiley.

Walras, L. (1954) *Elements of Pure Economics*, trans. W. Jaffé, Holmewood, Ill: Richard D. Irwin.

Ward, B. (1972) *What's Wrong with Economics?*, New York: Basic Books.

Weber, M. (1978) 'Konfuzianismus und Taoismus', in M. Weber, *Gesammelte Aufsätze zue Religionssoziologie*, I, Tubingen: J.C.B. Mohr.

Wicksell, K. (1901) *Lectures in Political Economy*, first published in English 1934. London: Routledge.

Wiles, P.J.D. (1961) *Price, Cost and Output*, 2nd edn, Oxford: Blackwell.

Wiles, P.J.D. (1968) *Communist International Economics*, Oxford: Blackwell.

Wiles, P.J.D. (1970) Review of F. Pryor, and rejoinder to Pryor *Weltwirtschafliches Archiv*.

Wiles, P.J.D. (1972) 'The Necessity and Impossibility of Political Economy', *History and Theory*.

Wiles, P.J.D. (1974) *The Distribution of Income, East and West*, Amsterdam: North Holland.

Wiles. P.J.D. (1977) *Economic Institutions Compared*, Oxford: Blackwell.

Wiles, P.J.D. (1979–80) 'Ideology and Methodology', *Journal of Post-Keynesian Economics*.

Wiles, P.J.D. (1981) *Die Parallelwirtschaft*, Cologne: Bundesinstitut für Internationale und Ostwissenschaftliche Fragen.

Wiles, P.J.D. (1982) 'Are There Any Communist Economic Cycles?' in *ACES Bulletin*, Tempe, Arizona.

Williams, J.B. (1967) 'The Path to Equilibrium', *Quarterly Journal of Economics*.

Williamson, O.E. (1975) *Markets and Hierarchies: Analysis and Anti-Trust Implications*, Glencoe: Free Press.

Williamson O.E., Wachter, M.L. and Harris, J.E. (1975) 'Understanding the Employment Relation: The Analysis of Idiosyncratic Exchange', *Bell Journal*.

Wootton, B. (1955, 2nd edn 1962) *The Social Foundations of Wage Policy*, London: Allen & Unwin.

Worswick, G.D.N. (1972) 'Is Progress in Economic Science Possible?', *Economic Journal*.

Young, P. (1969) 'Unifying Elements in the Theories of the Firm' *Quarterly Review of Economics and Business*.

Contributors

Mark Blaug is Professor of the Economics of Education at the University of London Institute of Education, and author of *Economic Theory in Retrospect*, and *The Methodology of Economics*.

Rod Cross is Lecturer in the Department of Economics at the University of St Andrew's.

Terence Gorman, like many others, uses the time mathematics saves in reading economics to indulge a taste for history and other social sciences, and admires the faith, but doubts the logic, which assures some whose lack of mathematics hides it from them, that modern economics is bunk.

Oliver Hart is Professor of Economics at the London School of Economics. He has published in the area of economic theory, with particular reference to the economics of uncertainty and incentives. He is a former managing editor of the *Review of Economic Studies*, and a Fellow of the Econometric Society.

Andrew Hartropp is Lecturer in Economics at Ealing College of Higher Education, London.

David Heathfield is Senior Lecturer in Economics at the University of Southampton. He has published works on production, inflation and econometric modelling.

Martin Hollis is Professor of Philosophy at the University of East Anglia. He is co-author, with E.J. Nell, of *Rational Economic Man: A Philosophical Critique of Neo-Classical Economics* and author of *Models of Man*.

Terence Hutchison is Emeritus Professor of Economics of the University of Birmingham, and the author of *Knowledge and Ignorance in Economics* and *The Politics and Philosophy of Economics*.

Frederic Lee is Visiting Professor in Economics, University of California, Riverside.

Louis Lévy-Garboua is Professor of Economics at the University of Paris, Senior Research Officer at the Centre de Recherche pour l'Etude et l'Observation des Conditions de Vie (CREDOC), and Director of the research programme on Sociological Economics granted by the Centre National de la Recherche Scientifique.

Brian McCormick is Professor in the Division of Economic Studies at the University of Sheffield and General Editor of Penguin Modern Economic Texts.

David Marsden is Lecturer in Industrial Relations at the London School of Economics.

Michio Morishima is Professor in the Department of Economics at the London School of Economics, and former President of the Econometric Society. He has published studies of Marx and Walras and a history of Japan.

Dennis Mueller is Professor of Economics at the University of Maryland, USA and the author of *Public Choice*.

Robert Neild is Professor in the Faculty of Economics, University of Cambridge.

Hiroyuki Odagiri is Professor at the Institute of Socio-Economic Planning, University of Tsukuba, Japan. His publications include works on the theory of the firm and industrial organization.

Morris Perlman is Senior Lecturer in Economics at the London School of Economics.

Sir Austin Robinson was Professor of Economics in Cambridge University 1950–65, editor of the *Economic Journal* 1944–70, and Secretary of the Royal Economic Society 1945–70.

Guy Routh was formerly Reader in Economics at the University of Sussex, and is the author of *The Origins of Economic Ideas* and *Economics: An Alternative Text*.

Peter Wiles is Professor of Russian Social and Economic Studies, University of London, and author of *Economic Institutions Compared*.

Name Index

Subject Index